CW00727331

The Europeanization of National Polities?

int u e
integrated and united

Series editors: Maurizio Cotta and Pierangelo Isernia
(CIRCaP – University of Siena)

Books in the series include:

The Europe of Elites
A Study into the Europeanness of Europe's Political and Economic Elites
Edited by Heinrich Best, György Lengyel, and Luca Verzichelli

The Europeanization of National Polities?
Citizenship and Support in a Post-Enlargement Union
Edited by David Sanders, Paolo Bellucci, Gábor Tóka, and Mariano Torcal

European Identity
What the Media Say
Edited by Paul Bayley and Geoffrey Williams

Citizens and the European Polity
Mass Attitudes Towards the European and National Polities
Edited by David Sanders, Pedro Magalhães, and Gábor Tóka

The Europeanization of National Polities?

Citizenship and Support in a Post-Enlargement Union

Edited by
David Sanders, Paolo Bellucci, Gábor Tóka,
and Mariano Torcal

OXFORD
UNIVERSITY PRESS

OXFORD

UNIVERSITY PRESS

Great Clarendon Street, Oxford OX2 6DP

Oxford University Press is a department of the University of Oxford.
It furthers the University's objective of excellence in research, scholarship,
and education by publishing worldwide in

Oxford New York

Auckland Cape Town Dar es Salaam Hong Kong Karachi
Kuala Lumpur Madrid Melbourne Mexico City Nairobi
New Delhi Shanghai Taipei Toronto

With offices in

Argentina Austria Brazil Chile Czech Republic France Greece
Guatemala Hungary Italy Japan Poland Portugal Singapore
South Korea Switzerland Thailand Turkey Ukraine Vietnam

Oxford is a registered trade mark of Oxford University Press
in the UK and in certain other countries

Published in the United States
by Oxford University Press Inc., New York

© The several contributors, 2012

The moral rights of the authors have been asserted
Database right Oxford University Press (maker)

First published 2012

All rights reserved. No part of this publication may be reproduced,
stored in a retrieval system, or transmitted, in any form or by any means,
without the prior permission in writing of Oxford University Press,
or as expressly permitted by law, or under terms agreed with the appropriate
reprographics rights organization. Enquiries concerning reproduction
outside the scope of the above should be sent to the Rights Department,
Oxford University Press, at the address above

You must not circulate this book in any other binding or cover
and you must impose the same condition on any acquirer

British Library Cataloguing in Publication Data

Data available

Library of Congress Cataloging in Publication Data

Data available

Typeset by SPI Publisher Services, Pondicherry, India
Printed in Great Britain
on acid-free paper by
MPG Books Group, Bodmin and King's Lynn

ISBN 978-0-19-960234-6

1 3 5 7 9 10 8 6 4 2

Series Editors' Foreword

In a moment in which the EU is facing an important number of social, economic, political, and cultural challenges, and its legitimacy and democratic capacities are increasingly questioned, it seems particularly important to address the issue of *if* and *how* EU citizenship is taking shape. This series intends to address this complex issue. It reports the main results of a quadrennial Europe-wide research project, financed under the 6th Framework Programme of the EU. That programme has studied the changes in the scope, nature, and characteristics of citizenship presently underway as a result of the process of deepening and enlargement of the European Union.

The IntUne Project—Integrated and United: A Quest for Citizenship in an Ever Closer Europe—is one of the most recent and ambitious research attempts to empirically study how citizenship is changing in Europe. The Project lasted four years (2005–9) and it involved thirty of the most distinguished European universities and research centres, with more than 100 senior and junior scholars as well as several dozen graduate students working on it. It had as its main focus an examination of how integration and decentralization processes, at both the national and European level, are affecting three major dimensions of citizenship: *identity*, *representation*, and *scope of governance*. It looked, in particular, at the relationships between political, social, and economic elites, the general public, policy experts, and the media, whose interactions nurture the dynamics of collective political identity, political legitimacy, representation, and standards of performance.

In order to address these issues empirically, the IntUne Project carried out two waves of mass and political, social, and economic elite surveys in eighteen countries, in 2007 and 2009; in-depth interviews with experts in five policy areas; extensive media analysis in four countries; and a documentary analysis of attitudes toward European integration, identity, and citizenship. The book series presents and discusses in a coherent way the results coming out of this extensive set of new data.

The series is organized around the two main axes of the IntUne Project, to report how the issues of identity, representation, and standards of good governance are constructed and reconstructed at the elite and citizen levels, and how mass–elite interactions affect the ability of elites to shape identity, representation, and the scope of governance. A first set of four books will examine how identity, scope of governance, and representation have been changing over time respectively at elites, media, and public level. The next two books will present cross-level analysis of European and national identity on the one hand and problems of national and European representation and scope of governance on the other, in doing so comparing data at both the mass and elite level. A concluding volume will summarize the main results, framing them in a wider theoretical context.

M.C. and P.I.

Contents

Contents

Contributors

Paolo Bellucci is Professor of Comparative Political Behaviour at the University of Siena, Italy

Eduard Bonet is Researcher at Pompeu Fabra University, Spain

Marina Costa Lobo is Researcher at the Social Sciences Institute of the University of Lisbon, Portugal

Andrija Henjak is Lecturer at Department of Political Science, University of Zagreb, Croatia, and Marie Curie Fellow, Department of Government, University of Essex, United Kingdom

Pedro C. Magalhães is Researcher at the Social Sciences Institute of the University of Lisbon, Portugal

Radoslaw Markowski is Professor of Political Science, Polish Academy of Sciences and Warsaw School of Social Sciences & Humanities, Poland

Hans Rattinger is Professor of Comparative Political Behaviour at the University of Mannheim, Germany

David Sanders is Professor of Government at the University of Essex, United Kingdom

Fabio Serricchio is Lecturer in European Union Politics at the University of Molise, Italy

Markus Steinbrecher is DAAD Visiting Assistant Professor at Northwestern University, Evanston, IL, USA

Gábor Tóka is Professor of Political Science at Central European University, Hungary

Mariano Torcal is Professor of Political Science at Pompeu Fabra University, Spain

Corina Wagner is Chair of Comparative Political Behaviour at the University of Mannheim, Germany

1

Introduction: Antecedents and Consequences of European Citizenship

Paolo Bellucci, David Sanders, Gábor Tóka, and Mariano Torcal

The deepening and widening of the European project that has taken place since the end of the West–East international divide in the early 1990s has significantly changed the role played by public opinion and citizens' orientations in the development of the European polity. The title of a recent article 'From Permissive Consensus to Constraining Dissensus' (Hooghe and Marks 2008) aptly summarizes the trajectory of a growing involvement of public opinion and of member states' citizens in this process. For four decades, the European polity grew in a technocratic fashion, driven primarily by political elites whose national electoral constituencies lent substantial, if superficial, support to the seemingly distant and slow advances in economic integration. However, the European issue was generally not salient at the mass level and, most importantly, it was substantively different from the lines of political conflict that prevailed domestically in most member states. As such, debates over the status of the emerging European Union were generally of little consequence for national patterns of party competition.

The relative insulation of European integration from domestic politics began to erode with the development and later affirmation of Europe as a political community, the adoption of a common currency, the EU's evolving multilevel system of governance covering an increasing number of policy areas, and its enlargement to encompass twenty-seven member states. In the unfolding of this process, it became evident that the original 'permissive consensus' (Lindberg and Scheingold 1970; Wilgden and Feld 1976) granted by Europeans showed signs of waning. From the early 1990s onwards, polls showed declining levels of support for European integration. Turnout in European elections fell progressively. National referendums produced

1

unexpected results that slowed down the ratification of treaties, and even aborted a drafted European Constitution in 2005. European issues became a matter of intense domestic contestation with the emergence of Eurosceptic populist parties. Mainstream social-democratic and conservative parties were exposed to difficulties in accommodating European integration within their traditional ideological outlooks. At the same time, national and European politics became more intertwined: domestic considerations began to influence party preferences over Europe, while European politics progressively altered traditional patterns of political contestation (Marks and Steenbergen 2004). As a result, popular preferences now tend to constrain, more than in the past, the actions of political, bureaucratic, and economic elites in the European arena.

All of this may speak relatively well to the condition of democracy in the European Union, especially in light of past concerns over the 'democratic deficit' of supranational institutions. That popular preferences contribute to shape parties' stances over European integration may entail a reduction of the gap between (more cosmopolitan) elites and mass publics, and enhance the responsiveness and legitimacy of both national and supranational institutions. Yet, at the same time the European project has inevitably become more controversial, as the opinion climate towards it has changed in tone, from one of prevalent enthusiasm to (in some instances) growing scepticism. Why this has happened is a matter of debate although it is clearly possible that the European Union's slow reaction to the challenges of globalization and to economic stagnation has played an important role. More important, however, is the fact that the European Union has been progressively portrayed by its critics as a problematic source of globalization, rather than as a possible remedial strategy for dealing with it. On this more critical account, the EU's economic integration process, its tighter budget constraints, the introduction of the common currency, policy harmonization, internal (and external) immigration, and greater cultural and religious heterogeneity have all represented increasingly serious threats to national sovereignty and to domestic traditions and customs.

The passage from an economic-trade community to a political union has ostensibly affected traditional mass perceptions of Europe, which was previously seen mainly as a provider of economic benefits associated with a larger single market. More recently, both mass publics and political elites have increasingly expressed concerns over the fact that, although membership in a supranational political community entails benefits and opportunities, it also—inevitably—involves constraints and costs. This raises important questions about the contours and the structure of the allegiances that European Union people maintain with their national and supranational political communities. To the extent that Europeans share a 'we-feeling' sentiment and develop an allegiance to supranational institutions, the constraints and limitation to states' sovereignty, together with any emerging economic threats and fears of cultural heterogeneity, can be accommodated within a common European framework. Such a process of accommodation would operate in the same way that, in national political systems, diffuse support for the political regime (legitimacy) compensates for performance shortcomings on the part of governments (Easton 1975). On the other hand, if the sense of European allegiance remains underdeveloped, or falters, the prospects of European integration may dim under the assault of either nationalist and populist concerns or simple dissatisfaction with the perceived results of integration, which, with greater intensity, are being voiced within member states.

Since the formation of the European Economic Community in 1957, there has been much academic and elite-level speculation about the development of a common popular European-wide allegiance and about what it means, or might mean, to be 'a European citizen'. Normative political theorists have pondered the tensions between traditional notions of national citizenship that are rooted in an existing *polis* and the prospects for developing a European citizenship in a situation where no (European) *polis* as such exists (Weale 2007). Neo-functionalist scholars of European integration have speculated that a sense of European citizenship might develop progressively as the institutions of the European Community strengthen and extend their policy range (Lindberg and Scheingold 1970). European elites, guided in part by the thinking of legal scholars, have taken the practical step of extending, through the Treaty of Maastricht, formal legal European citizenship to the citizens of all EU member states.

But is the European Union developing as a political community in the eyes of its 'citizens'? Have people acquired allegiances and loyalties towards the EU that do not conflict with their national counterparts? Is there any evidence that European mass publics are developing a sense of belonging to a single European *demos*? During the 1990s, the geographical widening and the functional deepening of European integration have greatly advanced, producing a complex, multilevel system of governance. Much research has been conducted on the political, institutional, and economic consequences of this process. Less attention has been paid, however, to the issue of whether and how this is affecting people's allegiance to national and supranational polities, and on how those allegiances might be connected. Numerous studies (reviewed in the following chapters) have extensively analysed public support for European integration and its determinants, while fewer have inquired into the structure of the belief system that citizens hold on Europe (Thomassen and Schmitt 1999; Scheuer 1999, 2005; Westle 2007a). Here we broaden the latter focus, to consider *European citizenship*, which we regard as an interconnected set of attitudes towards the supranational arena, as perceived by citizens of EU member states, which may uphold their commitment to the European polity. Further, and reversing the causal order assumed by neo-functionalism, we next ask ourselves what consequences such allegiance might have, not only for traditional national identities, but also for popular support for European integration and for political engagement with the EU. In this volume we pursue three main goals.

- The first goal is descriptive. We empirically trace the contours of a concept—European citizenship—on which previous public opinion research is unsystematic. We measure its dimensions and assess its spread across Europe, i.e., the extent to which Europeans share an allegiance with the European polity and perceive its legitimacy.
- The second goal is explanatory. We explore the individual level and contextual determinants of European citizenship and test systematically the explanatory power of a set of (sometimes rival) theoretical perspectives.
- The third goal is both theoretical and empirical. We inquire into the consequences that European citizenship attitudes have for support for the European integration and on the likelihood of getting involved with European politics by voting at the European Parliament elections.

The analyses we report are based on a cross-national mass survey conducted in 2007 (and replicated in 2009) within the larger research project of *IntUne—Integrated and United: A Quest for Citizenship in an Ever Closer Europe*—that was financed under the 6th Framework Programme of the EU. IntUne studies the changes in the scope, nature, and characteristics of citizenship in Europe as an effect of the process of deepening and enlargement of the European Union. It looks at the relationships between elites, public opinion, and media, whose interactions nurture the dynamics of collective political identity, political legitimacy, representation, and standards of performance. In order to address these issues, IntUne conducted two waves of political and social elite, experts, and mass public surveys on these issues in eighteen countries. The research described in this volume is based on the analysis of the citizen surveys conducted in sixteen member states (we focused therefore on current EU citizens, and excluded the surveys carried out in Serbia and Turkey). The questionnaire administered to representative samples of citizens in these countries and information on the fieldwork are reported in the Appendix.

The explanandum: European citizenship

We centre our analysis on the beliefs that member states' citizens share towards the European polity. We focus on people's sense of European citizenship under the working hypothesis that this is distinct from their generalized support (or lack of it) for European integration. Of course, expressing loyalties to a polity-in-the-making requires that at least certain features of the polity be already consolidated. Some polity-building must inevitably have taken place before allegiance to it can develop. Once this threshold is reached, however, we expect to find a distinction between allegiance to the European polity and support for integration, with a likely causal link flowing from the former to the latter. In principle, evidence relating to changes in public opinion over time could be used to assess the potentially reciprocal historical dependence between the development of support for European unification and the extent of popular allegiance to EU institutions. However, systematic testing of this sort of relationship is difficult to effect in practice because of a lack of both long-term data and adequate survey items. A companion volume to this research (Magalhães et al. forthcoming), which analyses all the available evidence, in fact shows that EU attitudes exhibit little trend over time. Measures of European identity, in particular, have remained remarkably stable over four decades and, contrary to both functionalist and identitarian theorists' expectations, it does not appear that European allegiance follows increases in European integration (Isernia et al. forthcoming). In these circumstances, we proceed on the strong prior assumption that support for a supranational political system—an evaluative judgement of the desirability of developing one—needs to be distinguished from popular allegiance to it. Our analysis thus builds on Scheuer's (2005) seminal research on the 1994 European Elections Study cross-sectional data, which showed a separation between European identification and support for European unification. As we will indicate later, the empirical findings reported here are entirely consistent with this core hypothesis.

Why do we focus on European citizenship? Previous research has investigated the structure of citizen attitudes, analysing how people perceive European institutions. Thomassen and Schmitt (1999), drawing on democratic theory rooted in the analysis of the nation state, pointed to the relevance of two dimensions for the study of Europeans' belief structures: legitimacy and representation.

We build on and broaden this perspective both theoretically and empirically, recognizing that perceiving that a political system is legitimate and expressing loyalty to its institutions are among the attributes of citizenship. Historically, such perceptions have been grounded in the nation state, which has endowed its members with a bundle of rights and obligations that have expanded in scope and nature over time, from civic to political to social (Marshall 1950). The obvious question is to assess whether it is plausible to extend such a notion, which is so strongly intertwined with the national welfare state, to the European supranational polity.

Debates about the meaning and sources of citizenship are constantly evolving. Traditional theorizing about citizenship, which proceeded from liberal, communitarian, and republican perspectives, has been challenged by new approaches, in particular by notions of transnational and multicultural citizenship (Kymlicka 2002; Pattie, Seyd, and Whiteley 2004). Both of these approaches recognize that a de-territorialization of politics has occurred (Benhabib 2002) and that the power of nation states has shrunk, as transnational institutions have emphasized universal rights and globalization has increased migration and cultural heterogeneity. In consequence, citizenship rights are no longer tied to national and territorial boundaries (Pattie, Seyd, and Whiteley 2004: 12).

Our perspective on citizenship is less radical, and does not assume that European citizenship must necessarily be of the transnational type. We acknowledge that, given that the EU gradually emerged from consensual agreements among states, 'European citizenship is bound to coexist (probably for a long time) with well-established national definitions of citizenship' (Cotta and Isernia 2009: 82). Since its very inception, in fact, the European Community has nurtured the seeds of a European citizenship and the 'language of citizenship' has progressively found its legal codification in the various treaties (Cotta and Isernia 2009: 74). These (most explicitly the Treaty of Amsterdam) incorporated national definitions of citizenship and laid out further European-specific rights, such as the right to free movement for individuals, the right to make direct appeal to the European Court of Justice and, obviously, the right to vote in European Parliament elections.

We regard European citizenship as being composed of three core elements (Benhabib 2002; Cotta and Isernia 2009): Identity—the extent to which people feel a sense of belonging towards Europe; Representation—the extent to which they consider that the EU represents their economic and political interests; and Scope of Governance—the extent to which they believe that the EU should be primarily responsible for decision-making in important policy areas.

Identity is a key component of citizenship. The willingness to act in a polity depends not only on the extent to which people have been granted legal rights but, crucially, also on the extent they *feel* that they are full members of the community. This happens when consciousness of membership of a group goes hand in hand with the perception of the salience of that sense of belonging, that is when the awareness of the existence of a 'common fate' relevant to people's personal lives becomes widespread. Asking whether a political European community exists means therefore asking first whether a common political identity—a *demos*—has been built (or 'imagined') by its members.

A second component of European Union citizenship stems from the perceived legitimacy of the political institutions, that is, the feeling that institutions are *representative* of the needs and desires of the members of a polity. Representation, the instrument through which citizens exercise their rule in democratic systems, requires that members of a polity be heard and that their interests, values, and preferences are pursued responsively by political actors and institutions. Citizenship attitudes grow when a common political identity is matched by feelings that people are being represented by political institutions and authorities.

Finally, Scope of Government refers to the jurisdiction of the *demos* exercised by representative political authorities. In national contests, this lies ultimately in the state itself, even though subnational institutions may be responsible for some policy competencies. In the multilevel context of the European Union, scope of government refers to people's preferences over the extent to which EU institutions must be endowed with ruling powers, and to which level (regional, national, European) primary policy responsibility should be attributed. In this context, feelings of EU citizenship should be associated with perceptions that EU institutions have a right to exercise political authority.

In this volume, we operationalize these dimensions of citizenship employing both traditional and innovative survey items that we discuss in detail in subsequent chapters. Our general goal is to ascertain the extent to which feelings of citizenship are shared by contemporary European publics. In particular we examine:

- the extent to which a European identity is developing across the EU and the sources of the feeling of common belonging;
- how far and why citizens regard the institutions of the EU, and those of their national and subnational political system, as representative and accountable;
- how far and why EU citizens wish to see extensions to (or reduction in) the scope of EU governance.

Overall these different dimensions of EU citizenship can be regarded as constituting a distinctive European 'political culture', the contours of which—across member states and individuals—allow us to assess the degree of legitimacy that the European project enjoys at the end of the first decade of the twenty-first century. In addition, these current measures of the extent of European citizenship may also serve as a yardstick with which to compare the 'state of the Union' in the future.

The broad causal logic of the analyses conducted in this volume is illustrated graphically in Figure 1.1. The first part of our causal analysis seeks to explain why European mass publics vary in the extent to which they feel a sense of European citizenship—in the extent to which they feel a sense of European identity, in how far they feel represented by European institutions, and in their preferences for EU policy competence in different policy areas. The

Figure 1.1. The causal sequence investigated in the volume

second part focuses on the impact of these three citizenship dimensions on people's 'support' for the EU itself and on their preparedness to vote in European elections. As the figure suggests, we also consider the feedback effects that EU support and participation have on people's sense of European citizenship.

Sources of European citizenship

Scholars of European politics have relied on several theoretical approaches to explain the development of European integration, from the earlier neofunctionalist focus in the 1960s to the multilevel governance and Europeanization perspectives in the 1990s (Checkel and Katzenstein 2009). Scholarly efforts—and also disagreements, as exposed for instance in the debate over the intergovernmental or supranational nature of the European project—have obviously been stimulated by the transformation that the deepening of the integration process has brought to the object of study. As Hooghe and Marks have observed: 'The European Union is an extremely versatile institution. It is an international regime that facilitates economic exchange; it is a supranational polity that exerts political authority over its citizens; and it is part of a system of multilevel governance that encompasses national politics' (Hooghe and Marks 2005: 436).

Public opinion researchers have devoted considerable effort to understanding the reasons and motivations behind people's rejection of or support for European integration. They have pondered the likely impact on public opinion of the evolving nature of the European community of the widening of powers and prerogatives of European Union institutions, and of the domestic politicization of the European issue (with the ensuing challenges, and opportunities, that it poses for national political actors). In response to these developments, empirical research on the determinants of support for European integration and of European attitudes among mass public has shifted its theoretical focus, moving from early reliance on models based on cognitive mobilization and cosmopolitan values (in the 1970s) to a rational choice approach examining popular perceptions of economic interests (in the

1980s); and, later on, to include the perspectives of national rational institutionalism, political cues mobilization, and of identitarian-affective reasoning.

Such diverse theoretical foci are not incompatible with each other, and none has so far superseded the others. This is unsurprising. A multi-paradigmatic perspective is more likely to reflect both the complex multifaceted European reality and the complexity of individual and collective opinion formation in democratic polities. This eclectic approach is mirrored in the efforts of contemporary empirical social science to integrate previously assumed irreducible paradigms of political behaviour: socio-structural, choice-based, and affective-based. Hooghe and Marks (2005), analysing 2000 Eurobarometer data, have shown that several of the previous perspectives contribute jointly to the overall explanation of support for European integration, reflecting the heterogeneity of individuals (moved by different motivations according to their status and orientations) and the influences exerted by the variety of national (economic and political) contexts in which they live.

Our own analysis of European citizenship relies on a range of theoretical perspectives to develop testable hypotheses about its sources. Here we explore a somewhat uncertain territory, as previous political science empirical research on European citizenship is relatively scarce, sometimes based on small-N quasi-experimental data or more often focused, given the limited data availability, on a restricted range of theoretical *explanans*. We are in the fortunate situation of being able to test directly and to compare the explicative power of different theoretical perspectives relying on the IntUne cross-national survey, where we have purposely inserted an array of items explicitly devoted to their operationalization. We have also included in these data a set of important country-level aggregate variables to test, in a multilevel design, the potential effect of some contextual factors. The chapters of this book, although with different emphasis according to the dependent variable of interest (EU Citizenship, EU Identity, EU Representation, EU Scope of Government, EU Support, and EU Engagement), test the impact of four major theoretical perspectives: *Cognitive Mobilization, 'Hard' Instrumental* (economic and institutional) *Rationality, 'Soft' Cueing Rationality,* and *Affective Identity.* Each chapter provides a selective review of research mostly relevant for the previous theories: hence, we provide here only a brief general overview of each of them.

Cognitive Mobilization, a perspective associated with early analyses of European support, posits that people's individual resources and their value orientations affect attitudes towards Europe. In the early phase of European integration, comparisons of 'cosmopolitism' with 'parochialism' appeared to be a promising line of inquiry, in which European mass publics appeared to be developing 'European attitudes' that would transcend the nation state. Value orientations such as 'postmaterialism' were seen as the result of a process of cognitive mobilization, that was itself brought about by increasing levels of affluence, education, knowledge, and political interest in post-war Europe. Later extensions and broadening of this perspective focused on political attentiveness, political awareness,[1] and sophistication as requisites for general political engagement, which in turn were found to be important predictors of many political attitudes and behaviours. Cognitive mobilization theory therefore points to individual resources (primarily: education, interest, and knowledge) and media exposure as relevant sources of political engagement and opinion formation. These, matched by life experiences that allow people to have direct experience of Europe and of its institutions, are seen as important sources of a sense of European citizenship and of favourable European attitudes and engagement.

It is not surprising that the early focus of European integration on economic and trade coordination stimulated scholars to analyse the costs and benefits accruing from it. Extensive research has been therefore inspired by a second theoretical perspective, that of *'Hard' Instrumental Rationality*, which centres on the mechanisms of choice that are faced by individuals. Relying on strict rational choice assumptions, numerous studies have explored the individual and contextual correlates of attitudes towards Europe. At the individual level, the opportunity to improve (or weaken) one's working status and conditions in a unified European market are linked to evaluations of the European project. Likewise, citizens of countries who benefit economically from the single market (either in terms of trade or in net financial transfers from the EU) are considered likely to develop positive attitudes towards Europe. More generally, both 'egocentric individualism' and 'sociotropic utilitarianism' imply relatively simple calculations about the benefits/costs that accrue from Europe as a basis for evaluating it. But choice is not uniquely an attribute of markets. Choice might also be involved in the development of identities and, more broadly, citizenship. Forms of instrumental attachment may indeed result from perceptions of benefits (in a variety of realms, from economic interest to personal esteem, prestige, or status) from membership in a group. However, rational calculations of cost and benefits cannot be reduced solely to pure economic utilitarianism. Citizens might also use hard instrumental calculations when it comes to institutions. Different national institutional arrangements perform differently and that differential performance may in turn produce losers and winners: this might also influence the way citizens evaluate the performance of EU institutions (Hix 2007). It follows that perceptions of effective benefits combined with choice-based processes of

---

[1] For the full discussion of this concept see Zaller (1992).

identification may directly sustain (or undermine) European allegiance and citizenship beliefs.

However, the levels of knowledge and political awareness that underpin *informed* rational choices are not necessarily distributed evenly among people, who are typically heterogeneous as to the availability of resources of time or interest required in order to become informed. The *'Soft' Cueing Rationality* perspective assumes that people can nevertheless overcome this limitation and act reasonably in a context of 'low-information rationality', employing cognitive shortcuts and 'heuristics'. 'Cueing rationality' points therefore to a possible strategy that people may follow in order to form or change opinions on issues for which information is vague or costly. They rely on—they take cues from—objects with which they are familiar—other individuals, institutions, or political parties. Hence, in evaluating the European Union, people can rely on the position promulgated by their preferred political party; they can derive their 'European position' from their own left–right ideological position; or they can base their assessment on their perceptions of (and degree of trust in) their own national political institutions. Previous research has shown that these sorts of cue originate mainly within the national system. This is partly because people are more familiar with it but also because political leaders and parties' competitive strategies make such cues salient and available to people. However, there is evidence that the images of the European Union and of its institutions, as framed and channelled by national mass media, also provide important sources of cueing information (Díez Medrano 2003; De Vreese et al. 2006). This said, there is no consensus in the existing scholarly literature on the mechanisms through which such cues operate. Our discussion of *Soft Cueing Rationality* accordingly distinguishes between *transfer* and *substitution* cues. Transfer cues involve *projecting* one's feelings about domestic political objects directly to the European sphere (for example: I have confidence in the workings of my national parliament, so I also have confidence in the operation of the European Parliament). Substitution cues involve making judgements about European institutions that compensate for domestic national institutional failings (for example: I have no confidence in my national parliament, so I will express confidence in European institutions). We use this distinction to help explain how and why certain cues exert differential effects on the various dimensions of citizenship and EU engagement.

The fourth major theoretical perspective we use to examine the sources of European citizenship is the *Affective-Identitarian* approach. Social science research has long since recognized the importance of loyalties and identities as enduring sources of social and political behaviour, as well as considering the emotional underpinnings of a variety of individual choices. Although identitarian explanations have been considered since the inception of public opinion research on Europe, this approach has achieved greater prominence in the wake of the rising Euroscepticism that followed the Maastricht Treaty. The ensuing arguments about the EU's challenge to state sovereignty and the dangers of growing cultural homogeneity articulated by populist and anti-EU parties were explicitly targeted to hit people's hearts and feelings rather than just addressing the state of their pocketbooks. From this perspective, strong feelings of national identity were at first thought to constrain the development of favourable European attitudes. Later theoretical and empirical research relaxed this assumption. At the same time, the relationship was recognized as being more complex and contingent, involving two important features that condition the relationship between national and European identities: their reciprocal dependence; and the *meanings* associated in people's minds with national and European identity. Research has therefore explored the exclusive/inclusive nature of identities, and the ascriptive/achieved contents of such allegiances. The former contrast hints at the possible coexistence of multiple and compatible allegiances, while the latter refers to the bases upon which national and supranational identities are constructed (with ascriptive meanings referring to pre-political attributes of nationality such as language, ancestry, and religion, and achieved meanings referring to civic-political attributes such as rights and institutional involvement). Both these differences have been shown to impinge on European attitudes, although their effective impact is still debated and remains a controversial issue, to which we provide additional, new evidence.

Throughout this book we constantly refer to these four possible sources of EU citizenship and engagement, assessing the extent to which they rival or complement each other in providing well-rounded explanations of people's attitudes across Europe. Beyond this, other explanatory factors also enter our analysis, both as individual-level controls and as part of our efforts to assess the impact of the social and political contexts in which European citizens live. We accordingly incorporate in our models, as we said above, a range of national (economic, social, political) characteristics to ascertain the extent to which system-level features impinge upon individual attitudes. We employ them in multilevel analyses to test the extent to which systemic characteristics such as fiscal transfers and governance quality interact and condition individual-level attitudes.

Plan of the volume

This research is the joint effort of a 'European' group of scholars and this volume the outcome of a collective endeavour. Although multi-authored, this book is not an edited collection of interconnected but intrinsically separate essays. Rather, we aimed at writing a cohesive piece of research that would read as unitary, not only in the style but specifically in the way we have built and tested our hypotheses, and in the way concepts are measured and models developed. To this aim, we engaged in extensive discussions that produced an agreed—in some instances after harsh disagreement—operationalization of variables, scales, and indexes that have been used systematically throughout the chapters. The reader will judge whether we have hit the target. The Appendix documents the various stages of variables construction and describes the methodology employed. Below we describe how our argument unfolds and the organization of the book.

Chapter 2—*Conceptualizing and Measuring European Citizenship and Engagement*—presents our dependent variables. It discusses the ways in which the various dimensions of European Citizenship and of Engagement have been theorized and measured. As to Citizenship, a six-factor analytic solution emerges from analysing a large number of survey responses across sixteen EU countries. The six factors are: Identity, Institutional Confidence, Political Efficacy, Current Policy Scope Preferences, Future Policy Scope Preferences, and Preferred Geographical Scope. This solution is robust and consistent across a range of individual characteristics and types of EU member state, including length of EU membership and Western versus Eastern tradition. This pattern of consistency continues when the six factors are mapped onto the three theoretical dimensions of Citizenship (Identity, Representation, and Scope of Government), thus showing that citizens' attitudes are clearly structured along these dimensions. The descriptive picture of European citizenship that emerges is one of a nuanced balance, in which medium levels of European identification are associated with mixed evaluations of the policy responsiveness of EU institutions and of EU policy competence. The final part of the chapter discusses our two measures of European Engagement: overall support for the EU itself and people's preparedness to participate in elections to the European Parliament.

Chapter 3—*Developing Operational Measures of the Explanatory Variables*—details the main explanatory variables (and associated measures) that are employed in subsequent chapters as independent, control, or intervening variables. The chapter presents a typology of explanatory variables based on the *Cognitive Mobilization, 'Hard' Instrumental Rationality, 'Soft' Cueing Rationality*, and *Affective Identity* perspectives. It shows how these sometimes competing and sometimes complementary theoretical positions can be effectively operationalized in terms of a set of exogenous variables that are employed in subsequent chapters to explain variations both in EU Identity, Representation, and Scope, and in EU Support and Engagement. Both individual-level 'micro' variables which measure political attitudes and behaviour, and 'macro' variables that describe the diversity of social or political contexts comprising the European Union, are analysed and their variance across Europe assessed by EU accession wave and by (West versus East) region.

Chapter 4—*Explaining European Identity*—analyses individual and national differences in the intensity of European identity and provides an assessment of the many factors that sustain or hinder the development of a European identification among the citizens of EU member states. A model of the intensity of EU identity—comprising feelings of EU belonging and their salience, according to social identity theory—is elaborated. This model considers the various perspectives outlined above, and their distinctive explanatory power across the European public is examined. It is found that socio-structural individual-level characteristics as well as system-level features have a modest impact on identity. Cognitive mobilization and instrumental 'rational' considerations are far more important in framing the image of Europe and in determining the extent of identification with it.

Chapter 5—*Institutional Trust and Responsiveness in the EU*—analyses the second dimension of European citizenship, Representation. It focuses on people's evaluation of the EU Parliament and Commission and on the perceived responsiveness of European Union institutions. It is argued that as citizens become more acquainted with the EU, instrumental motivations acquire greater importance *vis-à-vis* affective heuristics in evaluating the mechanisms of political representation in the Union. The chapter explores the role of egocentric and sociotropic evaluations, national political cues, and political awareness—all contingent upon economic and political system-level characteristics—in determining people's trust in and perceived responsiveness of the EU. The chapter concludes that evaluations of EU institutions and their perceived responsiveness depend on three main factors: affective support, instrumental sociotropic support, and evaluations of national institutions. The distinctive role that these three attitudes play in increasing or decreasing the level of EU institutional trust is conditioned by the quality of the governance, the balance of the fiscal transfers, the level of political awareness, and the level of 'EU politicization'.

Chapter 6—*The Scope of Government of the European Union: Explaining Citizens' Support for a More Powerful EU*—discusses the third dimension of citizenship: Scope of Government. It analyses people's perceptions of and expectations for current and further EU policymaking capacity. It is argued that Scope captures mainly a political, prospective, and input-oriented dimension of citizenship. Accordingly, instrumental rationality, which is rooted in perceptions of EU benefits, should have little impact on people's attitudes towards EU policy scope. This is because people's retrospective instrumental calculations about perceived benefits might well be at odds with their judgements about the desirability of future policy scope. I may feel that I have benefited from the EU in the past because its policy scope was *restricted* and that these benefits would be at risk if policy scope were to be extended. This in turn implies that people's preferences for EU Policy Scope will be driven mainly by political and identitarian factors. The results reported show that domestic political cues, confidence in EU institutions, and feelings of (exclusive) national identity are strong individual-level predictors of Scope of Government attitudes. The impact of these factors is in turn reinforced by system-level factors, such as domestic polarization over EU integration and the quality of government at the national level.

Chapters 7 and 8 shift the focus of the discussion to the *consequences* of EU citizenship. Chapter 7—*Explaining Support for European Integration*—deals with the impact of citizenship attitudes on popular support for European integration. This issue has been extensively investigated in previous research. The distinctiveness of this new analysis is that it allows an empirical testing of a wide set of theoretical claims that are advanced in the literature but whose explicative contributions have only seldom been assessed comparatively, due to data limitations. Further, their contribution is tested against that provided by the dimensions of citizenship previously analysed. Last, modelling of systemic-level features and of their interactions with individual-level variables is carried out to adjudicate between rival theoretical perspectives. The findings show that citizenship attitudes are important determinants of people's overall evaluation of EU integration, without any significant variation across Western, Southern, and Eastern Europe.

Chapter 8—*Explaining Turnout in European Parliament Elections*—focuses on a key behavioural component of EU engagement, and ascertains the extent to which EU-related attitudes, and in particular citizenship attitudes, explain electoral participation. Citizenship explanations are therefore tested against a host of traditional determinants of EU turnout, including instrumental calculations, partisan cues, sense of civic duty, affective commitment, and demographic characteristics. Voters/non-voters are grouped in four types, according to whether they voted in both EU and national elections, did not vote in either, or voted in one election but not in the other. The analysis shows that, with the partial exception of Identity, European attitudes are *not* important predictors of turnout in European Parliament elections. Traditional explanations—mainly associated with political and cognitive mobilization—are far more important, thus pointing out that low turnout does not signal specific anti-European sentiments.

The final analytical Chapter 9—*Towards an Integrated Model of EU Citizenship and Support*—relaxes the recursive perspective that has informed the previous analyses, and explicitly models reciprocal causal effects, providing a comprehensive and integrated account of EU Citizenship attitudes on EU Support. While preceding explanatory chapters are all based on single-equation models—in which a given dependent variable is assumed to be affected by a set of exogenous explanatory factors—here a system of equations is estimated in which instrumental variables are employed to sharpen the understanding of possibly reciprocal causal effects between Citizenship and Support. The analysis makes explicit controls for the impact of different levels of political sophistication on the part of different individuals. The results suggest three main conclusions. First, of the three dimensions of citizenship that we explore, Representation appears to be the most important: the net effects of Representation on EU Identity and EU Policy Scope are far greater than the effects of Identity on Representation and Scope or of the effects of Scope on Representation and Identity. Second, once the 'endogenous' links between Identity, Representation, and Scope are carefully controlled for, all four of the theoretical perspectives whose impacts have been tested throughout the book appear relevant for understanding EU Citizenship. However, the strongest influences are associated with instrumental rationality and heuristic rationality variables. Third, although some intercorrelation exists between Citizenship and Support, estimates controlling for this endogeneity show that Support is dependent on Citizenship rather than vice versa. This confirms the utility of the broad recursive modelling strategy outlined in Figure 1.1.

The concluding chapter provides a summary review of the main themes and empirical findings developed throughout the book. Although levels of citizenship and engagement vary across countries and contexts, the processes affecting perceptions of EU citizenship and engagement appear to operate in a broadly similar fashion across all of the countries of the EU. European mass publics tend to think about the EU in remarkably similar ways. Their sense of EU citizenship may not yet have 'caught up' with the formal legal citizenship that all EU citizens enjoy. This said, there is a real, measurable emerging sense of European citizenship, which complements rather than contradicts feelings of national citizenship among mass publics in all member states, and which counterbalances a developing Euroscepticism in some EU countries. This structure, moreover, appears to be relatively stable. The empirical results reported in the final part of the chapter show that, in spite of the global economic crisis that affected EU nations after 2007, levels of perceived EU Citizenship and Support remained at very similar levels in the 'follow-up' IntUne survey that went into the field in 2009. To the extent that the EU can continue to deliver clearly perceived benefits to its citizens and to the extent that its institutions effectively represent citizens' needs and preferences, hard and soft instrumental calculations suggest that the sense of EU citizenship and EU support will be maintained in the future.

2

Conceptualizing and Measuring European Citizenship and Engagement

David Sanders, Paolo Bellucci, Gábor Tóka, and Mariano Torcal

There are clearly many alternative ways of thinking about the idea of citizenship. From a legal perspective, citizenship is something that can be formally conferred upon an individual in virtue of her/his possession of certain characteristics, and which typically engenders the acquisition of certain rights. For some political theorists, the notion of citizenship is intimately bound up with the idea of the *active* citizen, the individual who participates in the *demos*—the political system—in order to fulfil her/his political obligations to the community. Our approach to citizenship in general, and to European citizenship in particular, focuses primarily on the views of the citizens themselves. Just as national and European Union laws recognize the coexistence of 'national' and 'European Union' citizenships, so we also recognize that individuals can think of themselves, to varying degrees, as citizens both of their own country and of the EU. Accepting this potential 'duality' of conception on the part of the individual, we follow Benhabib (2002) and distinguish among three key components of citizenship at the national and European levels:

- *Identity*—the extent to which the individual identifies her/himself as a member of the (national or European) *demos*;
- *Representation*—the extent to which s/he feels her/his interests are represented by (national or European) political institutions; and
- *Scope of Governance*—the extent to which the individual considers (national or European) political institutions should be engaged in policymaking and implementation in different policy areas.

In this chapter, we describe and justify a range of European and national-level indices that we have developed for measuring individuals' feelings of

Identity and Representation, and their assessments of Scope of Governance. We also describe how we measure the related notion of 'EU Engagement', which we conceptualize as involving both behavioural and attitudinal components. Part 1 of the chapter provides the necessary contextual background and outlines the survey of mass opinion in sixteen European countries that we use in order to measure the different dimensions of European (and national) citizenship and EU engagement. Part 2 describes a series of factor analyses that we conducted using these data. The results show that, throughout the countries surveyed, citizens' attitudes map very clearly onto the three conceptual dimensions of Identity, Representation, and Scope to which we have referred. In Part 3, we show that there are consistent country-by-country variations in the levels of these three measures, and that these variations are linked systematically to the time at which different countries joined the EU. Finally, in Part 4, we describe our measures of 'EU Engagement', in which we focus on turnout in EU elections and overall 'support for the EU'. In subsequent chapters, we develop models that seek to account for individual- and country-level variations in these various perceptions and behaviours.[1]

The contextual background and the sixteen-nation survey

The creation of the European Economic Community in 1957 was fundamentally an elite-driven project. The elites of the member states who supported the EEC were largely convinced by the neo-functionalists' ideas of 'spillover'. The core notion was that functional cooperation at the supranational level in certain pivotal policy areas—such as coal, steel, and agriculture—would prove so successful that businesses, interest groups, and perhaps even public opinion, would press for the extension of supranational decision-making in other policy areas. The gradual extension of supranational policy competence did indeed develop in line with neo-functionalist expectations. It was reinforced, moreover, by a series of intergovernmental agreements—the Single European Act in 1986, the Maastricht Treaty of 1992, and the Amsterdam Treaty of 1999—that aimed to broaden and deepen the policymaking capabilities of (what had become) the EU. For much of the late twentieth century, public opinion in most member countries (with the notable exceptions of the UK and, to a lesser extent, Denmark) was broadly supportive of the European project. As revealed in a long-running series of Eurobarometer surveys from

---

[1] Unless otherwise noted, all data presented in this chapter refer to the complete set of 16,133 respondents from sixteen EU countries interviewed for the IntUne survey in spring 2007. For question wording, weighting, and missing data issues the reader is referred to the technical Appendix of the book.

1970 onwards, mass publics broadly recognized the benefits that the EEC/EC/EU had brought. When asked, large majorities of the populations of most member states clearly proclaimed their approval of the EU and their sense that, on balance, their countries—and often they themselves—had benefited from EU membership.

In the twenty-first century, however, public opinion towards the EU has not been quite so positive. The accession of new member states and the extension of the scope of the Union's policy competence appear to have raised doubts, among some EU mass publics, about the wisdom of further extending the European project. This decline in EU support among mass populations has thrown into relief the disparity between mass and elite opinion about the future course of European integration. But even if support for the EU has dipped in recent years, it does not necessarily follow that the EU's citizens do not feel a sense of allegiance to the EU. This is what our analysis tries to explore. The populations of all EU member states automatically became EU citizens as a result of Maastricht, gaining common rights that were formally extended at Amsterdam. What we examine here is whether these citizens by default actually think of themselves as citizens of the EU.

As indicated above, the theoretical notion of citizenship that we employ derives from the work of Benhabib (2002). In these terms, subjective feelings of citizenship towards any given *demos* consists in a combination of a sense of identity, feelings of representation, and beliefs about the proper scope of government attributable to the *demos*. A *demos* is typically defined as the political system, traditionally a nation state, that exercises sovereignty—decision-making and judicial authority—over the population living within its borders. In an age of multilevel governance, the notion of the *demos* necessarily becomes more fluid. In principle, it could be applicable at subnational, national, and supranational levels simultaneously in a given geographical area—depending on the extent to which these three differing levels of government exercise some sort of judicial and political authority over the people living within that area. Citizens have a relatively strong subjective sense of citizenship if they identify with the *demos*, feel that their interests are strongly represented by the decision-making authorities within the *demos*, and believe that the competence of those authorities to make policy in different areas is appropriate. Their subjective sense of citizenship is relatively weak in the absence of any or all of these three characteristics.

In order to establish how far European citizens exhibit a sense of EU citizenship, we conducted interviews with representative samples (N~1000) of the populations of sixteen EU member states. The interviews were conducted by telephone in March 2007 by TNS-Gallup, using random digit dialling in order to identify respondents. The data were weighted to ensure that each national sample was demographically representative of the population of the country surveyed. Each respondent was asked a series of questions designed to elicit the extent to which s/he exhibited a sense of European, as well as national, citizenship. They were also asked a range of other questions relating to possible factors that could influence citizenship at these different levels. These other questions, and the theories that underpin their use, are discussed in the next and subsequent chapters. The questionnaires and the weighting and general measurement procedures that we use in order to analyse the data are described in the Appendix. These procedures include the use of multiple imputation techniques for substituting item-non-response missing data with sensible estimates. These techniques enhance the representativeness of the overall sample analysed because they ensure that individuals with relatively weak or uncertain views on particular issues—those who answer 'don't know' or 'no opinion' or 'refuse' in response to a particular survey question—are not excluded from the analysis. For any given variable, multiple imputation techniques use all of the information in the dataset to estimate the most likely 'active' response category for each of the individuals who would otherwise be recorded as 'missing data' on that variable. The use of these techniques means that there are no missing (don't know; no opinion; refusal) cases in the survey measures that we report here—even though the original survey questions, as outlined in the Appendix, did allow for such responses by respondents.

In the remainder of this section, we describe the survey questions and responses that we use to measure our three core concepts of European

Table 2.1. Responses to survey questions about European Identity

Panel A	Not at all	Not very much	Some-what	Very much
Question:				
How much does being a European have to do with how you feel about yourself in your day-to-day life?	26.0	26.3	34.7	13.0
How far do you feel that what happens to Europe in general has important consequences for people like you?	7.0	21.0	45.2	26.8
People feel different degrees of attachment to their town or village, to their region, to their country and to Europe. What about you[r attachment to Europe]?	10.7	25.0	42.1	22.7

Panel B	[Czech etc.] only	[Czech etc.] and European	European and [Czech etc.]	European only
Do you see yourself as . . .:				
1992	39.5	49.7	6.8	4.1
2003	41.2	47.0	7.9	3.9
2007	39.5	48.6	7.9	4.0

Source: Westle (2007b) for 1992 and 2003, and the 2007 INTUNE survey data.

Note: Table entries are percentages based on the entire cross-national sample, with demographic weights for sampling bias and equal weight for each country.

Identity, Representation, and Scope. In providing this descriptive account, we do not discuss the *structure* of these attitudes or the way in which the *response patterns differ* across different EU countries. These are tasks that we undertake, respectively, in sections 2 and 3 below.

Table 2.1 describes the range of measures that we used to assess the extent of each individual's sense of *European Identity*. We asked our respondents, first, about the extent to which 'being a European' mattered to their everyday lives. As Panel A of the table shows, just under half of our respondents (48 per cent) considered that it mattered either 'somewhat' or 'a great deal'; over half intimated that 'being a European' mattered 'not very much' or 'not at all'. In response to a more indirect question about European identity, some 72 per cent of our respondents felt that they were affected by 'what happens to Europe'. This higher level of identification with Europe was also reflected in the responses to a question that we asked about people's attachment to Europe—as opposed to their local, regional, and national attachments. The relevant marginal distribution in Table 2.1 indicates that two thirds of respondents felt either 'somewhat' or 'very' attached to Europe—a figure slightly higher than that observed in surveys conducted in both 1991 and 2003. The average score on a 1–4 scale reported by Westle (2007b) from the Eurobarometer series is 2.46 in 1991 and 2.64 in 2003, while with our 2007 data the equivalent score is 2.77. Finally, as Panel B of Table 2.1 shows, when asked explicitly to compare their sense of national identity with their sense of being European, well over half of respondents indicated that they saw themselves as at least partially European and some 4 per cent saw themselves as being 'European only'. As can be observed in this same table, this 2007 distribution is almost identical to that observed in previous EU-wide surveys conducted in 1992 and 2003. It suggests that levels of EU identity have remained relatively stable over at least the last decade and a half. Taken together, these measures suggest that there is a reasonably enduring sense of European identity among European mass publics, although it is clearly neither fully developed nor universal. As we discuss below, this sense of identity is in fact consistently structured across the full range of types of EU member state.

Table 2.2 describes our measures of *EU Representation*. Panel A focuses on two of the key EU institutions, the Commission and the Parliament. We asked our respondents to indicate, on a 0–10 scale, how much they trusted each of these institutions 'to usually take the right decisions'. The response patterns show most respondents clustered around intermediate levels of trust. In later chapters, we compare these levels of EU institutional trust with people's trust in their own national political institutions. Here we merely note that the average level of trust for the (democratically elected) EU Parliament was virtually identical to that for the (appointed) Commission: both received a mean score of 4.8 on the trust scale.

Table 2.2. Responses about European Representation

Panel A	No trust at all							Complete trust			
	0	1	2	3	4	5	6	7	8	9	10
Trust in European Parliament	8.1	2.9	5.9	8.9	10.4	24.0	13.2	12.8	8.9	2.2	2.7
Trust in European Commission	7.7	3.1	6.2	9.0	10.4	23.7	13.6	12.9	8.6	2.2	2.5

Panel B	Strongly disagree	Disagree	Can't choose	Agree	Strongly agree
Those who make decisions in the European Union are competent people who know what they are doing	10.0	23.1	4.7	48.3	13.9
Those who make decisions in the European Union do not care much what people like me think	7.6	21.3	3.0	37.7	30.4
Those who make decisions in the European Union ignore our country's interests.	7.0	24.7	4.9	4.3	23.1

Panel C

Satisfaction with the way democracy works in the European Union:

Very dissatisfied	Dissatisfied	Satisfied	Very satisfied
8.5	27.1	58.3	6.1

Note: Table entries are weighted percentages based in the entire 16-country sample.

Panel B of Table 2.2 reports the results of asking our respondents a series of more specific questions about EU decision-makers. Their overall views were mixed. A clear majority (62 per cent) agreed that EU decision-makers are 'competent people who know what they are doing'. However, clear majorities also felt that decision-makers 'do not care much what people like me think' (68 per cent) and that they 'do not take enough account of our country's interests' (67 per cent). Finally, Table 2.2 Panel C shows quite a high level of satisfaction with the way democracy works in the EU, with some 64 per cent of respondents saying that they are either fairly or very satisfied. This compares favourably with an average of around 50 per cent satisfaction for the period between 1973 and 1990 and an average of around 55 per cent between 1998 and 2005 (Bellucci, Memoli, and Sanders forthcoming). Taken together, these results suggest that while EU citizens are broadly satisfied with the general representative functioning of the EU, they have reservations about the responsiveness of the European institutions to their own and to their countries' interests.

Our respondents' attitudes towards the proper *Scope of EU Governance* are shown in Table 2.3. Panel A reports people's preferences for regional- or national- versus EU-level governance in six relatively high-salience policy areas. The majority of respondents preferred regional or national decision-

Table 2.3. Preferred Scope of European Governance

Panel A	EU-level only	EU and some other level	Only some other level or none
Which level of government should be currently responsible for each policy:			
Unemployment	21.6	6.0	72.7
Health	19.1	4.5	76.4
Environment	43.4	7.3	49.3
Crime	37.3	7.5	55.3
Agriculture	28.1	5.4	66.4
Immigration	40.5	5.3	54.2

Panel B	Strongly disagree	Disagree	Can't choose	Agree	Strongly agree
Support for future extension of EU policy scope to:					
A unified tax system	19.2	19.6	5.0	31.8	24.5
A common system of social security	8.4	14.1	3.4	40.6	33.4
A single EU foreign policy	7.5	14.8	4.6	42.8	30.3
More regional development aid	3.7	8.2	2.2	44.1	41.7

Panel C

Support for a larger geographic scope of the EU

Turkey's EU membership is:	A bad thing	Neither good nor bad	A good thing
	49.1	18.6	32.3

Enlarging the EU to include new countries:	Very much against	Somewhat against	Somewhat in favour	Very much in favour
	12.9	23.2	46.6	17.3

Note: Table entries are weighted percentages based in the entire 16-country sample.

making in each area, though this preference was stronger in the Unemployment and Health policy domains, where, respectively, 73 and 76 per cent preferred regional or national solutions. The preference for EU-level policy was strongest in relation to the Environment (43 per cent supported EU solutions) and Immigration (41 per cent support). Surprisingly—given the prominent role of the CAP in EU spending—only 28 per cent favoured EU-level policy-making for Agriculture.

In addition to asking about the proper scope of *contemporary* EU policy, we also asked our respondents to think about their preferences 'over the next ten years'. The results are reported in Table 2.3, Panel B. Here, a rather different picture emerges. Clear majorities of respondents favour 'a unified tax system for the EU' (56 per cent support), 'a common system of social security' (74 per cent support), 'a single EU foreign policy' (73 per cent), and more EU regional aid (86 per cent). This suggests that in certain critical policy areas, the EU's citizens would welcome more EU involvement in decision-making—even if they are not yet ready to abandon regional and national decision-making in some of those same areas. Finally, as Panel C of Table 2.3 shows, we also enquire about people's preferences for the geographical scope of the EU itself. Here, the picture is relatively straightforward. A majority of Europeans are in favour of a larger EU, as long as that larger EU excludes Turkey.

Where does this leave us? In essence, this brief review of the empirical referents of our three conceptual dimensions of EU citizenship produces a mixed picture of the 'European citizen'. A majority of our survey respondents display some sort of European identity. In terms of representation, a majority considers EU policymakers to be competent, but they are broadly neutral in their view of EU institutions—and on balance negative in their assessments of EU policymakers' responsiveness. With regard to policy scope, the majority prefers regional and national decision-making now, but they would favour greater EU involvement in several key areas in the future. Given this rather mixed picture, how confident can we be that the survey results we have presented reflect a genuine set of political attitudes? Is there a clear empirical structure that underpins the collection of responses that we have described— and which corresponds to the simple identity/representation/scope schema that we deploy? We explore these questions in the next section.

The structure of European mass attitudes towards the EU

There are numerous statistical techniques available for exploring attitude structures—including uni- and multidimensional scaling, unfolding, and correspondence analysis. Here, we employ one of the simplest and most straightforward techniques: non-orthogonal exploratory factor analysis. There are two main reasons for choosing this approach. First, we are interested in determining whether or not the latent structure of our citizenship data corresponds to the broad theoretical categories of identity, representation and scope implied by Benhabib's (2002) conceptual analysis (see above). Exploratory factor analysis imposes no prior expectations on what dimensions of citizenship are identified in the data. A non-orthogonal solution also allows for the possibility that the different dimensions of citizenship are correlated with one another.

Table 2.4 reports the results of an oblimin factor analysis of the twenty-two survey items that were described in Tables 2.1 to 2.3. The table suggests a six-factor solution that can be interpreted very easily because each measured variable loads highly on just one factor (cf. the loadings printed in *bold*). Thus, for example, the four Identity measures—'Feels European', 'Attachment to Europe', 'Europe affects me', and 'European versus national identity'—all

Table 2.4. The dimensions of European Citizenship (rotated oblimin factor loadings)

Factor	1	2	3	4	5	6
Variables defining the 'Representation—Institutional Confidence' factor						
Trust in EU Parliament	*0.866*	0.134	0.170	0.286	−0.146	−0.208
Trust in EU Commission	*0.875*	0.134	0.168	0.264	−0.141	−0.204
EU democracy	*0.626*	0.080	0.254	0.273	−0.208	−0.184
EU decision-makers are competent	*0.631*	0.055	0.226	0.159	−0.250	−0.080
Variables defining the 'Scope of EU Policy—Now' factor						
Unemployment	0.027	*0.660*	0.131	0.132	−0.089	−0.043
Immigration	0.136	*0.609*	0.176	0.114	−0.154	−0.122
Environment	0.122	*0.671*	0.111	0.166	0.008	−0.116
Crime	0.052	*0.671*	0.135	0.094	0.007	−0.026
Health care	0.041	*0.659*	0.131	0.061	−0.093	−0.070
Agriculture	0.122	*0.645*	0.119	0.157	−0.009	−0.130
Variables defining the 'Scope of EU Policy—Future' factor						
Unified tax system	0.124	0.180	*0.726*	0.133	−0.128	−0.088
Common social security system	0.176	0.169	*0.780*	0.133	−0.182	−0.020
Single EU foreign policy	0.251	0.152	*0.695*	0.209	−0.071	−0.003
More regional aid	0.287	0.076	*0.589*	0.148	−0.391	0.127
Variables defining the 'EU Identity' factor						
Feels European	0.295	0.114	0.150	*0.708*	−0.065	−0.207
Attachment to Europe	0.354	0.140	0.227	*0.684*	−0.093	−0.137
Europe affects me	0.089	0.048	0.092	*0.627*	−0.100	0.015
Feels European versus national	0.189	0.231	0.136	*0.608*	−0.112	−0.177
Variables defining the 'Scope of EU: Geography' factor						
Favours Turkey in EU	0.160	0.090	0.113	0.094	*−0.835*	−0.119
Favours EU enlargement	0.327	0.094	0.280	0.213	*−0.800*	−0.069
Variables defining the 'Representation—Political Efficacy' factor						
EU ignores our interests	−0.154	−0.125	−0.033	−0.132	0.125	*0.813*
EU doesn't care about people	−0.234	−0.079	−0.041	−0.161	0.041	*0.791*

Note: Table entries are factor loadings estimated for the entire 16-country sample. Coefficients exceeding 0.5 in absolute value are printed in italics.

load over r = 0.61 on Factor 4 and below r = 0.29 on all other factors. Similarly, the two Geographical Scope variables—'Favours EU enlargement' and 'Favours Turkey in EU'—load highly on Factor 5 and weakly on all other factors. This pattern extends to all six factors, suggesting that the solution is well determined. Note also that the relative contribution of each factor to the total amount of variance in the model—as measured by the rotation sums of squared loadings—is fairly similar across all six factors, with the sum of squared loadings after rotation ranging between 1.6 and 3.0 for each factor. This suggests that the ordering of the factors (in particular, of the first four factors) is not especially significant—rather, that they are all of broadly similar statistical importance.

In substantive terms the implications of Table 2.4 are clear. European public attitudes towards EU citizenship are structured in a manner that corresponds broadly to Benhabib's conceptual distinctions of identity, representation, and scope—though with one or two additional wrinkles. As anticipated, there is certainly a single European Identity factor—Factor 4—which underlies respondents' answers to all four of our survey questions about feelings of European identity. In terms of Representation, there are clearly two factors or 'subdimensions'. The first representation subdimension concerns 'Confidence in EU decision-making', as reflected in the loadings on Factor 1, where high loadings are observed for trust in the EU Parliament and Commission, for satisfaction with EU democratic processes, and for the competence of EU decision-makers. A second representation subdimension relates to a general sense of Political (In)efficacy at the EU level, as reflected in the loadings on Factor 6. This factor clearly reflects people's feelings about the responsiveness of EU policymakers to their own needs and to their country's interests.

In relation to beliefs about the Scope of EU Governance, three subdimensions emerge. The first, picked up in Factor 2, concerns attitudes towards the proper 'Scope of EU policymaking now'. Here, respondents' attitudes across six different policy areas (environment, crime, unemployment, health, agriculture, and immigration) are clearly underpinned by a single pro/anti-EU dimension: people who favour EU involvement in any one policy area tend to favour EU involvement in the others. The second scope subdimension is reflected in Factor 3 and concerns attitudes towards the Future Policy Scope of the EU. Here, respondents' views are underpinned by a general preference/aversion for an *extension* of EU policy scope over the next decade or so. The final scope subdimension is picked up by Factor 5, which, as noted, summarizes respondents' attitudes towards the geographical enlargement of the EU. In short, Table 2.4 shows that European mass attitudes towards EU citizenship have a *single* Identity dimension; *two* Representation subdimensions (Confidence in Institutions and Political Efficacy); and *three* Scope of Governance subdimensions (Policy Scope Now, Policy Scope Future, and Geographical Scope). In the following discussion we explore the robustness of this six-factor characterization of mass attitudes and describe the cross-national variations in the average scores observed on these different factors.

The robustness of the six-factor structure of citizenship attitudes

It is possible that the sort of factor solution shown in Table 2.4 could describe an overall, pan-European, pattern that conceals significant variations at a lower level of aggregation. For example, the structure of attitudes among publics in Western Europe could be very different from those observed among the more recent member states in the East. Similarly, the attitude

Table 2.5. Consequences of estimating the factor solution separately for Western vs Eastern Europe and for Men vs Women (factor loadings in different subsamples)

Attitude item in the factor analysis	Loadings on which factor	All	West	East	Men	Women
Trust in EU Parliament	Representation—	0.87	0.88	0.88	0.87	0.88
Trust in EU Commission	Institutional Confidence	0.88	0.87	0.85	0.86	0.87
EU democracy		0.63	0.66	0.60	0.65	0.62
EU decision-makers are competent		0.63	0.65	0.55	0.63	0.61
Unemployment	Scope of EU Policy—Now	0.66	0.65	0.67	0.67	0.65
Immigration		0.61	0.61	0.61	0.62	0.60
Environment		0.67	0.65	0.70	0.68	0.66
Crime		0.67	0.65	0.71	0.67	0.67
Health care		0.66	0.65	0.68	0.65	0.66
Agriculture		0.65	0.63	0.68	0.65	0.64
Unified tax system	Scope of EU Policy—	0.73	0.76	0.66	0.74	0.71
Common social security	Future	0.78	0.79	0.76	0.79	0.77
Single foreign policy		0.70	0.69	0.70	0.68	0.71
More regional aid		0.59	0.56	0.64	0.58	0.59
Feels European	Identity with EU factor	0.71	−0.70	0.69	0.72	0.70
Attachment to Europe		0.68	−0.70	0.69	0.67	0.70
Europe affects me		0.63	−0.58	0.69	0.66	0.59
European vs national		0.61	−0.62	0.59	0.60	0.69
Favours Turkey in EU	Geographical Scope	−0.84	−0.84	−0.81	−0.84	−0.84
Favours EU enlargement		−0.80	−0.79	−0.78	−0.80	−0.80
EU ignores country's interests	Representation—Efficacy	0.81	0.80	0.82	0.81	0.82
EU doesn't care about people		0.79	0.79	0.77	0.80	0.78

Note: Table entries are loadings, in various subsamples, on the factor corresponding to the concept indicated in the second column. The column labelled 'All' reproduces the italic loadings reported in Table 2.4.

structure of men could be very different from that of women, or that of older people very different from that of the young. We tested a range of different possibilities by estimating the factor model shown in Table 2.4 for subsets of East and West European countries, for subsets of countries grouped according to the time period in which they joined the EEC/EU, for a range of different socio-demographic variables (men versus women, young versus old, and so on), and for each country sample individually.

An illustrative set of results is reported in Table 2.5. The column labelled 'All' reports the pattern of significant loadings shown in the six-factor solution from Table 2.4. Thus, the loading (0.886) for 'Trust in EU Parliament' in the 'All' column in Table 2.5 is the loading of that variable on the Representation—Institutional Confidence factor from Table 2.4. Similarly, the loading (0.671) for 'EU should make policy—Environment' is the loading of that variable on the 'Scope of EU Policymaking—Now' factor from Table 2.4; and so on. Two key features of Table 2.5 should be noted. First, each disaggregated grouping (West/East, men/women) produces the same six-factor solution as the overall, aggregated sample. Second, the *pattern* of factor loadings is virtually identical across all the different groupings—including when similar disaggregated analyses are run for Accession Wave (to the EU), age cohort, education level, and religion.

Very similar results are obtained, in analyses not reported here in detail, when factor solutions are estimated for 'Accession Wave' of joining the EU (Founder member; Joined in 1970s; Southern Wave; Post 1994); for 'old' (45 and over) versus young respondents; for 'high education' (A-level qualifications or higher) versus 'low education' (below A-level or equivalent); and for religion (Catholic, about half of the sample) versus not. Even when separate factor solutions are estimated for each country individually, the same broad pattern is observed. In ten of the sixteen countries sampled (Bulgaria, Denmark, Estonia, France, Britain, Greece, Italy, Portugal, Slovakia, and Slovenia), exactly the same six-factor solution as that reported in Table 2.4 is observed. In Belgium, Germany, and Spain, a seven-factor solution is observed, with five of the factors identical to Table 2.4, but with the 'EU Policy Scope—Now' factor split into two subdimensions. In Hungary and Poland, a comparable seven-factor solution is also observed, though here the 'Representation—Institutional Confidence' factor splits into two subdimensions. Finally, in Austria, a five-factor solution is found, in which Institutional Confidence and EU Efficacy combine to form a single Representation factor. The details of these various solutions, however, are less important than the overall picture they portray. The broad pattern of EU citizenship attitudes characterized in Table 2.4 is extremely robust to variations in sample specification. As anticipated in our earlier discussion, citizenship attitudes across the EU would appear to be very clearly structured in terms of Identity, Representation, and the Scope of Governance.

Variations in the levels of EU Identity, Representation, and Scope

We noted earlier that an oblimin factor solution of the sort shown in Table 2.4 allows for the possibility that the different underlying factors may be correlated with each other. This was certainly the case with our six-factor solution. Table 2.6 reports the intercorrelations among our six citizenship dimensions. Note that we do not use the factor scores derived directly from the factor solution itself in order to construct these intercorrelations. Although factor scores have some attractive features (for example, they all have means of zero) their ranges can in principle vary quite widely, which means that comparing scores across factors and cases can be misleading. In the analysis here, we accordingly use 'constant range scales'—one such scale corresponding to each factor—as described in the Appendix. These constant range scales are constructed by combining the variables that load highly on each factor in a way that ensures that each scale has the same 0–10 range. The correlations

Table 2.6. Correlations among constant range scale measures of six dimensions of European Citizenship

	Identity	Representation— Institutional Trust	Representation— Efficacy	Scope— Now	Scope— Future
Representation— Institutional Trust	0.37				
Representation— Efficacy	0.21	0.25			
Scope—Now	0.21	0.15	0.13		
Scope—Future	0.27	0.29	0.08	0.26	
Scope—Geography	0.18	0.28	0.14	0.11	0.27

Note: Table entries are bivariate Pearson correlation coefficients; all significant at p < 0.001

between the constant range scales and the original factor scores are all greater than r = 0.95. The huge advantage of constant range scales is that country A's average score on scale X can be directly and usefully compared either with country B's average on X or with A's average score on scale Y. The intercorrelations among the constant range scales in Table 2.6 show that, although the factors are related, they are only weakly correlated with each other. Even the strongest correlation, between 'Representation—Institutional Trust' and EU Identity, is only r = 0.37; the remaining intercorrelations are all below r = 0.3. Clearly, if an individual scores unusually high (or unusually low) on one citizenship dimension, it does not follow that s/he will also be very distinctive on another. In short, although there are likely to be some connections among the different dimensions of EU citizenship (as, indeed, we show in later

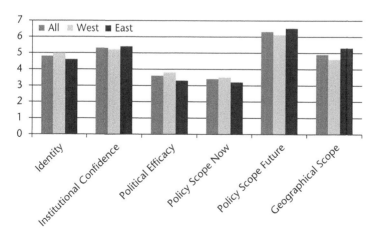

Figure 2.1. Average Scores on 0–10 constant range scales for six dimensions of European Citizenship. Overall average compared with Western and Eastern European respondents' perceptions

chapters), those dimensions are certainly sufficiently distinct and distinctive to merit separate, differentiated, analysis here.

Figure 2.1 reports the EU and West/East Europe average scores, across the sixteen countries surveyed in the IntUne mass survey, on our six 'constant range' measures of EU Identity, Representation, and Scope. Several conclusions are suggested by the figure. First, although levels of EU Identity are roughly the same as the level of 'EU Representation—Institutional Confidence' (both average around 5 on the 0–10 scale), the second measure of EU Representation—Political Efficacy—is noticeably lower, averaging around 3.6 on the 0–10 scale. EU citizens, in short, exhibit reasonable levels of confidence in the rectitude of EU institutions but they do not feel commensurately efficacious in determining political outcomes. Second, EU citizens display a variegated pattern of preferences in respect to the EU's Scope of Governance. They are generally reserved about the policy areas in which the EU ought to be involved *now* (average score = 3.4), but they are fairly comfortable about extending its policy scope in the future (average score = 6.3). In terms of the geographical expansion of the EU, their views are midway between these two 'extremes' (average score = 4.9). A third set of conclusions from Figure 2.1 relates to the differences between East and West Europe. The differences between East and West are relatively modest on all six citizenship measures, with EU Identity and Political Efficacy being slightly higher in the West, and Institutional Confidence and Preference for Geographical Expansion being slightly higher in the East. Given their longer membership of the EU, it is perhaps not surprising that Identity and Efficacy levels should be higher in

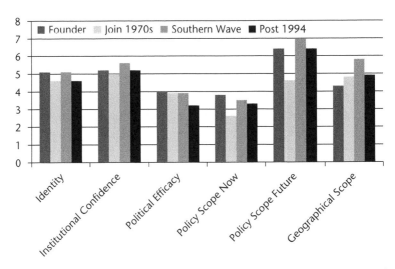

Figure 2.2. Average Scores on 0–10 constant range scales for six dimensions of European Citizenship. Broken down by Accession Wave

Western European countries. Similarly, given their relatively recent accession to the EU, people in the Eastern states are more likely to be sympathetic to the inclusion of people living in new candidate states whom they might expect would share similar aspirations.

A similar pattern to that shown in Figure 2.1 is also evident in Figure 2.2, where the average scores on the six citizenship measures are broken down further—by 'EU Accession Wave'. As Figure 2.2 shows, regardless of the time of joining the EU, Identity and Institutional Confidence levels again tend to be 'middling' and similar to each other, while Efficacy levels and Future Policy Scope preferences tend to be weaker. To be sure, Identity levels and support for current and future EU Policy Scope are noticeably lower among the 1970s joiners (presumably reflecting the relatively high levels of Euroscepticism in both the UK and Denmark). Nonetheless, there is not much difference among Founder, Southern Wave, or Post-1994 respondents in terms of any of the six citizenship dimensions. With the possible exception of the 1970s joiners, therefore, people living in countries that have joined the EU at very different times take a broadly similar view of the EU in terms of Identity, Representation, and the proper Scope of Governance. There are, of course, some differences in levels on the various scales but none is particularly marked; there are certainly more similarities than there are differences among the different accession waves.

Figure 2.3 attempts to clarify the overall position even further. It reports the results of (a) combining the two Representation measures (Institutional Confidence and Political Efficacy) into a single Representation scale, and (b) combining the three Scope measures (Policy Scope Now, Policy Scope Future,

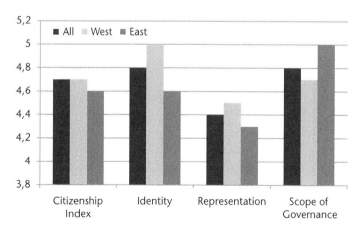

Figure 2.3. Average scores on simplified measures of EU Citizenship, Identity, Representation and Scope. Overall averages compared with Western and Eastern European respondents' perceptions

and Geographical Scope) into a single Scope of EU Governance scale. (Each of these combined scales is calculated as the arithmetic average of the component measures.) The three 0–10 scales (Identity, Representation, and Scope) are then combined (again as the arithmetic average) into a single 0–10 Citizenship Index. Unsurprisingly, as the figure shows, the Citizenship Index averages out the 'highs' and 'lows' on its constituent dimensions. The relatively high average levels of Identity and Scope (both 4.8) are counterbalanced by the relatively low average level of Representation (4.4). The overall Citizenship average for respondents in the East is lower (4.6), though not by much, than the average for the West (4.7). The key conclusion suggested by Figure 2.3, however, is that Identity and Representation levels are clearly higher in the West than they are in the East, while the East's preference for EU Scope of Governance is clearly stronger than that in the West. Being from a country that has been part of the EU family for a longer period clearly engenders both a stronger sense of European identity and a stronger sense that EU institutions can effectively 'represent' people's interests. Being from an Eastern, generally post-Communist member state—where domestic political institutions are often seen as weak and unreliable—clearly encourages a stronger preference for EU governance. These are important empirical patterns, which, it turns out, continue to be observed when a range of statistical controls and modelling techniques are applied to the data. We explore them in considerable detail in later chapters.

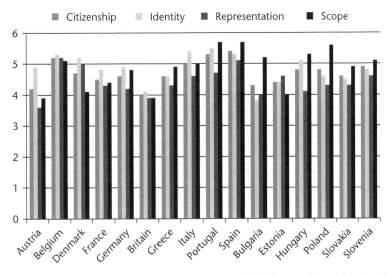

Figure 2.4. Average scores on simplified measures of EU Citizenship, Identity, Representation and Scope. Broken down by country

Finally, Figure 2.4 presents the average Identity, Representation, Scope, and overall 'Citizenship' scores for each country separately. There are few surprises in the patterns reported. As suggested in relation to Figure 2.3, Representation levels tend to be lower than the corresponding Identity and Scope levels in all the countries surveyed. The countries with the lowest EU Citizenship scores are Austria, Britain, Bulgaria, and Estonia, though this pattern is mitigated by the fact that European Identity is relatively high in Austria and the preference for EU Policy Scope is relatively high in Bulgaria. Of the long-standing EU member states, Britain—perhaps because of its imperial legacy and transatlantic ties—remains the most hesitant in developing a sense of European citizenship. The highest Citizenship levels are observed in Belgium (where Identity, Representation, and Scope levels are all relatively high) and in Spain and Portugal (where more variegated patterns are evident, with disproportionately strong preferences for EU Policy Scope). We consider the reasons for these country differences in detail in later chapters. However, three simple arguments commend themselves as possible explanations for the upper and lower tails of the overall distribution shown in Figure 2.4. Britain's failure to develop a strong sense of European citizenship probably reflects its lingering imperial pretensions and the continuing transatlantic focus of its political and economic discourse. Belgium's stronger sense of European citizenship could reflect the fact that the EU's institutional home is located in the Belgian capital itself. And the enthusiasm of the Spanish and Portuguese could be a simple consequence of the considerable economic progress that those two countries have made since joining the EU. We attempt to model the impact of these and other factors on Identity, Representation, and Scope in Chapters 4 through 7. We also examine how all of these things relate to the extent to which people are prepared to 'engage with' and to 'support' the EU itself.

Measuring EU engagement: EU support and electoral turnout

There have been extensive scholarly analyses of cross-national patterns of EU support and of turnout in 'second-order' European elections. The broad conclusions suggested by these earlier analyses are that support for the EU is dependent on a combination of instrumental rationality, party cues, and progressive values (see, for example, Gabel and Palmer 1995; Gabel 1998c; Carey 2002), while turnout in European Parliament elections reflects a combination of rationality, affective commitment to Europe, and sense of civic duty (see, for example, Schmitt and van der Eijk 2003; van der Eijk and Franklin 2009). Our analysis supplements these studies by providing a more extensive set of measures of European Identity, Representation, and Scope that can be used to explain *why* individual European citizens choose to express support (or the lack of it) for the EU and *why* they decide to vote (or not) in elections to the European Parliament. In theoretical terms, we follow Easton (1953) and conceptualize support as a diffuse resource that is targeted primarily at either the regime or the political community or both.

We measure EU support with a single item which asks respondents to use a 0–10 scale to tell if their opinion is closer to the idea that holds that EU integration has 'already gone too far', or to the other pole that it should be 'further strengthened'. Figure 2.5 reports the average EU support score (5.6) across all the sixteen countries surveyed and compares it with the equivalent averages for the different EU accession waves. As the figure shows, the differences among the different waves are relatively small. Support is close to the mean among founders (5.7) and post-2003 accession states (5.5; this drops to 5.3 when Austria is added to the group as in Figure 2.5); below the mean among 1973 and 1995 joiners (5.1 and 4.1, respectively); and above the mean in Southern Wave states (6.6). Table 7.1 in the subsequent chapter on EU support shows the more detailed country-by-country pattern and finds that EU support is highest in Portugal, Italy, Greece, and Spain, and lowest in Austria and Britain.

Expressed attitudinal support for the EU, however, is only one aspect of political engagement. We also asked our respondents whether (and how) they had voted in the previous round of elections to the European Parliament (EP), held in 2004. In asking whether or not respondents had voted in 2004, we were more interested in their *general dispositions towards voting in European elections* than we were in their actual voting records. (In fact, vote recall is known to be an inaccurate measure of a previous vote. See for example,

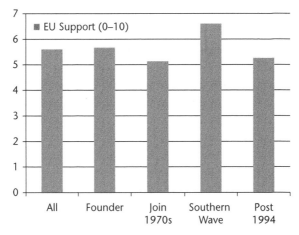

Figure 2.5. Average scores on 0–10 scale of EU Support. Europe-wide average compared with average scores of each EU Accession Wave

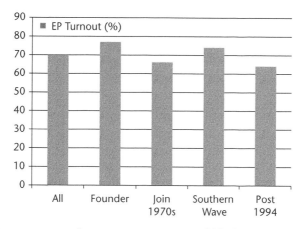

Figure 2.6. Average reported percentage turnout in 2004 European Parliament elections. Broken down by Accession Wave

Sanders and Price 1995.) Figure 2.6 summarizes these dispositions, comparing the overall average reported turnout across our surveyed countries with the equivalent average scores in the different accession waves. The pattern is in fact very similar to that reported for EU support in Figure 2.5. Founders and Southern Wave joiners score above the EU average, while 1970s joiners and post-1994 joiners score below it. The details of this pattern are also shown in Table 8.1 of our subsequent chapter on turnout, which gives the country-by-country reported turnout scores and compares them with actual turnout in the 2004 European elections. Indeed, reported turnout was higher than actual turnout everywhere, except in Belgium, where voting was compulsory. The highest levels of over-reporting were in the post-1994 accession states, most of which had only joined the EU immediately prior to the 2004 EP elections, giving relatively little opportunity for political parties effectively to mobilize voters to participate. All of this suggests that reported turnout in 2004 can be regarded as an additional—primarily attitudinal rather than behavioural—measure of an individual's political engagement with the EU.

Our final (negative) measure of (lack of) EU engagement consists in identifying those individuals who say that they voted in their own country's previous national elections but that they did not vote in the 2004 EP elections. We wish to distinguish between this group and those respondents who say that they voted in both national and European elections, since the former group are clearly *voters* (as opposed to habitual non-voters) who report that they abstained in the last EP election. This suggests that, although they are politically engaged nationally, these 'EP abstainers' are not (so) politically engaged at the European level. As such, they merit special attention since there may be

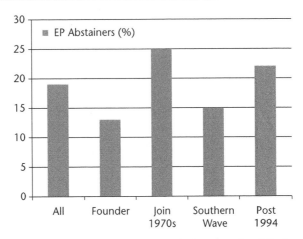

Figure 2.7. Percentage of voters in last national election who failed to vote in 2004 European Parliament elections; by Accession Wave

specific reasons—related perhaps to notions of citizenship as developed here—that lead them to avoid involvement in EU-level electoral politics. Table 8.2 in our subsequent chapter on turnout reports the percentages of respondents who reported voting/not voting in national and in European elections. In the IntUne sample as a whole, about 15 per cent reported voting in neither, and 3 per cent in only EP elections. We are not directly interested in either of these subgroups here. Rather, we are interested in what might distinguish those who vote in elections at both national and European levels (about two thirds of all respondents) from those 'voters' who abstain from EP voting (16 per cent of all respondents).

Figure 2.7 compares the rates of EP abstention across the different accession waves. The numbers reported represent the percentage of *voters* who abstained at EU level rather than the percentage of *all respondents*—thus, for example, the overall average figure indicates an EP abstention rate among voters of 19 per cent (calculated as 16 per cent of 16 per cent + 66 per cent). The differences in EP abstention rates across the accession groups are quite marked. Among Southern Wave voters, abstention is only 15 per cent and among founders only 13 per cent. This rises to 22 per cent among post-1994 joiners and to 25 per cent among 1970s joiners. In short, as with EU Support and EP Reported Turnout, EP abstention rates suggest that founder and Southern Wave states contain the most enthusiasm for the European project, and that 1970s and post-1994 states contain the least. These are themes to which we return in subsequent chapters, where we attempt to unpack what it is about these different groups of states that invokes such differentiated responses towards the EU on the part of their citizens.

Summary and conclusions

In this study we conceptualize citizenship as a multidimensional set of beliefs about political institutions and the citizen's relationship to them. We have shown in this chapter that there is strong individual-level evidence, derived from representative mass surveys in sixteen EU countries, that citizens' attitudes map on to our three core conceptual dimensions of citizenship—Identity, Representation, and Scope of Governance. Our analysis shows that regardless of individual characteristics (such as gender, age, or religion) and regardless of 'type of EU member state', the same basic six-factor EU citizenship attitude structure is observed. This structure consists of a single Identity dimension, two representation dimensions (Confidence in Institutions and Efficacy), and three scope dimensions (Policy Scope Now, Policy Scope in the Future, and Geographical Scope). We suggested that each of these six dimensions can be analysed separately but that, in addition, they can also be combined to produce simpler, aggregate measures of Identity, Representation, and Scope, as well as a single, overall measure of the individual's sense of 'EU citizenship'. In subsequent chapters, we develop models that seek to explain why these attitudes vary across countries and across individuals.

The final purpose of this chapter was to develop measures of the extent of different individuals' 'engagement with the EU'. Superficially, our measures of engagement appear to involve both an attitudinal and a behavioural component: attitudinal in terms of 'support for the EU'; and behavioural in terms of turnout in (and abstention from) European Parliament elections. Given the limitations of vote recall data, and in particular the lack of correspondence between turnout recall among our respondents and actual turnout in the 2004 EP elections, we prefer to use both the 'EU support' and the 'turnout recall' measures as *attitudinal* measures of EU engagement. Accordingly, we employ three measures of EU engagement. These involve, first, a general measure of EU support that reflects the respondent's views of the impact of the EU on her/ his own country and the extent to which the process of European unification should be strengthened. Second, it involves the respondent's reported participation in the 2004 EP elections. Our core assumption here is that those who 'recall' having voted are more likely to be 'engaged' with the EU than those who do not (and vice versa). And finally, we use a negative measure of EU engagement that consists in differentiating between individuals (a) who voted in their last national elections *and* the 2004 EP elections and (b) who voted nationally but *abstained* from voting in the EP elections. We are interested in this group because they are clearly engaged with national politics but are unengaged with the EU.

In the rest of this book, we employ these different measures variously as dependent and independent variables. Initially, we are interested in *explaining* patterns of citizenship, and we accordingly treat our measures of Identity, Representation, and Scope as dependent variables that require explanation. In later chapters, we seek to explore the possible causal connections among these different citizenship dimensions, and as a result we treat them as both dependent and independent variables. Finally, since we are also interested in assessing the possible *consequences* of feelings of EU citizenship, we employ our measures of Identity, Representation, and Scope as independent variables in models where we seek to explain patterns of EU engagement and abstention.

3

Developing Operational Measures of the Explanatory Variables

Corina Wagner, Markus Steinbrecher, and Hans Rattinger

Introduction

The previous chapter outlined the key theoretical and empirical dimensions of European citizenship. This chapter shifts the focus to the factors that might explain why European citizenship varies, in its different dimensions, across both individuals and countries. It provides a description of the main individual-level and country-level characteristics that have been proposed in the various theories developed to explain the evolution of public orientations towards the European Union. As the measurement of these different characteristics is not straightforward, the operationalization of the relevant concepts is discussed here. The direct empirical testing of the various explanatory theories, which makes use of the diverse set of variables reviewed here, is conducted in subsequent chapters.

The independent variables that we review in this chapter are presented in two groups. The first involves individual-level 'micro' variables that measure political attitudes and reported behaviour. Differences between countries, accession waves, and the Western and the Eastern parts of the EU are highlighted. We base our description of individual-level characteristics on the typology of theoretical approaches that was described in Chapter 1. We accordingly distinguish among variables that operationalize *'hard' instrumental rationality* effects; those that measure *'soft' cueing rationality* effects; those that reflect *affective and identitarian* effects; and those that involve *cognitive mobilization*. Second, we describe a series of aggregate-level, 'macro' variables that capture the diversity of political, economic, and social contexts that exist in the different countries of the European Union. Differences across countries, between countries by EU accession wave, and between Western and Eastern (and occasionally, Southern) countries are described, in order to suggest a number of contextual hypotheses that are further explored in subsequent chapters.

Description of micro, mass-level characteristics

As noted above, current research on the influence of attitudinal variables on EU support can be categorized according to four main approaches. The 'hard' *instrumental rationality* approach sees the individual as self-interested and assumes that EU support in its different dimensions stems from an individual cost/benefit calculation of the consequences of integration (see, among others, Gabel and Palmer 1995; Gabel and Whitten 1997; Gabel 1998c, 1998b). Accordingly, citizens will support the integration project if policy outcomes result in a net benefit for them personally, for a group they belong to, or for their country. This would imply that support for the EU could be actively crafted by political elites, if they succeed in delivering the gains expected by their respective mass publics (Gabel and Palmer 1995: 13). The instrumental rationality approach runs parallel to the idea of the EU as a mainly economic organization, whose right to exist was originally prompted by its potential to improve the standards of living of its citizens (Loveless and Rohrschneider 2008: 8).

This instrumental rationality theory has been challenged on two main grounds. It is suggested, first, that its citizens are not pure utility maximizers and, second, that they are rarely well informed enough to make the sort of careful cost/benefit analysis that the hard rationality approach prescribes. Thus, researchers in the school of *cue-taking* or *heuristics-based (bounded) rationality* assume that attitudes towards a distant object like the EU are rooted in 'other, more firmly held and extensively developed, political beliefs that are the result of citizens' experiences with domestic political reality' (Anderson 1998: 573). According to this approach, Europe's citizens resort to 'proxies' (Anderson 1998: 574), 'cues' (Hooghe and Marks 2005: 420), or 'cognitive short-cuts' (Hooghe and Marks 2005: 425) in order to fill their knowledge gap and to understand and to evaluate the EU. These shortcuts typically involve citizens using assessment categories and mechanisms from the national level in order to make judgements about the new supranational arena (Wessels 1995: 124–6). What remains unsettled within this discussion, however, is the question of whether citizens perceive the EU as a simple extension of domestic politics (Anderson 1998) or whether they use the latter as a basis of comparison for evaluating the former (Sánchez-Cuenca 2000; Rohrschneider 2002) with the help of other attitudinal heuristics.

With the EU becoming active in more and more non-economic policy areas and with its development as a distinct polity that sits above the national level, the *affective/identitarian* approach has become prominent (see, among others, Carey 2002; McLaren 2002; Hooghe and Marks 2004, 2005). Instead of presuming mechanisms of rationality, this line of thought draws on the psychology of group identities and loyalties. It considers how cultural factors and individual political feelings are engaged in order to form opinions about the EU and the integration process. In a political system of multilevel governance it becomes more and more difficult to pursue distinct (national) group interests. Boundaries between communities are blurred, and norms of 'us' and 'them' erode (Hooghe and Marks 2005: 423). It can be argued on theoretical grounds, on the one hand, that multiple identities can be mutually reinforcing (Marks 1999; Citrin and Sides 2004) and, on the other, that the possession of one identity can undermine another or others (Carey 2002). It requires precise and systematic empirical enquiry to determine which of these effects— if either—actually operates in practice.

The importance of cognitive involvement with the European project, and support for that project, is an implicit part of all the theories mentioned above. However, *cognitive mobilization* is also regarded as having a distinct and independent impact on EU support (Inglehart 1970, 1977a; Inglehart, Rabier, and Reif 1987; Janssen 1991). Information on any system of multilevel governance, such as that constituted by the EU, is often supplied at a fairly high level of abstraction, which makes it difficult for ordinary citizens to understand. In these circumstances, cognitive skills enable the individual to obtain and process this sort of information, while communication skills and information can bridge the distance between the abstraction of Europe and the personal lives of individuals. The core idea is that cognitively mobilized individuals will be more open to and more engaged with politics generally, will be more cosmopolitan in their world views and, by implication, more sympathetic to the overall European project.

In order to gain a better understanding of the potential these attitudes might have in explaining the overall level of EU citizenship and cross-national variation in it, the above classification is generally used throughout this volume. That said, there are some chapters where the authors either use additional variables or else, for reasons specified in those chapters, reassign a given variable to a different schematic category. In this chapter, we provide descriptions of the main variables that are used as exogenous predictors. For a discussion of the main dependent variables, which are themselves used in some chapters as independent variables, see Chapter 2. The general issues of endogeneity and possible reciprocal relationships between variables are explored in Chapter 9.

Instrumental rationality

The classical theory of instrumental rationality draws on the perception that people link their attitudes towards Europe to the result of an individual cost/ benefit calculation about the advantages and disadvantages of membership of the Union. As shown in Table 3.1, we use three straightforward measures of the perceived benefits of integration and one more general evaluation of national economic conditions to capture the possible instrumental roots of support for the EU.

The first column in Table 3.1 shows the mean of the *EU benefit* factor. This variable is an additive scale constructed from two questions that ask for an assessment of whether the respondent's home country and 'people like the

Table 3.1. Mean values of Instrumental Rationality indicators by Country

	EU benefit factor	EU personal benefits	EU national benefits	Economic perceptions
	(0–10)*	(0–1)	(0–1)	(1–5)
Belgium	6.7	0.52	0.82	2.9
France	5.0	0.38	0.63	2.3
Germany	4.9	0.39	0.59	3.1
Italy	6.6	0.55	0.76	2.3
1957 entrants together	5.5	0.44	0.66	2.7
Denmark	7.1	0.61	0.81	3.6
Great Britain	4.2	0.35	0.49	2.4
1973 entrants together	4.5	0.38	0.52	2.5
Greece	6.9	0.55	0.84	2.1
Portugal	6.9	0.57	0.82	2.1
Spain	7.5	0.65	0.85	2.7
1981/6 entrants together	7.4	0.63	0.85	2.5
Austria	4.9	0.41	0.57	3.2
Western states together	5.7	0.46	0.67	2.6
Estonia	6.6	0.54	0.78	3.4
Hungary	4.5	0.40	0.50	1.9
Poland	6.3	0.46	0.80	2.8
Slovakia	6.7	0.55	0.79	3.1
Slovenia	5.8	0.39	0.78	2.9
Bulgaria	5.1	0.37	0.65	2.6
Eastern states together	5.9	0.45	0.73	2.7
All 17 states together	5.7	0.46	0.68	2.6
Variance explained by Country	6.8**	—	—	11.5

* Figures in brackets indicate the range of each scale. In this table and in all others in this chapter, all micro variables are weighted by standard national demographics. In general, higher values express a more pro-European position.
   The row 'Eastern states together' is equivalent to '2004/7 entrants' together. 'Variance explained by Country' gives the percentage of total variance explained by country.
** A regression of the EU benefit index on 16 country dummies yields an r2 value of 0.068. The equivalent model for Economic Perceptions yields r2 = 0.115. Similar models are employed to produce the 'Variance explained by Country' scores reported in all the tables of this chapter.

respondent' have benefited from EU membership.[1] This scale is designed to capture each individual's cost/benefit calculation about EU membership from both sociotropic and egocentric viewpoints. On the whole, the evaluations seem to be positive since the European average is 5.7 on a scale from 0 to 10. The highest values are found in the Southern European countries, the lowest in Great Britain and Hungary. This calculation seems to be not only a matter of individual variation, as 6.8 per cent of the overall variance can be explained by country groups. Looking more closely at the components of this scale, it can be seen that they are measured on a scale from 0 to 1 and, thus, the mean can be interpreted as the percentage of people judging that the EU has benefited 'people like me' or the nation, respectively. The European mass public is almost evenly divided in this context, with 46 per cent seeing the EU as having delivered a net benefit. The inhabitants of the larger countries, such as Germany, France, and Great Britain, as well as those of the new members Slovenia and Bulgaria, are the most discontented with a mean of below 40 per cent taking a positive view. Spain leads, with 65 per cent of its citizens believing that people like them have gained from EU membership. Comparing these values with respondents' sociotropic assessments of the benefits of EU membership for their respective countries, it is striking that the European mean, as well as the mean in each country, exceeds that of personal benefits by more than 10 percentage points, and in the case of Belgium and Slovenia by more than 30 percentage points. Overall, over two thirds of Europeans believe that EU membership is a good thing for their respective home countries. This is particularly the case among citizens of the countries of the 1981/6 enlargement, among whom almost three quarters (73 per cent) make a positive cost/benefit calculation for their countries.

Another way of thinking about economic benefits is to consider respondents' perceptions of the general economic situation of their respective countries. The broad conjecture here is that people who believe that the domestic economy is doing fairly well (badly) will be more (less) sympathetic to the EU project since that project increasingly sets the parameters for economic activity and growth. As Table 3.1 shows, the mean score (on a 1–5 scale) for all the countries sampled is 2.6, though this varies from a low of 1.9 for Hungarians to a high of 3.6 for the Danes. Some 11.5 per cent of the variance in these economic evaluations can be explained by the country of residence of the respondent, which indicates that the evaluation of the national economy is moderately determined by conditions in the country.

---

[1] The variables correlate at 0.51, the reliability coefficient Cronbach's alpha is 0.67.

Heuristics-based rationality

As noted above, the soft or bounded rationality approach builds on the assumption that in order to process information on such a remote and complex object as the EU, people tend to fall back on attitudes or opinions that focus primarily on the domestic political arena. What kind of attitudes do citizens use as political cues or heuristics? A first possibility is that people perceive the EU political arena and its institutions through their attitudes towards national (and local) institutions (e.g., Anderson 1998; Sánchez-Cuenca 2000; Rohrschneider 2002). The *national institutional confidence* variable, which varies between 0 and 10, taps this dimension. It is an index consisting of measures of 'external political efficacy', satisfaction with democracy, and institutional trust (see Table 3.2).[2] Across the EU, confidence in national institutions is not very pronounced, as is indicated by the mean score of 4.4. It is especially low in those countries that have only recently joined the EU (mean = 3.5). However, the level of confidence is partly dependent on the respondent's country of residence; 8.5 per cent of the variance in the confidence measure can be explained by this information. Against the background of this general position, the second and third column of Table 3.2 distinguish between the values of two of the component variables of the index, *trust in the national parliament* and *trust in the national government*. Both are measured on the same scale, from 0 to 10, so the index and its components can be easily compared. On average, Europeans judge their national parliaments and national governments very similarly. The highest deviations are found in France and in Hungary, where the difference is 0.6 points on the scale. Interestingly, in these two cases and also in general, people in the old member states tend to trust their parliaments more than their governments, whereas citizens of the new member states are more positively inclined towards their governments. However, it is also clearly the case that the evaluation of the parliaments is more dependent on national conditions than is that of the national governments—as the explained variance figures of 10.6 and 6.5 per cent in columns 2 and 3 of Table 3.2 respectively attest.

As discussed earlier, the relationship between trust in national and in EU institutions is not straightforward. Two mechanisms are conceivable. On the one hand, given their relative inexperience with Europe, people might just *transfer* their domestic evaluations of institutions to the European arena; positive assessments of national institutions may simply be extended to positive assessments of European institutions and the whole political system of

---

[2] The scale's reliability (Cronbach's alpha) is 0.77; the absolute value of the corrected item-total correlation is not lower than 0.29.

Table 3.2. Mean values of heuristic indicators by Country: Confidence, Trust, and Identification

	National institutional confidence	National parliament trust	Government trust	Identification with pro-EU party	Identification with incumbent party
	(0–10)	(0–10)	(0–10)	(1–7)	(1–7)
Belgium	5.4	5.6	5.5	4.9	0.23
France	4.7	5.1	4.5	4.7	0.22
Germany	4.4	4.3	4.4	5.1	0.53
Italy	4.0	4.4	4.3	4.5	0.28
1957 entrants together	4.4	4.6	4.5	4.8	0.36
Denmark	6.1	6.4	6.0	5.0	0.42
Great Britain	4.4	4.3	4.2	4.3	0.28
1973 entrants together	4.5	4.5	4.4	4.4	0.29
Greece	4.2	4.2	4.3	5.1	0.30
Portugal	4.3	4.2	4.1	5.1	0.24
Spain	4.9	5.1	4.9	5.2	0.27
1981/6 entrants together	4.7	4.8	4.7	5.2	0.27
Austria	4.9	4.6	4.6	5.0	0.43
Western states together	4.5	4.6	4.5	4.8	0.33
Estonia	5.1	4.8	5.1	4.7	0.34
Hungary	3.9	3.4	4.0	4.9	0.16
Poland	3.6	2.5	2.6	4.4	0.11
Slovakia	4.6	4.6	4.8	4.4	0.23
Slovenia	4.6	4.4	4.5	4.4	0.11
Bulgaria	2.9	2.2	2.6	4.9	0.33
Eastern states together	3.5	2.9	3.1	4.5	0.16
All 17 states together	4.4	4.4	4.3	4.8	0.30
Variance explained by Country	8.5	10.6	6.5	8.0	7.80

Note: National Institutional Confidence is a composite index, comprising responses to questions about satisfaction with national democracy, sense of external efficacy (or institutional responsiveness), and trust in national parliament and government. These indicators are combined to form a 0–10 scale. For details, see Appendix A.

the EU (Anderson 1998). Low trust in national institutions would in turn hamper EU support. On the other hand, people might regard national institutional settings and EU institutions as mutually exclusive alternatives, with one *substituting* for the other. So, if people lack confidence in their own national institutions, they might only see a gain from turning towards Europe and could thus be rather supportive of Europe. In this line of thought, those content with their national institutional setting would rather stick with what they have at home because they fear a worsening of the situation if Europe accrues more power (e.g., Sánchez-Cuenca 2000; Rohrschneider 2002). Which of these putative mechanisms operates is a matter of empirical testing that is discussed in subsequent chapters of this volume.

Another important heuristic at the national level that occupies a central position in the individual belief system is partisanship. Representing a stable affection towards a political party, it structures individual perceptions of politics. When forming their opinions about an issue, party supporters often adapt their position to that taken by 'their' party. This also applies to evaluations of the European Union (Franklin, Marsh, and McLaren 1994; Wessels 1995: 130–4; Anderson 1998; Steenbergen and Jones 2002: 228). There are two ways of assessing the impact of party cue-taking on the formation of EU-related opinions. First, individual positions on European integration issues might be a reflection of people's identifications with parties that are either in favour of or opposed to the EU. Our measure of *identification with a pro-EU political party* is based on the Chapell Hill index of the pro/anti position of the party with which the individual identifies (see Hooghe et al. 2008).[3] The index ranges from 1 to 7, where 1 denotes identification with a strongly anti-EU party and 7 denotes identification with strongly pro-EU party. The European mean score of 4.8 is well above the midpoint of the scale, in the pro-EU direction. No country falls below this midpoint, though the lowest scores are generally found in the countries of the 2004 enlargement wave.

A second way to estimate the possible effects of national partisanship on EU attitudes is to consider whether or not each respondent identifies with the governing party(ies) in her/his respective country. As national governments (through the Council of Ministers) continue to have an important say in the formulation of EU policy, it is plausible to assume that support for the governing party or parties might have an effect on mass attitudes towards Europe (Anderson 1998: 577; Gabel 1998b: 339; for a discussion on qualifications of this thesis, e.g., Ray 2003b). We have accordingly created a dummy variable that scores 1 if the individual identifies with (one of) the governing party(ies) and 0 otherwise. Table 3.2 shows that there are considerable differences across countries in the percentage of people that identify with parties in the incumbent government. In Western Europe, roughly a third of the population exhibits such an identification. The share varies between a quarter and more than a half identifying with the incumbent in Germany. In the East, the average country scores are much lower, averaging around 16 per cent.

A further set of soft-rationality heuristic indicators is outlined in Table 3.3. In the European context, the left–right ideology dimension is a known tool that some individuals use in order to understand and assess their complex political environment. The self-placement scale we use here varies from 0 to 10, where 0 means the left and 10 means the right. As Table 3.3 shows, the European mean of the scale is 5, exactly the midpoint of the scale at 5. This is also the category that contains the most cases (not shown), which suggests the ideological moderation of many voters in Europe. Cross-national average

---

[3] Missing values due to no identification, no naming of party, or no available placement of the party are replaced by the neutral position (4).

Table 3.3. Mean values of heuristic indicators by Country: Ideology, Social versus Competitive Europe, and Globalization

	Left–right ideology	Left–right ideological extremity	Social versus competitive Europe	Globalization is a threat
	(0–10)	(0–10)	(0–1)	(1–4)
Belgium	5.0	4.6	0.68	2.5
France	5.0	6.7	0.43	2.7
Germany	4.8	4.2	0.69	2.6
Italy	4.9	7.8	0.64	2.5
1957 entrants together	4.9	5.9	0.61	2.6
Denmark	5.4	6.1	0.63	2.3
Great Britain	5.0	3.0	0.58	3.0
1973 entrants together	5.0	3.3	0.58	2.9
Greece	5.4	6.7	0.80	2.8
Portugal	4.8	5.7	0.69	2.8
Spain	4.5	7.2	0.75	2.4
1981/6 entrants together	4.7	6.9	0.75	2.6
Austria	4.8	3.2	0.73	2.4
Western states together	4.9	5.6	0.63	2.6
Estonia	5.5	4.1	0.67	2.5
Hungary	5.5	5.5	0.62	3.0
Poland	5.6	5.8	0.75	2.6
Slovakia	5.0	5.2	0.72	2.6
Slovenia	4.7	6.0	0.76	2.3
Bulgaria	4.6	6.4	0.76	2.6
Eastern states together	5.3	5.7	0.73	2.6
All 17 countries together	4.9	5.6	0.65	2.6
Variance explained by Country	1.4	3.6	—	3.0

deviation from this European mean is relatively small and only 1.4 per cent of the variance can be explained by country.

There has been an important scientific debate on the relationship between left–right position and support for the EU (Wessels 1995; Hooghe and Marks 2004; Steenbergen and Marks 2004; Hix 2007). One line of thought assumes that the supranational character of the EU appeals more to those with a leftist ideology, with its potential and will to regulate economic and social conditions (Inglehart 1977a: 351–2; Hooghe and Marks 1999; Gabel and Anderson 2004; Wessels 2004: 258–9). Others have argued that it is people who are at either extreme of the ideological spectrum who are most likely to be critical of the European project (Hooghe, Marks, and Wilson 2004: 122–6). To address this latter discussion, we employ a variable that measures the respondent's distance from the neutral midpoint on the left–right scale. Our *left–right ideological extremity* variable is calculated as the squared deviation of left–right self-placement from the midpoint of the scale. The European mean for this variable is 5.6, implying that ideological extremism is not very widespread in the seventeen countries analysed here. Almost three quarters of the sample is within two points of the neutral category (not shown). In general, the inhabitants of the Southern European states display the highest levels of ideological polarization.

A further heuristic shown in Table 3.3 relates to the type of EU that respondents would prefer to see develop in the future in terms of a trade-off between the achievement of a competitive all-European market versus the provision of pan-European norms regarding welfare provision. We have accordingly created a dummy variable that codes respondents who agree that 'the main aim of the EU should be to make the European economy more competitive in world markets' as 0, while those who agree that 'the main aim of the EU should be to provide better social security for all its citizens' are coded as 1. The distribution of this variable shows that the majority of Europeans (65 per cent) would prefer the EU to concentrate on expanding and embedding the welfare system. The difference on this issue between Western and Eastern European countries is noticeable, with some 73 per cent of respondents in the East preferring a 'social EU' compared with only 63 per cent who take this position in the West. Finally, Table 3.3 reports the distribution of opinion with regard to perceptions of the threat represented by globalization.[4] The distribution of this variable displays a European mean of 2.6 on the 1–4 scale. Country differences on this variable are hardly discernable, with only 3.0 per cent of the variance being explained by country.

To recapitulate: any or all of the above attitudes could be potential cues that citizens use in order to form their opinions about the EU. However, the extent to which each of them actually contributes to the formation of these opinions remains an open empirical question. Does a positive assessment of national institutions support or hamper a positive regard of the European political system? Have left groups become Europhile or are they more Europhobe than the average? Can Europe fulfil the economic mission wanted by the people or does it prohibit it? Is the EU perceived as a potential shield for

---

[4] This attitude was measured in a split design, with three question variations. Part of the sample was asked 'Nowadays, people, money, and ideas travel across national boundaries very quickly. Because of this, a number of [nationality] believe the country now faces serious threats to our national security. What do you think? Is this a very serious threat, a somewhat serious threat, not a very serious threat, or not a threat at all?', another part 'Nowadays, people, money, and ideas travel across national boundaries very quickly. Because of this, a number of [nationality] believe the country now faces serious threats to our economic well-being and jobs. What do you think? Is this a very serious threat, a somewhat serious threat, not a very serious threat, or not a threat at all?', and another part 'Nowadays, people, money, and ideas travel across national boundaries very quickly. Because of this, a number of [nationality] believe the country now faces serious threats to our cultural values and way of life. What do you think? Is this a very serious threat, a somewhat serious threat, not a very serious threat, or not a threat at all?'. These splits were combined in one variable.

the threat of globalization or not? These questions are addressed empirically in subsequent chapters.

Affective/identitarian orientations

There are several ways in which different local, regional, national, or supranational identities could affect people's EU-related attitudes (Hooghe and Marks 2005; de Vries and van Kersbergen 2007; McLaren 2007a). On the one hand, a strong feeling of an exclusive national or subnational identity could *compete* with an emotional attachment to Europe and thereby hamper enthusiasm for European integration (e.g., Carey 2002). On the other hand, it is equally possible that those who believe that their European identity complements their commitment to a national or subnational entity will tend to be EU supporters (Marks 1999; Citrin and Sides 2004).

In order to investigate this question empirically, we use three different identity measures that are reported in Table 3.4. Our combined index of *national identity* was constructed by adding the variables (each measured on a 1–4 scale) which express the strength of attachment to the *local*, *regional*, and

Table 3.4. Mean values of Affective Orientation indicators by Country, Part 1

	National identity	Local attachment	Regional attachment	National attachment
	(0–10)	(1–4)	(1–4)	(1–4)
Belgium	7.1	3.2	3.1	3.1
France	7.6	3.2	3.2	3.4
Germany	7.9	3.5	3.3	3.4
Italy	7.9	3.3	3.3	3.5
1957 entrants together	7.8	3.3	3.3	3.4
Denmark	7.5	3.3	2.8	3.7
Great Britain	7.1	3.1	3.1	3.2
1973 entrants together	7.1	3.1	3.0	3.3
Greece	7.9	3.3	3.3	3.6
Portugal	8.2	3.4	3.4	3.6
Spain	7.2	3.3	3.1	3.2
1981/6 entrants together	7.5	3.3	3.2	3.3
Austria	8.4	3.5	3.5	3.6
Western states together	7.6	3.3	3.2	3.4
Estonia	7.9	3.4	3.2	3.6
Hungary	8.5	3.5	3.4	3.7
Poland	8.4	3.5	3.4	3.6
Slovakia	7.4	3.3	3.1	3.3
Slovenia	8.3	3.5	3.4	3.7
Bulgaria	8.8	3.6	3.6	3.7
Eastern states together	8.3	3.5	3.4	3.6
All 17 states together	7.7	3.3	3.2	3.4
Variance explained by Country	4.4	2.4	3.3	5.2

national community. The individual component variables correlate with the combined scale fairly strongly (between r = 0.41 and r = 0.64) and the reliability (Cronbach's alpha) of the scale is a reassuring 0.72. The national identity average scores in Column 1 of Table 3.4 shows an all-European mean of 7.7 (on 0–10 scale), though the average score is slightly lower in Western Europe (7.6) than it is in the East (8.3). Only 4.4 per cent of the variance of this variable is explained by country, suggesting that variations in national identity are to a large extent independent of country.

Beyond the *levels* of national and subnational attachments described in Table 3.4, it is useful to enquire into the *nature* of these attachments, as summarized in Table 3.5. To understand what makes up national identities, respondents were asked what it means to them to be German, Italian, Danish, or whatever. They were asked to rate how important different characteristics were in this respect. A factor analysis (not reported) reveals that these attitudes are structured along two dimensions. The first factor can be described as mapping a traditional *ascribed* national identity. The defining variables here are the importance of being a Christian, of being born in the respective country, and of having parents with the respective nationality.

Table 3.5. Mean values of Affective Orientation indicators by Country, Part 2

	Ascribed national identity	Achieved national identity	General Trust	Trust in other Europeans
	(0–10)	(0–10)	(0–10)	(0–10)
Belgium	4.8	7.9	5.8	5.8
France	4.5	8.5	5.3	5.4
Germany	5.7	8.3	5.1	5.2
Italy	7.1	8.5	5.3	5.8
1957 entrants together			5.2	5.4
Denmark	5.0	8.1	6.4	6.3
Great Britain	5.4	8.3	5.3	5.2
1973 entrants together			5.4	5.3
Greece	7.4	8.2	4.6	5.2
Portugal	6.4	8.7	5.0	5.1
Spain	5.9	7.9	5.5	5.5
1981/6 entrants together			5.2	5.4
Austria	5.4	8.7	5.6	5.6
Western states together	5.7	8.3	5.3	5.4
Estonia	5.7	8.5	5.2	5.1
Hungary	5.9	8.4	5.0	5.3
Poland	7.5	8.0	4.7	4.9
Slovakia	6.2	7.6	5.1	5.4
Slovenia	5.5	8.4	5.2	5.6
Bulgaria	7.9	8.7	4.6	5.2
Eastern states together	7.1	8.1	4.8	5.0
All 17 states together	5.9	8.3	5.2	5.3
Variance explained by Country	11.4	2.4	2.9	1.9

The second factor groups variables together that correspond to an *achieved* notion of national identity. These comprise the importance of respecting the laws and institutions of the country, the need to master an official language, and the ability to exercise citizens' rights and duties, like active participation in national politics. The two sets of variables were accordingly used to create two additive scales—*ascribed national identity* and *achieved national identity*, both of which range from 0 to 10.[5] The averages of these scales in the different countries can be seen in Table 3.5. On the whole, the perception that national identity can be *acquired* is more widespread in Europe than the belief that national identity has to be *ascribed*. Additionally, whereas country differences on the importance of *achieved* characteristics for national identity are hardly discernible, Europeans in the different countries disagree on how decisive ascriptions are for constituting national identity, with 11.4 per cent of the variance being explained by country differences. Ascribed traits are more important for Eastern and Southern states: there is a 3.4 point difference between the lowest scale score (France: 4.5) and the highest (Bulgaria: 7.9).

Identification with and the sense of belonging to a political community presuppose mutual trust (Loveless and Rohrschneider 2008: 12). To measure *general trust*, we constructed a scale using individual-level items that tap (a) social trust[6] and (b) trust in fellow nationals, in other Europeans and in non-Europeans. The constructed general trust scale has a reliability of 0.75 and it correlates with the component variables between 0.41 and 0.68. It ranges from 0 to 10, with 0 meaning that the person has no trust at all and 10 that the person has complete trust. The average for all seventeen countries is 5.3, which we regard as rather low. Substantive differences between East and West Europeans are discernible, with a mean level of trust of 5.3 in the West and only 4.8 in the East. The fact that a model with the country of residence as the explanatory variable set explains only 2.9 per cent of the variance indicates, however, that trust varies mostly *within* rather than *between* countries. It is also interesting to compare this index of general trust with the values of the component that measures *trust in other Europeans* and which is measured on the same 0–10 scale. The values are quite similar in most countries for both types of trust. Larger differences can be observed for Italy, Greece, and Bulgaria, where trust in other Europeans exceeds the level of general trust. At this point, inevitably, we are unable to tell what these levels and distributions of affective orientations mean for individual support for the EU. Again, further

---

[5] The ascribed national identity scale has a reliability of 0.74, the achieved national identity scale of 0.44.

[6] This general indicator is discussed separately later within the theoretical framework of cognitive mobilization.

empirical analysis is required—which is precisely what is undertaken in later chapters.

Cognitive mobilization

The final set of theories examined in this book suggests that those highly cognitively mobilized are less parochial in their outlooks, and thus more comfortable with and supportive of the EU (see Tables 3.6 and 3.7). The first relevant variable is the feeling of *external* political efficacy, which reflects the subjective assessment of the extent to which political authorities and institutions are responsive to citizen demands (Campbell, Gurin, and Miller 1954). As this attitude reflects the degree to which the individual perceives political behaviour as worthwhile, it is often considered to be a good indicator for self-initiated political involvement (Inglehart 1977a: 297–319). In relation to attitudes towards the EU, the expectation is that those who feel more involved in politics are also more enthusiastic about European integration. Note,

Table 3.6. Mean values of Cognitive Mobilization indicators by Country, Part 1

	Political influence	Media exposure	Political sophistication	EU knowledge	Political Interest
	(0–10)	(0–10)	(0–10)	(0–4)	(1–4)
Belgium	2.5	6.1	5.8	2.4	2.7
France	2.5	6.2	6.2	2.4	2.9
Germany	1.9	7.1	5.1	2.0	2.5
Italy	2.3	7.0	4.7	1.7	2.5
1957 entrants together	2.2	6.7	5.3	2.1	2.6
Denmark	4.0	7.1	6.3	2.2	3.1
Great Britain	1.9	6.0	4.7	1.7	2.5
1973 entrants together	2.1	6.1	4.8	1.7	2.6
Greece	3.1	5.7	5.0	2.1	2.4
Portugal	2.1	6.5	4.7	2.0	2.3
Spain	2.5	6.8	4.6	1.8	2.4
1981/6 entrants together	2.5	6.6	4.7	1.9	2.4
Austria	2.4	6.7	6.0	2.7	2.6
Western states together	2.3	6.6	5.1	2.0	2.6
Estonia	1.7	7.0	4.5	1.6	2.5
Hungary	1.7	6.4	5.0	2.1	2.5
Poland	1.5	5.6	4.7	1.9	2.4
Slovakia	1.5	5.5	5.0	2.1	2.4
Slovenia	1.2	6.0	6.1	2.7	2.6
Bulgaria	1.0	6.0	4.1	1.6	2.3
Eastern states together	1.5	5.8	4.7	1.9	2.4
All 17 states together	2.1	6.5	5.1	2.0	2.6
Variance explained by Country	3.5	4.1	6.1	5.6	3.9

Table 3.7. Mean values of Cognitive Mobilization indicators by Country, Part 2

	Social trust	EU visits	Non-electoral participation
	(0–10)	(0–5)	(0–10)
Belgium	5.6	2.0	1.8
France	5.1	1.1	2.2
Germany	4.8	1.2	2.1
Italy	4.6	0.6	1.6
1957 entrants together	4.8	1.0	2.0
Denmark	6.6	1.9	2.3
Great Britain	4.8	1.2	2.0
1973 entrants together	5.0	1.2	2.0
Greece	3.2	0.4	2.1
Portugal	4.4	0.9	1.7
Spain	4.8	0.6	1.3
1981/6 entrants together	4.5	0.6	1.5
Austria	5.2	1.7	1.8
Western states together	4.8	1.0	1.9
Estonia	5.1	1.0	0.9
Hungary	4.3	0.7	0.8
Poland	4.2	0.5	0.8
Slovakia	4.0	1.4	0.9
Slovenia	4.2	2.2	1.7
Bulgaria	3.3	0.2	0.6
Eastern states together	4.1	0.6	0.8
All 17 states together	4.7	1.0	1.7
Variance explained by Country	3.9	7.2	4.5

however, that on the scale used here, which measures efficacy with a single indicator, Europeans score extremely low: the mean is only 2.1 on a 0–10 scale. In the East, it is even lower, though only 3.5 per cent of the variance can be explained by country.

Our second measure of Europeans' cognitive involvement concerns their exposure to communication networks (Inglehart 1970: 49–53). The relevant theory here is that more intensive use of political media might make the EU more familiar and, by implication, more appealing. The *media exposure* index is constructed with items that measure how often the respondent watches the news on TV and reads about politics in the newspaper; it also varies between 0 and 10.[7] For most people in Europe, keeping oneself updated on politics by the media seems to be a ritual thing; the European mean (6.5) is well above the midpoint of the scale. The country-means do not differ strikingly.

Cognitive mobilization is also captured by an index of *political sophistication* (Inglehart 1970: 53–4). It combines an index of factual knowledge about the

---

[7] The statistical parameters—Cronbach's alpha is 0.31 and Pearson's r is 0.19—might not support the addition of these two variables. But the variables fit very well together with respect to the content, so they are added up to construct the variable media exposure.

EU and self-reported interest in politics.[8] The European average of this index (5.1) hits almost exactly the midpoint of the 0–10 scale and thus indicates a moderate level of political sophistication. Political sophistication is slightly lower in those countries which have only recently joined the EU and in the South. Overall, 6.1 per cent of the variance on this index is due to cross-country variation. An inspection of the components of the scale separately is also instructive. The *EU knowledge* variable indicates that the average European can give the right answer to two out of four questions on the EU (hence a scale from 0 to 4). Here, however, significant differences between countries and regions are not observable. Unsurprisingly, perhaps, self-reported *interest in politics* exceeds factual knowledge; the European mean of 2.6 is well above the midpoint of the scale which goes from 1 to 4. Again, however, Europeans are similar in their reported interest levels.

The distribution of *social trust*, along with our remaining cognitive mobilization measures, is shown in Table 3.7. The social trust measure, which reflects feelings of integration into a community, varies from 0, which corresponds to the belief that 'you need to be very careful in dealing with people' to 10, which corresponds to the belief that 'most people can be trusted'. The underlying assumption is that higher social involvement might help to increase support for the EU. If this is the case, then the cross-national differences shown in Table 3.7 suggest that the preconditions for the EU are more challenging in the Eastern part of Europe. The mean there is 0.6 points below the European mean of 4.7. Bulgaria, in particular, stands out with its low level of social trust (3.3), whereas Denmark displays the highest, with 6.6. Despite these extremes, the level of social trust is dependent on country variations to only a small extent.

Drawing on the popular wisdom that travel broadens the mind, another interesting variable to look at in the explanatory family of cognitive involvement is the number of visits the respondent has made to other European countries within the last twelve months.[9] Apparently, the visits to other countries seem to be more common for residents of smaller countries, e.g., Slovenia, Belgium, or Denmark, which have an average of about two visits.

The final measure of cognitive mobilization shown in Table 3.7 relates to *non-electoral participation*. The index employed here combines information about the extent to which the respondent has recently been politically active in a party, voluntary organization, or group that promoted a public issue, or by boycotting products for political reasons (see Table 3.7).[10] As might be

---

[8] Concerning the reliability and inter-item correlation, similar considerations apply as in the case of media exposure.

[9] The upper limit of the scale is 5, indicating five visits or more.

[10] Cronbach's alpha (0.52) and the correlations of the individual variables are not very high, but the values are still sufficiently high to conclude that the variables scale on a single dimension.

expected, the level of non-electoral political participation is extremely low. The European average is 1.7 on the scale from 0 to 10. In most countries that have joined the EU only recently it does not even exceed 1. To illustrate the levels, the most active country in the sample is Denmark with a mean of 2.3. With these uniformly low values, individual non-electoral participation is to a large extent independent of the national context.

Description of macro, country-level characteristics

The countries in Europe differ with regard to their historical, political, and economic contexts. The influence that the characteristics of countries might exert on the respective residents' perceptions of the EU has been the object of research in numerous studies (Hooghe and Marks 2005; Loveless and Rohrschneider 2008). The analysis here uses several aggregate variables to test for the possibility of context dependency. The variables that we employ are drawn from official statistics and other academic sources[11] and describe either the historical-political or the economic context. Tables 3.8 and 3.9 display the relevant national-level data for the countries where interviews were conducted in our mass survey.

Table 3.8. Historical-political context

	Duration of membership	Democratic history	Quality of governance	Public social expenditure	Partisan divide over Europe
Belgium	51	101	−0.2	29.7	1.3
France	51	102	−0.5	31.5	1.7
Germany	51	72	0.1	29.4	0.8
Italy	51	59	−1.5	26.4	1.6
Denmark	33	87	0.6	30.1	1.5
Great Britain	33	102	0.1	26.8	1.6
Greece	26	62	−1.4	24.2	1.7
Portugal	21	46	−0.8	24.7	1.1
Spain	21	61	−1.0	20.8	0.8
Austria	12	74	0.3	28.8	1.6
Estonia	3	31	−0.7	12.5	1.0
Hungary	3	17	−1.1	21.9	0.8
Poland	3	25	−1.7	19.6	1.9
Slovakia	3	17	−1.3	16.9	1.1
Slovenia	3	17	−0.9	23.4	1.0
Bulgaria	0	17	−2.1	16.1	1.2

[11] The main sources are Eurostat and the World Bank.

Table 3.9. Economic context

	GNI	Trade Openness	Net transfers from EU
Belgium	40,710	74.0	−0.3
France	38,500	67.2	−0.2
Germany	38,860	65.1	−0.3
Italy	33,540	58.6	−0.1
Denmark	54,910	71.8	−0.3
Great Britain	42,740	56.3	−0.1
Greece	29,630	60.8	2.4
Portugal	18,950	76.1	1.6
Spain	29,450	65.6	0.4
Austria	42,700	75.9	−0.2
Estonia	13,200	74.1	1.5
Hungary	11,570	74.0	1.7
Poland	9,840	75.8	1.8
Slovakia	11,730	80.5	1.2
Slovenia	20,960	71.5	0.3
Bulgaria	4,590	59.6	1.2

Table 3.8 shows that our sample includes countries with varying lengths of EU membership (in years until 2007). Each accession wave is represented: there are four founding members, Belgium, France, Germany, and Italy; two out of three members joining in the Northern enlargement, Denmark and Great Britain; and all three countries of the Southern enlargement that occurred in the 1980s. Austria, in turn, represents the EFTA enlargement of 1995. Five countries from the 2004 Eastern enlargement, Estonia, Hungary, Poland, Slovakia, and Slovenia, as well as one of the newest members, Bulgaria, are also included. This classification of the countries is important because it is plausible to assume that support for the EU and its determinants might vary by the length of membership (e.g., Kaltenthaler and Anderson 2001: 149–50; Schmitt 2003: 64).

The duration of membership is also partly reflected in the information about *Communist past*[12] and the length of *democratic history*, which is measured by the number of years in which the country was under a democratic regime in the period since 1900. The oldest democracies are Great Britain and France with a democratic experience of more than a century; the youngest are the Eastern countries Hungary, Slovakia, Slovenia, and Bulgaria.

Various scholars have noted the direct (Sánchez-Cuenca 2000) and conditioning (Rohrschneider 2002) impact of the political performance of a country on EU support. To capture this in different dimensions, we included various indicators of political performance. The variable *Quality of Governance* in Table 3.8 is a single comprehensive estimate based on the first principal component

---

[12] Germany with its divided history is coded 0 and thus has no Communist past.

of the World Bank indicators for *control of corruption, government effectiveness, political stability, rule of law, regulatory quality,* and *voice and accountability* for the twenty-seven member states for the time span from 2002 to 2007.[13] The table indicates negative, that is, relatively low, values for the *Quality of Governance* index for several European countries. Denmark, according to this measure, has the best quality of governance, with a value of 0.6, and Bulgaria has the worst, with a value of -2.1. Another aggregate indicator of political performance that might affect EU attitudes is the size of social expenditure (Sánchez-Cuenca 2000: 158–9). The variable *Public Social Expenditure* measures this as the percentage of each country's GDP in 2005.[14] While this share lies between 25 and 30 per cent in most West European states, most East European countries only spend around 20 per cent or even less on these expenditures. It is plausible to assume that these different levels of quality of governance and development of the welfare state could help to explain cross-national variations in support for European integration.

Another aspect of the political context that is of potential relevance for support for European integration in the different countries is the extent of *elite division over the EU issue*. If a dispute exists on the topic between elites, political cues are more likely to be resorted to by citizens when it comes to forming their EU opinions (Hooghe and Marks 2005: 425–6). The *Partisan Divide over Europe* variable tries to measure the elite division in the different states by a country-by-country standard deviation of a variable describing the parties' positions on European integration, weighed for the parties' vote share in the national election most prior to 2007.[15] The last column in Table 3.8 shows the distribution of this aggregate variable. Obviously, parties seem not to disagree very much on which stance to take on European integration in Germany, Spain, and Hungary. Conversely, Polish parties seem to differ substantially on such issues. This clearly implies that there is potentially important cross-national variation in terms of public debate about European integration.

Besides historical and political experiences, macroeconomic forces have also been analysed as influences on EU support (Eichenberg and Dalton 1993, 2007). There are several indicators in our dataset to measure economic structure and performance. From the inception of the EU, welfare gains were presented as a basic rationale for European integration. Countries are accordingly characterized, first, by economic characteristics like their gross national

---

[13] This factor explains 85 per cent of the variance of the six variables. The first principal component has a correlation exceeding 0.9 with all World Bank indicators but political stability, for which the correlation drops to 0.7.

[14] The missing value for Portugal was replaced using the value from the preceding year as a predictor.

[15] When vote information is not available for separate coalition partners, vote percentage is calculated on the basis of the proportion of seats in parliament held by the coalition partner.

income (GNI) (Eichenberg and Dalton 2007: 130). The differences in the *GNI*, in dollars per capita, between the countries in the dataset are considerable (see Table 3.9). The value varies between $54,910 for Denmark and $4,590 for Bulgaria. Generally, GNI levels are significantly lower in the Eastern and Central European countries than in the Western states.

When connecting support for European integration to economic performance it is especially interesting to take into account the countries' economic activity with(in) the EU. The share of trade with other European Union countries, i.e. the share of imports and exports with the EU compared to the overall trade, can be understood as an indicator for the dependence of the national economy on the EU. If this is high, one would expect the inhabitants of that country to call for further integration, which renders trade relations more efficient (e.g., Eichenberg and Dalton 1993; Gabel and Palmer 1995; Kaltenthaler and Anderson 2001; Eichenberg and Dalton 2007). By 2007, intra-EU trade was obviously high in all member states, but substantial differences could be observed. Slovakia had the highest value on our *Trade Openness* measure with 80.5 per cent of all imports and exports being traded with other EU members, and Great Britain the lowest.

Finally, the benefits of European integration can be evaluated by considering net financial transfers between individual member states and the EU. This involves the balance of total contributions to the EU budget from the given member state and its revenues from the EU budget (which derive mostly from the Common Agricultural Policy and the Cohesion Fund). This last variable in Table 3.9 differentiates net contributors from net recipients by indicating the percentage of the GNI that each country received from the EU budget in 2007. Negative numbers signal net contributors. The Western European countries (taken without the Southern European members) have an average net contribution of 0.3 per cent, while most East European members receive just below 2 per cent. Greece is the largest net recipient with 2.4 per cent of its GNI directly accounted for by EU contributions. As is also the case with trade relations, it is reasonable to expect that net budget transfers condition the different nationals' perceptions and judgements of European integration (e.g., Schmitt 2003: 64; Hooghe and Marks 2005: 421).

All in all, our macro variables reflect Europe's diversity in political and economic context and speak to the theoretical arguments discussed above. Cue-taking theory mainly argues that citizens perceive Europe against the background of their nation and compare European with domestic conditions. They accordingly take pro- or anti-EU cues from domestic political actors, which are reflected here at the macro level in our measures of the historical and political context. Instrumental rationality mainly conjectures that Europeans, when judging European integration, consider economic outcomes; this is where indicators for economic performance, as presented in Table 3.9

are brought to bear. As we saw above, the objective country contexts in Europe are diverse with regard to historical experience, political performance, and economic conditions. It is clearly possible that these background conditions affect citizens' judgements of the EU in its different dimensions. The extent of this context dependency is explored in the following chapters.

Conclusion

Scientific research on public attitudes towards European integration has kept pace with the development of the attitude object—the EU. During recent decades, different theories of support have been put forward, discussed, tested, and criticized. Our objective here is to submit them simultaneously to rigorous empirical testing and to relate them to European citizenship, defined in its different dimensions (see Chapter 2). We draw on theories that define instrumental or cueing considerations, affective orientations, and cognitive mobilization as determinants at the individual level. With regard to hard rational calculations, respondents were asked to deliberate about the personal and national benefits that result from membership of the EU and to judge retrospectively on the development of the economic situation. To gauge the prerequisites for cue-taking, citizens were asked to express their confidence in national institutions and were characterized according to their partisanship and ideological stance. Their preferences with regard to the welfare state as well as their perceptions of the threat posed by globalization were also recorded. In the field of affective orientation, we tried to capture attachments to national and subnational entities to assess their ascriptive versus achieved configurations, and to measure the extent both of their general trust and their social trust in fellow Europeans. Lastly, we sought to describe European citizens with regard to their cognitive mobilization, which involved 'objective' characteristics such as the level of *media exposure* and *political sophistication*, but also people's subjective feelings of *political responsiveness*. Our measures of cognitive mobilization also included visits to other European countries and participation in political organizations and actions. The measurement of all these factors relies on indicators and instruments that have generally stood the test of time in decades of survey research. Hence the stage is now set for substantive analyses of our newly collected data and for answering the research questions of this book.

4

Explaining European Identity

Paolo Bellucci, David Sanders, and Fabio Serricchio

The goal of this chapter is to analyse the determinants of the feelings of mutual belonging that Europeans share and to assess the factors that affect the formation of European identity. Defining European identity is not, however, straightforward since both its actual and preferred contours are the subject of lively political and scientific debates. On the one hand, taking national identity as the point of comparison, it has frequently been argued that the European Union faces difficulties in becoming a proper polity because it cannot command people's primary loyalty in the way the nation does, particularly in the sense that Europeans do not share a single common history, ethnicity, or culture. On the other hand, it can also be argued that European identity need not be framed in strict accordance with the various national identities that have emerged historically, especially since a 'common path' of national identity development is lacking. From this perspective, both Smith's (1998) differentiation between 'civic' and 'ethnic' sources of national identity, and the social psychological distinction between ascribed (inherited) and acquired (by choice) social identities (Huddy 2001), point to the possible development of a distinctive European identity that is both different from, and more nuanced than, 'simple' national identities.

In this chapter we focus on the task of measuring European identification empirically and assessing its determinants. We conceptualize European Identity as a collective identity that involves not only an attachment of individual citizens to the EU itself but also as an encompassing individual self-perception of being a member of a salient social group or community—Europe—that includes multiple political and social dimensions. In the first section of this chapter we discuss our operationalization of the dependent variable—European Identity. In the second, we observe its variance across the peoples of Europe. It is shown that social structure is only modestly related to the strength of European identity, although this pattern systematically varies across EU member states. In the third part, we review the main explanatory theories that have been elaborated to explain the development of European identity. In the fourth, we test a model which assesses their explicative power. In the concluding section, we discuss the implications that the sources of European identity have for EU citizenship.

European identity as a political and social identification

In the years between the 1991 Maastricht Treaty and the 2007 Lisbon Treaty the issue of European identity was a matter of intense politicization and controversy, with 'cosmopolitan' and 'national-populist' declinations of identity projects being juxtaposed (Checkel and Katzenstein 2009: 11). Outward-looking, cosmopolitan European identity stresses political rights and citizenship, while national-populist European identity focuses on cultural authenticity. Political contestation has therefore risen on the very issue of the distinctive features—the origins—of Europe. This is not surprising: political identities differ from other collective identities on the basis of the particular shared beliefs that encourage leaders and mass publics to demand sovereignty and express loyalty (Hermann and Brewer 2004: 6). There is no agreement on the role that the development of a collective identity plays in the European project—whether such an identity is a *prerequisite* for legitimate governance or an *evolving* attachment that goes hand in hand with political and institutional integration. Moving from normative to scientific inquiry, we attempt in this chapter to identify the contours and determinants of identification with Europe as expressed by public opinion, recognizing that, as Castiglione (2009: 29) argues, 'the construction of European political identity does not necessarily rest on a definite conception of what it is to be European' and that Europeans might indeed be involved in exciting 'identity experiments' (Holmes 2009). In uncertain territory, we start from where empirical research on European identity has proceeded.

While early public opinion research assumed that European identity was a component of more general attitudes towards European integration—often interpreted as being synonymous with support (Inglehart 1970, 1977b)—later research has explicitly interpreted European identity as a sense of membership in a political community that is distinct from general support for the EU itself (Duchesne and Frognier 1995; Scheuer 1999). Recently, more complex conceptualizations have appeared, analysing the structure of the belief system that citizens hold towards Europe (Scheuer 2005; Westle 2007b). Yet, these accounts, due to the limitations of available survey data, have generally been forced to rely on evidence that somehow blurs the distinction between support and identity, concepts that overlap to only a limited extent and which indeed appear to be theoretically and empirically distinct. In defining identity, we follow Tajfel and Turner (1986) regarding it as a *feeling* of attachment to a salient group. With reference to Europe, we assume that this implies attachment to a salient supranational community. Support, in contrast, is an *evaluation* of the legitimacy of the political community (Easton 1965); in the European context, an evaluative judgement on the desirability of developing a European polity. Support, therefore, implies a judgement while identity is a psychological-affective sentiment. This has an important bearing on the present research, as we hypothesize for the moment that identity, and more broadly citizenship, is conceptually distinct from and causally antecedent to support. This is an issue that we confront explicitly in Chapters 7 and 9.

Past research has measured 'support' for Europe with the Eurobarometer 'classical' items of *unification/dissolution*, *membership*, and *desired speed* (Niedermayer 1995; Norris 1999). The more scant research on identity has relied on instruments tapping *belonging*, *territorial attachment*, and *future feelings* (Citrin and Sides 2004; Sinnott 2005; Moreno 2006).[1] We draw on and widen this perspective, relying on social identity theory. According to this perspective, social identity is 'that part of the individual's self-concept which derives from his *(sic)* knowledge of his membership of a social group (or groups) together with the value and emotional significance attached to that membership' (Tajfel 1981: 255). Collective identities accordingly have two dimensions: (a) the consciousness of membership of a group or *belonging*; and (b) the value and emotional weight attached to such belonging, that is, its *salience*. Identification is the output of a process that implies the joint presence of belonging and salience. This perspective explains how an individual can incorporate a group membership into her/his self-concept, which is when group membership becomes emotionally important and relevant. This allows us, in turn, to distinguish identification as a 'mere affinity/empathy' from 'identification as self-conception' (Green et al. 2002). This basic process applies in principle to a variety of collective identities, and has been employed in particular to explain the development of partisan identification and national identity. We consider that it is also appropriate to an inquiry into the development of a European identity.

Our measure of European Identity, then, is directly inspired by social identity theory, and is aimed at tapping specifically perceptions of both *belonging to* and the *salience of* Europe. European belonging is measured by the two long-serving Eurobarometer questions:

---

[1] Eurobarometer questions include: (A) To which one of the following geographical units would you say you belong to first of all (town, region, country, Europe, world)? (B) People may feel different degrees of attachment to their town, region, country, or to European Union. How attached do you feel to ... (C)? In the near future, do you see yourself as (nationality) only, (nationality) and European, European and (nationality), European only?

A. People feel different degrees of attachment to their town or village, to their region, to their country, and to Europe. What about you? Are you very attached, somewhat attached, not very attached, or not at all attached to Europe?

B. Do you see yourself as ...? (1) Nationality (e.g., Italian) only; (2) (nationality) and European; (3) European and (nationality); (4) European only?

European salience is measured by two questions which have been elaborated from Lilli and Diehl (1999)'s National Identity reformulation of the Collective Self-Esteem Scale originally proposed by Luhtanen and Crocker (1992):

C. How much does being a European have to do with how you feel about yourself in your day-to-day life?

D. How far do you feel that what happens to Europe in general has important consequences for people like you?

As we have already shown in Chapter 2, these four variables intercorrelate in a systematic and stable way across Europe and can be combined into a single (0–10) constant range scale index of European Identity.

European identity across the peoples of Europe

The overall average score on European Identity occupies a middle position on the 0–10 scale. The average value of 4.8 reveals a tendency of the European public surveyed to hold a moderate rather than a strong allegiance to Europe. The curve depicting their distribution (see Figure 4.1) shows a longer left tail, suggesting that a larger proportion of Europeans clusters on moderate levels of European identification. As the figure shows, a quarter of Europeans have a value below 3.3 while the 75 per cent percentile is set at 5.8, slightly above the average. This is not surprising. Rather, it is in line with comparable previous evidence on the diffusion of perceptions of European 'belonging' (Duchesne and Frognier 1995; Westle 2007b). Around 65 per cent of Europeans in our survey feel attached to Europe, a level comparable to the average of 62 per cent registered by Eurobarometer between 2000 and 2007, up from 55 per cent registered in the earlier decade. Unfortunately, no previous survey evidence is available concerning the *salience* of Europe to its citizens, so we cannot assess whether what we observe about the importance of Europe for people's lives in 2007 (48 per cent report that feeling European is important in their day-to-day life, and 72 per cent feel Europe carries important personal consequences for themselves) has or has not increased over time.[2] These data may simply

---

[2] The available Eurobarometer question closest to our notion of salience taps the extent to which Europeans think of themselves not only as national citizens but also as citizens of Europe. In 1992, 50 per cent of the citizens of the six founding members of the EU never thought of themselves as Europeans (Scheuer 1999).

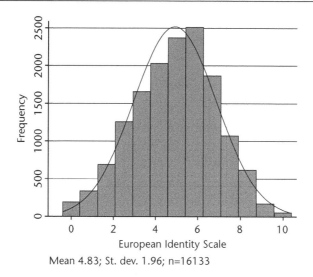

Figure 4.1. Distribution of European Identity (0–10 scale)

suggest that among EU member-state nationals the notion of Europe is readily available and accessible to people's minds, and not devoid of an emotional loading. However, it is of interest to note that the 'salience' component of the index of European Identity has a greater intensity (a value of 5.2 on the 0–10 scale) than the 'belonging' component (with an average value of 4.2). This means that in our overall index of European Identity salience weighs slightly more than attachment.

In order to provide some understanding of the previously unknown distribution of the intensity of European salience, we can illustratively compare across our sample the pattern of the two measures—their average national scores. As Figure 4.2 shows, the two components are related: the greater the attachment to Europe, the more intense the level of salience. This is obviously expected (the aggregate correlation is high, r = 0.55) since the original variables load on the same factor dimension at the *individual level*, as we know from Chapter 2. But we also observe a substantial variance in the pattern of association between *countries*, which reflects the underlying variability within each polity. For instance, at one extreme, British citizens consider that Europe is quite salient, but they also exhibit relatively low levels of European attachment. This is reflected in the relatively high value of the standard deviation of the distribution of their index of European Identity (2.04)—clearly higher than the average standard deviation (1.96). At the opposite end of the spectrum, Italians' level of European attachment is similar to their level of expressed European salience, producing a much lower standard deviation (1.72). Some countries (e.g., Hungary, Belgium, Denmark) show a pattern similar to

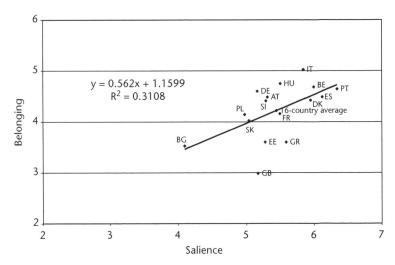

Figure 4.2. Distribution of European Belonging and European Salience (0–10 scale) across Europe

that of Italy. Others (e.g., Slovakia, Estonia, Greece) follow that of UK. There-fore, there is a significant variation in the intensity of European Identity, which is neither universal nor equally distributed, as the standard deviation of the overall distribution—1.96—hints. This is reassuring in terms of the validity of the measure we use, which shows a healthy variability both within and between countries.

Many factors could lie behind the intensity with which a person identifies with Europe, including both individual characteristics and features of the context—the nation—in which s/he lives. Before laying out specific hypoth-eses that might explain the individual propensity to express an identification with Europe, it is useful to explore descriptively how European Identity varies both according to respondents' social and political characteristics and accord-ing to macro-level national attributes.

A perusal of Table 4.1 reveals that European Identity does not strongly and systematically co-vary with social structure.[3] Gender and age, for instance, do not appear to exert a strong influence on the intensity of European attach-ment. Even education is able to distinguish across European identity levels only moderately (the Eta coefficient is 0.18). However, being young and educated does appear to raise the level of identification with Europe—students represent the social group with the highest level of EU identification (5.2), in

---

[3] In assessing the strength of these associations we must of course be careful, since the large N on which they are computed makes them statistically significant even when the differences are not substantively large.

Table 4.1. Socio-demographic correlates of European Identity

	Mean within group	Standard deviation within group	Correlation (eta) with variable
Overall	4.83	1.96	
Gender			0.070***
Female	4.70	1.93	
Male	4.97	1.99	
Age			0.043***
18–24	4.95	1.86	
25–34	4.93	1.88	
35–44	4.84	1.90	
45–54	4.85	1.95	
55–64	4.77	2.01	
65 +	4.70	2.11	
Education			0.179***
Elementary	4.33	2.03	
Secondary	4.57	1.98	
Intermediate	4.95	1.85	
University	5.36	1.90	
Occupational status			0.042***
Employed	4.85	1.96	
Not employed	4.43	1.95	
Occupation			0.134***
Self-employed	5.15	2.00	
Non-manual employee	4.93	1.89	
Civil servant	5.25	1.83	
Manual employee	4.45	1.91	
Student	5.19	1.75	
Retired	4.64	2.08	
Unemployed	4.43	1.95	
Other inactive	4.58	1.94	
Religion			0.132***
None	4.93	2.03	
Catholic	4.97	1.88	
Orthodox	4.23	2.04	
Protestant	4.81	1.92	
Muslim	4.09	2.09	
Other	4.92	2.16	
Religion attendance			0.043***
Never	4.79	2.06	
Seldom	4.88	1.94	
Often	4.78	1.92	
Interest in politics			0.230***
None at all	4.07	2.04	
Not very much	4.59	1.85	
Some	5.05	1.86	
A lot	5.53	2.03	
Left–right ideology			0.082***
0–2	4.87	2.04	
3–4	4.94	1.94	
5	4.66	1.97	
6–7	4.93	1.88	
8–10	4.98	1.93	

N = 16133.
*** p<.001

Note: Table entries are the mean and standard deviance of the eleven-point European identity scale for each group and the correlation between European identity and given grouping variable.

keeping with previous research on cosmopolitan values (Inglehart 1977b). Weak associations are also observed in relation to occupation. People in employment display only slightly higher levels of identification with Europe (4.8) than unemployed people (4.4) and, surprisingly, manual (supposedly the 'losers' of economic integration) and non-manual workers' levels of attachment are similar (respectively, 4.5 vs 4.9). We find, then, no strong evidence of a possible 'class cleavage' as suggested by other scholars, though it is confirmed that interactions with European people and institutions increase the salience of Europe, here highlighted by the stronger attachments of civil servants (5.2) (Fligstein 2009). Table 4.1 also demonstrates that the relationship between European identity and religious denomination is weak (Eta is 0.13, the same as for occupation). Stronger levels of identification are observed among Catholics and atheist/agnostics, while it is lower among Orthodox and Muslims.[4] However, the differences are minimal according to religion attendance: intermittent religious practice slightly increases European identity, which is weaker among both devout and non-religious people.

Table 4.1 also reports the association between Identity and a series of political variables. These are included here to provide a general illustrative description of the correlates of Identity, even though their expected causal implications are not considered until later. Not unexpectedly, *political engagement* increases the strength of European identification (Eta = 0.23), while there is a weak correlation with left–right self-placement (Eta = 0.08). In fact, radicals, of both left and right, express slightly *higher* levels of identification than people with centrist ideological leanings. EU integration was traditionally supported by centrist mainstream parties and opposed by radical left- and right-wing parties (the former based on defence of social regulation of the market and the latter on the defence of prerogatives of nationality). Our finding here is in fact in line with other recent research on EU support (Scheuer and van der Brug 2007). This suggests that we may be witnessing a possible evolution of partisan attitudes towards the EU in which the European project is being progressively accepted by both the left and right of the political spectrum—though it remains to be seen whether or not the particular pattern that we observe here continues in the future.

Overall, the message that this preliminary analysis conveys is of a very modest impact of social structure on EU identification and a somewhat stronger influence of political engagement. Of course, the fact that we are observing

---

[4] These preliminary results—which may relate to debates on the Christian roots of Europe—must be treated with caution. Actually the Muslims' lower support derives from an interaction with nationality: their EU identity is lower in Bulgaria, 3.8—where they are mostly numerous and whose national average level of identification is lower—while German and Danish Muslim minorities show levels of European Identity higher than average, i.e., 4.9 and 5.2.

Table 4.2. Mean and dispersion of European Identity (0–10 scale) across Europe

Country	Mean	St. dev.
Portugal	5.49	2.01
Italy	5.43	1.72
Belgium	5.34	1.97
Spain	5.30	1.83
Denmark	5.19	1.74
Hungary	5.12	1.63
Austria	4.90	2.06
Germany	4.88	2.00
Slovenia	4.85	1.79
France	4.83	1.98
Average of 16 countries	*4.83*	*1.93*
Greece	4.59	1.86
Poland	4.56	1.83
Slovakia	4.53	1.88
Estonia	4.44	2.03
Great Britain	4.08	2.04
Bulgaria	3.81	2.12

bivariate associations may conceal spurious relationships, which may disappear once control and intervening variables are taken into account.

The previous analysis of individual-level variations in European Identity can be supplemented by taking into account the national context where respondents live. As Table 4.2 and Figure 4.2 show, from this perspective the variance in the level of European identification appears somewhat greater, since it varies from a low score of 3.81 in Bulgaria to a high of 5.49 in Portugal. Southern European countries (Portugal, Italy, Spain) and Belgium are at the top of the ranking, while the Eurosceptic UK joins Eastern European nations at the bottom. The evidence from Table 4.2 and Figure 4.3 suggests that, contrary to Bruter's (2005) claim, the level of European identity is not dependent on the duration of a country's membership of the European Union. Rather, it appears that the relationship is non-linear: people living in Southern countries which acceded to the EU in the 1980s show, on average, a higher level of identification—comparable to that of the founders—than earlier accessions in the 1970s. This said, more recent joiners of Eastern Europe do indeed exhibit a lower level of identification (Table 4.3). Note that the differences among the mean scores shown in Table 4.3 are significant at the individual level (even if the association of Eta = 0.13 is fairly tenuous) but not at the aggregate country level.[5] This is not the case when we consider member states that have experienced a Communist regime, whose populations may have high expectations but share fewer experiences with those

[5] Of course aggregate etas, with reduced N, are always higher than individual-level etas. Some caution is therefore necessary in comparing individual- and aggregate-level etas across Table 4.3.

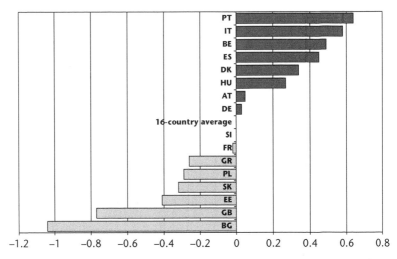

Figure 4.3. Differences in European Identity (0–10 scale) between countries (average country score minus overall average score)

Table 4.3. Mean values on index of European Identity (0–10 scale) by Length of EU Membership, Communist Past, Quality of Governance, and Trade Openness

	E-Identity (mean)	St. Dev.	Eta (individual level)	Eta (aggregate level)
Overall	4.83	1.96		
Accession			0.13***	0.55
Founder	5.12	1.94		
Join 1970s	4.63	1.97		
Southern Wave	5.13	1.94		
Post 1994	4.60	1.96		
Communist Past			0.11***	0.47
No	5.00	1.97		
Yes	4.55	1.93		
Quality of Governance			0.03***	0.13
High	4.89	2.00		
Low	4.76	1.91		
Trade Openness			0.05***	0.13
High	4.71	1.96		
Low	4.93	1.99		

*** p<.001

Note: Eta values measure—at the individual and country level—differences among means with associated levels of statistical significance.

living under a consolidated democratic regime. The 'Communist Past' variable in Table 4.3 depresses EU identification, with an association at the individual level (Eta = 0.11) that is confirmed at the system level (Eta = 0.47). In addition, people living in polities with a higher 'Quality of Governance' express a somewhat higher EU identification.

Finally, Table 4.3 suggests a small but significant difference in the intensity of identification according to the openness of the countries' economies: contrary to our expectations, living in a country greatly dependent on external trade does not increase the level of European identification. This finding probably reflects the fact that the wealthiest and most open economies in Europe also have important domestic markets that provide a degree of shelter from international economic fluctuations and which therefore allow their citizens to have a greater degree of confidence in processes of internationalization. We note again, however, that all of these bivariate relationships are potentially spurious and should not be overinterpreted at this stage. The assessment of their actual impact on EU identity can only be gauged via a multivariate analysis where individual and contextual effects can be simultaneously evaluated, which will be carried out later in this chapter. We turn now to laying out some hypotheses on the factors that might lead to the development of a European identification.

The sources of European identity: theoretical perspectives and research hypotheses

Historical, philosophical, and normative analyses on the political, cultural, and social identities of Europe abound (for a review, see Weiler 1999; Lowenthal 2000; Stråth 2002). However, systematic empirical research on the contours and determinants of European identification among mass publics is somewhat scarcer, since the vast literature that has analysed public attitudes on Europe has focused mainly on support for the integration process rather than on identity. A reading of previous empirical research points to four theoretical perspectives that have been developed over time—in response to the evolving nature of the supranational European arena, the expansion of its functions, and also to the changing attitudes of European citizens. These range from *cognitive mobilization* to *instrumental rational* perspectives, from *political mobilization* to *affective/identitarian* explanations. All of them, in principle, are capable of shedding light on the determinants of European identification.

The first theoretical perspective—associated with early analyses of support for European integration—focuses on the individual resources and value orientations that are held to affect mass attitudes toward Europe (Inglehart 1977b, 1979). These are primarily *cognitive mobilization* variables, such as knowledge of (the former) European Economic Community, exposure to information, and the holding of 'postmaterialist' values. In short, according to the cognitive mobilization perspective, 'cosmopolitanism' was a key source for developing allegiance to a political project that would transcend national and parochial borders. Early empirical research on European identity showed a positive correlation with cognitive mobilization: higher levels of education, urban residency, and political engagement were all found to be positively associated with feelings of EU identity by Duchesne and Frognier (1995). Extensions to the cognitive mobilization model have focused more explicitly both on individual resources (education and individual political efficacy) and the sort of life experiences, such as political engagement, work abroad, and speaking foreign languages that allow people to interact on a regular basis with other Europeans (Fligstein 2009). These resources and life experiences are seen as a prerequisite of favourable attitudes toward Europe that are further enhanced by media exposure. According to this approach, the mass media plays a key role by providing visibility ('image building') to a relative abstract entity such as Europe (Díez-Medrano 2003; Bruter 2005), thus acting as a source of mobilization of citizens.

A second theoretical approach—*instrumental rationality*—is also associated with the analysis of support for EU integration. The early economic-trade focus of European integration made it reasonable to study the determinants of public attitudes to the EU in terms of rational calculations about the individual and collective costs and benefits accruing from Europe (Eichenberg and Dalton 1993; Gabel 1998c). Individuals who perceived that they themselves and/or their respective countries had, on balance, benefited from EU membership were much more likely to support the European project. 'Egocentric individualism' (the individual's position in the labour market, which determines whether or not s/he is a winner or a loser from the free movement of capital and labour), 'sociotropic utilitarianism' (the country's competitive advantage/disadvantage from lessening trade barriers), and 'perceptions of group interests' being threatened in the allocation of welfare benefits by immigration have all been found to constitute important sources of EU attitudes (McLaren 2006).

It might appear that this sort of 'rational' approach is quite distant from research on social identities. However, identification can also be an instrumental choice. As Kelman argues (1969: 281), 'An individual is instrumentally attached when he *(sic)* sees the system as an effective vehicle for achieving his own ends and the ends of other system members'. It follows that people who view EU membership as a sustained source of personal and/or national benefit may develop a higher intensity of attachment to Europe. This finding is consistent with the findings of Ruiz-Jimenez et al. (2004), which show that instrumental motivation correlates with European identification. This idea is reinforced by social identity theory, which highlights the motivational underpinnings of identities and the importance of subjective perceptions of the value of group membership (Huddy 2001). According to Huddy (2003), choice-based processes of identification with a group can be based on a variety of motivations, including the desire for social mobility, relative deprivation, perceptions of realistic group interests, and even shared symbolic concerns. In principle, therefore, identification with Europe may be driven by a multiplicity of 'rational choice' factors, spanning from direct economic interests to the desire to enhance the economic and political effectiveness of the nation in a larger supranational group, to the desire to acquire a higher international status.

The third perspective introduces *political mobilization* factors and *judgemental heuristics*. The main idea here is that mass perceptions of Europe are defined in national political arenas and that parties, political elites, and the mass media may 'cue' voters in their views towards Europe and its institutions (Hooghe and Marks 2005). Previous research has shed light on the importance of the role that the institutions of the EU play in the formation of a common identity. Chryssochoou (1996) finds that a low identification with Europe is explained by a perception of distance from and lack of control over EU politics.[6] More generally, however, institutions and identities are connected through complex mechanisms which involve possible *socialization* and *persuasion* effects (Hermann and Brewer 2004: 14–16). The strength of possible socialization effects reflects the salience of EU institutions for people's lives. As in the previous cognitive mobilization model, the more that people interact with EU institutions or their representatives, the greater the likelihood that the EU will be perceived as a 'real' entity, providing shared experiences which enhance group identity and a sense of community. The strength of persuasion effects in turn reflects the intensity and character of the portrayal of EU institutions, directly or indirectly, by the mass media; the more intense and positive the portrayal, the greater the extent to which the EU's institutions will be seen as legitimate and the greater the sense of EU collective identity among European mass publics.

But how are these perceptions and identities formed? According to Anderson (1998), people use 'proxies' or cognitive shortcuts based on a variety of heuristics to structure their views on Europe. Empirical support for a range of such heuristics has been reported in a number of previous studies of the determinants of EU *support*. These include quality of democratic governance (Sánchez-Cuenca 2000), democratic satisfaction (Rohrschneider 2002), national institutional trust (Anderson 1998), images and trust of European institutions[7] (Laffan 2004; Bruter 2005), and partisan identification (Ray

---

[6] Likewise Catellani and Milesi (1998) point to the relevance of political efficacy in the development of a European identity.

[7] This perspective is also echoed in recent social-psychological research, which proposes a media mobilization model which gives content to an abstract entity such as Europe, based on the concept of entitativity (Campbell 1958) which explains how people develop allegiance to abstract entities. Castano et al. (2003) and Castano (2004) argue that European visibility is provided by the

2003a). However, there is also evidence to suggest that when they are employed to explain measures of European *identity*, political variables such as party identification, left–right position, and satisfaction with democracy seem unable to explain European identity (Duchesne and Frognier 1995).

More importantly perhaps, there is no consensus in the literature on how and through which mechanisms these various heuristics operate. Cognitive shortcuts enable people to make (reasonably) reasoned choices in a context of low information (Popkin 1991) by relying on easily available and accessible cues in response to complex and/or distant stimuli. So in principle it is easy to understand how in forming evaluations of, and attachments to, Europe people may rely on the European stance taken by their preferred parties or on their image (positive or negative) of EU institutions and actors as represented in the media. Less straightforward is how to assess the direction of the cueing in the case of people's perceptions and evaluation of national institutions. On the one hand, people *satisfied* (dissatisfied) with the performance of national institutions may extend their *trust* (distrust) to European institutions (Anderson 1998). On the other hand, it is equally possible that dissatisfied people—or people living in low quality of governance polities (Sánchez-Cuenca 2000)—may translate their *negative* domestic evaluations into greater *confidence* in European institutions, seen as a source of modernization/ improvement of national governance. Therefore, as argued in Chapter 9, *transfer* or *substitution* heuristics may operate in opposite directions. Transfer heuristics *project* towards Europe positive or negative feelings and evaluations that originate from the domestic system, while substitution heuristics look to Europe to *compensate* for unaddressed domestic national shortcomings or failings. We consider both of these possibilities in the models developed here.

The broadening of the European project in the wake of the 1992 Maastricht Treaty, combined with some dissatisfaction over the performance of pure economic models of support for European integration, moved scholarly attention in the early 1990s toward *identitarian/affective* processes. The identity perspective gives to national (and subnational) attachments a crucial role in constraining European identity and, more generally, European attitudes. However, the role of national identity in explaining European attachments is, again, ambivalent. Duchesne and Frognier (1995) find a positive relationship between national identity and EU attachment. In contrast, Carey (2002) and McLaren (2002, 2006) find that national identification hinders

---

interaction between individual psychological attitudes—such as perception of proximity, common fate, similarity, and boundness—and the role of supranational institutions which build an image of Europe (Díez-Medrano 2003). Also Bruter (2005) focuses on the role of EU institutions—and of media—in shaping European identity.

favourable attitudes towards Europe. Hooghe and Marks (2005) show that only 'exclusive' national identity attenuates European support.

There are, then, two main questions confronting the possible impact of national (and regional) identity on the intensity of European identification: their possible reciprocal dependence, and the precise character of national identity. As to the first, national identity constrains and limits European identity to the extent that the former competes with the latter (exclusive identity). This constraining effect does not operate, however, if multiple 'inclusive' identities coexist. Available political psychology empirical research tends to agree that national, subnational, and European identities are mainly inclusive identities that can relatively easily coexist, although it is less clear what the balancing mechanism is that allows these multiple identities not to conflict (Mlicki and Ellemers 1996; Huici et al. 1997; Castano, Yzerbyt, and Bourguignon 2003; Citrin and Sides 2004). To be sure, social identity research has long since shown the coexistence of multiple (cross-cutting) social identities that are relatively independent of each other. Hermann and Brewer (2004: 8) point to a possible hierarchy of attachments. They contrast a model of 'clear separation' (where there is no overlapping membership) with a 'nested' model (where everyone in a smaller community is also member of a larger community) and a 'cross-cutting' model (where some, though not all, members of a group are also members of another group). Their ideas in turn have been developed to accommodate even more fluid identity combinations, as in the 'marble-cake model' proposed by Risse (2004), which adds the ideas of 'salience' and 'coherence' to cumulative multiple attachments (see also Duchesne and Frognier 1995).

The character of national identity is the second important factor highlighted in the identitarian perspective. To what extent might a national allegiance hinder the development of a European one? Scholarly research has approached this question in terms of the contents/meaning of national *vis-à-vis* European identity. On the one hand, according to Ruiz-Jimenez et al. (2004), national and European identity need not conflict because of their different natures and sources. Ruiz-Jimenez argues that national identities are primarily viewed in *ascriptive* (cultural and ethnic) terms, whereas supranational European identities are primarily viewed in *achieved* or acquired (political and civic) terms. This implies that there need be no tension between national and European identities—because they focus on different things. On the other hand, Haller and Ressler (2006) suggest that this distinction is of relevance also for *national* identity. They show that the meanings that Europeans attribute to national identity alone do indeed entail a distinction between ascribed characteristics (national ancestry, birth in country, citizenship) and achieved, action-related components (respecting national institutions and laws, mastering a national language). Battistelli and Bellucci (2002) find that, in the Italian case, it is mainly the meaning subjectively assigned to feelings of national attachments that constrains/facilitates the development of an identification with Europe. Citizens who rely on ascribed factors (cultural traditions) in defining their national identity exhibit weaker identification with Europe than citizens who rely on acquired traits of national attachment (political institutions, rights). While the relationship between national and European identity is not uncontested, then, it is clear that there are potentially important causal connections between them that require systematic empirical exploration. The key issue is whether national identities seriously constrain the development of European identity or whether there are forms of European and national identity that can readily coexist.

A final consideration relevant to identity development is the pattern of relationship among different types of national attachment. According to 'categorization theory' (Turner 1985), in-group/out-group distinctions lie at the core of social relations. The development of an awareness of belonging to a group requires a perception of differentiation. European integration alters 'national' categorizations, since former reciprocal (national) out-groupers (should) become in-groupers. European identity, from this perspective, would then be nurtured by mutual trust among Europeans and, to an extent, by a perceptual closure *vis-à-vis* other communities, variously defined according to (increasingly shared) cultural, political, and/or economic common interests. In this vein, Citrin and Sides (2004: 165) argue that European identity consists of an 'individual's self-concept shared with some but not all other people', a 'we-feeling' sentiment based on mutual trust among members of a group (Deutsch 1957).

Many of the possible explanatory factors which the various perspectives outlined above consider relevant for the development of a European identity were purposely inserted in our survey instrument. We are thus in a position to assess their actual explanatory power. The model we test, which is summarized in Table 4.4, is based on four sets of variables that seek to operationalize the previously discussed theoretical perspectives.

For the cognitive mobilization model, our predictors include both behavioural and attitudinal variables. The former embrace education, media exposure, political engagement, and visits to EU countries; the latter, political influence and political sophistication.[8] In essence, we hypothesize that the development of EU identity should be fostered by citizens' active involvement in the social and political sphere, and by indirect (through the media) and direct (by travelling) knowledge and experience of European peoples and institutions. The underlying rationale is therefore that of both

---

[8] All variables, with the exception of education and visits to EU countries, are multi-item constructs scaled to 0–10. See Ch. 3 and data appendix for their definition.

Table 4.4. Bivariate correlations between European Identity and selected independent variables

	Pearson's R
Cognitive Mobilization Theory	
Education	0.18**
Political Influence	0.23**
Media Exposure	0.18**
Political Sophistication	0.28**
Visited EU Countries	0.19**
Non-Electoral Participation	0.16**
Instrumental Rationality Theory	
EU Personal Benefits	0.41**
EU National Benefits	0.34**
Retrospective Economic Evaluation	0.15**
Political Mobilization/Cueing Rationality Theory	
EU Institutional Trust	0.36**
EU Representation—Efficacy	0.21**
National Institutional Confidence	0.30**
Pro-EU Party Identifier	0.15**
Left–Right Ideology	−0.00
Left–Right Extreme	0.05**
Affective/Identitarian Theory	
Trust other Europeans	0.27**
National Attachment	0.12**
Regional Attachment	0.09**
Town Attachment	0.05**
Achieved National Identity	0.13**
Ascribed National Identity	−0.09**
Macro-Contextual Variables	
Communist Past	−0.11**
Trade Openness	−0.04**
Quality of Governance	0.06**

N = 16.133
** p < .01 (2-tailed)

Note: Entries are Pearson correlation coefficients.

'cosmopolitanism' and of a 'social capital'-rich citizenry, which empower people with the resources necessary to understand, evaluate, and develop feelings of attachment to a relatively distant supranational community. The bivariate correlations in Table 4.4 show that each of the variables considered is associated positively with our measure of European identity.

A cosmopolitan outlook is obviously not the only path to European allegiance. Instrumental-rational motivations may also sustain it. This highlights the notion of 'choice' as a key factor in developing identities, an aspect often overlooked by social identity research (Huddy 2001: 131). Motivation is hypothesized to be of great importance, especially in acquired identity, as it has been argued European identity is likely to be. The contribution of Europe to the improvement of personal and collective life conditions should therefore constitute an important instrumental source of EU allegiance. Accordingly, perceptions of the personal and collective benefits that accrue from EU membership represent the next block of explanatory variables in our model, as potential predictors of the intensity of identification.[9] The bivariate correlations in Table 4.4 suggest that these are strong predictors, together with a general evaluation of the economic situation, although this latter correlation appears weaker.

Turning to the third perspective, political mobilization, we model here the heuristics people may employ in forming European attachment. The first two variables—trust in European institutions (EU Institutional Trust) and feelings of being represented by them (EU Representation—Efficacy)—tap the overall image that people have of EU political institutions and their legitimacy, gauging institutional confidence and representation efficacy. Both variables, which are multi-item constructs scaled 0–10 as outlined in Chapter 2, correlate moderately with our index of European Identity, suggesting that favourable attitudes towards the institutions of the EU do increase identification. Note that a caveat must be advanced here since these variables constitute our formerly discussed indexes of Representation which together with Identity and Scope we assume represent independent dimensions of European Citizenship. A risk of endogeneity is clearly present, since we are inserting measures of representation to explain identity. However, this appears to be a safe assumption since, as we show in Chapter 9, representation is largely exogenous to identity.

The third political mobilization variable we include in our model is National Institutional Confidence, an additive construct scaled 0–10, which ascertains the level of confidence people hold regarding their *national* institutions and governance.[10] As discussed above, there is evidence from previous studies to support both 'transfer' and 'substitution' cueing effects. The bivariate positive association between national institutional confidence and EU identity described earlier implies that trust and satisfaction with national governance are 'transferred' directly to feelings of European attachment. However, in order to test the possibility that both transfer and substitution cueing occur, we interact national institutional confidence with *low* levels of Quality of Governance. Our supposition here is that in national contexts where the Quality of Governance is low, substitution cueing is more likely to occur. Our expectation is that where governance quality is low, the effect of National Institutional Confidence on strength of EU identity will be positive; where governance quality is high the effect will be attenuated or even negative.

---

[9] See Ch. 3 and data appendix for variables coding.

[10] This variable combines additively, after a factor analysis showing clearly unidimensionality, six questions probing trust in national parliament/national government/regional/local government, satisfaction with the working of democracy in nation, national decision-makers' competence, and care of people. See Appendix.

Finally, we include two variables that tap heuristics directly associated with partisan attitudes: (1) identifying with a party with a pro- or anti-European stance; and (2) individual political ideology, measured through self-placement on a 0–10 Left–Right scale. Parties differ both in their support for the European project and in the salience they assign to it in their competitive electoral strategies (Steenbergen and Scott 2004). But do voters perceive this, and is this perception transferred to their individual European allegiances? The bivariate correlation with European identity in Table 4.4 suggests that, contrary to the literature previously reviewed, party cueing is a promising hypothesis: being a partisan of a Eurosceptic(-phile) party does depress (increase) one's own identification with Europe. More controversial is the assumption that left–right ideology also carries a European-related content. Disagreement among scholars is wide, and different models of party contestation have been proposed (Steenbergen and Marks 2004). At the mass level, however, the common finding (van der Eijk and Franklin 2004; Scheuer and van der Brug 2007) is of a substantial *independence* of *support* for European integration from left–right ideology. On the other hand, shifting from evaluation (EU support) to affect (European identity), the preliminary bivariate correlations in Table 4.4 lend at least some moderate support to the hypothesis that the left–right heuristic is indeed associated with identification.

The last theoretical perspective we explore relates to other identitarian/affective variables. We include attitude towards other Europeans, attachment to national and subnational communities, and the content of national identity. As to the first variable, 'Trusting other Europeans' operationalizes that 'we-feeling' sentiment, or 'sense of community', which transactionalism associates with political integration (Deutsch 1957) and which is also implied by the in-group/out-group distinction of categorization theory (Turner 1985). Sense of European community—measured through expressed trust for the nationals of other named EC countries—was not very pronounced before 1990 (Niedermayer 1995). In our study, a general measure of trust towards 'people in other European countries' has an average value of 5.4 on a 0–10 scale, with the value of the 25 percentile set at 5, showing that a majority of people surveyed expressed a medium-high level of trust towards other European nationals. We expect European identity to be stimulated by mutual trust among Europeans. This hypothesis is *prima facie* supported with our data, as is shown by the relatively strong bivariate correlation in Table 4.4 between European we-feeling and identification.

The next block of affective variables includes attachment to the nation, to the region, and to the town. The bivariate correlations with European identity in Table 4.4 lend support to the previously discussed hypothesis of coexisting multiple identities. The pattern of correlation with European identity shifts from stronger to weaker correlations as the level of attachment narrows in focus. The correlation with national attachment is $r = 0.27$; with regional attachment, it is $r = 0.12$; and with local attachment, it is $r = 0.05$. This confirms the findings of previous experimental research and appears to be consistent with a nested model of inclusive identities, according to which there would be a hierarchy of attachments conceived of as concentric circles (Bruter 2005). The last variable that we include among the affective component in the model of European identity is the character or 'configuration' of *national* identification. We hypothesize that European identity should be stronger among individuals who define their national identity on acquired traits rather than on ascribed ones.[11] This is based on the assumption that there will be less conflict between national and European identities that are expressed primarily in civic—achieved—terms than there are between national and European identities that are expressed primarily in ethnic-linguistic—ascribed—terms.

Finally our model includes a standard battery of sociodemographic controls and a set of macro variables that describe the historical, political, and economic context in which our respondents live. These latter include Communist Past, Quality of Governance, and Trade Openness of the national economy.

The determinants of European identity

Table 4.5 reports our estimates of the effects of the model described in Table 4.4 on strength of European Identity. Estimation is by OLS, corrected for the clustering of the respondents by country, where individual-level variables are associated with macro-contextual ones. The model fit is satisfactory and most of the variables associated with the different theoretical perspectives are significant. None of the coefficients on the individual-level control variables reach traditional levels of significance and, among the macro-contextual controls, only Communist Past does. This means that, in the context of the estimated model, social structure and varying economic and political system-level attributes do not add any additional insight once the effects of attitudinal and behavioural predictors of European identity are simultaneously estimated. This may at first appear surprising, given the previously observed differences in the levels of European identification across EU member states. On the other hand, it points out that, once the many paths which may lead to identity development are analytically delineated and estimated, the peoples of Europe share a common pattern. The observable

---

[11] See Appendix, section 2 for variables definition.

Table 4.5. Results of OLS regression with European Identity as dependent variable[a]

	Coeff.	Beta°
Cognitive Mobilization		
Education	0.07** (0.02)	0.03
Political Influence	0.05*** (0.01)	0.06
Media Exposure	0.02* (0.01)	0.03
Political Sophistication	0.08*** (0.01)	0.10
Visited EU Countries	0.10*** (0.02)	0.08
Non-Electoral Participation	0.03** (0.01)	0.03
Instrumental Rationality		
EU Personal Benefits	0.83*** (0.05)	0.21
EU National Benefits	0.39*** (0.05)	0.09
Retrospective Economic Evaluation	0.04 (0.02)	0.02
Political Mobilization/Cueing Rationality		
EU Institutional Trust	0.20*** (0.02)	0.19
EU Representation—Efficacy	0.04*** (0.01)	0.05
National Institutional Confidence	−0.07** (0.02)	−0.07
Pro-EU Party Identifier	0.01 (0.01)	0.01
Left–Right Ideology	0.00 (0.01)	0.00
Left–Right Extreme	0.00 (0.00)	0.01
Affective/Identitarian		
Trust other Europeans	0.06*** (0.01)	0.07
National Attachment	0.16** (0.04)	0.06
Regional Attachment	0.17*** (0.03)	0.07
Town Attachment	−0.08** (0.02)	−0.03
Achieved National Identity	0.07*** (0.01)	0.06
Ascribed National Identity	−0.02* (0.01)	−0.03
Demographic Control Variables		
Male/not	0.00 (0.04)	0.00
Age	0.00 (0.01)	0.03
Age Squared	−0.00 (0.00)	−0.02
Unemployed/not	0.01. (0.09)	0.00
Manual/not	0.01 (0.07)	0.00
Catholic/not	0.06 (0.06)	0.01
Macro-Contextual Variables		
Communist Past/not	−0.73* (0.30)	−0.18
Trade Openness	0.00 (0.00)	0.08
Quality of Governance	−0.08 (0.23)	−0.03
Macro-Micro Interaction		
Quality of Governance LOW* National Institutions Confidence	0.09* (0.05)	0.03
Constant	4.7*** (0.40)	
Rmsea°	1.64	
Adj. R-sq°	0.30	

N = 16133
*** p<.001
** p<.01
* p<.05

Notes: [a] Entries are regression coefficients with panel-corrected standard errors in parentheses. Higher values of independent variables mean greater intensities/positive evaluations.
Computed without correction for multiple imputation.

country differences originate from combining the different configurations of attitudinal and behavioural *antecedents* of identification rather than from country-specific features. In the logic of most-dissimilar system design, within-nation variance appears more relevant than its between-nation counterpart. The notable exception to this is 'Communist Past' which, net of all of the other variables taken into account, retains its reductive influence on European affective allegiance.

What, then, explains the intensity of identification with Europe? We discuss first the contribution that each variable brings about within each theoretical perspective, and then compare the overall contribution that each perspective makes to the development of European identification.

All of the *Cognitive Mobilization* variables impact positively, as expected, on European identity. In terms of 'political engagement' variables, attitudinal orientations exert stronger effects than behavioural engagement. The coefficients for political sophistication (b = 0.08) and political influence (b = 0.05) are in fact greater than that for non-electoral participation (b = 0.03) (all measured on identical 0–10 scales). In terms of 'cosmopolitanism', personal life experience in other EU countries significantly increases identification, which is also supported by media exposure—although its influence appears plausibly lower—and by higher educational levels. These results are fully in line with theoretical expectations and with previous research, pointing to the importance of individual resources and social activism as predictors of European allegiance. Of course, the simple fact that such resources are unevenly distributed across the population and that, as we have seen in Chapter 3, only a minority of Europeans enjoys very high levels of cognitive mobilization implies that this source of identity cannot be the unique basis on which European identification can be built.

Instrumental Rationality adds significant explanatory leverage to the overall picture, both for high and low cognitively mobilized. The estimated model shows that both sociotropic and egocentric evaluations of the benefits accruing from EU membership strongly influence the intensity of identification with Europe. Feelings of attachment are therefore sustained by reasoned evaluations, showing the importance of choice in acquiring and holding identity, and giving it meaning. Perceptions of receiving benefits from Europe appear, then, an important and independent source of (instrumental) attachment to Europe. Among Europeans, personal considerations prevail over collective ones by a ratio 2:1, as shown by the regression coefficients (EU Personal Benefits, b = 0.83; EU National Benefits, b = 0.39), and together they describe an important part of the story. Note that the contingent evaluation of the economic situation at the time of the survey does not show a significant impact on European identity. This is in contrast to what has been observed in the past concerning the relevance of the economic cycle for popular support for European integration.

With regard to the *Political Mobilization* perspective, the results in Table 4.5 show the relevance of some of the hypothesized heuristics but also the irrelevance of others in shaping European identification. Recall that according to this approach, people should develop their attachment to Europe based both on their images of European institutions and on the cues coming from domestic politics. The model estimates clearly show the importance of EU institutions—see the significant coefficients of EU Institutional Trust (b = 0.20) and 'EU Representation—Efficacy' (b = 0.04). In terms of domestic political cueing effects, the partisanship and ideology terms fall short of statistical significance, even though their bivariate correlations with European identity were (spuriously) positive. Thus, controlling for the effects of other variables in the model, the pro-/anti-European outlook of the preferred party does *not* transfer onto individual European attachment. Likewise, left–right individual orientations do not translate into a direct significant effect on European identification.

However, one heuristic based on national politics does have a clear and strong impact on European identity: confidence in national institutions. Its direct impact shows a *negative* relationship with our dependent variable. Accordingly, the higher the trust people have for their political system, the lower (b = –0.07) their attachment to Europe. This shows clearly that a *substitution heuristic* is at work, a finding that buttresses the notion that it is dissatisfaction rather than satisfaction that boosts European attachment. This in turn implies a vision of Europe as a source of improvement for faltering national governance. Note, however, that before accepting entirely this result, it is useful to look at the macro-micro interaction we inserted in the model between Low Quality of Governance[12] (a macro-contextual variable whose direct effect is, as we have already seen, not statistically significant) and National Institutional Confidence. This interaction term's coefficient is positive (b = 0.09). This means that for individuals who trust their national institutions *and* who live in a country with a low Quality of Governance, the strength of European identity is *augmented*. Conversely, for an individual holding a high national institutional trust and living in a high Quality of Governance polity, the intensity of attachment to Europe is *attenuated*. The contextual factor, therefore, *mediates* the impact of the individual attitude. This finding can reconcile previous existing and contradictory evidence on

---

[12] For ease of interpretation the continuous variable Quality of Governance has been recoded into a dummy variable, assigning to Low Quality (coded 1) the countries with a score equal or below the 20 per cent percentile and coding 0 all others. Findings do not change if we set different thresholds or if interaction is computed on the original continuous variable.

the relationship between European attitudes and national confidence, by focusing on the polity features. The impact can be visually inspected (since interaction effects are not straightforward to gauge) by plotting the post-predicted values of European identity (based on the equation of Table 4.5, and setting all other variables at their mean value) according to the level of National Institutional Confidence and of the Quality of Governance, observed at the median value, and at values above the 80 per cent percentile and below the 20 per cent percentile[13] (Figure 4.4). For people living in countries with above-the-median values of Quality of Governance, there is a clear and strong negative relationship between European identity and national confidence. The slope of the line is still negative, but flatter, at the median value of governance, while the slope becomes positive for people living in worse Quality of Governance polities. In these countries, a transfer effect is at work, and higher trust in national institutions translates into moderate attachment to Europe. Therefore in countries whose Quality of Governance is high, European identification is stronger among citizens who are distrustful of/dissatisfied with the working of their national institutions, while in low Quality of Governance democracies the most trustful in national institutions are the people who show relatively higher identification with Europe.

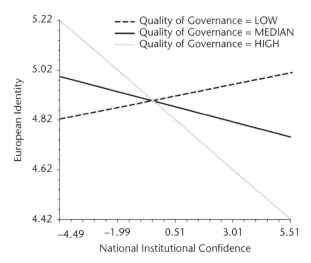

Figure 4.4. European Identity and National Institutional Confidence according to Quality of Governance (estimates derived with the model shown in Table 4.5)

[13] Findings are unaltered if we set different thresholds for Quality of Governance: for instance predicting European identity for individuals living in countries having the four lower, four higher, and in-between values of the Quality of Governance index; or in 25 per cent percentile, 75 per cent percentile.

The image of European institutions is a heuristic that, as we have antici-pated, significantly shapes European identifications. Both trust and efficacy exert effects on our dependent variable, with EU Institutional Trust showing a greater impact (b = 0.20) than EU Efficacy (b = 0.05)—and since both are measured on 0–10 scales, the coefficient magnitudes are directly comparable with one another. Overall they gauge the competence and legitimacy of European institutions and their responsiveness to people's needs. Trust in European institutions and the perception that they *represent* individual and national interests enhance European Identity—and, as we show in Chapter 9, appear to be substantially exogenous to it. Moreover, the fact that EU Institu-tional Trust exerts a greater impact than EU Efficacy supports the hypothesis that the institutions of the European Union have begun to achieve an 'iden-tity hegemony' in which Europe has come to denote 'the political and social space occupied by the EU' (Risse 2004: 255). The image of being European, in short, is defined largely by (trust in) EU institutions. At the same time, the limited sense of efficacy felt by most Europeans (the average value is 3.6, on a 0–10 scale) hints at the continuing importance of the 'democratic deficit' in constraining European identification.

Turning to the *Affective/Identitarian* variables, the estimates reported in Table 4.4 show that all have significant effects on identification with Europe. As expected, Trust other Europeans, the 'we-feeling' sentiment of proximity and reciprocal confidence, significantly increases identification (b = 0.06). In relation to national and subnational attachments, the results suggest a more elaborated frame than the one envisaged by earlier bivariate correlations. Those earlier findings allowed us to speculate on the coexistence of multiple and nested identities. Our multivariate results show that this is true only for national and regional attachments: feelings of national (b = 0.16) and regional (b = 0.17) attachment co-vary positively with European identification, but local (town) attachment does not (b = –0.08). People who strongly identify with local community appear to have a lower level of attachment to Europe, implying that Parochialism can hinder attachment to Europe. The overall implication, however, is that national and regional attachments do not con-flict with European identification; rather the different attachments comple-ment each other, perhaps reflecting the involvement of state and regional apparatus in the European multilevel policymaking.

Rather than threatening national traditions and peculiarities, then, Euro-pean attachment is fostered by them. However, the meanings associated with national identity vary across individuals. The hypothesis that people who rely more on *ascribed* factors in defining their national identity would hold *weaker* attachment to Europe than those assigning greater weight to *achieved* compo-nents in national feelings is clearly supported. Indeed, among the latter the impact is strong and positive (b = 0.07) while among the former it is negative, although weaker (b = –0.02). The implication of these relationships can be easily gauged in the graphs that show the post-predicted values of European identity (again based on the equation of Table 4.5, and setting all but relevant variables at their mean value) according to the strength with which they adhere to achieved and ascribed declinations of national identity. In order to further control for different historical trajectories and legacies of state building we show the results on a country-by-country basis (see Figure 4.5): in each country the relationships show a strong growing level of European identity the higher the ascribed intensity and the lower (albeit less strongly so) the achieved one.

Where does this discussion leave us? We have seen that most of the variables hypothesized to impinge upon European identification have statistically significant effects and in most cases in the expected directions. European attachments are fostered by cognitive, attitudinal, and behavioural political mobilization. Identification is also instrumentally explained by egocentric and sociotropic perceptions of the benefits that accrue from EU membership. Attachment is driven by positive images of Europe and by a combination of national institutional trust and lower quality of governance. Last, a shared we-feeling sentiment among Europeans supports a superordinate identification that does *not* conflict with national identity. These are the main findings on the determinants of European identity that the analysis of the IntUne comparative survey offers us, so far. Does this mean that all the four theoretical perspectives which have inspired the empirical analysis carry an equal explanatory power? Or in explaining identity, are some perspectives more relevant than others? In other words, is there a driving force that should be singled out as the mover of European citizens in the path towards, if ever, a stronger attachment to Europe or, conversely, which might be singled out for an eventual decline in European attachments? We can approach an answer by trying to assess the relative importance that each perspective brings about in terms of its 'unique' explanatory contribution.

Different research strategies are available for this task, from simpler to more complex ones: from block regression—which allows the measurement of the change in the variance explained by sets of variables entered subsequently—to structural equation modelling, which tests the contribution of latent constructs among variables included in a given model. We have chosen a straightforward strategy, which does not compel us to make strong assumptions either on the ordering of the variables or on the covariance structures.[14] We have accordingly constructed for each theoretical perspective a variable that additively combines the ones that were represented in each theory, rescaled them

---

[14] We can report that the results we reach are overall, although not identical, congruent with what we find employing the alternative strategies.

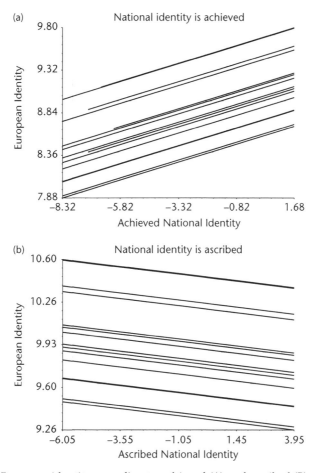

Figure 4.5. European identity according to achieved (A) and ascribed (B) meanings of national identity (estimates for individual countries derived with the model shown in Table 4.5)

to a 0–10 index,[15] and then used these new variables as predictors in a new estimation. The identical scale of these new variables allows us to compare their causal strength and explanatory power. Table 4.6 reports the findings. Clearly, all theories bear on the dependent variable. *Cognitive Mobilization*, however, has the strongest impact on European identity (b = 0.27), followed by *Instrumental Rationality* (b = 0.21), *Political Mobilization* (b = 0.15), and

---

[15] The resulting indexes have the following reliability scores (Crombach's Alpha): Cognitive Mobilizations, 0.69; Instrumental Rationality, 0.58; Political Mobilization, 0.53; Affective/ Identitarian, 0.61.

Table 4.6. Results of an OLS regression with a simplified model with European Identity as a dependent variable[a]

	Coeff.	Standard error
Cognitive Mobilization	0.27***	0.02
Instrumental Rationality	0.21***	0.01
Political Mobilization/Cueing	0.15***	0.02
Affective/Identitarian	0.15***	0.02
Demographic Control Variables		
Male/not	−0.01	0.04
Age	0.00	0.01
Age Squared	−0.00	0.00
Unemployed/not	0.01	0.09
Manual/not	−0.00	0.07
Catholic/not	−0.01	0.06
Macro-Contextual Variables		
Communist Past/not	−0.73*	0.30
Trade Openness	0.00	0.00
Quality of Governance	−0.08	0.23
Constant	4.7***	0.40
Rmsea°	1.68	
Adj. R-sq°	0.27	

N = 16133. *** p<.001
** p<.01
* p<.05

Notes: [a] Entries are unstandardized coefficients with standard errors corrected for clustering reported. Computed without correction for multiple imputation.

Affective/Identitarian factors (b = 0.15). In shaping Europeans' allegiance to Europe, being cognitively mobilized has an impact nearly double that carried by identity considerations. Instrumental attachment weighs slightly more than the extent to which people are cued by their images of Europe and of their national institutions. Overall, feelings of European allegiances evidently do have roots in the experiences that citizens share of their respective political systems. One might ask how it could be otherwise, since the construction of the European Union has been driven by national politics. But citizens balance these bottom-up drivers with their own emotional and cognitive involvements, where reason and affect interact in building a (new) identification.

We do not claim that this insight reveals the causal structure of people's thinking. Nor do we claim that it describes in every detail the ways people reason and relate themselves emotionally to Europe. In fact, as we explore in later analyses in this volume, different motivations sustain other dimensions of European engagement. However, as far as psychological attachments are concerned, our analysis does suggest the extent to which the many paths to identity development contribute to an understanding of one important aspect of European Citizenship. The following chapters explore the other dimensions of Citizenship and later we will further explore the reciprocal relationships among them.

Summary and conclusion

This chapter has provided an assessment of the many factors that lie behind the development of a European identification among nationals of EU members states. Our definition of European identity departs from previous research. We have striven to account for two dimensions which, according to social identity theory, constitute a social and political identity: the feeling of belonging to a group and the salience of such membership. Their combination results in an index of European identification which has been our dependent variable throughout this chapter.

It may have come as no surprise to some readers that EU member states' citizens have a rather *moderate* level of identification with Europe. On the other hand, and maybe surprising for others, we have shown that this identification is readily accessible to people, and that their feelings of belonging are not separated from their perceptions of the salience of Europe itself. Many Europeans have some identification with their supranational community, although there is a significant variance in the intensity with which that attachment is felt.

But why do people identify with Europe? Normative and philosophical perspectives abound, and often provide well-argued, self-contained justifications for why people should or should not feel attached to Europe, in ways similar to or different from the attachments that they have for their own nations. Europeans might indeed be engaging themselves in what Holmes (2009) has aptly defined as 'identity experiments'. We have approached this question differently, by inquiring into the factors that can be thought to be the causal antecedents of identity development among European mass publics. Taking an empirical route does not, however, make the task simpler. Multiple, sometimes conflicting, theoretical perspectives have been proposed, in a situation where systematic empirical research on European identity is actually fairly limited. We identified four paradigms/theories that in the past have been brought to bear on public attitudes both towards European integration and, less often, towards Europeans' feelings of belonging to Europe: cognitive mobilization, instrumental rationality, political mobilization, and affective/identitarian. We operationalized these perspectives using survey items that have been asked of samples of European citizens and employed them in an explanatory model of European attachment.

Our results show that each perspective accounts for some important paths in identity development, although not all of the detailed hypotheses we tested were supported by the evidence. Some general findings stand out. First, socio-structural factors have little leverage in explaining individual intensity of European identification once we accurately model the relevant causal linkages. Second, countries' system-level features also fail to impact significantly, and within-system variance appears far greater than its between-system counterpart. However, one notable exception to this pattern is the influence exerted, once all linkages are estimated, of 'Communist Past': citizens in these countries appear on average to identify less with Europe even after all individual-level determinants are factored out in our model. Third, cognitive mobilization appears to exert a major influence on the strength of our respondents' identification with Europe. Individual resources, social and political engagement, experiences abroad, and media exposure all impact positively on European attachments. But these are relatively scarce resources among Europeans. Fourth, Identity is also sustained (or attenuated) by choice, as instrumental considerations of the benefits (or costs) accruing from Europe compose and frame the image of Europe. Fifth, Identity is further enriched by people's perceptions of the efficacy and representativeness of European institutions, perceptions that play a central role in defining what Europe is. Sixth, and in contrast, trust in other Europeans—the we-feeling sentiment that incorporates former outgroupers—enhances identifications beyond institutional representativeness, and clearly adds a social dimension to European identity that complements the political one.

The causal structure we have modelled appears to describe parsimoniously the determinants of European Identity. However, we should ask ourselves how robust such explanation is. We have put European Identity under the magnifying glass and examined its multifaceted antecedents. In the broader perspective of European Citizenship—the one this volume holds to—some of those may turn out to be intervening factors or may change causal direction or even lose relevance. We do not expect that this structure will necessarily hold fully when other dimensions of citizenship are simultaneously considered. We might discover the need then to refurbish our explanations, a task that we undertake in later chapters. For the time being, however, that's the story.

5

Institutional Trust and Responsiveness in the EU

Mariano Torcal, Eduard Bonet, and Marina Costa Lobo

Introduction

Representation has traditionally been regarded as one of the pillars underpinning the concept of citizenship and democracy (Pitkin 1967; Manin 1997; Przeworski 2010). For Dahl, 'one of the key characteristics of a democracy is the continued responsiveness of the government to the preferences of its citizens' (Dahl 1971: 1). In representative systems of government, those who have been selected to govern must be seen as legitimate by citizens. In recent years, the question of the quality of representation has become an increasingly important topic for the European Union. This is due to the fact that EU integration has advanced considerably and impinges on many aspects of European citizens' life. As the ambit of EU policymaking grows, to what degree do citizens consider EU institutions legitimate, and where do such attitudes stem from?

This chapter attempts to answer these questions. We seek to account for the trust that electors deposit in the supranational institutions which make collective decisions in their name. In order to do so, several aspects of representation are investigated. As is normally the case, degree of trust is used as an indicator of the quality of representation. Thus, in this chapter we consider the correlates and explanatory factors of trust in two different EU institutions, namely the European Parliament (EP) and the European Commission (EC). By looking at these two institutions, we are able to gauge whether the nature and degree of trust varies, depending on whether the institution is directly elected or not. In addition, we explore the quality of representation in the EU by investigating the level of EU responsiveness as perceived by European citizens. Following the dimensional analysis of Chapter 2 and the descriptive presentation of the current levels of trust and responsiveness presented in Chapter 3 of this volume, a central question emerges: what can explain these assessments of the EU institutions and the mechanism of representation, as well as the differences observed among the citizens of different member states? That is the question we address in this chapter.

This chapter seeks to make several contributions to the extant literature. For the first time, several different measures of representation (trust in the EP, trust in the EC, and perceptions of EU responsiveness) are investigated together as dependent variables. Each model is tested for the three dependent variables to provide a much broader understanding of the factors influencing institutional trust and other attitudes when evaluating the mechanisms of EU representation. A further advantage of our approach resides in the fact that independent variables identified as important explanatory factors are reanalysed in a proper contextual, multilevel setting. This again is an attempt to take account of the complex reality of the EU political system, which is the prototype of a multi-level political system.

We will start from the premise that many citizens typically tend to fall back on basic attitudes and values to form their opinions on politics because they *lack information* (Zaller 1992: 24). Indeed, a theory of human behaviour based on limited cognitive abilities has become increasingly popular among a growing number of political scientists as they explore public opinion, voting behaviour and elite decision-making (Lupia 1992, 1994; Lupia and McCubbins 1998; Popkin 1991; Sniderman, Brody, and Tetlock 1991). The assumption is that people choose to adopt some heuristic-based strategy for making decisions and forming judgements about the EU institutional setting. This starting assumption, we believe, is valid when assessing the ways in which electors form opinions on national politics, and even more so on European politics.[1]

It is a well-established fact that Europeans actually have little information about the EU (Janssen 1991: 454; Franklin, Marsh, and McLaren 1994: 458) and much less about the functioning of its fundamental institutions (Hix 2007: 147). As such, they tend to rely on three basic attitudes towards the EU in order to express their trust in the EP: the subjective perceived benefits of the EU, affective and identitarian support for the EU, and finally trust in national institutions (Torcal, Muñoz, and Bonet forthcoming). However, the use of these different attitudes has not been consistent over time (Hix 2007). As citizens improve their knowledge of the EU in general and EU institutions in particular, they tend to rely more on perceived subjective benefits (and

---

[1] This is normally the case for citizens' opinions on foreign policies (Hurwitz and Peffley 1987: 1114).

other political cues) and less on affective heuristics when it comes to trusting the EP (Torcal, Muñoz, and Bonet forthcoming).

It seems then that citizens' support of the EU and its institutions is becoming increasingly linked to subjective evaluations of EU general outcomes. This trend is the logical consequence of the declining process of the so-called 'permissive consensus' (Lindberg and Scheingold 1970; Wilgden and Feld 1976), which has been waning since the Maastricht Treaty and Economic Monetary Union (EMU) came into force (Eichenberg and Dalton 1993; Niedermayer 1995; Franklin, Marsh, and McLaren 1994; Dalton and Eichenberg 1998; Hix 2007).[2]

This chapter starts by considering whether the attitudes normally used to explain trust in the EP are equally valid to explain levels of trust in another important EU institution, namely the European Commission (EC), and, in general, to evaluate the mechanisms of political representation in the EU. The nature of the IntUne dataset used in this volume also allows us to determine whether subjective instrumental calculations are based mostly upon subjective egocentric calculations (an interpretation defended by the pure individualistic instrumental rational approach), or rather, are derived primarily from perceptions of sociotropic institutional rationality (Hooghe and Marks 2005: 422).

This analysis also examines the impact of other political cues, such as trust in national institutions as an expression of trust in EU institutions and citizens' perception of EU responsiveness (Anderson 1998; Sánchez Cuenca 2000; Rohrschneider 2002 and 2005; Christin 2005; Hix 2007). However, as we will see, this effect is not the same for all the countries in Europe. Attitudes that are relevant to European integration vary according to a range of contextual national political factors (Duch and Taylor 1997; Ray 1999, 2003a, and 2003b; Hug and Sciarini 2000; Sánchez Cuenca 2000; Brinegar and Jolly 2005; Hooghe and Marks 2005; Rohrschneider 2005). Accordingly, the impact of *trust in national institutions* upon trust in EU institutions might also vary as a consequence of a set of national factors. We will see, following this logic, how the quality of democratic governance might affect the intensity of the relationship between this particular *national* political cue and trust in the EU institutions.

An additional factor we consider is the possible impact of political awareness on support for the EU and its institutions.[3] As Hooghe and Marks (2008) and Kriesi (2008) have recently argued, political awareness of the consequences of EU integration is the first step towards politicization of the EU issue and a possible cause of the emergence of the so-called 'constraining

---

[2] For a different position on this deterioration process see Janssen (1991).
[3] For the discussion of this concept see Zaller (1992: 20–3).

dissensus' about EU integration. Yet individual political awareness alone does not produce a uniform attitudinal change; its effects are shaped by the impact of EU policies (Anderson and Reichert 1996; Gabel 1998b, 1998c; Díez Medrano 2003; Brinegar, Jolly, and Kitschelt 2004; Eijk and Franklin 2004; Christin 2005; Hix 2007). At the same time, political awareness interferes in the aforementioned relationship between trust in national institutions and EU institutions.

Finally, opinions on political integration depend on party political cues (Steenbergen and Jones 2002; Ray 2003a and 2003b; Steenbergen and Scott 2004). Despite the lack of a true and stand-alone European party system, national parties have been assuming, with greater or lesser success and with varying degrees of true commitment, the politicization of the EU issue. They have also sought to structure European policy by including the EU issue in domestic political agendas (Gabel and Hix 2004; Hooghe, Marks, and Wilson 2004; Hooghe and Marks 2008). Thus, the evolution and future prospects of the EU will depend on the role that political parties play as mediators between citizens and the whole political process (Ray 1999 and 2003a). Accordingly, the final part of the chapter concentrates on the effect political parties have on the degree to which citizens evaluate EU institutions, as well as the associated mechanisms of representation.

Rediscovering the importance of heuristics and attitudinal cues

In this section, we test the importance of basic EU attitudinal cues in people's evaluations of EU institutions. We do this not only for the EP but also the EC, as well as for people's perceptions of the responsiveness of the EU. To understand the importance of these attitudinal cues, we include two variables to test the effects of instrumental subjective evaluations, one for the sociotropic component and one for the egocentric component. We also add a group of control variables, namely: four socio-demographic variables (gender, age, education, a dummy variable coding for the unemployed); an indicator of support for European identity to draw a distinction between pure affective support for the EU and the inclusionary or exclusionary identitarian nature of support for the EU;[4] political interest; and social trust. Social trust is allegedly the central element in a complex virtuous circle, in which the prevalence of attitudes and norms of reciprocity and generalized morality among individuals in a given

---

[4] As has been discussed elsewhere, scholars tend to link identification with the national community and support for exclusionary norms to perceptions of European integration as a threat (Kriesi et al. 2008). Some argue, however, that national identiy reinforces European identity (Citrin and Sides 2004; Díez Medrano and Gutiérrez 2001; Díez Medrano 2003).

political system tends to facilitate collective action and favour good governance, which in turn creates favourable conditions in which social, political, and institutional trust can flourish (Almond and Verba 1963; Coleman 1990; Putnam 1993, 1995a, and 1995b; Fukuyama 1995; Kumlin and Rothstein 2005). We also include the left–right scale in the model because, as some scholars have suggested, European integration might be subsumed into the left–right dimension (Tsebelis and Garrett 2000), the dominant factor defining national party competition among Europeans. Additionally, Anderson (1998) argues that the issue of European integration cuts across the lines of traditional left–right divisions and so the relevant distinction will be between supporters of establishment parties and supporters of anti-establishment parties, which are often Eurosceptical (for similar arguments, see Hooghe and Marks 1999 and 2001; Aspinwall 2002; Hix 2007). Finally, we include a general indicator of exposure to political information, measured in terms of media exposure, to test the importance of the use of attitudinal cues, regardless of the level of exposure to general political information (national or international).

The baseline model tested—Model 1—includes all the aforementioned variables. In the full model—Model 2—we include the four above-mentioned EU attitudinal variables. Table 5.1, which contains the results of the estimation for Model 1, displays the importance of some traditional variables in explaining trust in EU institutions and trust in EU mechanisms of representation in general. It shows the significant and positive effect of social trust, political interest, and media consumption in explaining trust both in the EP and in the EC. The results are similar for EU responsiveness, with the exception that

Table 5.1. Factors explaining EU Institutional Trust and EU Responsiveness (Model 1, OLS Clustered Estimators)

	Trust EU Parliament		Trust EU Commission		EU Responsiveness	
	Coef.	SE	Coef.	SE	Coef.	SE
Male	−0.152***	(0.048)	−0.193***	(0.051)	0.148***	(0.047)
Age	−0.045***	(0.007)	−0.039***	(0.006)	−0.032***	(0.008)
Age SQ	0.000***	(0.000)	0.000***	(0.000)	0.000***	(0.000)
Education	0.467***	(0.121)	0.326**	(0.130)	0.237**	(0.093)
Unemployed	0.042	(0.136)	−0.147	(0.151)	−0.193	(0.124)
Media Consumption	0.030**	(0.010)	0.035**	(0.013)	0.023	(0.017)
Social Trust	0.223***	(0.020)	0.222***	(0.022)	0.139***	(0.017)
Interest in Politics	0.151***	(0.049)	0.109**	(0.048)	0.059	(0.053)
Left–right	−0.018	(0.061)	−0.034	(0.059)	−0.037	(0.056)
Left–right SQ	0.004	(0.005)	0.005	(0.005)	0.003	(0.005)
European Identity	0.410***	(0.110)	0.439***	(0.108)	0.616***	(0.102)
Intercept	4.231***	(0.245)	4.338***	(0.231)	3.352***	(0.313)
N	16,133		16,133		16,133	
R^2	0.09		0.09		0.04	

interest in politics and media consumption are not statistically significant. Moreover, European identity seems to have a positive relationship with the three dependent variables, as has been shown in other chapters of this volume. However, the model in general explains little: R^2 is very low, reaching only a poor 0.09 at most.

Model 2, which adds the four EU attitudinal cues to the baseline model 1 (see Table 5.2), presents encouraging results. Adding these variables substantially increases the goodness of fit in two cases, with R^2 rising to as much as 0.39 for the EP and 0.35 for the EC. The goodness of fit for EU responsiveness is much lower. The four attitudinal cues are significant for all the models, except for sociotropic EU instrumental evaluations in the model for EU responsiveness. The inclusion of these variables also renders some of the preceding variables statistically non-significant, such as media consumption and interest in politics. However, EU identity remains a significant predictor as well as social trust, albeit to a lesser degree.

The OLS cluster estimators displayed in Table 5.2 also reveal that egocentric perceptions of EU benefits have the weakest impact in explaining trust in EU institutions. Surprisingly, however, these perceptions have the strongest effect when it comes to explaining EU responsiveness. Additionally, the coefficients show that the affective component of diffuse support for the EU, so relevant for creating the 'permissive consensus' in the past, is actually the least relevant of the attitudinal cues in explaining trust in the EC and second-least relevant, after sociotropic evaluations, in explaining trust in the EP. This confirms the

Table 5.2. The effects of attitudinal cues on EU Institutional Trust and EU Responsiveness (Model 2, OLS Clustered Estimators)

	Trust EU Parliament		Trust EU Commission		EU Responsiveness	
	Coef.	SE	Coef.	SE	Coef.	SE
Male	−0.147***	(0.048)	−0.232***	(0.041)	0.095*	(0.051)
Age	−0.022***	(0.007)	−0.018**	(0.007)	−0.017*	(0.008)
Age SQ	0.000**	(0.000)	0.000*	(0.000)	0.000*	(0.000)
Education	0.281**	(0.103)	0.146	(0.095)	0.076	(0.075)
Unemployed	0.261*	(0.120)	0.039	(0.130)	−0.086	(0.125)
Media Consumption	−0.008	(0.009)	0.001	(0.012)	−0.001	(0.017)
Social Trust	0.040**	(0.013)	0.080***	(0.017)	0.079***	(0.013)
Interest in Politics	−0.021	(0.041)	−0.010	(0.030)	−0.008	(0.042)
Left–right	0.025	(0.045)	0.019	(0.034)	−0.004	(0.042)
Left–right SQ	−0.001	(0.004)	−0.002	(0.003)	−0.001	(0.004)
European Identity	0.173*	(0.087)	0.208**	(0.087)	0.423***	(0.083)
Trust Nat. Parl./Gov.	0.435***	(0.031)	0.334***	(0.022)	0.088***	(0.019)
EU benefits nation	0.382***	(0.127)	0.530***	(0.095)	0.095	(0.081)
EU benefits me	0.169*	(0.086)	0.218**	(0.073)	0.643***	(0.060)
EU Support	0.198***	(0.019)	0.193***	(0.021)	0.140***	(0.020)
Intercept	1.579***	(0.254)	1.797***	(0.229)	1.874***	(0.295)
N	16,133		16,133		16,133	
R^2	0.39		0.35		0.10	

dwindling importance of this affective component in explaining trust in EU institutions (Torcal, Muñoz, and Bonet forthcoming). Trust in national institutions (in national parliaments for the EP, and in national governments for the EC) is significant and positive, and especially important for trust in the EC and EP, confirming at first glance that trust levels appear to be interconnected across institutional tiers. A more detailed discussion on this topic will follow.

These results serve to reconfirm the importance of attitudinal cues in explaining citizens' evaluation and trust of EU institutions as well as their mechanisms of representation, despite the inclusion of a number of controls, such as EU identity, degree of political exposure, social trust, ideology, education, employment situation, and other basic attitudes and variables. Even so, the model fit is much better as regards trust in the two institutions (EP and EC) than for the general measure of EU responsiveness. Yet despite this, the same variables are significant for each of the three dependent variables.

The role of national institutions

It would appear from the preceding results that Europeans might simply be transposing their own views on national institutions and their performance to form their evaluations of EU institutions. This finding echoes previous observations that underscore the importance of national cueing factors (political and institutional) in forming attitudes towards the EU (Anderson 1998; Sánchez Cuenca 2000; Rohrschneider 2005). These are the so-called national political cues models, whereby attitudes towards the EU are seen as an extension of domestic politics (Hooghe and Marks 2005: 420).[5] However, we need to explore this relationship further since existing research on this issue seems to be highly controversial. While some argue that degrees of trust at different levels of government are positively correlated, others argue quite the opposite: in particular, that lower evaluations of national institutions *vis-à-vis* European ones will foster support for European institutions by reducing the perceived costs of transferring power to the latter (Anderson 1998: 577). Nevertheless, both hypotheses could be right because the impact of national institutions on opinions regarding the EU could vary depending on a set of national contextual factors (Franklin et al. 1994 and 1995; Anderson 1998; Hooghe and Marks 2005: 420).

---

[5] There might be more 'national' mediating factors, such as party competition and the evaluation of national incumbents (Duch and Taylor 1997; Gabel 1998c; Ray 1999, 2003a, and 2003b; Hug and Sciarini 2000), national or subnational identities (Díez Medrano and Gutierrez 2001; Kriesi et al. 2008) and, finally, the evaluation of national representative institutions (Anderson 1998; Sánchez Cuenca 2000; Rohrschneider 2002 and 2005; Christin 2005).

One of the factors that might intervene in this relationship is the quality of national governments (Sánchez Cuenca 2000; Rohrschneider 2002). The IntUne dataset allows us to test this hypothesis with reliable data, as we attempt to assess the nature and direction of the relationship between national and EU evaluations in the context of varying levels of Quality of Governance. Therefore, the same baseline model as the one presented in Table 5.2 was run but including only trust in national institutions (parliament or government). The sample was split in two groups, distinguishing between countries with below- and above-average rankings for the Quality of Governance indicator (World Bank data).

The results of this estimation are displayed in Table 5.3 and show that trust in national parliaments is positively related to trust in the EP at both low and high levels of Quality of Governance. However, in countries with low Quality of Governance, a 1 point increase in the 10-point scale of trust in national parliaments implies an increase of almost 0.5 points in the 10-point scale of the dependent variable, whereas in countries with higher levels of trust in their national parliament, this effect is higher. So, we can conclude that there is essentially a simple transportation of individual trust from national to EU arenas, regardless of the levels of Quality of Governance, although the intensity of the transportation seems to be higher in countries with higher levels of trust in national institutions. Thus, general levels of trust in the EU have more to do with levels of trust (and political disaffection) toward all institutions at the national level than with a real evaluation of the functioning and performing of EU institutions.

Table 5.3. Factors explaining Trust in the EP by Quality of Governance (OLS Clustered Estimators)

	Countries with low Quality of Governance		Countries with high Quality of Governance	
	Coef.	SE	Coef.	SE
Male	−0.005	(0.054)	−0.286***	(0.052)
Age	−0.022**	(0.006)	−0.049***	(0.010)
Age SQ	0.000**	(0.000)	0.000**	(0.000)
Education	0.328***	(0.072)	0.230**	(0.072)
Unemployed	0.177	(0.160)	−0.018	(0.136)
Media Consumption	0.021	(0.018)	0.010	(0.019)
Social Trust	0.085***	(0.015)	0.077***	(0.016)
Interest in Politics	0.160***	(0.042)	−0.075**	(0.021)
Left–right	0.123*	(0.059)	0.004	(0.070)
Left–right SQ	−0.008	(0.004)	−0.002	(0.006)
European Identity	0.341	(0.185)	0.581***	(0.085)
Trust Nat. Parl.	0.485***	(0.031)	0.605***	(0.038)
Intercept	2.299***	(0.263)	2.658***	(0.208)
N	9120		7013	
R^2	0.33		0.43	

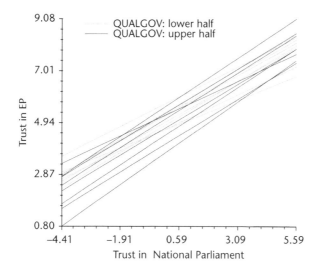

Figure 5.1. Slopes for the relationship between Trust in National Parliaments and Trust in the EP (based on a multivel model with random intercept and random slope for Trust in NP)

In order to confirm the above findings more formally, a multilevel model was run on exactly the same premises as the ones for Table 5.3 above. The results of the model's estimation are not shown due to space limitations, but Figure 5.1 shows the different slopes of the relationship of trust in the national parliaments and trust in the EP. As expected, the slopes vary but are always positive, showing that there is a consistent positive relationship for all countries regardless of the level of the Quality of Governance. Thus, our findings contradict those studies which advocate the changing nature of support, depending on the levels of support for national institutions (Anderson 1998; Sánchez Cuenca 2000). Nonetheless, there is a pattern at work: for those countries with high levels of Quality of Governance (grey lines), the relationship between trust levels at national and supranational level is stronger, i.e. the slopes are steeper, than for those with low levels of Quality of Governance (black lines).

The role of political awareness

It has been argued that the growing impact of these subjective instrumental evaluations on support for the EU is the result of both greater political awareness of the consequences of the EU and the politicization of the EU issue. As Hooghe and Marks (2008) and Kriesi (2008) have stated, political awareness of the consequences of EU integration is the first step towards politicization of the EU issue.[6] As discussed by Easton (1965 and 1975) specific support or subjective instrumental support can exist only in societies whose institutions allow authorities to be held accountable for their actions and their consequences. Accordingly, each political object could be supported by either or both diffuse/affective and specific/instrumental arguments, although the latter depend on each individual's level of political knowledge, sophistication, and subsequent acquiescence.

In this section, we deal with two aspects of political awareness. Firstly, we study the interactive relationship between EU events and political awareness when it comes to explaining some citizens' attitudes toward the EU. As we show, the effect of political awareness on trust in EU institutions depends on the nature of those events and how they distinctively affect the economic condition of each member state. Secondly, and continuing the discussion from the preceding section, we show that the transposition effect of trust in national institutions towards trust in EU institutions depends on the level of political awareness. This is also observed with the perceived responsiveness of EU citizens.

Political awareness and economic events

Political awareness of the EU among citizens is growing as the consequences of the integration process become more salient (Hooghe and Marks 2008; Ray 2003a: 990). But how does this political awareness affect basic attitudes toward the EU, such as trust in EU institutions? We contend that the effect of political awareness on citizens' attitudes toward the EU is not uniform across countries, and depends on a set of contextual factors.[7]

Political awareness by itself does not increase support for the EU and, therefore, explains neither trust in EU institutions nor their mechanisms of representation. In our view, the effect of political awareness on EU attitudes depends on the effects of certain policies and EU decisions, such as the balance of net fiscal transfers to each member state and important elements that may condition other significant attitudes toward EU integration (Anderson and

---

[6] See also Eijk and Franklin (2004: 48).

[7] There is an extensive literature dealing with the distinctive effect of certain contextual factors on the formation and evolution of citizens' support for the EU, suggesting that attitudes toward the EU are conditioned by the different countries' share of EU trade (Gabel and Palmer 1995; Gabel 1998b); the Economic Monetary Union (EMU) and the Euro (Niedermayer 1995; Franklin, Marsh, and McLaren 1994; Dalton and Eichenberg 1998; Ray 2003a; Torcal, Muñoz, and Bonet forthcoming); inflation or unemployment levels (Eichenberg and Dalton 1993; Dalton and Eichenberg 1998; Anderson and Kaltenthaler 1996; Bednar, Ferejohn, and Garrett 1996; Gabel 1998c), and other specific EU policies that are producing economic and social winners and losers in each country (Gabel and Palmer 1995; Anderson and Reichert 1996; Gabel 1998c and 1998b; Hooghe and Marks 2005).

Reichert 1996; DíezMedrano 2003; Brinegar, Jolly, and Kitschelt 2004). To test this hypothesis, we estimate a multilevel model that tests the effects on trust in the EP of the *interaction* between political knowledge[8] and an aggregate variable that measures net fiscal transfers (Net Transfers) for 2007. Table 5.4 displays the results. As we can see in this model, the interaction between EU political knowledge and net fiscal transfers is statistically significant and positive (p = 0.008). This means that in countries where net fiscal transfers are negative, political awareness has a negative impact on levels of EP trust, while in countries where transfers are positive, political awareness has a positive impact on levels of EP trust. This relationship is visualized in Figure 5.1, where it is possible to observe the slope of the relationship for countries allocated at negative to low levels of net fiscal transfers (−0.16), mid-range (0.36), and at the high end of such transfers (1.580). Figure 5.2 shows that the relationship between trust in the EP and EU political knowledge is completely

Table 5.4. Trust in the EU Parliament as a function of Political Awareness and Net EU Transfers (multilevel model with robust standard errors)

	Trust EU Parliament	
	Coef.	SE
Intercept (β_0)		
Intercept (γ_{00})	4.783***	0.173
Net Transfers from EU (γ_{01})	0.091	0.154
Age	−0.029***	0.005
Age SQ	0.001***	0.000
Education	0.038	0.039
Unemployed	0.097	0.093
Manual	−0.048	0.063
Media Consumption	0.011	0.007
Social Trust	0.200***	0.007
Interest in Politics	0.105***	0.021
Left–right	0.068***	0.023
Left–right SQ	−0.005**	0.002
European Identity	0.225***	0.052
EU benefits nation	0.508***	0.063
EU benefits me	0.441***	0.050
EU Support	0.214***	0.008
Information on EU	−0.072**	0.032
Information on EU X Net Transfers from EU	0.086***	0.028
Level-1 N		16,133
Level-2 N		16
Random Intercept Variance		0.305
Random slope Information EU Variance		0.006
Level-1 variance		4.415

[8] Our index of EU political knowledge sums up the number of correct responses to four quiz questions about European Union politics; for details see the Appendix.

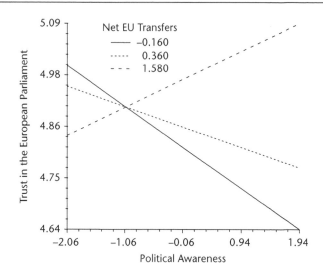

Figure 5.2. The effect of Political Awareness on EP Trust in countries with negative, positive and balance Net EU Transfers. (Slopes computed with a multivel model from Table 5.5)

different among these three groups of countries. Whereas at negative or low levels of net transfers the relationship is significant and negative, at high levels of net transfers the relationship is significant and positive.

These results are not only applicable for trust in the EP, but also for other EU institutions such as the EC. Table 5.5 below shows that the interaction coefficient is also significant and positive, although the relation in this case is weaker. Figure 5.3 presents the corresponding slopes derived from that model. Despite the fact that the same relationship is observed concerning the direction of the relationship between trust in the EC and political knowledge at different levels of net transfers to the EU, the slopes are less steep than in the previous model.

Political awareness and trust in national institutions

Following on from the preceding discussion on the effect of trust in national institutions on trust in the EP, we contend that the effect of political awareness on this attitude does not only depend on objective contextual factors such as the balance of net transfers, as discussed above, but political awareness may also condition the effect of other attitudinal cues, such as trust in national institutions. To test this possibility, we estimate the model shown in Table 5.7, which includes an interaction between political awareness and trust in national institutions. The results of this model's estimation, displayed

Table 5.5. Trust in the EU Commission as a function of Political Awareness and Net EU Transfers (multilevel model with robust standard errors)

	Trust EU Parliament	
	Coef.	SE
Intercept (β_0)		
Intercept (γ_{00})	4.864***	0.202
Net Transfers from EU (γ_{01})	0.033	0.179
Age	−0.022***	0.006
Age SQ	0.001***	0.000
Education	−0.042	0.042
Unemployed	−0.084	0.094
Manual	−0.044	0.062
Media Consumption	0.016*	0.008
Social Trust	0.197***	0.007
Interest in Politics	0.069***	0.020
Left–right	0.059**	0.023
Left–right SQ	−0.004**	0.002
European Identity	0.199***	0.053
EU benefits nation	0.542***	0.054
EU benefits me	0.454***	0.050
EU Support	0.203***	0.007
Information on EU	−0.081**	0.031
Information on EU X Net Transfers from EU	0.059**	0.027
Level-1 N		16,133
Level-2 N		16
Random Intercept Variance		0.418
Random slope Information EU Variance		0.005
Level-1 variance		4.339

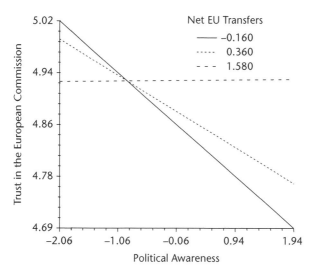

Figure 5.3. The effect of Political Awareness on EP Trust in countries with negative, positive, and balance Net EU Transfers. (Slopes computed with a multivel model from Table 5.6)

for the three dependent variables in Table 5.7, reveal that political awareness also intervenes in the aforementioned relationship between trust in national institutions and attitudes towards EU institutions, as well as perceptions of the degree of EU responsiveness. Moreover, the positive effect of political awareness is actually reversed when dealing with higher levels of trust in domestic institutions.

The marginal effects of this interaction are depicted in Figure 5.4. The relationship is unequivocal for all dependent variables (EP, EC, and degree of EU Responsiveness). As Brambor, Clark, and Golder (2006) have argued, to better evaluate the effects of an interaction, studying the marginal effects is actually more important than testing the significance of the estimated coefficients. The marginal effects displayed in Figure 5.4 show that the magnitude of the effect of trust in domestic institutions on EU institutions *declines* as political awareness increases. For EU Responsiveness, the magnitude of the effect increases, though it is noticeably weaker, reflecting the non-significance of the interaction term in the EU Responsiveness equation in Table 5.6.

These results show that political awareness does indeed interfere with the extent to which national attitudes affect EU attitudes. In general, political awareness increases the impact that trust in domestic institutions has on trust in EU institutions; nevertheless the increment is mitigated as the level of political awareness increases. In terms of EU responsiveness, the increment is larger as the level of political awareness increases.

Table 5.6. EU Institutional Trust, EU Responsiveness, and the interaction between Political Awareness and Trust in National Institutions (OLS Clustered Estimators)

	Trust EU Parliament		Trust EU Commission		EU Responsiveness	
	Coef.	SE	Coef.	SE	Coef.	SE
Male	−0.097*	(0.052)	−0.169***	(0.054)	0.151***	(0.048)
Age	−0.032***	(0.006)	−0.029***	(0.006)	−0.028***	(0.008)
Age SQ	0.000***	(0.000)	0.000**	(0.000)	0.000**	(0.000)
Education	0.444***	(0.129)	0.342**	(0.137)	0.228**	(0.104)
Unemployed	0.237	(0.151)	−0.005	(0.155)	−0.138	(0.129)
Media Consumption	0.010	(0.008)	0.021*	(0.010)	0.016	(0.016)
Social Trust	0.048**	(0.016)	0.091***	(0.019)	0.087***	(0.014)
Interest in Politics	−0.010	(0.039)	0.016	(0.031)	0.011	(0.041)
Left–right	−0.009	(0.062)	−0.013	(0.051)	−0.036	(0.054)
Left–right SQ	0.003	(0.005)	0.001	(0.005)	0.002	(0.005)
European Identity	0.352***	(0.106)	0.403***	(0.106)	0.591***	(0.100)
Trust Nat. Parl./Gov.	0.563***	(0.035)	0.458***	(0.015)	0.118***	(0.029)
Information on EU	0.176*	(0.086)	0.128	(0.078)	−0.041	(0.076)
Inf*Trust Nat. Parl.	−0.035***	(0.009)	−0.031**	(0.010)	0.016	(0.009)
Intercept	2.722***	(0.291)	3.052***	(0.212)	3.107***	(0.351)
N	16,133		16,133		16,133	
R^2	0.32		0.26		0.05	

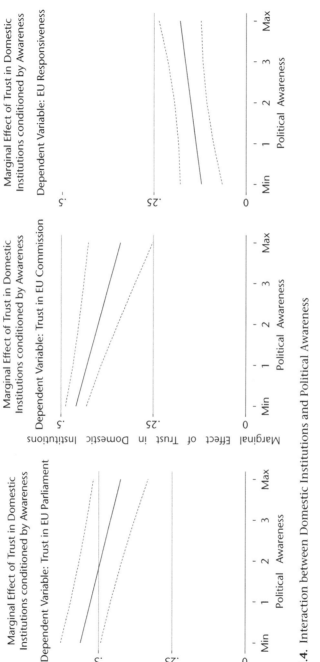

Figure 5.4. Interaction between Domestic Institutions and Political Awareness

Politicization and EU representation

Our final set of analyses of the relationship between EU politicization and trust levels in various institutions focuses on the role of national parties and the cueing role they play in determining trust in EU institutions and perceptions of EU responsiveness. As many scholars have claimed, the increasing effects of both instrumental evaluations and national politics are linked with the increasing politicization of the European integration process in many of the member states (Franklin, Marsh, and McLaren 1994; Hix 2007; Hooghe and Marks 2008). Naturally, political parties play a central cueing role in the process of increasing EU saliency (Ray 1999 and 2003a). As Hooghe and Marks (2005: 425) state, 'individuals who support a particular party will tend to follow that party's position on European integration' (see also Steenbergen and Jones 2002). Cues will, moreover, be at their strongest when elite groups dispute an issue (Ray 2003b; Hix 2007).

Table 5.7 shows the result of the estimation of the same baseline model reported in Table 5.2, but this time adding support for pro-EU parties. These results seem to confirm at first glance that voting for pro-EU parties increases support for EU institutions but not EU responsiveness. Political parties therefore act by liaising citizens and the EU institutions, but have no role to play in the perception of EU responsiveness.

Table 5.7. EU Institutional Trust and EU Responsiveness as a function of the Vote for pro-European parties by region (OLS Clustered Estimators)

	Trust EU Parliament		Trust EU Commission		EU Responsiveness	
	Coef.	SE	Coef.	SE	Coef.	SE
Male	−0.208***	(0.044)	−0.257***	(0.057)	0.091*	(0.045)
Age	−0.040***	(0.008)	−0.032**	(0.010)	−0.019	(0.010)
Age-SQ	0.000***	(0.000)	0.000***	(0.000)	0.000*	(0.000)
Education	0.213*	(0.105)	0.062	(0.096)	0.053	(0.086)
Unemployed	0.149	(0.123)	0.116	(0.139)	−0.048	(0.159)
Media Consumption	−0.011	(0.011)	−0.011	(0.012)	0.001	(0.018)
Social Trust	0.172***	(0.017)	0.174***	(0.018)	0.110***	(0.017)
Interest in Politics	0.073*	(0.039)	0.041	(0.036)	−0.015	(0.045)
Left–right	0.009	(0.043)	0.005	(0.037)	−0.017	(0.046)
Left–right SQ	0.001	(0.004)	0.000	(0.004)	0.000	(0.004)
European Identity	0.150	(0.100)	0.159	(0.100)	0.371***	(0.085)
EU benefits nation	0.527***	(0.131)	0.692***	(0.120)	0.145	(0.090)
EU benefits me	0.327***	(0.085)	0.335***	(0.071)	0.706***	(0.097)
EU Support	0.230***	(0.023)	0.221***	(0.021)	0.153***	(0.023)
Voted Pro-EU party	0.153***	(0.036)	0.148***	(0.031)	0.053	(0.038)
Intercept	1.965***	(0.423)	1.958***	(0.321)	1.832***	(0.283)
N	10,862		10,862		10,862	
R^2	0.23		0.24		0.10	

However, the question is whether pro-EU party cues might interfere with the effect of other attitudinal cues when it comes to expressing trust in EU institutions and EU responsiveness. More concretely, we are interested in testing whether instrumental cues play a more important role when parties polarize political conflict over the EU. To test this possibility, we estimate the same model, but add the interaction between these cueing attitudes and votes for pro-EU parties. Table 5.8 and Figure 5.5 present the results of the estimation and reveal that the egocentric variable 'EU benefits *me*' has a positive effect on trust in the EP, but this effect is only statistically significant for those who voted for Europhile parties. Indeed, the stronger the Europhile position of the party each individual voted for, the higher the effect of the egocentric instrumental calculation. Although not displayed here due to space limitations, the same pattern can be observed for the sociotropic variable 'EU benefits *my country*', confirming once more the increasing role of instrumental subjective attitudinal cues in expressing support for EU institutions when there are higher levels of political polarization (Torcal, Muñoz, and Bonet forthcoming). Nonetheless, the effects are not present for the other two dependent variables, namely trust in the EC, and the degree of responsiveness of EU institutions. We do not report the results of these analyses here but the findings are available from the authors on request.

Table 5.8. Trust in the EU Parliament as a function of the Vote for pro-European parties (OLS Clustered Estimators)

	Trust EU Parliament	
	Coef.	*SE*
Male	−0.208***	(0.045)
Age	−0.040***	(0.008)
Age SQ	0.000***	(0.000)
Education	0.211*	(0.105)
Unemployed	0.151	(0.122)
Media Consumption	−0.011	(0.011)
Social Trust	0.171***	(0.017)
Interest in Politics	0.072*	(0.040)
Left–right	0.009	(0.042)
Left–right SQ	0.001	(0.004)
European Identity	0.151	(0.099)
EU benefits nation	0.556*	(0.308)
EU benefits me	−0.173	(0.364)
EU Support	0.263***	(0.070)
Voted Pro-EU party	0.153*	(0.073)
VPro*EU benefits Nat.	−0.009	(0.064)
VPro*EU benefits me	0.088	(0.061)
VPro*EU Support	−0.006	(0.012)
Intercept	1.984***	(0.600)
N		10,862
R^2		0.23

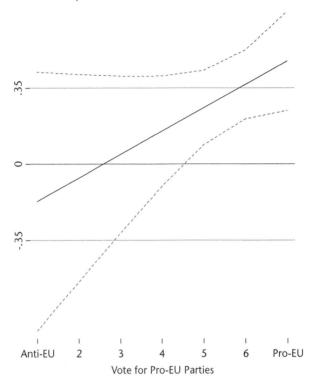

Marginal Effect of EU Benefits Me
conditioned by Vote for Pro-EU Parties

Dependent Variable: Trust in EU Parliament

Figure 5.5. Interaction between Instrumental Support for EU and Vote for Pro-EU Parties

The effect of politicization in post-Communist countries

One further qualification is necessary. When considering the role of parties as cueing agents, several studies have argued that there may be significant differences between older EU member states and the post-Communist entrants of 2004. It is claimed that post-Communist countries display a distinctive ideological interpretation of the EU integration process and its consequences—as a result of (a) idiosyncratic national political cueing in those countries, (b) the distinctive nature of the dimensions of party competition, and (c) the existence of different types of winners and losers of the integration process (Cichowski 2000; Tucker, Pacek, and Berinsky 2002; Rohrschneider and Whitefield 2004 and 2006a; Christin 2005; Marks, Hooghe, Nelson, and Edwards 2006). Given these country differences, it might be expected that people's approach to the evaluation of the EU should be different in post-Communist countries. We accordingly re-estimated the models shown in Table 5.7, but broken down by Eastern versus Western European countries. As a further check, we also considered the possibility that differential patterns of relationship might be observed in Southern Europe. The results of these estimations suggested that there was nothing particularly distinctive about the pattern of effects in any of these three European regions. The results of these analyses are available from the authors on request.

Conclusions

This chapter has sought to provide a fully fledged analysis of representation in the EU, a topic that has been the subject of previous studies. Yet this chapter also aims to make an important contribution to the subject by innovating at two levels. Most studies reduce the concept of representation to the study of one dependent variable, e.g. trust in the European Parliament. In this chapter, and following on from the discussion in Chapter 2, the complexity of the concept of representation is acknowledged. Throughout this chapter, three dependent variables have been considered, namely trust in the European Parliament, trust in the European Commission, and perceptions of the degree of responsiveness of EU institutions. Not only is the concept of representation thus given 'density', but the relationships between variables are considered in a multilevel context. This allows for the correct modelling of attitudes in a multilevel political setting such as the EU. In short, this chapter revisits some current theories about attitude formation of representation in the EU, but elaborates on them by testing these through interactions between macro and individual-level variables.

The role of heuristics and attitudinal cues in explaining attitudes toward the EP has been well established in previous research (Torcal et al. forthcoming). The first section of the chapter expanded on those findings by encompassing trust in the European Commission, as well as perceptions of institutional responsiveness. The results show that citizens tend to fall back on basic attitudinal cues when they have to express trust in the EP and EC, although not to the same extent when evaluating EU responsiveness. Additionally, the results showed that variables measuring affective attitudes towards European institutions are the least relevant of the cues, thus confirming the erosion of the 'permissive consensus' in citizens' attitudes towards the EU.

In the second part of the chapter, our analysis focused on attitudes towards-*national* institutions, the effects of which were modelled in the context of the Quality of Governance that each country enjoys. This is an important relationship to model given the lack of consensus in the field. Our findings unequivocally show that trust in national parliaments is positively related to trust in the EP at both low and high levels of Quality of Governance. The results show that there is a slight difference in the intensity of the strength of the relationship, which seems to be more marked in countries with higher levels of trust in national institutions. Thus, actual levels of trust in EU institutions have more to do with levels of trust in (or political disaffection with) *all* institutions at the *national* level than with a real evaluation of the functioning and performance of *EU* institutions. These results were confirmed both when the analysis was performed by running the regression on a split sample (distinguishing between low and high Quality of Governance), as well as in a formal multilevel model.

The third part of our discussion considered the contextual importance of *political awareness* when explaining attitudes towards EU representation. The effect of political awareness on EU attitudes varies according to the objective consequences of EU integration in each country, which can be measured in various ways. For our purposes, EU integration was measured by the balance of net transfers from the EU for each member state. We found that in countries where the balance of these net fiscal transfers is negative, political awareness has a *negative* impact on levels of EP trust, and in countries where transfers are positive, political awareness has a *positive* impact on levels of EP trust. The results are similar when trust in the EC is considered. We delved more deeply into the role of political awareness by showing that the effect of trust in *national* institutions upon trust in *EU* institutions is mediated by individual levels of political awareness regarding the EU. Additionally, we also showed that national institutions affect trust in EU institutions mostly for those who are at extreme positions on the political awareness scale.

The final part of our analysis considered the relationship between voting for pro-EU parties and EU attitudes. We showed that individuals who vote for pro-EU parties are not only more likely to have confidence in EU institutions; they are also more likely to use egocentric instrumental calculations in arriving at their assessments of those institutions.

Beyond the several individual findings outlined above, there are several unifying themes that this chapter contributes. The first is the changing nature of heuristics or attitudinal cues in explaining the nature of representation in the EU. We have shown that these are becoming increasingly instrumental, reflecting the growing importance of the consequences of EU policies in the formation of these attitudes. The second is the role played by national cues, namely national parliaments, in forming attitudes towards supranational institutions. It is clearly demonstrated that trust in national institutions is carried over to supranational institutions. There is no negative relationship between these two levels of trust.

Thus we find that the decline of the permissive consensus has made instrumental variables more important. Individuals use national cues as proxies for their attitudes towards Europe. The systematic similarity of results for two such different institutions as the EP and the EC attests to this fact. Yet it is also the case that with respect to perceptions of EU responsiveness, model fit statistics and the effects of many of the variables are less significant, suggesting that the complex nature of the concept of representation beckons future analyses to focus on this particular dimension.

6

The Scope of Government of the European Union: Explaining Citizens' Support for a More Powerful EU

Pedro C. Magalhães

Why do some people support the notion of having the institutions of the European Union setting and implementing policy in a variety of areas while others are more likely to reject it? Is this question important at all? To a large extent, the history of the European Union can be told as a succession of transfers of policymaking competencies and prerogatives from national governments to EU institutions, from the initial creation of common trade and agricultural policies to the more recent inclusion of areas such as monetary, immigration, and asylum policies under the supranational 'community pillar'. Although such increases in the scope of governance of the EU have not occurred at a similar or constant speed in all domains of policymaking, they have been mostly unidirectional and without significant retrenchments in the last decades (Börzel 2005).

As argued early on in the introduction to this volume, the question of what European citizens feel about these developments (and why) is a crucial one. Citizens' perceptions and attitudes about the scope of EU government are at the very heart of the notion of 'European citizenship'. Being and feeling a citizen of the EU must entail holding the belief that the European level of government indeed has the right to exercise some kind of political authority. The relationship between the claims on the part of European political elites and institutions at exercising that authority, on the one hand, and citizens' views about such claims, on the other hand, lie at the very heart of the legitimacy of the EU as a political system (Sinnott 1995: 275; De Winter and Swyngedouw 1999: 66; Hooghe 2003: 283; Lubbers and Scheepers 2005: 239).

It is therefore somewhat surprising that the literature on citizens' attitudes *vis-à-vis* Europe has chosen to devote comparatively little attention to the central issue of citizens' views about the EU's scope of government. Most of the theoretically influential empirical literature on public support for integration has focused on survey data about citizens' approval of their countries' membership in the EU and on the perceived benefits of integration, or, more recently, on variables such as 'support for unifying Europe', 'the desired speed of integration', 'the desired role of the EU in people's daily lives' or some combination of the former.[1] However, it is unclear whether the highly developed theorization that has already been produced to explain attitudes such as those described above also serves to explain a perhaps narrower, very concrete, but overly important aspect of the construction of Europe: citizens' support for increasing the powers and policy prerogatives of the EU. This is the main issue we will address in this chapter.

In the next section, we start by reviewing the evidence in the literature concerning explanations of public support for European integration. Then, we suggest several reasons why extant findings may not be entirely adequate to make inferences about what explains support for increasing the policymaking prerogatives of European institutions. We argue that such a dimension of European attitudes is, unlike others, specifically political, prospective, and impinging on the input-oriented legitimacy of the EU. Thus, as such, it is much less likely to be related to the real or perceived economic costs and benefits of integration. Instead, we suggest that support for an enlarged scope of policymaking in the EU is much more likely to be hampered by the input-legitimacy deficits of the EU, particularly those related to 'the lack of a pre-existing sense of collective identity, the lack of Europe-wide policy discourses, and the lack of a Europe-wide institutional infrastructure that could assure the political accountability of office holders to a European constituency' (Scharpf 1999: 187). Identity, political costs and gains, and EU representation, not economic calculation, should drive citizens' views about the EU's scope of government. In the third section, we test the hypotheses developed in this regard by using data on sixteen surveys conducted in EU member states under the IntUne project. Taking into account the clustered nature of the data, we start by examining the role of a set of individual-level variables that capture different approaches to public opinion about Europe, and then improve the model's specification by introducing several individual-level interaction effects, contextual factors, and cross-level

---

[1] For a review, see Brinegar and Jolly (2004).

interactions. In the last section, we discuss the theoretical and political implications of the findings.

Explaining attitudes about the EU's scope of government

Public opinion on European integration

In a wonderful synthesis of the existing literature on public opinion about European integration, Liesbet Hooghe and Gary Marks (2005) describe the three main approaches that have been most commonly used in this regard as focusing on 'calculation, community, and cues'. 'Calculation' refers to the notion that attitudes towards European integration are driven by citizens' evaluation of the economic costs and benefits brought about by European integration to themselves and their groups. 'Community' captures the idea that citizens' feelings about the social and political community to which they belong are also consequential for their views about the European Union, leading individuals who see themselves as belonging exclusively to a national community to perceive European integration as a fundamental cultural and political threat. Finally, 'cues' refers to the notion that, since individuals have little knowledge about European integration and its consequences (and few incentives to obtain it), they tend to resort to beliefs and attitudes related to a more accessible level of government (the domestic political system) in order to make judgements about Europe: their psychological predispositions about politics and their relationship with the party system, the cues emanating from the positions of political elites they see as reliable sources of information, or their own views about how their national political system works.

After surveying the literature and analysing some of the most recent available data, Hooghe and Marks conclude that all three approaches contribute to explain the motivations underlying public opinion on European integration. Citizens take into account individual and collective economic interests, especially by responding more positively to integration when they live in countries that are net beneficiaries of EU transfers, when they have higher levels of education (and are thus more likely to benefit from economic integration and free trade) and whenever they form a subjectively better perception of their country's and their own personal economic situation. The positions held by the parties they identify with also seem to be used as cues, and the extent to which political elites are divided on the European integration issue in any given country is also consequential. However, all these previous factors seem to be less relevant than those related to 'community': citizens who conceive of their national identity as exclusive of other territorial identities are much more likely to be hostile to European integration, particularly in contexts where the issue of integration is heavily politicized (McLaren 2002; Hooghe and Marks 2004 and 2005). According to Hooghe and Marks, the reason why identity has become, generally speaking, more important in explaining public opinion about the EU is linked to a transformation of the integration process: the scope and depth of integration have increased, integration is more and more seen as 'political' rather than merely 'economic', and the European issue has become increasingly politicized in domestic arenas and vulnerable to electoral considerations. In this context, anti-European parties have framed their positions on the basis of a nationalist stance, and citizens' feelings of exclusive attachment to their nation have become highly consequential for their support of EU membership (Hooghe and Marks 2008).

Hooghe and Marks's dependent variable is citizens' generic views about 'European integration'. It encompasses the principle of membership ('support for membership') and its desired speed and direction ('EU's future role in daily lives'). What happens when we move from this sort of *generic* view to the explanation of citizens' *concrete* views about the proper scope of government of the EU, i.e., about whether the European Union should hold more political and policy prerogatives at the expense of nation states? As we will attempt to show, it may not be enough, in this case, to say that all three—'community', 'cues', and 'calculation'—contribute to explain such views, even with 'community' playing the most important role. While attitudes such as support for one's country membership in the EU or the perception of the benefits brought about by that membership inevitably evoke retrospective considerations about economic losses and gains, linked to the EU's 'output-oriented legitimacy', views about the proper scope of government of the European Union are likely to evoke very different considerations on the part of citizens: prospective, related to *political* (rather than economic) losses and gains, and linked to the 'input-oriented legitimacy' of the EU as a political system.

This justifies why 'identity' should also be particularly consequential in this case, but suggests something more. First, when we shift our focus from generic views of integration to the EU's scope of government, considerations about economic costs and benefits should actually be mostly irrelevant to explain views about the scope of government of the EU. Second, political attitudes about *both* the national *and* the European political systems are likely to be at least as important as identity considerations in explaining attitudes towards the EU scope of government, and in a rather different way from that assumed by the 'cues' approach. In the next sections, we explain why that is the case.

From calculation to identity

The notion that citizens' attitudes towards integration are driven by their evaluation of the economic costs and benefits brought about by European integration has been taken to imply at least three things in the literature. First, citizens who are objectively less likely to benefit from economic integration and free trade—those with lower levels of education and lower-skills occupations—are less likely to be supportive of integration. Second, subjective perceptions of the economy can also be consequential for the level of support awarded to the EU in general and integration in particular: the more positive the views of how the economy is doing at home, the higher the support for integration. And third, citizens embedded in contexts—i.e., countries—where such benefits have been measurably higher should also be more supportive of integration (Gabel and Palmer 1995; Anderson and Reichert 1996; Gabel 1998b and 1998c; Christin 2005).

However, we should not expect these factors to produce the same sort of effects in what concerns citizens' views about the proper scope of government of the EU. Questions about whether membership is a 'good thing' or whether one's country has 'benefited' from integration, on the one hand, and about what powers the EU should acquire, on the other, evoke very different considerations from the point of view of what citizens see as the *status quo* on the basis of which developments can be evaluated. Judgements about the advantages or benefits of integration, particularly if asked of citizens of member states, are fundamentally retrospective and 'backward-looking', inviting individuals to evaluate how their personal situation or that of the groups to which they belong has been affected by EU membership. In other words, such questions largely invite individuals to look at the EU from the point of view of its 'output-oriented' legitimacy or effectiveness, i.e., its basic ability to produce social and economic welfare (Scharpf 1999). Obviously, from this point of view, the perceptions of current economic conditions, the net fiscal transfers received by the country as a result of membership, or even one's position in the labour market clearly line up as potential explanations of why citizens make a positive or negative judgement about the consequences of European integration.

In contrast, judgements about the convenience of having the EU acquire policymaking capacities are fundamentally different. First, they are prospective in nature. Although, in some policy areas, the EU's prerogatives have increased over time and have reached very significant levels (in matters such as the environment, agriculture, or monetary policy, for example), in most other areas those capacities remain rather modest (Börzel 2005; Alesina, Angeloni, and Schuknecht 2005). Thus, what is being asked of citizens in this case is, to a large extent, a 'forward-looking' judgement: whether they would agree to change the *status quo*, i.e., to transfer more policymaking prerogatives to the EU institutions in several areas where they enjoy little or none. Second, these questions directly evoke issues of national sovereignty, political power, and the locus of policymaking. In other words, they potentially invite citizens to think about the EU not only (or not so much) from the point of view of its output-oriented legitimacy but rather from the point of view of its input-oriented legitimacy: the extent to which a political system allows the equal participation of all in articulating their preferences, fosters the accountability of office holders to their constituencies, and is based on a belief shared by citizens in a common political identity (Scharpf 1999).

There are several implications of the previous points. The first is that 'scope of government' attitudes should be empirically distinct from those related to the benefits of integration or support for membership: individuals who perceive membership to have been positive for their country are not necessarily those who desire to increase the powers of the EU. The existing research does tend to support this notion. Applying a factor analysis to Eurobarometer data, Lubbers and Scheepers (2005) find precisely that while items such as the 'membership as a good thing' or the 'perceived benefits of integration' seem to belong to a single dimension of 'instrumental' attitudes, citizens' views about the EU's scope of government—their support for (or rejection of) European policymaking—empirically constitute a different dimension of what they call 'political' support (or its inverse, 'political Euroscepticism').[2]

The second implication is that economic cost/benefit considerations should not be particularly relevant in explaining people's willingness to see sovereignty transferred to the EU. Indeed, the little we know about the determinants of attitudes about the EU's scope of government suggests that might be the case. It is true that, in most of the few studies using 'scope of government' as a dependent variable, higher levels of education seem to be associated with preferences for EU policymaking.[3] However, that positive impact of education might also be seen as a vindication of the 'cognitive mobilization' hypothesis rather than the 'economic costs and benefits' one, especially because all other indicators of individuals' objective socio-economic circumstances (levels of income or their position in the occupational structure) fail to serve as relevant predictors of support for a broader scope of EU government. In fact, in a study using 2002 Eurobarometer data, McLaren (2007a) finds that *none* of the occupational variables (or even education, for that matter) displays a significant relationship with support for a broader EU scope of government in ten different policy areas. Similarly, subjective perceptions of the economy do rather

[2] For similar empirical findings about the dimensionality of attitudes towards Europe, see Chierici (2005).

[3] Using 1994 European Election Study data, de Winter and Swyngedouw (1999) find that individuals of the EU12 countries with higher levels of educational attainment do tend to be more supportive of having the European Union set policies on the issues they see as most important, while Rohrschneider (2002), using 1994 Eurobarometer data, also finds a positive relationship between education and support for an EU-wide government. Similar results are obtained in studies on support for EU policymaking on immigration (Luedtke 2005) or defence and security (Genna 2005).

poorly in this respect: Rohrschneider (2002) finds that citizens' 'support for an EU-government' is unaffected by perceptions of either national or household economic circumstances. These results also fit well with extant research using time-series aggregate data, which has shown that economic performance— GDP growth, unemployment, or inflation—all fail to predict trends in net support for policy integration (Magalhães forthcoming).

The third implication of the previous arguments is that the increasingly important role of identity in explaining generic views of integration also applies (and much more so) when the EU's scope of government is concerned. One of the deficits in the EU's input-oriented legitimacy is precisely the absence of a pre-existing sense of collective identity that might help in legit-imizing the centralization of powers in the EU (Scharpf 1999: 187). As the political prerogatives of the EU increase, these increases come into a potential collision course with the collective identity deficit. Existing findings do tend to confirm the special importance of identity in shaping views about the EU's scope of government. For example, De Winter and Swyngedouw find that 'those with an exclusionary national orientation are also least in favour of the EU decision-making' (1999: 65), a result confirmed by McLaren in her analysis of Eurobarometer data collected almost ten years later (2007). Using a some-what different approach to test this hypothesis, Luedtke concludes that, once feelings of European identity are controlled for, attachment to the national level of government is the strongest explanation of (lack of) support for a common EU policy on immigration (2005: 98). And Rohrschneider finds that national pride is negatively related to support for an EU-wide government (2002).

Taking democratic deficits seriously

However, discussing the issue of the EU's scope of government as a 'political' dimension of support for integration, evoking considerations about the (lack of) input-oriented legitimacy of the EU, involves something more than assum-ing the economic calculations should be mostly irrelevant or that political identity should trump them in explaining citizens' attitudes. It also involves assumptions that citizens' views about how democracy works in Europe and in their own countries should also play a major role in explaining whether they are willing to transfer sovereignty to the European Union.

The way most of the existing literature has treated the role of political attitudes in explaining opinions about integration is by assuming that citizens compensate for their lack of knowledge and their lack of fully developed attitudes about European institutions by judging them on the basis of atti-tudes and beliefs about their domestic political system. This is supposed to occur in two basic ways. The first is by assuming that citizens follow the positions of political elites, particularly from the parties to which they are psychologically attached and see thus as trustworthy sources of information about political reality. This leads to the expectation, for example, that individuals attached to parties with more pro-European positions should also be more likely to have made such positions their own (Steenbergen and Jones 2002; Ray 2003a and 2003b). Similarly, individuals who see themselves as leftist in ideological terms are likely to react to the fact that, in many European countries, European integration remains a left-wing project to the extent that it is associated with internationalism, in contrast to the nationalist and traditionalist reactions to Europeanization taken by right-wing parties (Huber and Inglehart 1995).

The second way in which individuals are supposed to deal with the lack of knowledge about integration and European institutions is by simply transferring their feelings about their national political system onto Europe. On the one hand, considering the central role of executives and ministers in representing one's country position in the EU, individuals attached to the incumbent party or parties are likely to transfer that specific support to a support for Europe (Gabel 1998b; Anderson 1998). On the other hand, lacking an ability to form independent views about the democratic quality of the EU's political system, citizens may transport their generalized goodwill (or the lack of it) *vis-à-vis* their national political institutions to the European integration project as a whole: 'satisfaction with the way democracy works gauges whether citizens are satisfied with the workings of political institutions in general regardless of whether they are national, subnational or supranational institutions' (Anderson 1998: 581).

However, there are several aspects of these arguments that seem problematic, especially when support for broader political powers for the EU is the dependent variable of interest. The first is the assumption that citizens' lack any definite, autonomous, or consequential views about the extent to which the European Union deserves their support as a political system. Early on in this volume, namely in Chapter 2, several findings are discussed that shed doubts on this assumption. Empirically, citizens' levels of trust in the European Commission and the European Parliament, their satisfaction with democracy in the EU, and their perception of the competence of the EU decision-makers form a single attitudinal dimension—*Confidence in EU institutions*—that is clearly distinct not only from other major clusters of European attitudes—such as those related to identity or scope of government or support for membership—but also from the dimension that is formed by the same items concerning *national* political systems. In fact, the analysis by Sanders and his colleagues in Chapter 2 even uncovers an additional autonomous dimension of generic political attitudes *vis-à-vis* the European political system, i.e., one that captures a sense of *European external efficacy*, reflecting citizens' feelings about the responsiveness of EU policymakers to their own needs and to their country's interests. And as some previous research suggests, although attitudes of diffuse support for domestic and the European political systems are undoubtedly related, it is not necessarily the case that the latter are a mere reflection of the former, particularly among those with greater levels of political knowledge: especially among these, it is argued, 'summary evaluations of the EU should be more strongly rooted in evaluations of the EU rather than evaluations of national actors and institutions' (Karp, Banducci, and Bowler 2003: 276).

Once we admit the possibility that (at least some) citizens may form independent attitudes about the EU's democratic performance as a political system, we can realize how those attitudes are likely to be particularly consequential in and of themselves in explaining support for a broader political role for the EU. We already saw that one of the implications of thinking about scope of government attitudes as impinging on issues of input-oriented legitimacy is that this turns identity into a potentially very important determinant of such attitudes. But the other implication is that attitudes about EU representativeness and responsiveness should also be particularly consequential. As Rohrscheider puts it (2002), by focusing on how economic factors explain integration, extant research has often neglected the possibility that mass support for integration is affected by citizens' views of how well the EU articulates their preferences and allows them equal chances at participating in decisions. What Rohrscheider finds, precisely, is that citizens' support for an EU-wide government is strongly affected by the extent to which they feel that decisions by European institutions are protecting their interests. Similarly, McLaren (2007a) finds that trust in EU institutions helps to predict support for shifting responsibilities to the EU in several policy areas.

Finally, this calls attention to the possibility that the basic 'transfer' hypothesis may be wrong not only by assuming that diffuse support for the EU is not a relevant attitude on its own but also by positing a *positive* relationship between views about national political systems and support for integration. There are reasons to believe that precisely the opposite may be taking place. Sánchez-Cuenca (2000), for example, finds that when trust in European institutions is taken into account, individuals who place greater trust in domestic political institutions are *less* (rather than more) likely to support 'increasing the rhythm of European integration'. Kritzinger (2003), although treating trust in European institutions as an endogenous variable, does end up finding a similar negative relationship between opinions of national domestic institutions and support for 'unifying Europe'. Rohrschneider (2002) detects a negative relationship between satisfaction with national democracy and support for an EU-wide government, while McLaren (2007a) finds that, holding trust in EU institutions constant, confidence in national political institutions (parties, government, and parliament) has an (albeit modest) negative relationship with support for policymaking at the EU level. Thus, instead of a mechanism through which citizens view national and European institutions under the same light and transfer a positive view of the former to a better evaluation of European integration, we have at least some evidence of an entirely different mechanism being in place: it is when they lend greater legitimacy and support to their national political institutions that citizens may become warier of shifting power to the EU.

In sum, then, taking input-oriented legitimacy and its deficits seriously means two additional things. On the one hand, that citizens do form opinions about the democratic performance of the European political system, the accountability it allows, and the responsiveness it exhibits, and that such opinions may be consequential for their views about the EU's scope of government. On the other hand, a 'European democratic deficit' is not necessarily found only at the EU level. Domestic political systems vary significantly in terms of the quality of governance they exhibit and not all citizens view their domestic political institutions as invariably accountable, representative, and responsive. 'Democratic deficits' are not an exclusive feature of the EU's political system, and citizens may be able and willing to weigh the costs and benefits of awarding more powers to the EU under this light, doing so *politically* rather than economically: 'the worse the political system works at home and the better at the supranational level, the smaller the risk involved in transferring national sovereignty to a supranational body' (Sánchez-Cuenca 2000: 148).

Analysing the IntUne data

Dependent variables: present and future EU scope

In the IntUne survey, representative samples of citizens in sixteen EU member states were asked about which level of government—regional, national, or European—should be responsible for a very diverse array of policy areas: fighting unemployment, immigration, environment, health care, agriculture, and the fight against crime. Although aggregate levels of support for the Europeanization of these policy areas varied more or less according to the findings of previous literature (Sinnott 1995; Dalton and Eichenberg 1998; Magalhães forthcoming)—highest aggregate support for environment and immigration, lowest for health and unemployment—factor analysis (see Chapter 2) confirmed that these questions capture a single dimension of respondents' attitudes towards the scope of government of the EU today:

people who favour the EU's involvement in any one policy area tend to favour EU involvement in the others.

We called this dimension *Present EU Scope,* since the survey also included an additional set of questions where respondents were primed to think about the scope of government from a more clearly prospective point of view ('thinking about the European Union over the next ten years or so'). In this case, the survey gauged their support for a future unified tax system, a common social security system, a single EU foreign policy, and a common regime of regional aid. Factor analysis reveals that answers to these four items also constitute a single dimension, independent from Present EU Scope, which we call *Future EU Scope.* As explained in Chapter 2, we constructed 'constant range scales'— one such scale corresponding to each factor—ensuring that both the dependent variables of interest here are measured in scale with the same 0–10 range, with higher values corresponding to greater support for increasing EU powers either now or in the future.

Independent variables

We employ four sets of independent variables to test hypotheses related to economic costs and benefits, identity, domestic political cues, and the role of political attitudes *vis-à-vis* representation in the EU's political system in explaining views about the scope of government in Europe. For economic costs and benefits, we include the respondent's level of education (in a four-point scale, from elementary to university), a dummy variable capturing whether the respondent is a manual worker (1) or not (0), and a five-point scale capturing the respondent's retrospective evaluations of the evolution of the economy in her/his country in the last twelve months, from 'got a lot worse' to 'got a lot better'.

In relation to identity, we employ a dummy variable capturing whether the respondent sees her/himself as 'exclusively national' (1) or both national and European or even exclusively European (0). We also follow Hooghe and Marks (2005) by also including an identity-related control variable, measuring, on a scale of 1 to 4 ('not at all attached' to 'very attached') the extent to which respondents feel attached to Europe.

The role of domestic political cues is captured by several different variables. On the one hand, ideology is measured by a conventional left–right ideological self-placement ten-point scale, where 0 is the position furthest to the left and 10 the position furthest to the right. On the basis of a question about party identification, we also created a variable that, for each individual attached to a particular party, was coded with the value of the mean position assigned by experts to that particular party's leadership on European integration (on a seven-point scale, where 1 means 'strongly opposed' and 7 'strongly in favour').[4] Another dummy variable, constructed again on the basis of the party identification question, distinguishes respondents who are attached to an incumbent party in their country at the time of the survey (1) from all others (0). Based on the factor analysis described in Chapter 2, we also employ a constant range scale built on the basis of a series of items that capture a generic view of the democratic quality of *national* domestic institutions, as perceived by citizens: trust in national and local government and in the national parliament; satisfaction with national democracy; and perceptions of whether domestic decision-makers are competent and care about what 'people think'.

Finally, we test the impact of attitudes towards the EU's political system by including two other already-mentioned scales emerging out of our initial analysis of the data. The first—*Confidence in EU institutions*—results from items measuring trust in the European Parliament and the Commission, as well as satisfaction with democracy in Europe and the competence of European decision-makers. The second—*European external efficacy*—results from two items: citizens' views about whether or not European decision-makers care about what respondents think and whether or not they take into account the interests of the respondents' countries.

Several control variables are also included. These are age, as an absolute value; whether respondents are male (1) or female (0); and, in order to separate the effect of education from that of cognitive mobilization, two additional controls: an index of political sophistication, based on responses to questions about levels of interest in politics and a quiz assessing levels of political knowledge; and an index of media exposure, based on responses to questions about the number of days per week respondents read about politics in newspapers and watch political news on television.

Table 6.1 shows the results of two linear regression analyses, with Present EU Scope and Future EU Scope as dependent variables. We used the pooled dataset of sixteen member states where IntUne surveys were conducted, with country samples equally weighted, and estimated regression models with robust standard errors. We also display standardized coefficients, to obtain a sense of the relative impact of each independent variable. Figure 6.1 displays the same results in a more intuitive way: it presents the beta standardized coefficients for the two regression models—for Present and Future EU Scope— by means of a dot plot with error bars, representing the 95 per cent confidence intervals for each coefficient.

---

[4] 2006 Chapel Hill Expert Survey dataset (Hooghe et al. 2008). Individuals attached to parties not included in the Chapel Hill dataset or without party identification were coded with value 4, the midpoint of the scale.

Table 6.1. Linear regression with Present EU Scope and Future EU Scope as dependent variables: model with individual-level variables, pooled dataset

	Present EU Scope			Future EU Scope		
	b	*s.e.*	*Beta*	*b*	*s.e.*	*Beta*
Intercept	3.35***	0.19		6.28***	0.20	
Economic costs and benefits						
Education	0.13**	0.04	0.04	−0.01	0.03	0.00
Manual worker	0.27**	0.10	0.03	0.08	0.07	0.01
National economic performance	0.09**	0.03	0.03	0.02	0.02	0.01
Domestic political cues						
Left–right self-placement	−0.04*	0.02	−0.03	−0.03**	0.01	−0.03
Pro-EU score of party ID	0.01	0.01	0.00	0.04*	0.02	0.02
Identification with incumbent	−0.06	0.07	−0.01	−0.001	0.07	−0.00
National political institutions	−0.05**	0.02	−0.03	−0.12***	0.01	−0.11
Attitudes towards EU politics						
Confidence in EU institutions	0.16***	0.02	0.11	0.30***	0.03	0.27
European external efficacy	0.07***	0.01	0.06	0.02**	0.01	0.02
Identity						
Exclusive national identity	−0.63***	0.06	−0.11	−0.33***	0.06	−0.07
Attachment to Europe	0.11*	0.05	0.03	0.24***	0.04	0.10
Controls						
Political sophistication	0.02	0.02	0.02	−0.001	0.02	0.00
Media exposure	−0.01	0.01	−0.01	0.01	0.007	0.01
Age	−0.004	0.003	−0.02	0.005*	0.002	0.04
Male	0.37***	0.07	0.06	0.33***	0.08	0.07

Note: Table entries are unstandardized (b) and standardized (beta) regression coefficients with clustered standard errors reported.
*$p<0.05$
**$p<0.01$
***$p<0.001$; N = 16,133; 16 countries, with country samples equally weighted; multiple imputation analysis; all independent variables group-centred.

Three main sets of findings deserve particular attention in light of the discussion in the previous section. The first is related to the variables capturing the relationship between economic costs and benefits and citizens' preferences about the EU's scope of government. Once we control for other relevant socio-economic and attitudinal attributes, differences based on individuals' level of education, perception of national economic performance, and whether they do manual work do tend to have a significant effect on their views about whether to assign policymaking prerogatives to the EU today. However, the sign of the coefficient for manual workers is actually *positive* in one of the regression models, contradicting one of the basic hypotheses behind the economic costs and benefits approach. Granted, there is a positive relationship between education and evaluation of national economic performance and Present EU Scope, but that relationship is very modest, especially when we compare the respective standardized coefficients with those pertaining to the variables capturing aspects of respondents' feelings of identity and

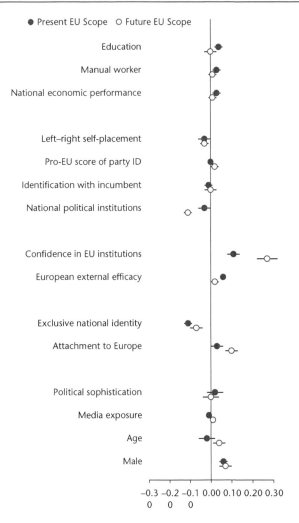

Figure 6.1. Dot plot representation of the standardized regression coefficients (error bars represent 95% confidence intervals)

EU representation. And finally, when the question is clearly posed in terms of increasing EU powers in the future, none of the 'economic costs and benefits' variables prove to be statistically significant correlates of support for a broader EU scope of government. Thus, it seems that economic explanations of differences in views about scope of government provide us very little leverage, and there is no evidence that they play any role at all when respondents are invited to think about the issue in more prospective terms. In contrast, the same clearly cannot be said for identity: whether respondents see themselves as being 'exclusively national' turns out to be one of the strongest (negative) correlates of views on Present EU Scope (albeit less so in what concerns Future EU Scope).

Second, evidence concerning the cueing hypotheses is not particularly encouraging. It is true that we are more likely to find leftists rather than rightists among supporters of a broader scope of government for the EU either today or in the future, as well as (in this case only in what concerns Future EU Scope) individuals attached to parties that are more supportive of integration. But again, these empirical relationships are invariably weak when compared to the role played by other variables.

Most importantly in relation to the 'political cues' approach, attitudes towards the domestic political system seem to matter in a way that is rather different from that hypothesized by the extant literature on support for integration. It is definitely *not* the case that individuals who support the government of the day or have more positive views of the democratic performance of their national political system are also more likely to endorse greater powers for the EU. On the one hand, identification with incumbent plays no visible role in driving these attitudes. On the other hand, one of the things that differentiates individuals with higher levels of support for the EU's policy-making role is precisely the fact that their views of national political institutions are *less* favourable, especially where support for EU policymaking in the future is concerned. In fact, in this case, the standardized coefficient is even larger than those found for either of the 'identity' variables.

The final relevant aspect of the results concerns views about democracy in the EU. The results confirm that, as we had suggested early on, identity is by no means the only attitudinal feature that differentiates respondents in terms of their support for a broader European scope of government. Respondents who are more favourable to a stronger political role for the EU are, on average, more likely to perceive European decision-makers as more responsive to their interests and, especially, to place greater trust in the institutions of the European Union. In the case of Present EU Scope, the standardized coefficient associated with 'Confidence in EU institutions' is as large (albeit, in the opposite direction) as that associated with 'Exclusive national identity'. And as for the prospective question, Confidence in the EU is clearly the strongest correlate of support for scope of government: one standard deviation in the scale of EU trust produces an increase of 0.27 standard deviations in support of a future broader policy scope of the EU.

A country-by-country replication of the analysis conducted for the pooled dataset reinforces these general conclusions. Table 6.2 shows the range of the values of the standardized coefficients found when the previous model is applied country-by-country, as well as the number of countries in which coefficients were statistically significant with $p < 0.05$ (sample sizes varied only between 1000 and 1082) with either a positive or negative sign. The

Table 6.2. Summary results of country-by-country regression analyses with Present EU Scope and Future EU Scope as dependent variables

	Present EU Scope				Future EU Scope			
	Lowest beta	Highest beta	Neg. with p<0.05	Pos. with p<0.05	Lowest beta	Highest beta	Neg. with p<0.05	Pos. with p<0.05
Economic costs and benefits								
Education	−0.06	0.15	0	6	−0.12	0.06	3	0
Manual worker	−0.06	0.10	0	5	−0.06	0.09	1	2
National economic performance	−0.04	0.10	0	3	−0.09	0.06	2	0
Domestic political cues								
Left–right self-placement	−0.11	0.07	3	2	−0.09	0.09	4	1
Pro-EU score of party ID	−0.13	0.06	1	1	−0.04	0.06	0	0
Identification with incumbent	−0.09	0.10	0	0	−0.09	0.08	2	1
National political institutions	−0.17	0.05	2	0	−0.18	0.00	8	0
Attitudes towards EU politics								
Confidence in EU institutions	0.04	0.22	0	9	0.13	0.45	0	16
European external efficacy	0.01	0.18	0	7	−0.06	0.09	0	2
Identity								
Exclusive national identity	−0.16	0.01	12	0	−0.20	0.03	9	0
Attachment to Europe	−0.07	0.18	0	4	−0.03	0.27	0	12

Note: Table entries are standardized (beta) linear regression coefficients of country-by-country regressions and counts of countries where coefficients of each independent variable achieved p<0.05 significance.

results can be easily summarized: the only variables that, in the majority of the country samples, constitute statistically significant correlates of views about the proper scope of EU powers in the theoretically predicted direction are the ones related either to identity or to attitudes about the EU's representational quality as a political system. Furthermore, in what concerns both Present and Future EU Scope, in no case do we find that views about national political institutions are positively related to our dependent variable, quite unlike the extant 'cues' literature would lead us to believe. Instead, we find the opposite: in all country surveys where the coefficient attached to the view of national political institutions was significantly different from zero, that coefficient was negative.

Early on, we also discussed the possibility that political knowledge might play a mediating role in the relationship between evaluations about national and EU institutions and views about integration: as it was argued, individuals with greater levels of political knowledge should be more likely to resort to their evaluations of the EU proper in order to form an opinion about integration, instead of resorting to their evaluations of domestic political performance. Table 6.3 shows the results of a test of this hypothesis for both Present and Future EU Scope. To our previous model, we added three interaction terms between political sophistication and the variables capturing

Table 6.3. Linear regression with Present EU Scope and Future EU Scope as dependent variables: model with individual-level variables and interaction effects, pooled dataset

	Present EU Scope		Future EU Scope	
	b	s.e.	b	s.e.
Intercept	3.35***	0.19	6.28***	0.20
Economic costs and benefits				
Education	0.12**	0.04	−0.01	0.03
Manual worker	0.27**	0.10	0.08	0.07
Retrospective national economic performance	0.09**	0.03	0.01	0.02
Domestic political cues				
Left–right self-placement	−0.04*	0.02	−0.03**	0.01
Pro-EU integration score of party ID	0.006	0.02	0.04*	0.02
Identification with incumbent party	−0.06	0.07	−0.002	0.06
National political institutions	−0.13**	0.05	−0.16***	0.03
Sophistication*National political institutions	*0.01*	*0.01*	*0.01*	*0.01*
Attitudes towards EU politics				
Confidence in EU institutions	0.20***	0.05	0.30***	0.03
Sophistication*Confidence in EU institutions	*−0.01*	*0.01*	*0.001*	*0.005*
European External Efficacy	0.02	0.02	−0.02	0.02
Sophistication*European External Efficacy	*0.01**	*0.004*	*0.01***	*0.003*
Identity				
Exclusive national identity	−0.62***	0.06	−0.32***	0.06
Attachment to Europe	0.12*	0.05	0.24***	0.04
Controls				
Political sophistication	−0.04	0.02	−0.07*	0.03
Media exposure	−0.01	0.01	0.013*	0.006
Age	−0.004	0.002	0.005*	0.002
Male	0.36***	0.07	0.32***	0.08

Note: Table entries are unstandardized (b) regression coefficients with clustered standard errors reported.
*$p<0.05$
**$p<0.01$
***$p<0.001$; N = 16,133; 16 countries, with country samples equally weighted; multiple imputation analysis; all independent variables group-centred.

attitudes towards political institutions: 'National political institutions', 'Confidence in EU institutions', and 'European external efficacy'.

The evidence for a mediating role of political sophistication is not particularly compelling. It is true that the interaction between 'Political sophistication' and 'European political efficacy' is significant, regardless of whether Present or Future EU Scope are the dependent variables of interest. Among individuals with the lowest level in the scale of political sophistication (zero), the impact of European external efficacy on support for broader powers for the EU is not significantly different from zero, but the same does not occur with the most sophisticated individuals. However, 'Confidence in EU institutions' is consequential for both dependent variables regardless of one's level of political sophistication, and there is no evidence that views about national political institutions are a stronger correlate of preferences for EU powers among the less politically sophisticated. This negative result is, in fact, less than surprising in light of the previous findings. The notion that individuals with lower levels of political knowledge should be more likely to use their support for national institutions to make judgements about the extent of EU powers assumes a 'transfer' mechanism. But what we had already found suggests that no such mechanism operates. Instead, the evidence favours the notion that individuals engage in something much more akin to a 'political costs and benefits' reasoning, rejecting losses of national sovereignty when they place greater trust in their national political systems and accepting them when they are most disaffected in relation to domestic politics. Such reasoning seems to be equally consequential across different individuals defined in terms of their level of political sophistication.

Introducing context

So far, we have focused exclusively on the individual-level correlates of preferences about the EU's scope of government. However, such preferences may also have relevant macro-level correlates. In other words, the contexts in which individuals are embedded may also help to explain levels of support for a more powerful EU, and may even help to account for variations in the coefficients associated with individual-level variables across countries. Some of the theoretical approaches we have been discussing propose that such effects do take place. 'Economic costs and benefits' approaches to mass support for integration, for example, have established that residents of countries who are net recipients of EU funds tend to be more supportive of European integration (Anderson and Reichert 1996; Brinegar and Jolly 2004; Hooghe and Marks 2005). On the other hand, approaches stressing the role of political cues have shown that, in countries where political elites are more divided on the integration issue, respondents' opposition to integration is likely to be stronger (Hooghe and Marks 2005). And in relation to identity, opposition to integration among those who feel exclusively national is particularly likely to be activated in political contexts where electoral competition has led to deeper divisions about Europe (Hooghe and Marks 2005).

Approaches focusing on the importance of national democratic performance have also assumed contextual effects. From this point of view, the 'transfer' hypothesis has never been proposed, but it remains unclear whether and in what way context might be consequential. Sánchez-Cuenca (2000), for example, shows an aggregate-level positive relationship between levels of corruption in the national political system (measured by Transparency International indicators) and support for integration, a relationship that persists when we treat corruption as a contextual variable explaining support for integration at the individual level. Rohrschneider (2002), however, using a proper multilevel analysis of the data, suggests that this contextual feature of national political systems—'institutional quality', which he captures by using International Country Risk Guide data—lacks any direct effect on support for an EU-wide government. Instead, he finds that the quality of domestic political institutions exerts a mediating effect: in countries where such quality is higher, citizens give greater weight to their perceptions of the EU's own democratic quality.

What support is there for these contextual hypotheses when we move to citizens' preferences about the EU's scope of government? Testing hypotheses about contextual effects with our data requires some initial qualifications. First, we only have sixteen countries, i.e., sixteen macro-level units, rather short of an ideal situation to test contextual effects. Second, the intraclass correlation coefficient, which can be estimated using the level-1 (individuals) and level-2 (countries) variance components of a null multilevel ANOVA, measures the extent individuals in the same country resemble each other in terms of their support for a broader EU scope of government as compared to individuals in different countries. For Present EU Scope, the ICC value is 0.07, while it reaches only 0.13 for Future EU Scope. Thus, most of the variation in citizens' support for either Present or Future EU Scope of Government is not between countries, but rather across individuals.

However, from this it follows neither that a multilevel analysis can be dispensed with nor that significant differences between countries (or between the effects of particular variables in different countries) are absent. We thus test the previous hypotheses, first, by adding three contextual variables to the model. The first is a score of *Quality of Governance* for each country for 2007, derived from a principal components analysis of the six indicators—control of corruption, government effectiveness, rule of law, regulatory quality, voice and accountability, and political stability—in the 2007 World Bank Governance data (Kaufmann et al. 2009). The second is the percentage of the Gross National Income that net transfers from the EU budget represented in each country in 2007. Finally, using again the Chapel Hill dataset, we introduce a variable capturing the degree of polarization in each party system around the European integration issue, by simply subtracting the lowest (anti-European) score of all parties represented in parliament to the highest (pro-European) score. We test two cross-level interaction effects: between party-system polarization on the integration issue and exclusive national identity, capturing the notion that 'political community' considerations may become more important when elite divisions are greater; and between transparency and attitudes towards representation in Europe, capturing the notion that support for a powerful EU is more shaped by views on the EU's democracy in those countries whose political systems work better.

Table 6.4. Multilevel linear regression (random intercept, fixed slopes) with Present EU Scope and Future EU Scope as dependent variables: model with contextual variables and cross-level interactions, pooled dataset

	Present EU Scope		Future EU Scope	
	b	s.e.	b	s.e.
Intercept	3.35***	0.18	6.27***	0.12
Level-2 predictors				
Quality of governance	−0.14	0.28	−0.87***	0.22
Net transfers from EU	−0.32	0.25	−0.07	0.16
Polarization on EU integration	−0.18	0.19	−0.23	0.12
Level-1 predictors				
Economic costs and benefits				
Education	0.12**	0.04	−0.01	0.03
Manual worker	0.27**	0.10	0.08	0.07
Retrospective national economic performance	0.09**	0.03	0.02	0.02
Domestic political cues				
Left–right self-placement	−0.04*	0.02	−0.03**	0.01
Identification with incumbent party	−0.06	0.07	0.006	0.07
Pro-EU integration score of party ID	0.005	0.02	0.04*	0.02
National political institutions	−0.13**	0.04	−0.16***	0.03
Sophistication* National political institutions	0.01	0.01	0.007	0.005
Attitudes towards EU's political system				
Confidence in European political institutions	0.20***	0.05	0.31***	0.03
Quality of governance* Confidence in EU inst.	−0.004	0.01	0.06*	0.03
Sophistication* Confidence in EU inst.	0.007	0.007	−0.002	0.004
European External Efficacy	0.02	0.02	−0.01	0.02
Quality of governance* European External Efficacy	0.004	0.01	0.02**	0.007
Sophistication* European External Efficacy	0.01*	0.004	0.007*	0.003
Identity				
Exclusive national identity	−0.62***	0.06	−0.33***	0.07
Polarization on EU integration*Exclusive national identity	−0.14*	0.06	−0.08	0.07
Attachment to Europe	0.11*	0.05	0.24***	0.04
Controls				
Political sophistication	−0.04	0.02	0.007	0.005
Media exposure	−0.01	0.01	0.01*	0.006
Age	−0.004	0.003	0.005*	0.002
Male	0.36***	0.07	0.32	0.08

Note: See note to Table 6.3.

As we can see in Table 6.4, none of the previous findings concerning individual-level correlates is affected by the introduction of macro-level variables and cross-level interactions. The economic costs and benefits approach still fails to account for variations in Future EU Scope, while the signs and sizes of the coefficients remain the same concerning Present EU Scope, allowing us to restate the previous conclusions concerning the comparatively weak (and in one case, counter-intuitive) relationships of these variables with support for a more powerful EU. Furthermore, we have now an additional finding concerning the economic costs and benefits approach. In contrast to what has been found in the extant literature in accounting for variation in other variables capturing support for integration, views about the EU's scope of government are apparently unrelated to fiscal transfers. Citizens living in countries where such net transfers represent a larger (positive) share of national income are neither more nor less likely to support increasing powers for the EU, now or in the future. Even more damagingly, the sign of the coefficients associated with this macro-variable is *negative*, increasing our confidence that this 'negative finding' is not merely a function of a small number of macro-level units.

In what concerns identity, the cross-level interaction term between party-system polarization around European integration at the system level and feelings of exclusive national identity is significant in the equation for Present EU Scope. What this means, taking into account the signs of the different coefficients, is that, for the lowest level of EU polarization, when all remaining variables are kept constant at their mean values, the predicted value of support for Present EU Scope drops approximately one point (in a scale from 0 to 10) when the value of exclusive national identity moves from 0 to 1; but for the highest level of EU polarization, that drop is slightly (albeit significantly) larger (1.4 points). In other words, as suggested already by the literature on generic support for integration (Hooghe and Marks 2005), there is some evidence that the extent to which political parties and elites are polarized on the European issue seems to make identity considerations more consequential for EU support.

Finally, there is another aspect in which the inclusion of macro-level variables and cross-level interactions improves model specification. It concerns the role played by views and facts about the quality of governance in the EU and in domestic political systems. First, the coefficient associated with the macro-level variable that captures the quality of governance in the different countries is negative in both cases and highly significant in the model for Future EU Scope. In other words, citizens who have less favourable views about the possibility of creating common EU policies in the future come disproportionately from countries where domestic governance institutions are more advanced and perform better. Reassuringly, this confirms previous results of analyses of net support for policy integration at the EU level using aggregate data (Ahrens, Meurers, and Renner 2007; Magalhães forthcoming).

Second, where Future EU Scope is concerned, the two cross-level interaction terms involving system-level measures of quality of governance and attitudes towards EU institutions have positive and statistically significant coefficients, with stronger results for confidence in EU institutions.[5] In other words, the

---

[5] We also tested an alternative specification of the model, replacing our Quality of Governance measure with the 2007 Corruption Perception Index as measured by Transparency International. The results were broadly similar.

impact of such attitudes on support for a broader future EU scope of government is not the same regardless of the domestic levels of quality of governance. As Rohrschneider proposed (2002), it is in those countries where the quality of governance is higher that the preferences about whether to transfer policy to the EU in the future seem to be more strongly related to views about the EU's political responsiveness and representativeness. In 'better-governed' democracies, perceptions about Europe's own democratic deficit are more consequential when it comes to making decisions about giving more powers to EU institutions.

Conclusion

The European integration process has faced well-known difficulties and challenges in the last decade and a half. Since Maastricht, positive views of membership among the citizenry have dropped (Çíftçí 2005), party-based Euroscepticism has increased in Western and Eastern countries (Szczerbiak and Taggart 2008), and efforts at institutional reform have repeatedly stumbled upon the obstacles placed by less than enthusiastic popular sentiment, as expressed in several negative referendum outcomes. Some have described these phenomena as a consequence of an extension of the EU's policy prerogatives well beyond the basic requirements of 'negative integration', i.e., the abolition of national barriers to the free movement of goods, capital, and people in a free and open European market. While such early economic integration enjoyed broad popular support, a new political and 'positive' integration in the wake of Maastricht has arguably been met with increased scepticism by citizens attached to their national identities, preferences, and policymaking traditions (Alesina and Wacziarg 1999 and 2008; Alesina, Angeloni, and Schuknecht 2005). For others, it is negative integration itself that has gone too far. With Maastricht and the creation of a common European monetary policy, bringing Europe closer than ever to an open, free, and unified market, citizens have reacted negatively to the budgetary consequences of monetary union (Eichenberg and Dalton 2007). And both perspectives on the causes of the current travails of the EU may just be capturing different aspects of the problem: while the 'excesses' of positive integration have been politicized by right-wing populist parties, the 'excesses' of negative integration have been turned into a mobilizing argument for left-wing radical parties (De Vries and Edwards 2009). In any case, there is agreement that at least part of this whole story must be related to a particular subset of public attitudes: people's views about the proper scope of government of the European Union in a multilevel system of governance. It is on this set of attitudes that we focused our attention in this chapter.

In his highly influential theorization about democracy and governance in the European Union, Scharpf pointed to a triple deficit of the EU, related to the lack of a common space of political debate and competition, the lack of a common identity, and the lack of mechanisms and practices ensuring representation and accountability at the European level. In this chapter, we argued that citizens' views about the proper scope of government in the EU were likely to be much more conditioned by factors related to such basic deficits than by considerations about the ability of integration to deliver growth and welfare, i.e., its ability to foster 'output-oriented legitimacy'. As we have shown, unlike what occurs when they are asked to judge the benefits of integration or whether membership has been a good thing for their country, Europeans seem largely to disregard economic cost/benefit considerations when asked to express preferences about how powerful the EU should be. Instead, they seem to be much more moved by sentiments about the political community to which they belong and, especially, by evaluations of democratic performance, responsiveness, and accountability of their political systems—both at the domestic and at the European level.

What are the main implications of these findings for the challenges posed to the legitimization of further powers and competencies to be awarded to EU institutions? First, it is important to note that, in spite of the unidimensionality we and others (Lubbers and Scheepers 2005) found concerning attitudes towards EU policymaking powers, aggregate levels of support do vary significantly across policy areas. As we have shown elsewhere (Magalhães forthcoming), and as the results of this survey confirm, there are several policy areas today in which clear majorities of citizens are broadly supportive of stronger policymaking for the EU in all or almost all member states, such as environmental policy, foreign policy, and addressing regional asymmetries. In some of these areas, the EU's policymaking role is already very significant, but in the cases where it is not—foreign policy is the obvious case in point—lack of popular support is certainly not the main culprit.

However, any sanguine view regarding the extension of the EU's scope of governance in some areas needs to be balanced with the findings of this chapter regarding the attitudinal explanations of support for European policy integration. On the one hand, in our sixteen-country sample, the percentage of respondents who feel 'exclusively national' averages 40 per cent, and ranges from 16 per cent in Italy to a whopping 67 per cent in Britain. Among those citizens, especially when they live in countries where a stronger polarization around the European issue has already developed in the party system, support for increasing the powers of the EU is scarce. And while there is no evidence that EU membership has been eroding exclusionary national identities or national pride, the same is not the case regarding the increasing salience and contentiousness of European integration in domestic political competition

(Hooghe and Marks 2006 and 2008). If this is the case, a significant segment of opposition to broader policymaking powers for the EU based on national identity considerations seems to be firmly in place.

If the challenges posed by national identity and its politicization in this respect are complex, the ones posed by the EU's institutional and democratic performance as perceived by citizens are no less daunting. As Chapter 2 in this volume shows, when we combine the two 'EU Representation' measures— 'Confidence in EU institutions' and 'European external efficacy'—into a single Representation scale, its average value is, in every single country, even below that of the EU Identity scale, suggesting that the 'democratic deficit' of the EU is even more pronounced than its 'identity deficit'. And as we saw, across our sixteen cases, citizens' levels of trust in European institutions, their satisfaction with democracy in the EU, and their perception of the competence of the European decision-makers emerged as the strongest and most consistent predictor of support for broader EU powers. Regardless of whether the EU can deliver growth, jobs, and development by means of broad initiatives such as the Lisbon strategy—a big if—the point is that the lack of 'input-based' legitimacy, not of 'output-based', is what seems to impede further support for policy integration in Europe.

This problem is compounded by the fact that, when thinking about whether to devolve powers to the EU, citizens engage in a political cost/benefit analysis in which the quality of governance in their domestic political systems also seems to play a role. Granted, there are countries we have examined— such as Poland, Hungary, Bulgaria, Spain, Portugal, or Italy—where the 'democratic deficit' is even more of a domestic than a European problem, and it is precisely there and among those who are most disaffected *vis-à-vis* domestic politics that support for a more powerful EU is stronger. However, the ability to ride on national dissatisfaction and the deficits of domestic governance to build a stronger Europe is limited. In spite of previous arguments about the increase of 'democratic dissatisfaction' with domestic politics in Western democracies (Klingemann 1999; Pharr and Putnam 2000), recent scholarship fails to confirm the existence of any general trends in this respect (Norris 2010). And there is no evidence that, at least since the mid-1990s, the quality of governance and democratic institutions in European countries has experienced any significant change either (Kaufmann et al. 2009). From this point of view, therefore, a divided Europe seems here to stay. In some countries and for some citizens, a broader scope of government for the EU seems a promising avenue to overcome national deficits in the quality of governance and policy delivery. For others, however, the EU seems to constitute, in quite the opposite way, a threat not only—or not so much—to national identity, but also to standards of policymaking, representation, and accountability that they do not wish to relinquish.

7

Explaining Support for European Integration

Gábor Tóka, Andrija Henjak, and Radoslaw Markowski

This is the first of two chapters that deal with the possible impact of the attitudes forming the dimensions of EU citizenship introduced in Chapter 2 and examined subsequently in this volume. In this chapter the focus falls on support for European integration and its dependence on three dimensions of EU citizenship. We aim to address three questions. First, we want to explore the links between people's positions on three dimensions of EU citizenship and their support for the European Union, and assess their respective merits in explaining support. Second, we examine the relative analytical strength of four sets of long-standing hypotheses concerning possible determinants of mass support for the European integration. We do this to explore whether, and in what ways, other expected determinants may affect EU support once the three key dimensions of EU citizenship feelings are controlled for. Third, we ask whether theories established in the West European context also explain reasonably well EU support in the Southern as well as East Central Europe. In this we seek to explore if there is a universal pattern of determinants of mass support for the EU, or whether support patterns exhibit some regional peculiarities, and if so, what drives them. Due to the special focus of the IntUne datasets on EU-related factors, we have a better opportunity than previous studies to simultaneously control for all of the theoretically relevant factors while assessing their direct impact on EU support.

Our theoretical framework and methodology closely follows those in previous chapters in this volume and rounds up the analysis about the roots and impact of European citizenship in EU politics. One rationale for the approach we use in this chapter stems from the current state of the art in the field of public opinion about European integration. A range of theories has been advanced in numerous studies published over two decades, with principal explanations based on factors ranging from economic-instrumental calculus, identity or affective attachment, political or other cues to cognitive mobilization. However, few of these studies attempted to test the full range of hypotheses and provide comparative assessment of the validity of individual explanations (for exception and overview see Hooghe and Marks 2005). We aim to fill this gap. We further aim to clarify, to the extent possible within this single chapter, the association between the variety of theoretical concepts and the real effects of their empirical measures. This is an important but rarely addressed issue, given that a wide range of theoretical propositions have been empirically tested using very similar or even the same set of variables, whose hypothesized effects often vary across studies. This makes the exact and unambiguous understanding of the effects of variables used less than straightforward. We warn that such issues should not be left unaddressed and that empirical studies would benefit from controlling for alternative propositions in a more comprehensive way. Such an analytical feat might be hard to achieve given the limitations in existing datasets. However, we hold that through the introduction of more contextual variables, and more careful modelling of interactions between contextual and individual-level variables, we should be able to assess the analytical merits of a broad range of often countervailing hypotheses.

A further motivation of our study is that the political changes of the recent past may have undermined the validity of some of the findings reported in the previous literature. After all, the last decade changed the context of EU integration probably more than any before. The 2004 enlargement brought to the Union countries with very different social, economic, and political circumstances. At the same time, the political context surrounding integration changed as immigration and globalization came to be perceived as social and economic threats by many in Western Europe. This triggered calls for a halt in the process of further enlargement and transfer of sovereignty from the national to the European level (Sides and Citrin 2007; Luedtke 2005; McLaren 2007b). The Eastern enlargement and the efforts to adopt the European constitution reshaped the structure of public opinion and the terms of public debate. The 'permissive consensus' between integrating elites and national mass publics all but disappeared, and questions about accountability and democratic deficit at the EU level got ever louder (Hooghe and Marks 2008; Katz 2001; Gabel and Palmer 1995). Mass support for European integration has supposedly followed these changes, reflecting the increasing politicization and the altered issue frames of European integration among mass publics (Hooghe and Marks 2008). The citizens of France, Ireland, Denmark, and the Netherlands rejected major treaties in referenda. Meanwhile, in some countries of East Central Europe, where integration generally had high support in the pre-accession period, citizens became somewhat more sceptical after membership was achieved (see, e.g., Table 7.1 below).

This chapter accordingly focuses on support for integration at a very recent time point and features explicit East–West comparisons utilizing a number of contextual variables to provide tests of previously advanced hypotheses. We formulate extensions of previous theories about how the roots of support for the EU might differ between Eastern and Western Europe, and where it may be more or less dependent on each of the dimensions of EU citizenship introduced in the previous chapters.

Since our goal is a comprehensive assessment using the full toolkit provided by the survey instruments developed in the literature on EU support so far, it may help the reader if our main findings are anticipated here. We find that overall evaluations of EU integration build on more specific attitudes related to Europe, above all the dimensions of EU citizenship introduced in Chapter 2. Once these more specific attitudes are taken into account, little influence seems to be exercised by factors like cognitive mobilization, domestic political cues, and national identity. Our findings point to a predominantly instrumental logic for EU support among citizens, with some further role played by EU identity and trust in Europeans as well as in EU and national institutions. The only direct effect of cognitive mobilization concerns the extent to which the influence of instrumental calculus is enhanced by citizens' political sophistication. The roots of EU support are remarkably similar across Western, Southern, and Eastern Europe, and the level of support is mostly explained by within- rather than between-country differences. The only striking cross-regional difference concerns the extent to which attitudes towards the EU are crystallized in the various parts of Europe. Citizens of the South and the East tend to have less well-developed attitudes towards EU support than West European mass publics. Moreover, if attitudes to integration were to become more crystallized, they would become very slightly less supportive than they are at this point.

The chapter is organized as follows. In section 1, we discuss theoretical expectations about the sources of support for European integration. Section 2 discusses how the observed level of support varies across countries, individuals, and recent years. Section 3 presents our first empirical tests about the sources of individual-level variation and considers if they vary across regions of Europe. Section 4 explores whether the determinants of EU support vary across member states in a systematic and theoretically plausible way. Section 5 concludes.

Propositions about the sources of support

Foundations of support for European integration have been the subject of intensive scholarly research (see Hooghe and Marks 2005 as well as the previous chapters of this volume for overviews). By and large, the individual-level determinants appear to include:

- *instrumental-utilitarian factors*, such as marketable skills and resources as the determinants of the individuals' ability to benefit economically from market integration; the flow of financial transfers between the EU and the member states; and the impact integration is likely to have on the performance of national economies and political systems (Anderson and Reichert 1996; Gabel 1998a, 1998b; Christin 2005);

- *cognitive shortcuts and cues* used to extrapolate views about European integration from positions held by preferred political parties; ideological orientations and partisan attachments; trust citizens have in national politicians and institutions; and economic conditions (see Anderson 1998; Aspinwall 2002; Hooghe and Marks 2005; Ray 2003a, 2003b; Rohrschneider and Whitefield 2006a, 2006b; but see Carruba 2001; Gabel and Scheve 2007; and Steenbergen et al. 2007 for some challenges to the cue-taking explanation);

- *affective/identitarian factors* such as national and European identity, including feelings of threat that integration may pose to it (McLaren 2002; Carey 2002; Luedtke 2005; McLaren 2007b);

- *cognitive mobilization* (i.e., political attentiveness and sophistication), which some studies found to have an influence on what level of government citizens see appropriate for collective action (Inglehart 1970; Gabel 1998b). Some recent studies also highlight the importance of the mass media, more precisely consonant media messages—positive and negative, and sometimes with delayed effects—on developments in support (Peter 2004; Bruter 2009; de Vreese 2007; de Vreese and Boomgaarden 2006; Vliegenthart et al. 2008);

- *political sophistication*, which can be seen as an indicator of cognitive mobilization, and may enhance or limit the impact of incoming new information and reasoned calculations (cf. Zaller 1992 on the general argument, and Chapter 5 of this volume for an application to attitudes towards the EU).

Reasons of space prevent us from offering a detailed review of all the related propositions and how different studies operationalized them, but our list of hypotheses at the end of the section is intended to cover nearly all propositions that received some empirical support in the prior literature and are testable with our current data. Our model-building is guided by three further considerations.

First, given that our dataset comprises just sixteen countries in a single year, we largely ignore the question of what determines aggregate (i.e., national) levels of support for integration. Yet we are particularly well positioned to explore how individual-level determinants of support vary across member states, even though the number of level-2 cases in the data is still too small to estimate random-coefficient multilevel models. We know from the previous literature that the impact of some determinants is contingent on context (see, e.g., Vössing 2005; Brinegar, Jolly, and Kitschelt 2004; Carruba 2001; Çíftçí 2005; Hix 2007; Kaltenthaler and Anderson 2001; Banducci, Karp, and Loedel 2003). For instance, Brinegar and Jolly (2005), Hix (2007), Hooghe and Marks (2005), and Ray (2004) find that in countries with higher welfare spending, left-wingers tend to be opposed to integration, but in countries with less welfare spending it is right-wingers who tend to oppose integration more. Furthermore, Christin (2005), Sánchez-Cuenca (2000), and Kritzinger (2003) find that support is higher among the lower skilled in countries where the performance of national political institutions or economies is inferior. Hooghe and Marks (2005) and Gabel (1998b), in turn, offer the compatible argument that labour is more supportive of free-trade regimes in labour-rich countries, while professionals and managers are more supportive of it in capital-rich ones. Finally, Garry and Tilley (2009) and de Vries and van Kersbergen (2007) find that economic benefits of integration can dampen the effect of exclusive national identity on opposition toward the EU, or conversely that economic anxiety can increase it. It is apparent that the hypothesized effects of some variables differ substantially between different theoretical accounts and are highly conditional on the socio-economic and political context. By implication, the patterns of support may vary substantially across countries.

Second, we are specifically interested in how far instrumental calculus, cues, identity, cognitive mobilization, or sophistication, relative to each other, have a bearing on EU support. Hence our own theorizing focuses partly on the allocation of various possible determinants among these broader categories. Consider first the Scope, Representation, and Identity dimensions of EU citizenship introduced in the previous chapters. We consider that support for a greater policy scope of EU government forms an instrumental/utilitarian foundation of generalized EU support because linking the two is merely a matter of making a simple logical connection between goals (a strengthened EU) and means (a greater EU capacity to make policy). General feelings about representation by EU institutions, in their turn, should impact EU support as cognitive shortcuts. Even if citizens cannot tell whether specific problems are more or less effectively solved at more highly aggregated levels of policymaking, citizens can have a general predisposition about whether particular institutions represent them well or not. They can use this dimension of citizenship feelings as a cue in judging whether they are willing to allocate those institutions more power or not. Finally, an affective EU identity obviously forms an identity-based foundation for EU support.

But some determinants of EU support discussed in the literature fall into more than one of the above conceptual blocks, and a few may even have opposite effects depending on whether they act as shortcuts or via reasoned calculus. For instance, some studies found that EU support increases as citizens' dissatisfaction with the performance of their national political systems and elites grows, presumably because the European Union is expected to correct the failings of national institutions (Kritzinger 2003; Christin 2005). This is an argument about instrumental calculus and expects that high trust in national governments and institutions reduces support for European integration—but only where good government prevails. However, since party elites and governments are typically more supportive of European integration than are their voters (cf. e.g., Mattila and Raunio 2006), trust in national institutions may actually increase support for European integration if citizens rely on partisan cues rather than a reasoned calculus about the value of increasing EU jurisdiction at the expense of trusted domestic actors. Thus, the main effect of satisfaction with the national political system is one of a cue and is expected to be positive—the usually pro-integration stance of incumbents receives more support when it is pursued by well-trusted national actors—while its interaction with the quality of government should have a negative effect due to the instrumental calculus that the power of well-functioning national institutions should not be surrendered to Europe.

Some known correlates of EU support are, however, really irrelevant for adjudicating between rival theoretical perspectives, and therefore we shall only include them as control variables. Consider first the clearest examples. Left–right ideology may influence support for integration via either a reasoned calculus of expectations about what policies will be promoted by a stronger EU, or cue-taking from trusted actors, or identity-based linkages. Similarly, cognitive mobilization theory would probably expect the better educated to be more supportive of Europe because of their less parochial perspective, i.e. their above-average belief in the feasibility of, and returns on collective actions at, higher and geographically more distant levels of political aggregation. However, the assumption of instrumental rationality would expect a similar correlation, since the better educated are more likely to possess marketable skills that are likely to be appreciated in the context of the broader economic market created by EU integration, and are also more likely to embrace those socially liberal values that formed a key basis for EU support among party elites, presumably in the expectation that these values will be promoted by integration (cf. Hooghe et al. 2002). Additionally, under benevolent assumptions about the overall impact of EU integration on society as a whole, information cost theory may see the positive impact of education on support for integration as a sign that education increases the probability of appreciating such collective net benefits of integration that accrue to the more and less educated to the same extent. Therefore, the impact of left–right attitudes and education—and indeed of any socio-demographic trait—on EU support cannot be seen exclusively as an indicator of either instrumental calculus, or the impact of cue-taking, cognitive factors, or identity. However, the latter should still be controlled for if we are to delineate the true influence of the theoretically more straightforward variables.

Yet, the interactions of such control variables like education with contextual characteristics can be telling about the validity of particular theories. For instance, in countries that greatly benefit from the flow of EU transfer payments integration may have a wide range of positive effects that accrue to more or less everyone, independently of the marketable skills and social liberalism that distinguish the better educated. Consequently, under the assumption of instrumental rationality, we can expect that the benefits of EU integration are less closely tied to education in such countries than in others. Therefore we will use certain macro-micro interactions to test particular theories even when the original variables making up an interaction term— such as education and net transfer payments—will, for reasons discussed earlier, only occur among the control variables of our statistical models.

Third, we are also concerned here with how sources of support for the EU may differ across regions of Europe. Previous studies of the East give surprisingly few starting points for this. They find that positive opinion toward the EU has above-average probability among supporters of the market economy and democratic values, as well as among those who have skills or income enabling their holders to compete on the market. Thus, it is presumably tied to a reasoned, if not necessarily correct, calculus that EU integration will advance the interests of such individuals (Caplanova, Orviska, and Hudson 2004; Cichowski 2000; Tverdova and Anderson 2004; Tucker et al. 2002). Status as a transitional winner or loser also contributes to how one looks at the EU (Tucker et al. 2002; Rohrschneider and Whitefield 2004), as does national identity (McManus-Czubinska et al. 2003), political efficacy (Tanasoiu and Colonescu 2008; Ehin 2001) and, maybe less consistently, partisan cues too (Rohrschneider and Whitefield 2006a, 2006b). Hence, at the individual level, the mechanisms behind support for integration in Eastern Europe seem similar to those at work in Western Europe (Marks et al. 2006). Baltic countries are a partial exception to this picture. Several studies found that fear among citizens about losing control over economic policy, changes in the position of Russian minority and loss of political independence keep support lower than in other CEE countries (Ehin 2001; Vetik et al. 2006). However, the above theories hardly exhaust the list of possible East–West differences, and we probe this question a little further below by adding some relatively new hypotheses to those found in the previous literature.

To begin with, EU accession is said to have had stabilizing effects on democracy and market economy in Eastern Europe and to have facilitated improvements in the quality of governance and the fight against corruption (Ethier 2003; Pop-Eleches 2007; Vachudova 2009; Schimmelfenning et al. 2003; Schimmelfenning 2008; Haughton 2007; Sadurski 2004; Epstein and Sedelmeier 2008; Sedelmeier 2008), and was also valued as a symbolic break with the authoritarian past and the 'return' to Europe (Szczerbiak and Taggart 2004; Sadurski 2004). Given this, we might expect support to be more broadly based in Eastern—and by the same token in Southern—Europe than in the West, since some effects of integration, like improved governance, can benefit nearly all. The same general mechanism may also operate because of the high trade openness of Eastern European countries. Their more open economies have a greater capacity to benefit from integration than closed ones, where the benefits of trade must always hurt some established interests. As is the case, several CEE countries, notably the Visegrad Four and Estonia, significantly upgraded their industries and reoriented their trade toward Western European markets, which markedly increased their potential to benefit from market integration (Crespo and Fonotoura 2007).

Opposition to integration in turn may be more strongly linked to national identity in the East than the West. It is sometimes argued that the more prolonged experience with foreign (German, Ottoman, Russian and later Soviet) dominance and a lesser matter-of-fact certainty about independent nationhood and statehood in the East might have boosted nationalist opposition to supranational political unions, foreign presence, and influence of any sort in these countries (Bunce 2005; Schopflin 1993; Todorova 1992; but see Shulman 2002).

In summary, we expect that:

1. *Reasoned instrumental calculus about the EU's role in achieving desired goals influences support for European integration* (Hypothesis 1, henceforth H1). Among the attitude variables in our analysis the perceived personal and sociotropic benefits of integration and support for a greater scope of EU government are clear instances of possible instrumental foundations. Other policy stances of citizens—such as whether they support a 'social' or rather a 'free market' Europe—could in principle be relevant too. However, given that at the time of our survey centrist grand coalitions of the left and the right seemed to have an unassailable hold on European policymaking, we expect that such policy attitudes had little across-the-board impact on EU support in spring 2007.

1a. *Interactions between country and individual characteristics are likely to qualify H1.* In particular, we expect the difference in support between manual workers and others to diminish in less affluent countries (Hooghe and Marks 2005; Gabel 1998a). Similarly, higher levels of welfare spending should reduce support for European integration among left-wingers and those who prefer Europe to promote a generous system of social welfare rather than a free market Europe—which is just a more precise operationalization of a theoretical proposition present in Brinegar et al. (2004), Brinegar and Jolly (2005), and Hooghe and Marks (2005). In addition, a high level of trust in domestic political institutions should create reluctance to transfer power to European institutions, but only if the quality of governance in a country is generally high. We would also expect that the benefits of integration are more widely distributed and thus that the impact of education on EU support is less pronounced than elsewhere in countries with recent experience of dictatorships, with more positive net transfers to the country from the EU budget, and with a lower quality of domestic governance institutions.

2. *Citizens use cues provided by trusted political actors and economic trends to gauge the merits of integration (H2).* We focus on three sets of cues. Positive perceptions of economic trends will increase EU support given that the *status quo* is the progressive deepening of integration through the play of market forces, acts of the European courts, and occasionally political decisions. Identification with political parties will increase or reduce support for integration depending on what stance the party in question has on European integration.[1] Trust in national institutions and feelings about representation by European institutions act as cues about the likely benefits of moving political choices to higher levels of aggregation; they will also increase EU support.

2a. The key caveat to H2 is that *the power of particular cues may vary across national contexts.* Cue-taking from preferred parties, in particular, may diminish with length of EU membership as citizens' personal opinions crystallize over time (Steenbergen et al. 2007). The effect of cue-taking should also diminish if preferred parties are internally divided about European integration in a way visible to voters (Gabel and Scheve 2007). Alternatively, cue-taking from preferred parties may vary by the degree to which parties offer clear alternatives, and thus allow the development of

---

[1] The extant literature (see, e.g., Ray 2003b and Rohrschneider and Whitefield 2006b) as well as previous chapters in this volume sometimes consider identification with a government party as a possible pro-integration cue too, given the supposedly more pro-European stance of the same parties in government than in opposition. However, when we did include this variable in the analyses reported in this paper we found that identification with incumbent parties—once we control for their stance on European integration—has, across our 16 countries, a small negative impact on EU support that turns statistically significant in some specifications. While this anomaly is substantively interesting on its own, it seems hard to account for it in terms of any one of the theoretical frameworks discussed in this chapter and therefore we decided to omit identification with incumbents from the analysis.

policy-based party–citizen linkages in matters of European integration (Popkin 1991; Lau and Redlawsk 2001). As we reasoned above, cue-taking from perceived representation by European institutions should diminish where the quality of national governance is higher.

3. *The strength of national identity reduces, while European identity and trust in fellow Europeans increase support for integration (H3)*. As Hooghe and Marks (2005) observe, it may be thought that it is not so much the strength of national identity but rather the exclusive nature of this identity that animates against the EU. We offer a new test of this proposition using the same measure of exclusive national identity, but this time pitting it against a more elaborate measure of national identity than Hooghe and Marks (2005) could use.

3a. *The effect of national identity may also vary*, e.g. we expect it to be especially strong in Eastern Europe, where, for reasons of history, citizens are particularly likely to view supranational institutions and foreign presence through an affective/identitarian lens. The effect of (exclusive) national identity may be particularly pronounced where parties are divided over Europe because anti-EU parties tend to mobilize along affective-identitarian lines (Hooghe and Marks 2005). A strong EU identity, in its turn, should be a stronger source of support for integration in those countries that have a longer experience with EU membership, as membership promotes institutional and discursive links between European identity on the one hand and the particular framework of the Union on the other.

4. *Cognitive mobilization may increase support for integration*, presumably because it makes citizens appreciate supranational venues for effective public-good provision more highly (H4). We expect this effect to occur with respect to such indicators of cognitive mobilization as internal efficacy, media exposure, political sophistication, social trust, visits to other European countries, and non-electoral participation, respectively. This goes back to Inglehart's argument that these factors reduce parochialism, which, if present, would reduce support for supranational institutions.

4a. It is possible that H4 was only valid in the period of the permissive consensus about Europe, i.e. when the best informed and most attentive sections of the EU citizenry were particularly strongly exposed to pro-EU elite arguments (cf. Peter 2004). Following this reasoning we can expect that precisely the most involved are the first to receive any new cues from elites (cf. Zaller 1992), and hence within-elite disagreements over Europe should have generated below-average support for integration exactly in this segment of the EU citizenry.

5. *Higher levels of political sophistication should increase the impact of instrumental calculation*—i.e. perceived benefits and support for a greater scope of European government—on EU support (H5). This is expected

because of the greater information needs of instrumental calculus than affective responses or cue-taking.[2]

Support for European integration: measurement and variance

The dependent variable of the present chapter is a highly generalized attitudinal predisposition towards European integration, i.e., whether citizens would like to have more or less of it. The reference point is thus the status quo; and we asked our respondents to express their preferences on the issue at hand without putting the latter in any particular frame, neither referring to specific issues of deepening or enlargement, nor particular perspectives of personal, national, or other interests. Instead, we raised the question in the most general way possible that nevertheless goes beyond soliciting mere evaluations of European integration as good or bad. This question ought to elicit a politically more considered response than mere approval of the status quo. It is a response that should be the best single proxy for likely voting behaviour in future referenda on European treaties, no matter whether they concern membership, secession, enlargement, or deepening.

The question that we use to measure our dependent variable reads like this: 'Some say European unification has already gone too far. Others say it should be strengthened. What is your opinion? Please indicate your views using [. . .] this scale, [where] "0" means unification "has already gone too far" and "10" means it "should be strengthened." What number on this scale best describes your position?' The bivariate correlations between the above measure of EU support on the one hand, and trust in the European Parliament and the Commission, as well as membership approval on the other, suggested that none of the latter items form a common scale with our dependent variable.[3] Indeed, the strongest of these three pairwise correlations within any of the sixteen countries was just 0.50 and the average correlation was only 0.27. The Cronbach alpha values for any of the two-item scales based on these items

---

[2] Some may wonder why we do not posit that the impact of cues and affective identity drop with citizen sophistication. Regarding the first, the reason is that cue-taking itself requires some prior political knowledge (Lau and Redlawsk 2001) and therefore reduced motivation among sophisticates to use shortcuts may be counterbalanced by their greater ability to use them. Regarding identity, we note that the incidence of affective responses is unrelated to cognitive skills (Marcus 2002) and hence there is no reason to find a weaker effect of identity among political sophisticates.
[3] Trust in institutions was measured on a 0–10 scale, while membership approval with responses to 'Generally speaking, do you think that (OUR COUNTRY)'s membership of the European Union is a good thing, a bad thing, or neither good nor bad?'

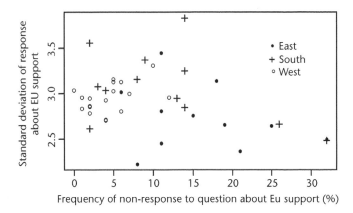

Figure 7.1. The polarization of public opinion about support for EU integration across 41 country-years

averaged a very modest 0.35 across the sixteen countries. Remarkably, the averages remained similarly weak when calculated only for a pair formed by membership approval and our dependent variable (average R = 0.31, average Cronbach alpha = 0.27). Thus we are confident that our dependent variable captures a distinct dimension of predispositions.

Figure 7.1 and Table 7.1 pool data from the 2007 IntUne survey with comparable figures from the 1999 and 2004 European Election Studies to examine the crystallization of attitudes on EU integration.[4] Figure 7.1 reveals a negative correlation (–0.32, significant at the 0.05 level) between the percentage of non-response to the EU support item with the standard deviation of the valid responses across the forty-one country-years appearing in the table. In other words, the more people have an opinion about the matter in a country at any given point in time, the more likely it is that their opinions will be relatively polarized rather than concentrated around a central tendency. Note that in Figure 7.1 the observations about the East European member states (indicated by solid circles) are nearly all concentrated near the bottom-right quadrant, while the South European observations (indicated by a cross) are spread somewhere between the Eastern and Western European

---

[4] The European Election Studies use compatible sampling methods and the same question wording to measure EU support, but the responses are recorded on a 1–10 rather than 0–10 scale as in the IntUne survey. For the purposes of comparability, we applied a linear transformation of the responses in the EES survey so that they also run from 0 to 10, and dropped those countries from the analysis that were not covered by the IntUne survey. The EES data and their technical documentation are publicly available from the www.europeanelectionstudies.net web address, and were collected in the immediate aftermath to the 1999 and 2004 elections to the European Parliament.

Table 7.1. The distribution of support for EU integration in the 2007 IntUne survey and in the 1999 and 2004 European Election Studies for countries included in the IntUne survey

Country	Mean response				Standard deviation				Non-response (%)		
	1999[a]	2004[a]	2007[a]	2007[b]	1999[a]	2004[a]	2007[a]	2007[b]	1999	2004	2007
Austria (AT)	4.67	3.65	3.95	3.94	2.93	2.96	2.87	2.86	4	1	2
Belgium (BE)	4.88	4.80	5.43	5.44	3.31	3.16	2.86	2.85	10	5	2
Denmark (DK)	4.64	4.79	5.73	5.71	3.03	2.81	2.71	2.71	5	6	4
France (FR)	5.95	5.14	5.21	5.20	2.96	3.04	2.95	2.94	12	0	2
Germany (DE)	6.01	4.95	5.38	5.40	2.84	3.13	2.79	2.78	1	6	2
Gr. Britain (GB)	4.12	3.53	4.52	4.54	3.00	3.13	2.72	2.71	7	5	4
Greece (GR)	6.92	6.22	6.63	6.61	3.37	3.56	3.08	3.07	9	2	3
Italy (IT)	6.23	5.73	6.69	6.67	2.67	2.95	3.04	3.03	26	13	4
Portugal (PO)	6.20	5.65	6.82	6.68	3.83	3.25	2.85	2.86	14	14	14
Spain (ES)	6.19	5.90	6.52	6.51	3.16	2.49	2.62	2.62	8	32	2
Bulgaria (BG)	–	–	5.36	5.27	–	–	2.50	2.54	–	–	32
Estonia (EE)	–	5.11	4.84	4.70	–	2.76	2.66	2.67	–	15	19
Hungary (HU)	–	5.51	5.26	5.29	–	2.81	2.37	2.37	–	11	21
Poland (PL)	–	6.01	6.43	6.37	–	3.14	2.46	2.45	–	18	11
Slovakia (SK)	–	5.61	5.51	5.49	–	2.65	2.23	2.23	–	25	8
Slovenia (SI)	–	5.99	5.72	5.71	–	3.45	3.02	3.01	–	11	6

[a] without multiple imputation of missing values
[b] after multiple imputation of missing values

ones. In other words, the percentage of non-response tends to increase, and the polarization of responses drop, as we move from Western to Southern and then to Eastern Europe. Thus, in the latter parts of the continent, popular opinion seems to be less crystallized on the question of further integration.

One reason for non-responses may be that the wording of the EU support item creates asymmetric choices for supporters and opponents of integration. For the first, a choice is offered between changing or maintaining the status quo, while for the EU-sceptic side the question is more about the intensity of opposition than a choice between reversing the integration process and maintaining the status quo. Whether the constrained choices on our survey item may have made some opponents of integration decline answering can be best investigated by comparing the density distribution of the original responses along the 0–10 scale with the distribution of our multiple imputed estimates for the likely opinions behind the non-responses (see the Appendix of this book). Multiple imputation makes guesses about the most likely responses of the respondents who did not answer a particular question given their responses to all other questions in the IntUne study and is therefore eminently suitable for gauging latent opinion.

In a majority of the sixteen countries, more of the imputed values for the non-responses than of the original valid responses should fall towards low values on our dependent variable, suggesting that non-response was indeed more frequent among people with low support (cf. Table 7.1). In Austria, Denmark, Bulgaria, Estonia, Poland, and in all four Southern European countries the difference between expressed and latent opinions is not only in this direction but is also statistically significant (at the $p = 0.05$ level, chi-square tests not shown), while only in Great Britain is the mean level of

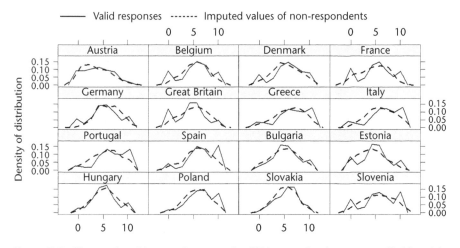

Figure 7.2. Observed and imputed support for EU integration by country (0–10 scale)

estimated EU support significantly higher among those who did not respond to the question at hand than among those who did. Overall, however, the estimated predisposition of the non-respondents lean in a centrist direction everywhere except in Austria, and thus most non-responses indeed stand for uncertain and ambiguous opinions (see Figure 7.2).

Table 7.1 helps to place our 2007 data in a dynamic perspective. In most countries, non-response to the question about EU support dropped over time, which suggests that a slow crystallization of opinions is taking place. This process did not lead to a growing polarization of opinions though. If anything, a remarkably large drop occurred in the within-country variation (standard deviation) of the responses between 1999 and 2007 everywhere except in Poland (which moved in the opposite direction) and Austria, France, Germany, and Italy, where we observe only small and trendless fluctuations in the degree of division over Europe among citizens in the given period. Even more remarkably, the polarization of opinion dropped not only within, but also across, member states.

Turning to the level of EU support, we observe a large drop of support among the then member states between 1999 and 2004, but that support for EU integration then increased in most member states in the years following the Eastern enlargement. This trend was particularly strong in some of the most Eurosceptic member states like Denmark and the UK, but was accompanied by a drop in EU support in some East European countries, which, in the main, had above-average levels of EU support back in 2004. The results of this variation in national trajectories is that by 2007 there was less within-country, but also less between-country difference of opinions on the future of European integration. Indeed, only half of the sixteen countries in our sample deviated by more than half a point from the cross-national mean (5.63) on our 0–10 scale. These were the somewhat less Europhile Austria, Estonia, and Great Britain on the one hand, and more Europhile Greece, Italy, Poland, Portugal, and Spain on the other.

Focusing on the 2007 data only, we find that less than 8 per cent of the total variance in EU support across the sixteen countries and 16,133 individuals in our analysis can be explained by cross-country differences, i.e. by regressing EU support on a series of dummy variables uniquely identifying each country.[5] The seven country-characteristics listed among our control variables in Table 7.2 (Communist Past, Quality of Governance, Net EU Transfers, Gross National Income, Welfare Spending, Length of EU Membership, and Partisan Divide over Europe) appear to explain over half of the 8 per cent cross-country variance, but this explanatory power is more apparent than real, as only

---

[5] The exploratory analyses reported in this paragraph are not displayed in the tables but are available from the authors upon request.

Quality of Governance registers a consistently significant effect across our various analyses. Taken alone, the tendency for better governed countries to be less supportive of further integration accounts for just 2 per cent of the total variance, or, in other words, a quarter of the cross-national differences that we find in 2007. Differences in support between Eastern, Southern, and Western Europe are more substantial and account for nearly 5 per cent of the total variance. However, these differences cannot be explained in terms of our theoretically informed macro variables (like the quality of governance at the national level), and boil down almost entirely to the notably higher levels of EU support in the South (i.e. Greece, Italy, Portugal, and Spain) than either in the West (Austria, Belgium, Denmark, France, Germany, and Great Britain) or the East (Bulgaria, Estonia, Hungary, Poland, Slovakia, and Slovenia).

What concerns us here most, however, is not the explanation of the rather muted cross-national differences in support but an understanding of the country-specific roots of the still very pronounced divisions in the mass public within literally every member state. These divisions, indicated by an average within-country standard deviation of 2.7 in 2007, are substantial in their size in spite of the recent drop. Indeed, as van der Eijk and Franklin (2006) noted, they are much larger than comparable divisions on the left–right dimension in Europe. Remarkably, the shape of these divisions within individual countries remains rather stable over time (cf. Figure 7.3). Thus, in the next two sections we turn to multivariate statistical analyses of the propositions about the sources of EU support advanced in section 1.

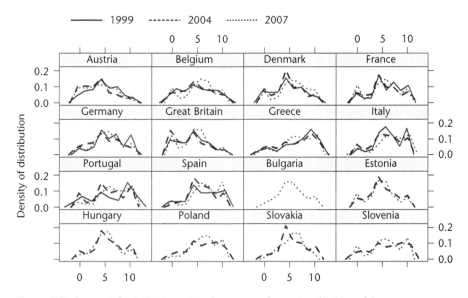

Figure 7.3. Support for EU integration by year and country (0–10 scale)

Empirical tests

Table 7.2 lists our numbered hypotheses and identifies the relevant independent variables. This follows the above discussion at the end of section 1, and only adds to that the list of control variables employed in our analysis. The variables in the analysis are described elsewhere in the volume (see Chapter 3 and the Appendix). The only extra note that is necessary here is that our EU Representation variable is the average score on the EU Institutional Trust and EU Efficacy scales introduced in Chapter 2, and EU Scope is the average of the EU Scope Current, EU Scope Future and EU Geographical Scope scales.

The control variables in our analyses are of two sorts. First, all our models except number 9 control for sex, age, education, religion, self-employment, manual work, and left–right position because some of the previous literature found differences in support for the EU along these lines. These effects are not directly relevant for the theoretical propositions that our analysis focuses on, but we evidently need to control for their possible confounding effects while examining the theoretically relevant hypotheses. Second, some of the propositions examined in the next section pertain to macro-micro interactions that

Table 7.2. Hypotheses and independent variables included in the analysis

Hypothesis	Variables	Effect
H1	EU Personal Benefits, EU National Benefits, EU Scope	+
H1	Social or Competitive Europe	none
Caveats to H1	Education* Communist Legacy	–
Caveats to H1	Education* Quality of Governance	+
Caveats to H1	Education* Net EU Transfers	–
Caveats to H1	Manual Worker* Gross National Income	–
Caveats to H1	Social or Competitive Europe* Welfare Spending	–
Caveats to H1	National Institutional Trust* Quality of Governance	–
H2	Economic Perceptions, Pro-EU Party Identifier, National Institutional Trust, EU Representation	+
Caveats to H2	Pro-EU Party Identifier* Length of EU Membership	–
Caveats to H2	Pro-EU Party Identifier* Partisan Divide over Europe	+
H3	National Identity, Exclusive National Identity	–
H3	Trust Other Europeans, EU Identity	+
Caveats to H3	National Identity* Communist Past	–
Caveats to H3	Exclusive National Identity* Communist Past	–
Caveats to H3	National Identity* Partisan Divide over Europe	–
Caveats to H3	Exclusive National Identity* Partisan Divide over Europe	–
H4	Political Influence, Media Exposure, Political Sophistication, Social Trust, Visited EU Countries, Non-Electoral Participation	+
Counter to H4	[each indicator of cognitive mobilization]* Partisan Divide over Europe	–
H5	[each indicator of (country-specific) benefits]* Political Sophistication	+
No hypotheses (control variables)	Sex, Age, Age squared, Education, Catholic, Manual Worker, Left–Right Ideology, Left–right Extremism, Communist Past, Quality of Governance, Net EU Transfers, Gross National Income, Welfare Spending, Length of EU Membership, Partisan Divide over Europe	any or none

Table 7.3. The fraction of within-country variance in EU support explained by various sets of individual-level variables in three regions taken separately and together

Model	Variable groups included	West	South	East	All
1 (baseline)	controls only	0.039	0.014	0.011	0.014
2 (instrumental)	controls + H1	0.260	0.127	0.136	0.176
3 (cues)	controls + H2	0.167	0.058	0.067	0.093
4 (identity)	controls + H3	0.178	0.066	0.068	0.097
5 (cognitive mob.)	controls + H4	0.082	0.022	0.023	0.034
6 (mixed)	controls + H1 + H2 + H3 + H4	0.308	0.149	0.157	0.204
7 (mixed with sophistication)	controls + H1 + H2 + H3 + H4 + H5	0.309	0.152	0.159	0.205
8 (all but EU citizenship)	model 7 w/o EU citizenship dimensions	0.241	0.088	0.085	0.131
9 (EU citizenship only)	just three dimensions of EU citizenship	0.262	0.125	0.138	0.179
Number of cases in the analysis		6,013	4,014	6,106	16,133

may explain cross-country differences in what individual-level variables influence EU support in various countries. Correct statistical tests of these effects require controls for the macro variables entering these interactions. In this section, however, we present and discuss models that only include individual-level variables and ask if instrumental calculus, cue-taking, identity, or cognitive factors explain better the very substantial within-country differences in support for integration, and whether the three regions of Europe differ with respect to the explanatory power of these theories.[6] Such differences can only be assessed with correct estimates of the statistical errors, which we facilitate with estimating all regression models with adjustments for multiple imputation of missing values using the *mim* package (see Carling, Galati, and Royston 2008) as well as for the clustering of observations by country.

Table 7.3 summarizes the results for nine different models. The baseline Model 1, for instance, only includes our individual-level control variables about the respondents' sex, age, age squared, education, religion (Catholic or not), manual work, left–right position, and the extremity of this left–right position (i.e., its squared deviation from the middle point of the 0–10 scale). The combined explanatory power of these variables is shown in the first row and appears uniformly modest in all three regions of Europe: just below 4 per cent in the West, and a little over 1 per cent in both the South and the East, as well as across all sixteen countries combined. The other six models add the substantively interesting groups of predictor variables. Thus, Model 2 refers to instrumental calculus, i.e. it adds to the baseline model the perceived personal and national benefits of EU membership, the EU Scope variable, and an

---

[6] To this effect, all variables in this analysis were centred at their country mean, that is we subtracted the country mean from each independent as well as dependent variable, leaving aside that less than 8 per cent of its total variance that, as we saw in section 2, can be attributed to cross-country differences (results in Table 7.3).

attitude item tapping preferences for a 'social' rather than common-market Europe; in other words, the four individual-level variables listed under the H1 in Table 7.2. Similarly, Model 3 refers to the four variables on cue-taking listed under H2 in Table 7.2, and so forth. Since information cost theory posits interactions between variables that, taken in isolation from each other, are already part of Models 2 and 5, the distinct contribution of this perspective (and thus of Model 7) to explaining EU support has to be evaluated against the already demanding standard set by Model 6, which combines all other theoretical perspectives in a mixed model. Finally, Models 8 and 9 are estimated to assess the relative contributions of the three dimensions of EU citizenship attitudes—Identity, Representation, and Scope—*vis-à-vis* all other variables to the explanatory power of Model 7.

Two striking trends appear in the tables. First, there are very large differences between the West and the other two regions in the explanatory power of any of the models. This means that established theories of individual-level roots of EU support fit the reality of Western Europe far better than that of the South or the East. At the same time, however, there are equally striking similarities across the three regions in the relative performance of the different models *vis-à-vis* each other. Instrumental calculus stands out as the strongest influence in all three regions. Identity and cues come next and each shows an appreciably larger explanatory power than cognitive mobilization. Considering the information costs of instrumental calculus via Model 7 increases the explanatory power of that model only negligibly. Last but not least, a comparison between Models 7, 8, and 9 reveals that the three EU citizenship variables and their single interaction explain appreciably more variance in EU support than the other fifty variables and interaction terms of Model 7 combined. In fact, the latter only add, depending on region, a modest 2 to 5 per cent to the variance that is already explained by the citizenship factors, suggesting that these more specific orientations towards Europe almost fully mediate the impact of all determinants of support for European integration postulated or discovered in the previous literature.

The best tentative explanation for this constellation is that the foundations of EU support do not differ very fundamentally between the three regions, at least not in terms of their affinity to these four theoretical perspectives. Where the West does differ from both the South and the East is in the stronger structuring of citizen attitudes to integration. This interpretation is consistent with the regional patterns in the polarization of opinions and frequency of non-responses to our question about EU support discussed in section 2 above, and could plausibly be related to the higher levels of cognitive mobilization and longer experience with democratic discourse and free opinion formation in the West than in the two other regions of Europe.

We note that the three regions are also similar in sustaining considerable overlaps between the explanatory powers of the different models. The *prima facie* explanatory power of instrumental calculus can be gauged through the difference between the R-squared for Models 1 and 2.[7] For the West, for example, this difference is a whopping 0.221. The comparable figure in the West for the *prima facie* influence of cues is 0.128, for identity 0.139, and for cognitive mobilization 0.043. However, the sum of these individual contributions and the maximum possible influence of the control variables (0.221 + 0.128 + 0.139 + 0.043 + 0.039 = 0.569) is a far cry from the actual estimate about their combined influence (see the R^2 = 0.308 figure for the West at Model 6). This gap suggests that about half the apparent work done by the variables belonging to any of these four theoretical models may well be shared by variables belonging to rival models. Again, the fact that similar, albeit slightly smaller, overlaps can be noticed in the data for the South and the East give further support to the idea that there is a similarity of attitude structures, but a difference in the extent of structuring that emerges in belief systems about the EU in the West on the one hand, and the East and South on the other.

Given the overlaps between the explanatory powers of the rival models, we have to consider the parameter estimates of the ultimate combined Model 7 as the best guide to which individual variables are the most influential within the individual groups speaking to the different theories. Table 7.4 provides the relevant estimates, once again both broken down by regions and for all sixteen countries combined. Simple calculus can show that there is not a single coefficient in this unwieldy table where the pairwise difference between any two regions, or between one region and all three combined, would show a statistically significant difference: even the biggest difference, which is between the South and the West in the impact of perceived benefits to the nation, stays within sampling error. The important determinants of EU support appear to be the same across the three regions, even if their impact does not necessarily pass conventional levels of significance within every one of our regional subsamples. That is to say, our three citizenship factors—EU Scope, EU Representation, and EU Identity—stand out as consistent influences from among the indicators of instrumental, cue-taking, and identitarian factors. This may be so partly because these variables—unlike some others appearing in the table—already incorporate information from several individual items, and are therefore more reliable measures of what they capture than, say, our simple dichotomous measure of exclusive national identity. However,

---

[7] By this *prima facie* explanatory power of a factor we mean the effect as it appears without controls for the influence of variables referring to rival theories, but after we somewhat conservatively adjust it for the maximum possible influence of the control variables.

Table 7.4. The individual-level determinants of within-country variance in EU support in three regions under Model 7 (OLS regression with panel-corrected standard errors)

	West		South		East		All 16 states	
	b	(s.e.)	b	(s.e.)	b	(s.e.)	b	(s.e.)
EU National Benefits	1.22[a]	(0.36)	0.04	(0.18)	0.59	(0.28)	0.62[a]	(0.21)
EU Personal Benefits	−0.22	(0.35)	0.21	(0.25)	−0.02	(0.24)	−0.08	(0.16)
EU Scope	0.24[a]	(0.07)	−0.10	(0.14)	0.10	(0.15)	0.12	(0.08)
Social or Competitive Europe	0.25[a]	(0.06)	0.30[a]	(0.07)	0.24[a]	(0.07)	0.29[c]	(0.04)
Economic Perceptions	0.01	(0.03)	−0.06	(0.03)	0.04	(0.06)	0.00	(0.03)
Pro-EU Party Identifier	0.11[a]	(0.04)	0.10[a]	(0.02)	0.03	(0.05)	0.08[b]	(0.02)
National Institutional Trust	0.02	(0.04)	0.07	(0.02)	−0.02	(0.05)	0.03	(0.02)
EU Representation	0.19[a]	(0.04)	0.09	(0.06)	0.13[a]	(0.04)	0.14[c]	(0.03)
National Identity	−0.04	(0.02)	−0.03	(0.03)	0.01	(0.03)	−0.02	(0.02)
Exclusive National Identity	−0.23	(0.11)	0.01	(0.07)	0.06	(0.14)	−0.05	(0.08)
Trust Other Europeans	0.15[b]	(0.01)	0.11	(0.04)	0.06	(0.01)	0.10[c]	(0.02)
EU Identity	0.11[a]	(0.03)	0.08	(0.07)	0.12[a]	(0.03)	0.10[c]	(0.02)
Political Influence	0.03	(0.02)	−0.01	(0.01)	−0.02	(0.03)	0.01	(0.01)
Media Exposure	0.04	(0.01)	0.03	(0.01)	0.01	(0.02)	0.02	(0.01)
Political Sophistication	−0.10[a]	(0.05)	−0.23[a]	(0.05)	−0.17[a]	(0.06)	−0.17[c]	(0.04)
Social Trust	0.01	(0.02)	−0.04	(0.02)	0.03	(0.02)	0.00	(0.01)
Visited EU Countries	0.05	(0.03)	0.02	(0.05)	−0.01	(0.03)	0.03	(0.02)
Non-Electoral Participation	−0.01	(0.02)	0.03	(0.01)	0.02	(0.02)	0.01	(0.01)
EU National Benefits* Sophistication	−0.06	(0.06)	0.11	(0.07)	−0.01	(0.03)	0.02	(0.03)
EU Personal Benefits* Sophistication	0.08	(0.05)	−0.03	(0.04)	0.02	(0.04)	0.04	(0.03)
EU Scope* Sophistication	0.02	(0.01)	0.02	(0.02)	0.03	(0.01)	0.02[b]	(0.01)
Sex	−0.04	(0.13)	0.05	(0.14)	−0.03	(0.07)	−0.02	(0.06)
Age	−0.01	(0.02)	0.00	(0.01)	−0.02	(0.01)	−0.01	(0.01)
Age squared	0.00	(0.00)	0.00	(0.00)	0.00	(0.00)	0.00	(0.00)
Education	0.01	(0.05)	0.01	(0.06)	0.00	(0.06)	0.00	(0.03)
Catholic	−0.06	(0.06)	−0.09	(0.14)	−0.08	(0.10)	−0.07	(0.05)
Manual Work	−0.23	(0.17)	−0.38	(0.43)	−0.04	(0.17)	−0.17	(0.12)
Left–right Position	0.00	(0.03)	0.03	(0.01)	0.05	(0.02)	0.02	(0.01)
Left–right Extremity	0.01	(0.01)	0.02	(0.00)	0.01	(0.01)	0.01[c]	(0.00)
Constant	0.00	−0.01	0.00	(0.02)	0.00	(0.03)	0.00	(0.01)

[a] $p < 0.05$
[b] $p < 0.01$
[c] $p < 0.001$

Note: All estimates are adjusted for clustering by country and multiple imputations.

the overall picture hardly changes when we remove these three citizenship factors from the model: only the influence of National Institutional Trust (a cue-taking factor) and Trust [in] Other Europeans (that we classified as an identitarian consideration) increases appreciably, which hardly makes much of a difference in the theoretical conclusions that can be drawn. These results are available from the authors on request.

Expectations regarding the impact of instrumental calculus are mostly borne out by the findings. The apparently weaker effect of personal rather than national benefits echoes typical findings in the literature on economic influences on voting support. It is against expectations though that supporters of a 'social' rather than common-market Europe register above-average EU support in the West, because one may expect that integration in this policy area may actually imply a drop, rather than an increase, in welfare commitments in countries where levels of current social spending tend to be higher than in the South and the East. But at the same time citizens of Western Europe have less to fear from the consequences that the achievement of a 'social' Europe might have for the competitiveness of their national economies and the policy independence of national governments. Among the variables referring to cue-taking, perceptions of the economic situation and party cues do not appear to play much of a role once all other variables are taken into account in Model 7. Trust in European and national institutions clearly trumps these influences, possibly because they provide more direct cues—indeed they may capture reasons rather than cues that prompt EU support.

National identity has negligible direct effects on EU support. Only in Western Europe does the (negative) impact of Exclusive National Identity come close to reaching statistical significance, and National Identity *per se* nowhere reaches that far. What matters again are attitudes with a more immediate logical connection to integration support, namely the degree of identification with Europe itself, and trust in other Europeans. The results regarding the impact of cognitive mobilization, in their turn, defy expectations of consistently positive effects. Rather, political sophistication (a combination of interest in politics and political knowledge) is the only significant cognitive mobilization predictor variable. Moreover, while on the one hand it acts slightly to enhance the positive effects of instrumental factors (see the mostly insignificant but consistently positive interactions between Sophistication and EU Scope), its direct effect on EU support is negative in all regions and hovers around borderline significance in every one of them. Following our theoretical reasoning about the impact of cognitive mobilization above, it could be that this reflects the fact that it was the most politically knowledgeable section of EU citizens who were the most exposed and receptive to EU-sceptical arguments in the years prior to 2007. This explanation is consistent with the proposition that consonant Eurosceptic messages about Europe in the mass media have a delayed effect and at first affect the more attentive parts of the public (see Bruter 2009). Our finding may then signal a change of opinion climate whereby EU-critical voices are becoming over-, rather than under-represented among the more politically knowledgeable segments of the citizenry.

Last but not least, we find that socio-demographic variables have no direct effect on EU support across Europe once the above attitudinal factors are taken into account. Left–right location does have an effect, but in the opposite direction to that expected by conventional wisdom. Right-wingers were, *ceteris paribus*, slightly but not significantly more pro-integration than left-wingers among the citizens—a finding that is probably consonant with the balance of forces in the EU's representative institutions around 2007. However, it is unexpected that extremes on both the left and the right appear to be slightly more pro-EU than their centrist peers. A closer inspection of this puzzle confirms that this paradoxical finding remains present through all seven models, and across nearly all the sixteen countries independently of model specification and our treatment of missing responses. For instance, when EU support is regressed country by country on just left–right position and left–right extremism, the latter has the unexpected positive effect in all sixteen countries save Denmark, and this positive effect reaches a $p<0.05$ significance level in eight countries (Austria, Germany, Italy, Poland, Portugal, Spain, Slovakia, and Slovenia). The general cross-country pattern is depicted in Figure 7.4. This figure makes predictions from the empirical estimates obtained with our Model 1 for a fictitious country where the average citizen places her/himself exactly in the middle of the left–right scale and the country matches the average of our sixteen-country sample on all other variables. Given that our estimates are based on centred variables, the results are displayed in terms of deviations from the centred country mean (i.e., zero) of EU support. The reader should note that we expect fairly small differences—at most 0.4 point on an 11-point scale—to go together with left–right position, but that the extremes on either end are more pro-EU than the centre. As possible explanations, future research may consider the dissimilar representation of relatively extreme parties in the European rather than in the national parliaments, or the perception among citizens of extreme persuasion that the EU may be a vehicle of policy change compared to the status quo that—given their extreme position—they apparently disapprove.

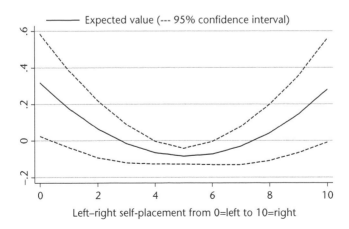

Figure 7.4. EU support by left–right ideology (cross-country estimates under Model 1)

Determinants of support and the national context

The remaining part of our analysis probes theories regarding the possible sources of cross-national differences in the individual-level determinants of EU support. Following the research design adopted in most of this volume as well as in section 3 above, we do so by testing specific *a priori* expectations about micro-macro interactions in our sixteen-country pooled cross-national data using clustered regression with fixed effects and the variables centred at their country means. This centering of the variables means that we evaluate the significance of all interactions at average values of all other variables in the model. Given our interest in the variance of within-country patterns and our scepticism that a sixteen-country dataset can tell us much about aggregate-level relations, the dependent variable, EU support, is also centred at its mean. Therefore the main effects of the macro variables are bound to be essentially nil in this analysis

The *a priori* expectations tested here are based on findings reported in the previous literature and our own attempts in section 1 at pushing the related theories a bit further within the logic of instrumental, cue-taking, and identitarian approaches. The empirical test adds all the micro-macro interactions referring to the various 'caveats' in Table 7.2 to our combined individual-level model (see Model 7 above). It turned out to be inconsequential for the findings, whether these interactions were added to Model 7 one at a time or all were included simultaneously. For simplicity, Table 7.5 presents the results obtained in the latter way and lists the variables in the same order as they appear in Table 7.2.

Starting the reading of the table from the bottom, note that the main effects of the macro variables that appear among the controls are indeed zero since our focus here is exclusively on the variance within the sixteen countries. The estimated impact of the individual-level control variables, as well as of the interactions of sophistication with the various instrumental motives of EU support, only change within sampling error compared to Model 7.

As will be remembered from the previous section, our 2007 results flatly contradict cognitive mobilization theorists who observed in the 1970s that politically more involved Europeans favour integration more strongly. We cannot find any support for the idea that the apparently changing impact of variables like political sophistication would have something to do with the diminishing 'permissive consensus' on matters of European policy. Only half the posited interactions between indicators of cognitive mobilization and party polarization over Europe go in the expected negative direction, and the only one that reaches statistical significance is wrongly signed: greater party polarization in a country appears to make the impact of visits to other EU countries more positive. All this makes little theoretical sense of course

Table 7.5. Individual- and cross-level determinants of within-country variance in EU support in the pooled sixteen-country data (OLS regression with panel-corrected standard errors)

	b	(s.e.)	beta
EU National Benefits	0.62[b]	(0.20)	0.10
EU Personal Benefits	−0.08	(0.18)	−0.01
Social or Competitive Europe	0.32	(0.27)	0.05
EU Scope	0.26[c]	(0.04)	0.17
Education* Communist Legacy	0.06	(0.09)	0.01
Education* Quality of Governance	0.04	(0.05)	0.01
Education* Net EU Transfers	−0.07[a]	(0.03)	−0.03
Manual Worker* Gross National Income	0.00	(0.00)	−0.02
Social or Competitive Europe* Welfare Spending	−0.01	(0.01)	−0.04
National Institutional Trust* Quality of Governance	0.08[b]	(0.03)	0.05
Economic Perceptions	0.00	(0.03)	0.00
Pro-EU Party Identifier	0.01	(0.09)	0.00
National Institutional Trust	0.08[a]	(0.03)	0.05
EU Representation	0.14[c]	(0.03)	0.09
Pro-EU Party Identifier* Length of EU Membership	0.00[a]	(0.00)	0.03
Pro-EU Party Identifier* Partisan Divide over Europe	0.01	(0.05)	0.01
National Identity	0.00	(0.06)	0.00
Exclusive National Identity	−0.27	(0.21)	−0.05
Trust Other Europeans	0.10[c]	(0.02)	0.08
EU Identity	0.11[c]	(0.02)	0.07
National Identity* Communist Past	0.04	(0.03)	0.02
Exclusive National Identity* Communist Past	0.26	(0.16)	0.03
National Identity* Partisan Divide over Europe	−0.03	(0.04)	−0.03
Exclusive National Identity* Partisan Divide over Europe	0.09	(0.18)	0.02
Political Influence	0.07	(0.05)	0.06
Media Exposure	0.01	(0.03)	0.01
Political Sophistication	−0.18[a]	(0.07)	−0.16
Social Trust	−0.03	(0.05)	−0.03
Visited EU Countries	−0.15[a]	(0.06)	−0.08
Non-Electoral Participation	0.07	(0.03)	0.06
Political Influence	−0.05	(0.04)	−0.06
Media Exposure	0.01	(0.02)	0.01
Political Sophistication* Partisan Divide over Europe	−0.04	(0.03)	−0.04
Social Trust* Partisan Divide over Europe	0.03	(0.04)	0.03
Visited EU Countries* Partisan Divide over Europe	0.14[a]	(0.05)	0.10
Non-Electoral Participation* Partisan Divide over Europe	−0.05	(0.03)	−0.05
EU National Benefits* Sophistication	0.01	(0.03)	0.03
EU Personal Benefits* Sophistication	0.03	(0.03)	0.06
EU Scope* Sophistication	0.02[b]	(0.01)	0.14
Sex	−0.02	(0.06)	0.00
Age	−0.01	(0.01)	−0.08
Age squared	0.00	(0.00)	0.07
Education	0.05	(0.04)	0.02
Catholic	−0.06	(0.05)	−0.01
Manual Work	0.02	(0.23)	0.00
Left–right Position	0.02	(0.01)	0.02
Left–right Extremity	0.01[c]	(0.00)	0.04
Communist Past	0.00	(0.04)	0.00
Quality of Governance	0.00	(0.02)	0.00
Net EU Transfers	0.00	(0.02)	0.00
Gross National Income	0.00	(0.00)	0.00
Welfare Spending	0.00	(0.00)	0.00
Length of EU Membership	0.00	(0.00)	0.00
Partisan Divide over Europe	0.00	(0.04)	0.00
Constant	0.00	(0.08)	

[a] $p < 0.05$
[b] $p < 0.01$
[c] $p < 0.001$

Note: All estimates are adjusted for clustering by country and multiple imputations.

beyond the overall conclusion that cognitive mobilization is not a positive influence on EU support. If this reflects a change compared to earlier times, then our data provide no support for the idea that this change was triggered by increasing policy differences between European political parties regarding integration. However, we could also speculate that this finding reflects a delayed effect on public opinion of a recent increase in negative media coverage of the EU issues which is first picked up by more sophisticated and attentive members of the public (see de Vreese et al. 2006; Bruter 2009).

Hooghe and Marks's (2005) proposition that a greater level of inter-party dissent on European integration increases the negative impact of exclusive national identity on EU support does not fare any better. The interaction of Partisan Divide over Europe with Exclusive National Identity has an effect in the expected direction but remains very far from any conventionally accepted level of statistical significance, and the interaction of Partisan Divide over Europe with National Identity does not do any better than that. What worked least from our theoretical expectations, however, is the idea that the impact of (exclusive) national identity on EU support may be particularly negative in post-Communist Europe. The regional comparisons in section 3 already raised doubts about this proposition, and in Table 7.5 we can see again that, if anything, the opposite is true. Though the positive effects of the National Identity with Communist Legacies and the Exclusive National Identity with Communist Legacies interactions are not significant, they come close enough to it to raise the possibility that it may be precisely in Eastern Europe where nationalist feelings exert a positive rather than negative influence on EU support. This finding may easily signify that joining the EU might have been considered as a final sign of break with the Communist past and Soviet dominance by more nationalist segments of the public in Eastern Europe.

Cue-taking theory has not been much more successful in generating viable propositions about cross-national differences either. Following Steenbergen et al. (2007) we expected that cue-taking from preferred parties diminishes over time as citizens' personal opinions crystallize. Yet we find the exact opposite: the length of a country's EU membership apparently *increases* the influence of party cues on EU support. Reasons for this anomaly may include our research design, which lacks an 'over time' component in the data analysed and thus only offers highly indirect cues about the possible causes of changes over time. However, should Steenbergen et al. (2007) be correct, it would have been expected that citizens of new democracies would be the most likely to follow party cues, and yet we find the exact opposite of that (for a possible explanation, see Markowski and Tucker 2005). It is possible that it is not the crystallization of citizens' opinion that matters more in old member states, but rather that citizens' knowledge of partisan exact positions about the EU is higher in old than in new democracies. This would be partially because of longer experiences with parties and their pronouncements on various issues, but also because, and this was very much evidenced at the time of pre-accession referendums, public proclamations about the EU from almost all relevant parties in East European member countries were largely, if not overwhelmingly, positive, while criticism was in most cases either muted or expressed in a very convoluted way (see Szczerbiak and Taggart 2004).

Theories of instrumental calculation do seem to work a little better, in that most of the relevant macro-micro interactions at least go in the expected direction. Specifically, and partly building on Brinegar and Jolly (2005), Hix (2007), Hooghe and Marks (2005), and Ray (2004), we expected that supporters of a 'social' EU would be likely to support Europe if welfare spending is low, but oppose integration if it is high in their own country. The interaction of Welfare Spending with Social or Competitive Europe is indeed negative as expected and might conceivably be stronger and statistically significant if our sixteen-country sample included more countries (e.g. from Scandinavia or the Low Countries) with relatively high levels of welfare spending. We also find that the impact of Education (i.e. the marketable skills) on EU support does vary mostly as we expected along macro variables that are conceivably related to how diverse the benefits of integration are likely to be. Yet all but one of these interactions are statistically non-significant. The exception concerns EU budget transfers, which should make the benefits of integration more widely visible and does indeed reduce the observed impact of education on support. Hooghe and Marks (2005) and Gabel (1998b) also proposed that manual workers are more likely to support market integration in labour-rich than in capital-rich countries. It is consistent with this that the interaction of Manual with GNI (gross national income) has a negative effect on support, but again the effect is far from significant.

Last but not least, we expected that National Institutional Trust as a cue has a direct positive effect on support for integration, but its effect turns negative where Quality of Governance is high, because in the latter situation instrumental calculus will suggest that integration will deliver worse, rather than better outputs. Yet what we find is that National Institutional Trust has a particularly positive influence exactly where the quality of governance is high. We suspect that the reason for this may be the even greater credibility of pro-integration national elites in countries with better than average governance, but the data at hand do not allow a more direct test of this proposition.

Conclusions

We find that overall evaluations of EU integration build on more specific attitudes related to Europe, particularly the dimensions of EU citizenship introduced in Chapter 2. Once these more specific attitudes towards Europe are taken into account, little influence seems to be exercised by other factors like cognitive mobilization, domestic political cues, and national identity. The only notable exceptions are provided by trust in national political institutions, which—contrary to some expectations—affect EU support positively, and especially in member states with high-quality governance. Apart from this small exception, our findings point to a predominantly instrumental logic for EU support among citizens. The roots of EU support are remarkably similar across Western, Southern, and Eastern Europe, and also the level of support is mostly explained by within- rather than between-country differences. The only striking cross-regional difference concerns neither the determinants nor the level of support for EU integration, but the extent to which attitudes to the EU are crystallized in the various parts of Europe. Citizens of the South and the East tend to have less crystallized attitudes towards EU support than the West European mass publics. One important implication of our models is that if attitudes to integration were to become more crystallized, they would become very slightly less supportive than they are at this point.

Generalized support for EU-integration can only be a multifaceted phenomenon due to the ever-changing, multipurpose, self-reflexive, and indeed democratic nature of the EU itself. As the EU evolves, its organization, policy agenda, and framing in public discourses all adjust to problems and opportunities as perceived by stakeholders. It is only natural, then, that the determinants of EU support can vary over time, across countries and across individuals. A key purpose of our volume has been to make this complexity analytically more tractable by distinguishing between three key dimensions of EU citizenship: identification with the community, support for the scope of the organization, and having a voice in it and feeling to be represented by its institutions. In this chapter we argued that the three citizenship dimensions of identity, scope, and representation correspond to the families of affective-identitarian, cue-taking and instrumental explanations for EU support. When entered in the analysis together, they add considerably to explained variance: a model including only the three citizenship factors among the predictors explains 18 per cent of the within-country variance of EU support across the sixteen countries, while our full combined model shown in Table 7.4 with its twenty-nine independent variables explains just 2.5 per cent more. The EU citizenship factors can also be plausibly linked to theoretically different perspectives about the roots of EU support. Crucially, most other variables familiar from the extant literature simply have insignificant effects on attitudes towards integration once the EU citizenship variables are taken into account. Indeed, in Table 7.5 only the perceived benefits of European integration to the respondent's country, trust in national institutions, and trust in other Europeans register significant Euro-wide effects on support that are not captured by the inclusion of the three citizenship variables in the analysis. It could of course be argued that citizenship attitudes are causally too close to support for European integration, but previous chapters aptly demonstrated how the varied dimensions of citizenship are influenced in plausible ways by differing (though overlapping) sets of factors themselves. The three dimensions of EU citizenship, our results suggest, can explain nearly as much of the variance of EU support as a wide array of theories and previously identified correlates do. Their impact on EU support is, of course, hardly unexpected.

Overall, our findings suggest that established theories and their logical derivatives do reasonably well in providing a model of EU support that fits all regions of the EU. Cognitive mobilization should not be counted among the possible roots of support in contemporary Europe any longer. Instead, instrumental calculus of the link between policy preferences and further integration, identification with Europe, and cue-taking from parties and institutional performance are the key cornerstone of the hybrid model that we arrive at, and the relative influence of these groups of factors is fairly consistent across the diverse regions of Europe. By the standards of mass attitude research, the model explains a very respectable amount of variance in Western attitudes towards integration, and fully mediates the impact of sociodemographic variables through specific attitudes. The model works less well for Southern and Eastern Europe, but circumstantial evidence suggests that this is more a consequence of low attitude crystallization in those two regions than the presence of substantially different roots of EU support in the newer member states.

The same theories seem to do markedly less well in explaining cross-national variation in what determines support here or there. One reason for this may be that this variance is in fact very limited and is barely more than some random noise around a common tendency. But we suspect that shortcomings of theory as well as the limitations of the data used in previous analyses may have also a played a role in this underachievement. Several of the interesting findings reported in the previous literature could not be replicated here given that we were able to exploit the richness of the IntUne dataset in attitudinal measures, in order to improve operationalization and to include a comprehensive set of control variables to the models. Our discussion and findings also point to some difficulties in clearly delineating information shortcuts from mechanisms of instrumental calculus and even identity, and unearthed large overlaps between the scope of explanation provided by one ostensibly different theoretical approach and another. If previous work in this field was often characterized by elaborate theories linked to a few rather ad hoc attitudinal indicators, here we encountered the opposite problem. Namely, the complex distinctions allowed by our attitudinal data were not always easy to link to established and productive theories of EU support. Theory-building in the past was probably constrained in this topic area by keeping an eye on a small range of proxy variables easily found in Eurobarometer surveys, and should gain from working out conceptual distinctions that can direct purposeful data generation and eventually generate predictions about how sources and levels of EU support may change over time.

8

Explaining Turnout in European Parliament Elections

Markus Steinbrecher and Hans Rattinger

Introduction

This chapter focuses on a key behavioural component of EU engagement—turnout in European Parliament elections. Participation in EU elections has been on the decline since the first elections in 1979. In 2004, turnout reached an all-time low of 45.7 per cent in the first European election after the accession of ten Southern, Eastern, and Central European countries. Turnout rates were especially low in the new member states. Less than 30 per cent of eligible voters went to the polls in Poland, Czech Republic, Slovakia, Estonia, Slovenia, Bulgaria, and Romania. This extraordinarily low level of turnout was rather surprising because electoral research has quite often reported a 'first-time boost' for 'new' elections (Franklin 2001: 312; Reif 1984: 7; van der Eijk, Franklin, and Marsh 1996). In addition, participation rates in the referendums prior to EU accession were much higher than in the election after accession to the EU in these countries. However, a look at the turnout rates in the United Kingdom (38.8 per cent), Portugal (38.6 per cent), and Sweden (37.8 per cent) reveals that low participation is a Europe-wide phenomenon.

The mass media and the public have often regarded low and declining turnout levels as symptoms of a crisis of the whole European project, interpreting it as a manifestation of Euroscepticism or even public Europhobia.[1] This interpretation is supported by the negative results of the referendums in the Netherlands (2005), France (2005), and Ireland (2008) on the Constitutional

---

[1] See, e.g., reports on the 2009 EP election in the *Süddeutsche Zeitung* (http://www.sueddeutsche.de/politik/799/471340/text/, accessed on July 10, 2009) and *The Economist* (http://www.economist.com/opinion/displaystory.cfm?story_id=13829453), accessed on July 10, 2009.

Treaty of the European Union and the Lisbon Treaty. Contrary to these popular assumptions, academic researchers have demonstrated, on the one hand, that European elections are elections of a specific kind, so-called second-order elections (Reif and Schmitt 1980; Reif 1997; Schmitt 2005). For such elections, turnout is lower because there is less at stake, resulting in a lower level of politicization and electoral mobilization. On the other hand, it has been pointed out quite often that the low level of participation in EU elections cannot be explained by negative evaluations of the European institutions, policymakers, policies, or the integration process itself (Oppenhuis 1995; Rosema 2007; Schmitt and Mannheimer 1991; Schmitt and van der Eijk 2003). However, there are other researchers who report precisely the opposite findings, namely, that negative attitudes towards European integration cause abstention from the European ballot box (Blondel, Sinnott, and Svensson 1998; Frognier 2002; Roth 2004).

While previous research relied on a limited number of attitudinal variables towards European integration, Chapter 2 has presented an innovative battery of measures of EU citizenship, combining the dimensions of identity, representation, and scope of governance (Benhabib 2002). This extensive battery of variables offers new opportunities for research on the impact of EU-related attitudes on turnout in European Parliament elections. Thus, one of the key goals of this chapter is to test whether these attitudinal dimensions help to explain electoral participation at the European level. The relative explanatory power of these EU-related attitudes will be assessed in comparison with traditional explanations of (EU election) turnout (instrumental calculations, partisan cues, sense of civic duty, affective commitment, and demographic profile).

This chapter is structured in the following way: section 2 introduces the dependent variables. Aside from European election turnout, electoral participation at the national level is included, too, since there are, as frequencies in section 2 show, strong differences in the willingness to participate in elections at both levels. Both turnout variables are combined to four voter types, so that this chapter distinguishes among citizens who vote in both EU and national elections, those who vote in neither, and those who vote in national or EU elections only. Section 2 also presents frequencies for the four voter types. The goal of section 3 is to offer a short theoretical background for the selection of all predictor variables that enter the logistic regression analysis in section 4. Aside from the dichotomous variable turnout in European elections, some of the voter types will be confronted with each other in logistic regression models. This comparison helps to understand the specific reasons for abstention at the European level and helps to minimize overreporting effects. As in previous chapters, national differences in the patterns of EU turnout are compared and explained, controlling for system-level characteristics.

Level of turnout and voter types

Vote intention and vote recall are the two main ways of measuring individual turnout in survey research. In the IntUne survey respondents were asked whether or not they participated in the last European election (2004) and in the respective last national election. A look at the level of reported turnout in national elections in Table 8.1 shows a clear gap between the countries in the East and the West, where electoral participation is definitely higher. However, there are also considerable differences among the West European countries. Electoral participation is relatively high in the countries that founded the European Union in 1957 and those that joined in the 1980s and the 1990s compared to the accession countries of 1973. This effect is produced largely by the United Kingdom which shows the lowest reported turnout rate (79.2 per cent) in the survey among all West European countries. However, the British level of reported electoral participation is quite high if one compares it with that of Bulgaria (64.2 per cent) or Poland (65.1 per cent).

Compared to national elections, the overall level of reported turnout is much lower in European elections (cf. the left- and right-side panels of

Table 8.1. Actual and reported turnout in 2004 European and most recent National Parliament Elections

Country	National Parliament Elections			European Parliament Elections		
	Reported	Actual	Difference	Reported	Actual	Difference
Austria	89.3	78.5	10.8	70.8	42.4	28.4
Belgium	88.7	91.9	−3.2	88.3	90.8	−2.5
Bulgaria	64.2	55.8	8.4	–	–	–
Germany	86.0	77.7	8.3	71.3	43.0	28.3
Denmark	91.1	84.5	6.6	73.6	47.9	25.7
Estonia	71.4	61.0	10.4	54.2	26.8	27.4
Greece	85.1	76.5	8.6	80.8	63.4	17.4
Spain	84.4	77.2	7.2	73.0	45.1	27.9
France	80.1	62.4	17.7	71.4	42.8	28.6
Hungary	79.2	67.8	11.4	75.5	38.5	37.0
Italy	89.1	83.6	5.5	78.5	73.1	5.4
Poland	65.1	40.6	24.5	48.3	20.9	27.4
Portugal	80.9	65.0	15.9	67.9	38.6	29.3
Slovenia	81.0	60.5	20.5	69.6	28.3	41.3
Slovakia	79.9	54.7	25.2	67.8	17.0	50.8
UK	79.2	61.3	17.9	57.8	38.8	19.0
Average	81.9	69.7	12.2	69.1	45.7	23.4
West	84.3	73.6	10.7	71.3	49.7	21.6
East (2004/2007 entrants only)	70.4	48.9	21.5	55.7	21.1	34.6
1957 entrants only	85.4	75.8	9.6	74.1	53.6	20.5
1973 entrants only	80.2	63.3	16.9	59.2	39.6	19.6
1981–6 entrants only	84.0	75.3	8.7	73.6	47.2	26.4
1995 entrants only	89.3	78.5	10.8	70.8	42.4	28.4

Note: Averages in the lower part of the table are weighted according to population size of states belonging to the respective group.

Table 8.1). Again, there are big differences between the countries which founded the EU or joined in the 1980s and 1990s on the one hand, and the accession countries of the 1970s and 2000s on the other (cf. the data by waves of accession in the lower panel of Table 8.1). Belgium and Greece clearly stick out with a reported turnout of more than 80 per cent while the rest of the West and South European countries except the United Kingdom (57.8 per cent) and Portugal (67.9 per cent) range between 70 and 80 per cent. Reported turnout rates in the East vary between 48.3 per cent in Poland and 69.6 per cent in Slovenia.

However, reported turnout tells only part of the story, since survey data are confronted with the problem of overreporting, the overestimation of turnout rates.[2] This phenomenon occurs in almost all surveys, both for European and national elections.[3] As research elsewhere indicates, vote recall (where respondents are asked to identify the party for which they voted) seems to be a more adequate and reliable measure for turnout at both European and national levels (Steinbrecher, Huber, and Rattinger 2007: 115–31). Table 8.1 shows that overreporting appears for both electoral levels and for all countries except Belgium where turnout is even underestimated at both electoral levels because of compulsory voting. The level of overreporting for national elections ranges between 5.5 percentage points (Italy) and 25.2 percentage points (Slovakia). However, overreporting is much higher for European elections: Italy, Greece, and the United Kingdom are the only countries where the difference between reported and actual turnout is smaller than 20 percentage points. In Slovakia and Slovenia this gap exceeds 40 percentage points. If one compares East and West European countries, overreporting is in general much higher for the former Communist countries. The fact that reported turnout is not necessarily an adequate measure of actual turnout in all cases leads to the conclusion that results of the analysis in section 4 may be distorted and might not depict the real relationship between the variables.

Although there is a difference between actual and reported turnout, electoral research has to use self-assessments by respondents, because vote validation with RDD sampling (Random Digit Dialling) is impossible. Thus, reported turnout will be the dependent variable in the following analysis and will

---

[2] There are three main reasons for this phenomenon: First, respondents lie on purpose, because they have internalised a societal norm that voting is the duty of a good citizen and thus perceive electoral participation to be socially desirable behaviour. Second, the design of the questionnaire, the questions, or the response categories might distort the respondents' answers (Schuman and Presser 1996). Third, respondents are unable to remember their behaviour correctly.

[3] Some examples help to illustrate that the problem also exists in surveys where measurement and realization of the behaviour are much closer together: in the European Election Study 2004 the Britons showed a turnout rate of about 58.4 per cent in the survey, while in fact only 38.8 per cent of the eligible British voters went to the ballot box. Over-reporting also occurs in the German Federal Election Study 2005, which displays a turnout of almost 88 per cent, while the turnout rate in the election was 77.7 per cent.

constitute the base for the calculation of voter types that help us to specify the reasons why abstention from the ballot box is higher in European elections. The figures reported in Table 8.2 have been calculated by cross-tabulating EU and national turnout variables, resulting in four *types of voters*. The first group votes in neither European nor national elections, representing 14.9 per cent of the whole sample. The second group of respondents (2.9 per cent of the sample) are those who reported voting in European elections only, but not in national elections. The third group, those who voted in national, but not in European elections, is a little bit larger than the first group (16.0 per cent). This group is very important, partly because it is relatively large but mainly because it represents (national) 'voters' who *abstained* in the last round of EP elections. It will be interesting to find out why these people participate in national but not in European elections. The fourth and last group combines those who participated in both types of elections and is clearly the largest, with 66.2 per cent of all respondents in the group. This means that a comparison of the third and the fourth group is of great value for the general research questions of this chapter.

Since the four voter types are calculated from both turnout variables, it is obvious that some of the differences between countries and groups of

Table 8.2. Voter types with respect to turnout in European (EPE) and national (NE) elections

	Abstain in both EPE and NE	Vote in EPE, abstain in NE	Abstain in EPE, vote in NE	Vote in both EPE and NE
Austria	8.7	2.0	20.5	68.8
Belgium	9.9	1.5	1.8	86.8
Bulgaria	11.7	2.3	17.0	69.0
Germany	7.8	1.1	18.6	72.5
Denmark	23.7	4.9	22.1	49.3
Estonia	13.0	1.9	6.2	78.8
Greece	13.1	2.5	13.9	70.5
Spain	16.4	3.5	12.2	67.9
France	15.2	5.5	9.3	69.9
Hungary	7.4	3.5	14.2	74.9
Italy	31.7	3.1	19.9	45.2
Poland	15.8	3.3	16.3	64.6
Portugal	16.0	3.0	14.5	66.6
Slovenia	15.9	4.2	16.3	63.6
Slovakia	18.0	2.8	24.1	55.0
Average	14.9	2.9	16.0	66.2
West	12.9	2.8	15.7	68.5
East (2004/2007 entrants only)	26.6	3.7	17.6	52.0
1957 entrants only	11.7	2.9	14.2	71.2
1973 entrants only	17.1	2.7	23.7	56.6
1981–6 entrants only	13.5	2.5	12.9	71.0
1995 entrants only	8.7	2.0	20.5	68.8

Note: Averages in the lower part of the table are weighted according to population size of states belonging to the respective group.

countries respectively mentioned above can also be reported here. As Table 8.2 shows, the main difference between East and West Europe is related to those who did not vote at both levels and those who participated in European as well as in national elections. While 26.6 per cent of East European respondents were general non-voters, only 12.9 per cent of the West Europeans said that they did not go to both ballot boxes. In contrast, 68.5 per cent of West Europeans took part in both elections, whereas only 52.0 per cent of the East Europeans did so.

Turning to the individual countries Belgium is, of course, the country with the highest share of people being active in both election types (86.8 per cent), followed by Greece (78.8 per cent) and Italy (74.9 per cent). The United Kingdom (55.0 per cent), Estonia (49.3 per cent), and Poland (45.2 per cent) are the countries with the lowest share of respondents in this group. In a majority of countries those who said that they only participated in national elections form the second biggest group. The United Kingdom (24.1 per cent), Estonia (22.1 per cent), Austria (20.5 per cent), and Poland (19.9 per cent) are the most striking examples. General non-voters are the second largest group in countries like Poland (31.7 per cent), Estonia (23.7 per cent), France (16.4 per cent), and Hungary (15.2 per cent). Those who took part in European elections only are the smallest group in all countries. Their share varies between 1.1 per cent in Denmark and 5.5 per cent in Hungary. Interestingly, this group is larger in East European than in West European countries.

Theoretical background and overview about explanations of turnout

The previous section has demonstrated that turnout in European elections is much lower than in national elections. The aim of this section is to introduce variables that help to explain individual electoral participation in both kinds of elections. The way in which the variables are presented differs from that used in other chapters. As in other chapters, the analysis here differentiates between the four groups of variables (hard rationality predictors, political cues, affective predictors, and cognitive mobilization variables) that were introduced in Chapter 3. In addition, however, following the general causal schema outlined in Chapter 1, EU-related attitudes are treated as a separate group of explanatory variables, divided into the dimensions of identity, representation, and scope of governance.

As mentioned above, it is possible that turnout in European elections at least is affected by support for the EU and the European integration process. This interpretation is in line with the theoretical assumptions of Easton (1965) as well as Almond and Verba (1963) who argue that the stability and performance of a democracy are dependent on the fundamental willingness of the citizens to support the political system. Thus, those who are satisfied with the European political system will go to the polls while those who are dissatisfied will stay at home. Lindberg and Scheingold (1970) extended this idea, distinguishing between 'diffuse/affective' support for the EU, which reflects overall approval of the EU integration process, and 'evaluative/utilitarian' support, which is based on a cost-benefit analysis of EU outputs and which requires higher levels of knowledge and sophistication. (For similar distinctions, see Inglehart 1977a; Inglehart and Rabier 1978; Niedermayer 1995; Anderson and Reichert 1996; Christin 2005.)

The EU-specific attitudes presented in Chapter 2 measure both of these aspects of support for the European political system. The index that combines perceptions of personal and national benefits from European integration is a useful measure of specific support, because these aspects are both clearly related to the output of the EU. We expect that effects of this benefits variable on turnout will be positive: those who think that they themselves and/or their country has benefited should be more active in the electoral process. We use the general EU support factor and the European Identity scale as measures of diffuse support, since these variables are not connected to specific actions or actors in the European political system, but to general aspects of the whole integration process. We expect both variables to influence turnout in European elections positively. Those who express general EU support and/or who identify with Europe should be more likely to vote in EP elections; those who exhibit low levels of EU support or lack a sense of European identity should abstain. Indeed, in a situation where there is a widespread consensus about the desirability of European integration in most of the member states and a consequent lack of competition among the parties in European elections, not casting a ballot is one possible way of expressing opposition to the European political system and the integration process (Schmitt and van der Eijk 2003: 281–2).

Aside from the demonstration of political support, another important function of elections in national politics is the distribution of power. The parties that won the national election and thus form the government consider their electoral victory to be a signal that they should implement the programme they presented to the voters during the campaign. This programme will thus be converted into certain policies. If one looks at European elections and at the role of the European Parliament, it is clear that despite the institutional reforms introduced since the Maastricht Treaty, European elections still do not have an effect on the formation of the European Commission and the selection of the President of the Commission. This lack of power is typically reflected in the character of the European election campaign, which is dominated by national issues and does not present front-runners for the future

Commission. This makes participation in these elections appear to be much less important than turnout in national elections. Hence, for some people, it can be a simple matter of rationality to abstain in elections to the European Parliament.

Another important aspect for electoral participation is the widespread perception of European citizens that the entire *EU* political process is less important than *national* institutions and processes. One reason for this perception is that citizens believe there is less at stake in European elections, an observation that led Reif and Schmitt (1980) to conclude that EP elections were rationally regarded by many citizens as 'second-order elections'. In order to operationalize these instrumental rational calculations, we use the Representation and EU Scope of Government indicators outlined in Chapters 2 and 3 of this volume. Our expectation is that both EU Representation and EU Policy Scope indicators will have positive effects on EP turnout.

However, affective commitment to Europe and instrumental evaluations of the integration process only tell part of the story of turnout. There are many other indicators that are powerful predictors of turnout at the national as well as at the European level. Hence, it is important to include these variables in the analysis, because they are rival explanations to the group of EU-related attitudes. These predictors, their related theoretical assumptions, and major empirical results can only be presented very briefly due to limitations of space. The presentation will follow the differentiation in four major theoretical approaches made in Chapter 3.

We include three *political cue* variables in the model. The first is party identification, derived from the social-psychological 'Michigan' approach to electoral analysis. Because the attachment to a party promotes psychological involvement in the political process, we hypothesize here that the stronger the party identification, the higher the probability that an individual will cast a ballot (Campbell et al. 1960: 97–8). The second political cue variable is left–right self-placement, which acts as a proxy for more general value orientations in this respect. People who place themselves on the right part of the continuum should be more active (Steinbrecher 2009: 185–214, 229–48), because they adhere to values and norms broadly supportive of the political status quo that generally promote higher levels of orthodox political participation (Knutsen 1995). The third cueing variable, relatedly, is the individual's sense of civic duty. The predicted effect of this variable is quite obvious. Those who consider voting to be a civic duty for a good citizen are clearly more willing to cast a ballot (Blais 2000).

Aside from the EU-benefit variable referred to above, the second group of predictors—*hard rationality* explanations—consists of a single indicator. This variable is national retrospective economic evaluations, which we expect to exert a positive effect on turnout. The direction of the effect here has to be considered against the background of the political support model presented at the beginning of this section. If economic conditions are perceived to be relatively good, this should be transformed into support for the political system and participation in elections (Killian, Schoen, and Dusso 2008).

National identity is the single *affective* predictor variable in the model. The causal connection with turnout in European elections is not obvious. If it is hypothesized that national and European identity are conflicting attachments, national identity should have a *negative* effect on turnout in European elections. In contrast, the impact should be *positive* if one accepts the possibility of complementary multiple attachments, in which European identity can be entirely consistent with holding other, national and regional identities (Duchesne and Frognier 1995; Westle 2003). The national identity variable is thus used to control for the effect of European identity, without any particular expectation as to the sign of its coefficient.

The fourth group of predictor variables introduced in Chapter 3 are indicators of *cognitive mobilization*, several of which can also be derived from the social-psychological approach (Campbell et al. 1960). The core idea is that higher political engagement—measured, for example, by political interest, political knowledge, or media consumption—leads to a higher probability of electoral participation (Campbell et al. 1960: 101f.). A second indicator of cognitive mobilization is political efficacy. The main hypothesis here is that the more positively an individual evaluates her/his capabilities and/or the responsiveness of the political system and its actors, the more probable it is that s/he will participate in elections (Campbell et al. 1960: 105).

Two other cognitive mobilization indicators cannot be connected to the social-psychological approach. *General trust*, an index that covers aspects of social trust and trust in different groups, relates to the social capital approach (Putnam 1993, 2000). People with higher degrees of trust are more active in the political process and thus more likely to vote in elections. Our final indicator of cognitive mobilization, based on the findings of various political participation studies (e.g., Kaase 1990; Milbrath 1965; Steinbrecher 2009) is *non-electoral political participation*. Those who are more active in general in the political process and use non-electoral forms of participation are also more likely to participate in elections (e.g., Inglehart 1977a).

Social structural variables are not as important as attitudinal variables for the prediction of individual electoral behaviour, but they need to be controlled for in any analysis of turnout (Steinbrecher et al. 2007: 210–18). We accordingly apply controls for class membership, religiosity, urbanization, gender, education, and age (the last being modelled as a potentially curvilinear function to reflect possible life-cycle engagement effects).

The overview of the turnout variables and the voter types presented in section 2 above showed that there are strong differences between countries.

Although it is possible that individual-level differences *could* explain all these country-level differences, it seems prudent to include macro-level variables in the analysis. This is especially so in view of the fact that previous research has identified several political system characteristics that explain national differences in the level of electoral participation (Blais 2000; Blondel, Sinnott, and Svensson 1998; Fauvelle-Aymar and Stegmaier 2008; Flickinger and Studlar 2007). These macro variables include the presence (or absence) of compulsory voting, Sunday voting, and postal voting,[4] which all help to boost turnout. Communist past is also included in the analysis to account for the different historical background of the countries in the IntUne sample and the strong differences in turnout levels between East and West Europe. Aside from these variables, net transfers from the EU budget are also included. The hypothesis here is that countries which gain monetarily from EU membership should show higher turnout rates, following the assumption that the electorate behaves rationally (Mattila 2003). We accordingly regard this particular macro variable as part of the group of 'hard rationality' variables.

Explanation of turnout in national and European Parliament elections

The primary interest of this chapter is to analyse the importance of the various EU-attitude dimensions presented in Chapter 2 for electoral participation. The first step of the analysis concentrates on the bivariate relationships between the different indicators of representation, identity, and scope of governance, on the one hand, and the turnout dummies and voter types, on the other (4.1 and 4.2). This is a preliminary step before the relative explanatory power of these dimensions will be assessed in comparison with several traditional explanations of turnout at the micro and the macro level that have been presented in section 3.[5]

---

[4] Simultaneous elections at other levels of the political system are also an important macro predictor of turnout, but had to be kept out of the analysis, because there was no information on the electoral level as well as on the scope (regional or national) of the simultaneous election. The position of the European election in the national electoral cycle and the (effective) number of parties are also valuable predictors of European election turnout, but had to be kept out of the analysis due to the limited number of country cases in the analysis.

[5] The whole analysis has been calculated by using weight variable w2, which means that countries are weighted according to their share of the entire sample. This is a deviation from the weighting strategy applied in the rest of the chapters. The reason for the application of a proportional weight is that turnout rates are also calculated proportionally, meaning that German turnout has a stronger impact on turnout in the whole of the EU than Estonian turnout, because of the differences in population size.

Bivariate relationship between Europe-specific attitudes and turnout in European elections

Table 8.3 presents differences between voters and non-voters for each of eight EU-specific attitudes that were outlined in Chapter 2. The eight indices are all measured on a 0–10 scale, where positive values for the differences indicate more positive evaluations among the voters. For example, in terms of perceptions of benefits from the EU, voters in EU elections score on average 0.7 scale points higher than non-voters. Negative values, in contrast, represent more positive evaluations among the non-voters, which appear quite rarely. One example is the attitude towards future enlargements. The mean value of non-voters is 0.15 scale points higher than that of voters in European elections.

Turning to the overall results, several inferences are suggested by Table 8.3. First, across the whole sample (column 1), with the sole exception of attitudes towards future enlargement referred to above, all of the measures record more pro-EU attitudes among voters than among non-voters. Second, the differences between voters and non-voters are clearly more pronounced in Western Europe (column 2) than in the East (column 3), though more than half of the differences in the East are not significant. This suggests that EU-specific attitudes should be less important for the explanation of electoral participation in the East and Central European accession countries of 2004. However, due to the high level of overreporting in these countries these results should be treated with caution. For the other groups of countries (columns 4 to 7) there are no peculiarities except for the scope of governance indicators,

Table 8.3. Differences in EU attitudes between voters and non-voters in European elections

	All 16 countries	West	East (2004/ 2007 entrants only)	1957 entrants only	1973 entrants only	1981–6 entrants only	1995 entrants only
EU efficacy	0.19***	0.07	0.49***	0.05	0.02	−0.08	0.58**
General EU support	0.59***	0.73***	0.10	0.54***	0.65***	0.45***	1.14***
EU benefit	0.70***	0.86***	0.15	0.59***	1.15***	0.67***	0.83**
Institutional trust EU	0.41***	0.42***	0.38***	0.40***	0.23**	0.51***	0.42**
EU policy scope—current	0.26***	0.34***	−0.08	0.22**	0.07	0.06	0.76***
EU policy scope—future	0.38***	0.51***	0.15	0.38***	0.13	0.28**	0.48**
Support future EU enlargements	−0.15**	−0.05	−0.04	0.13	0.41**	−0.08	0.11
EU identity	0.58***	0.53***	0.76***	0.39***	0.66***	0.34***	0.69***

Level of significance:
* $p < 0.05$
** $p < 0.01$
*** $p < 0.001$

Note: Table entries are the differences between the mean scores of voters and non-voters in the 2004 EP election, respectively.

for which significant differences seem to appear quite rarely. A third conclusion suggested by Table 8.3 is that the most marked differences relate to the representation and identity indicators. This in turn suggests these two citizenship measures should be more important in predicting turnout in European elections than the equivalent scope of EU government indicators.

Bivariate relationships between Europe-specific attitudes and different voter types

Table 8.4 contrasts the two key voter types; voters in European and national elections on the one hand and voters who only participate in national elections on the other. This comparison is important because both groups are politically active citizens, but one of the groups does not use the whole repertoire of participatory possibilities. If the assumptions about the positive effects of EU-related attitudes on turnout in European elections are correct, individuals who vote at both electoral levels should be more positively oriented towards the European integration process than those people who vote in national elections only. This is clearly the case for the whole sample, again with the exception of the future enlargement indicator (column 1). Differences among the two voter types are stronger in the EU-15 countries (columns 2, and 4 to 7). There are differences in strength between the various accession waves until the 1990s, but the overall pattern is the same. Those who vote at both electoral levels demonstrate more pro-European attitudes

Table 8.4. Differences in EU attitudes between voters in European and national elections and voters in national elections only

	All 16 countries	West	East (2004/ 2007 entrants only)	1957 entrants only	1973 entrants only	1981–6 entrants only	1995 entrants only
EU efficacy	0.21***	0.11	0.65***	0.09	0.17	−0.44**	0.92***
General EU support	0.72***	0.89***	−0.15	0.67***	0.76***	0.36**	1.55***
EU benefit	0.87***	1.10***	−0.32	0.90***	1.12***	0.71**	1.36***
Institutional trust EU	0.39***	0.43***	0.20*	0.38***	0.20*	0.47**	0.63***
EU policy scope— current	0.47***	0.57***	−0.09	0.37***	0.34**	0.25	0.94***
EU policy scope—future	0.47***	0.58***	0.00	0.25***	0.39**	0.44**	0.70***
Support future EU enlargements	0.07	0.18*	−0.17	0.07	0.64***	0.01	0.36
EU identity	0.61***	0.62***	0.54***	0.47***	0.66***	0.41***	0.87***

Level of significance:
* $p < 0.05$
** $p < 0.01$
*** $p < 0.001$

Note: Table entries are the differences between the mean scores of respondents who voted in both the last EP and the last national election and of those who voted only in national elections, respectively.

than those who cast only their national ballot. This again contrasts with the position of the new member states of 2004, where only three differences between both types are significant.[6] This suggests that EU-specific attitudes are less likely to be effective in predicting turnout in European elections in Eastern Europe than they are in the West.

The role of EU attitudes in multivariate models of European election turnout

The previous analysis has only applied a bivariate perspective on different measures of turnout on the one hand and eight EU-related attitudes on the other. But what happens in a multivariate analysis? Tables 8.5, 8.6, and 8.7 present three different models for the explanation of turnout in European elections. The dependent variable in these models is the dichotomous variable for participation in European elections, thus the models differentiate between voters and non-voters at the European level only. Using a clustered logistic regression analysis, Model 1 tests the strength of the effect of the eight EU-specific attitudes and hence provides the maximum share of variance in the dependent variable that this group of predictors is able to explain. Model 2 adds other individual-level variables to gauge the relative importance of the EU variables. Finally, Model 3 introduces macro variables to account for cross-country differences.

Table 8.5 shows the results for the entire sample. Model 1 explains, measured by Nagelkerke's R^2, 3.8 per cent of the variance of the turnout dummy variable. Two of the eight independent variables have significant positive effects. One predictor, the attitude towards future enlargements of the EU, has a negative effect. This corresponds to the previous findings of this chapter. Since all EU attitudes are coded on a scale from 0 to 10, the best predictor can be identified easily: the strongest effect is produced by the EU identity scale. Model 1 shows that the explanatory power of the eight EU-specific attitudes is very limited; however, Model 2 explains 25.6 per cent of the variation of turnout, mainly thanks to the attitudinal and social structural variables that have been added to Model 1. Among the eight EU-related variables that were already entered into Model 1, there is no item with a significant effect on the dependent variable. This means that, in contrast to the additional attitudinal and social structural variables, the effects of the EU-specific variables are negligible. The strongest predictors in Model 2 are strength of party identification and the feeling that voting is the duty of a good citizen, both part of the group of cueing variables. Additional positive effects originate from media consumption, non-electoral political

---

[6] Bulgaria is excluded because we only have information about participation in national elections for Bulgarian respondents.

Table 8.5. Logistic regression with turnout in European elections as the dependent variable

	Model 1		Model 2		Model 3	
	b	s.e.	b	s.e.	b	s.e.
EU efficacy	0.00	0.02	0.00	0.02	0.00	0.02
General EU support	0.04**	0.02	0.04	0.02	0.02	0.02
EU benefit	0.00	0.02	0.00	0.01	0.00	0.01
Institutional trust EU	0.04	0.03	0.00	0.03	0.00	0.03
EU policy scope—current	0.00	0.01	0.02	0.02	0.01	0.02
EU policy scope—future	0.02	0.02	0.01	0.02	-0.01	0.02
Support future EU enlargements	-0.06***	0.01	-0.02	0.01	0.02	0.01
EU identity	0.12**	0.04	0.02	0.03	0.04	0.03
Male			0.06	0.08	0.07	0.07
Age			0.03***	0.01	0.03***	0.01
Education			0.11	0.10	0.16*	0.08
Class			0.05	0.04	-0.01	0.04
Religiosity			-0.01	0.02	-0.02	0.02
Urbanization			0.02	0.04	-0.01	0.04
Duty to vote			0.16***	0.02	0.18***	0.02
Left–right ideology			0.00	0.01	0.01	0.01
Strength PID			0.28***	0.06	0.27***	0.05
Media consumption			0.06**	0.01	0.05**	0.01
Political sophistication			0.03	0.02	0.04*	0.02
Internal efficacy			0.03	0.02	0.02	0.02
Non-electoral participation			0.05*	0.02	0.05	0.02
General trust			-0.02	0.03	-0.02	0.02
National identity			0.04	0.03	0.04	0.03
Economic perception			-0.08*	0.04	-0.07*	0.03
Communist past					0.25	0.27
Compulsory voting					1.53***	0.14
Sunday voting					0.63***	0.06
Postal voting					0.34***	0.09
Net transfers from EU					-0.23***	0.06
Constant	-0.12	0.15	-3.81***	0.42	-4.54***	0.51
R^2	0.038		0.256		0.282	
N	16,505		16,178		16,178	

Level of significance:
* $p < 0.05$
** $p < 0.01$
*** $p < 0.001$

participation, and age. Economic perceptions have the only negative effect in Model 2: those with a more positive evaluation of the economic situation have a lower probability of participation. Overall, the results for Model 2 clearly show that abstention in European Parliament elections is only to a very limited degree caused by negative attitudes towards the EU and the integration process.

The inclusion of aggregate-level variables in Model 3 causes only minor changes in the strength of the effects for the individual-level variables. Strength of party identification and electoral duty are still the most important positive predictors of turnout, while there is still no EU-related attitude with a significant effect. Sophistication, which did not have a significant effect in

Model 2, gains significance, having a positive effect on turnout. Thus, indicators of cognitive mobilization are important for the explanation of turnout too. The whole model explains 28.2 per cent of the variation of the dependent variable, so that the macro variables have only limited additional explanatory value. One result is surprising: turnout is lower among the respondents from those countries which receive higher net transfers from the EU budget. This, in combination with the negative effect of economic perceptions, could imply that voters do not rely on hard rationality factors as expected when casting a ballot, but we have to be cautious with statements like that due to the high degree of overreporting in our dataset. The rest of the effects are in line with the expectations and assumptions stated earlier: turnout is positively affected by compulsory voting, Sunday voting, and the possibility of postal voting. All in all, Model 3 leads to the same conclusion as the results of Model 2. Negative attitudes towards the EU are not the reason for abstention in European elections.

But if there is no obvious effect of EU-related variables on turnout in European elections across the EU as a whole, is there any evidence of an effect if Eastern and Western European countries are considered separately? Table 8.6 reports the results of estimating the model shown in Table 8.5 for Western Europe only. The results are virtually identical to those reported for the whole sample. The crucial point is that, as in Table 8.5, the EU-related variables in Table 8.6 explain only 3.7 per cent of the variance in turnout, and all of those variables fail to yield statistically significant effects when appropriate controls are made, as in Model 3. Table 8.7 shows the equivalent results for Eastern Europe. Here, the position is slightly different, though not much. The EU-specific attitudes considered alone now explain 7.6 per cent of the variance in turnout, but none of these effects is significant when other appropriate variables are included in the (Model 3) specification. In short, in all parts of Europe, failure to vote in EP elections is clearly *not* a function of people's attitudes towards the EU.

EU-related attitudes and 'European election abstainers'

While the previous logistic regression analysis identified the factors that help to differentiate between voters and non-voters in European elections, we now compare the two decisive voter types presented earlier in this chapter, voters in national elections on the one hand versus voters in European and national elections on the other. The aim of this additional analysis is to see if EU-related attitudes help to explain why some of the people who vote in national elections decide to abstain from voting in EP elections. The dependent variable is again a dichotomous one. Voters in elections at both levels are coded as '1', while voters in national elections only are coded '0'.

Table 8.6. Logistic regression with turnout in European elections as the dependent variable. Results for West European countries only

	Model 1		Model 2		Model 3	
	b	s.e.	b	s.e.	b	s.e.
EU efficacy	−0.02	0.01	−0.01	0.02	−0.01	0.02
General EU support	0.05**	0.02	0.06*	0.02	0.04	0.02
EU benefit	0.01	0.02	0.01	0.01	0.01	0.02
Institutional trust EU	0.04	0.03	0.01	0.04	0.00	0.03
EU policy scope—current	0.01	0.02	0.03	0.03	0.03	0.02
EU policy scope—future	0.04	0.02	0.00	0.03	−0.02	0.02
Support future EU enlargements	−0.05***	0.01	−0.01	0.01	0.00	0.01
EU identity	0.08*	0.03	−0.02	0.03	−0.03	0.03
Male			0.09	0.08	0.09	0.08
Age			0.03***	0.01	0.04***	0.01
Education			0.07	0.11	0.12	0.08
Class			0.04	0.05	−0.01	0.05
Religiosity			0.02	0.02	−0.01	0.02
Urbanization			−0.02	0.03	−0.04	0.04
Duty to vote			0.15***	0.02	0.17***	0.02
Left–right ideology			0.00	0.01	0.00	0.01
Strength PID			0.25***	0.06	0.26***	0.06
Media consumption			0.06**	0.02	0.05**	0.02
Political sophistication			0.02	0.03	0.03	0.02
Internal efficacy			0.01	0.02	0.01	0.02
Non-electoral participation			0.05	0.03	0.05*	0.03
General trust			−0.05*	0.02	−0.04	0.02
National identity			0.06*	0.03	0.06	0.03
Economic perceptions			−0.05	0.04	−0.05	0.03
Compulsory voting					1.50***	0.15
Sunday voting					0.61***	0.06
Postal voting					0.34**	0.09
Net transfers from EU					−0.22***	0.05
Constant	−0.01	0.14	−3.62***	0.45	−4.31***	0.53
R^2	0.037		0.250		0.273	
N	14,192		13,866		13,866	

Level of significance:
* $p < 0.05$
** $p < 0.01$
*** $p < 0.001$

Using this new dependent variable measure, Table 8.8 reports the consequences of estimating the equivalent of model 3 in Table 8.5 for all of Europe, for Western Europe, and for Eastern Europe. The results are decisive and easily interpreted. As in Tables 8.5–8.7, none of the EU-related attitude variables exerts a significant effect on this more specific measure of turnout/abstention. As with the more general models of turnout, EU-related attitudes fail to explain why some individuals who, on the basis of their national voting patterns, might be regarded as 'voters' fail to vote in European elections. Whatever it is that induces people to vote or abstain in EP elections, it appears not to involve their perceptions and assessments of the EU itself. Traditional

Table 8.7. Logistic regression with turnout in European elections as the dependent variable. Results for East European countries only

	Model 1		Model 2		Model 3	
	b	s.e.	b	s.e.	b	s.e.
EU efficacy	0.06**	0.02	0.04	0.02	0.03	0.02
General EU support	−0.02	0.04	−0.02	0.03	0.01	0.03
EU benefit	−0.04*	0.02	−0.03*	0.01	−0.02	0.02
Institutional trust EU	0.07*	0.03	−0.01	0.04	0.00	0.03
EU policy scope—current	−0.04	0.02	−0.03	0.03	−0.05	0.02
EU policy scope—future	0.02	0.02	0.03	0.03	0.04	0.03
Support future EU enlargements	−0.02	0.03	−0.02	0.03	−0.01	0.03
EU identity	0.25***	0.04	0.11**	0.03	0.06	0.03
Male			−0.06	0.15	0.02	0.15
Age			0.03***	0.00	0.03***	0.00
Education			0.42**	0.12	0.37**	0.12
Class			−0.17	0.12	−0.13	0.10
Religiosity			−0.05	0.06	0.07	0.04
Urbanization			0.04	0.05	0.07	0.04
Duty to vote			0.19***	0.03	0.20***	0.03
Left–right ideology			0.02	0.04	0.02	0.04
Strength PID			0.38***	0.06	0.37**	0.06
Media consumption			0.04*	0.01	0.04	0.02
Political sophistication			0.09*	0.03	0.09*	0.03
Internal efficacy			0.08*	0.03	0.08*	0.03
Non-electoral participation			0.04	0.04	0.05	0.04
General trust			0.07	0.03	0.04	0.04
National identity			−0.02	0.03	−0.02	0.03
Economic perception			−0.10	0.05	−0.01	0.02
Postal voting					−1.84***	0.40
Turnout last national election					0.13***	0.02
Net transfers from EU					−1.52***	0.41
Constant	−0.95*	0.38	−4.47***	1.11	−10.19***	1.62
R^2	0.076		0.316		0.355	
N	2312		2312		2312	

Level of significance:
* $p < 0.05$
** $p < 0.01$
*** $p < 0.001$

predictors of turnout such as party identification, civic duty, and increased opportunities to vote in terms of Sunday voting are far more important.

Conclusions

The main goal of this chapter has been to analyse whether the typology of EU-related attitudes developed in Chapter 2 has a significant impact on turnout in European Parliament elections or not. The bivariate analysis showed that voters in the countries of the EU-15 are more pro-European than non-voters. The same applies for voters in elections to the European and the national parliament, in contrast to those who cast a national ballot only. Findings for the East and Central European accession countries of 2004 are mixed. Voters in European elections in these countries are at the same time more and less positively oriented towards European integration in comparison with the respective reference group. These different results were the reason for separate analyses of West and East European countries in the remaining part of the chapter.

In spite of this separation, the regression analysis has clearly demonstrated that abstention in European elections is not caused by anti-European attitudes. If appropriate controls are applied for other micro- and macro-level variables, the effects of EU-related attitudes are either insignificant or very small. The only EU-related measure that has any empirical impact is the European identity scale, especially in Eastern Europe. Traditional explanatory variables of turnout, such as the perceived duty to vote, strength of party identification, political sophistication, media consumption, and age, prove to be much more important predictors of turnout. This proves the dominance of political cue variables and indicators of cognitive mobilization. All in all, the results of this chapter provide promising news for European policymakers and the European integration process. Low turnout is not caused by anti-European sentiments and an alienation from the political system of the EU among the citizens. The recent wave of Euroscepticism, culminating in the negative referendums in France, the Netherlands, and Ireland, is therefore not reflected in the reasons for abstention in European elections identified in the analysis of this chapter. However, European Parliament elections do not provide as much support and legitimation for the European project as they could do. In the long run, this could possibly have negative consequences for the European integration process, especially if low turnout promotes the electoral success of anti-European parties (as in the 2009 election). Thus, it is an important task for future political science research to keep track of turnout and its determinants at the European level.

For political scientists the results of this chapter can be interpreted in different ways. First, European citizens are satisfied with the integration process, with the main actors in the European arena, and with the outputs of the European political system. On this interpretation, which is consistent with the sort of output-oriented theory of elitist democracy articulated by Schumpeter (1942), low turnout rates could be taken to signify satisfaction with the EU project rather than disillusion with it. A second interpretation could be that turnout in European elections is low because the citizens think that they are not important and less is at stake compared to national elections. This would be a rather traditional explanation, which was already integrated into the second-order election model by Reif and Schmitt (1980). Third, differences between actual and reported turnout revealed a large degree of overreporting,

Table 8.8. Logistic regression comparing voters in European and national elections with voters in national elections only, in all Europe, Western Europe, Eastern Europe

	All Europe		Western Europe		Eastern Europe	
	b	s.e.	b	s.e.	b	s.e.
EU efficacy	0.00	0.02	−0.01	0.02	0.09*	0.03
General EU support	0.03	0.02	0.04	0.03	0.00	0.03
EU benefit	0.01	0.02	0.03	0.02	−0.05*	0.02
Institutional trust EU	0.00	0.03	0.01	0.04	0.01	0.04
EU policy scope—current	0.02	0.03	0.04	0.03	−0.04	0.03
EU policy scope—future	−0.02	0.03	−0.02	0.04	0.00	0.02
Support future EU enlargements	0.01	0.01	0.01	0.01	0.00	0.04
EU identity	0.04	0.03	0.02	0.02	0.07	0.04
Male	0.08	0.09	0.08	0.10	0.19	0.22
Age	0.02***	0.01	0.02***	0.01	0.02**	0.00
Education	0.12	0.07	0.09	0.07	0.18	0.12
Class	0.00	0.06	0.00	0.07	−0.08	0.19
Religiosity	−0.01	0.02	0.00	0.02	0.06*	0.03
Urbanization	−0.01	0.04	−0.04	0.05	0.13*	0.06
Duty to vote	0.14***	0.02	0.14***	0.02	0.13***	0.02
Left/Right	0.00	0.01	0.00	0.02	0.01	0.04
Strength PID	0.19*	0.07	0.19*	0.07	0.20*	0.08
Media consumption	0.06*	0.02	0.07*	0.02	0.03	0.03
Political sophistication	0.02	0.03	0.01	0.04	0.07	0.03
Internal efficacy	0.02	0.02	0.01	0.02	0.06	0.03
Non-electoral participation	0.04	0.03	0.04	0.03	0.09*	0.04
General trust	−0.01	0.03	−0.03	0.03	0.06	0.05
National identity	−0.01	0.03	0.00	0.04	−0.05	0.03
Economic perception	−0.15***	0.03	−0.15***	0.03	−0.02	0.07
Communist past	0.28	0.25				
Compulsory voting	2.05***	0.28	2.04***	0.30		
Sunday voting	0.71***	0.09	0.67***	0.09		
Postal voting	0.07	0.08	0.06	0.08	−1.51***	0.20
Turnout last National election					0.12***	0.01
Net transfers from EU	−0.27***	0.07	−0.29***	0.08	−1.08***	0.18
Constant	−2.65***	0.55	−2.48***	0.60	−7.80***	0.66
R²	0.166		0.172		0.206	
N	13,281		11,671		1611	

Level of significance:
* p < 0.05
** p < 0.01
*** p < 0.001

especially for elections at the European level. If respondents pretend to behave in a socially desirable way, it is also possible that they give socially desirable responses with respect to their attitudes. Since there is a widespread consensus on European integration in most member countries of the EU, it is possible that anti-Europeans do not reveal their real attitudes and behaviour in surveys. In addition, it is conceivable that anti-European non-voters do not participate in Europe-related surveys, so that it is almost impossible for political and behavioural research to catch them. Fourth and most important, it is obvious from the results of the preceding analysis that turnout is already explained by cognitive mobilization variables like media consumption and political sophistication, and political cues, such as strength of party identification, and the feeling of a duty to vote. There is thus no need to include Europe-specific attitudes in an analysis of electoral participation at the European level, because it does not matter for a respondent's decision to cast a ballot what s/he thinks about Europe. For electoral research this implies these variables can safely be omitted from the analysis of turnout in European elections, following Ockham's razor: *'Entia non sunt multiplicanda praeter necessitatem'*.

9

Towards an Integrated Model of EU Citizenship and Support

David Sanders, Paolo Bellucci, and Gábor Tóka

In previous chapters, we developed a series of models of different aspects of European citizenship, support, and participation. In Chapter 2, we analysed the structure of public attitudes towards European citizenship. The analysis showed that there were six distinct attitude sets, connected with European Identity, Representation, and Scope of Governance. In Chapters 4 to 6, we explored the explanatory capabilities of four broad theories about the sources of these attitude sets: 'hard', instrumental rationality; 'soft', cue-based rationality; 'identitarian' approaches; and 'cognitive mobilization'. In Chapter 7, we examined how far these theories, combined with the different dimensions of citizenship, were capable of explaining patterns of *support* for the EU as a whole. Chapter 8 examined the extent to which voting in elections for the European Parliament is affected by these various European orientations as opposed to other, more personal and country-specific factors.

In this chapter we try to join these various strands together. Our first main aim is to map out the overall pattern of relationships that has been reported in previous chapters. The second is to explore the connections among the three core dimensions of European citizenship. This latter exercise is important from both methodological and substantive perspectives. In methodological terms, we need to establish that the various assumptions made in earlier chapters about the endogeneity and exogeneity of certain key variables are actually justified. We do this by developing a multi-equation model that explicitly tests for reciprocal causation among our three key dimensions of citizenship—identity, representation, and scope. In substantive terms, we investigate the differential impacts that the three dimensions of citizenship have on each other. In addition, however, we also pursue one of the sub-themes that emerged in previous chapters—how political sophistication affects the way that Europeans think about their emerging polity.

The first part of this chapter reviews the four main explanatory theories that we have employed in previous sections of this book. It revisits the hypotheses that these theories generate about the sources of Identity, Representation, and Scope of Governance. Section 2 outlines the modelling logic that we employ in order to arrive at an integrated analysis of the sources, character, and consequences of European citizenship. Since we have at least three sets of simultaneous hypothesized causal effects, we adopt a three-stage-least-squares (3SLS) instrumental variables approach, using robust standard errors, to generate estimates of the various coefficient magnitudes. Section 3 presents our integrated model of the sources of, and interconnections among, European Identity, Representation, and Scope. It shows that there are significant two-way reciprocal linkages among all three citizenship dimensions. Section 4 shows how these different citizenship dimensions collectively relate to support for the EU as a whole—and how they appear *not* to relate to participation in European elections. The fifth section engages in a systematic exploration of the role played by political sophistication in all of the above. It shows that sophisticated EU citizens differ significantly from their unsophisticated counterparts in terms of the weight they accord to both 'cues' and identitarian factors in the determination of their citizenship attitudes.

The dimensions of EU citizenship and their hypothesized sources

The factor analysis that we reported in Chapter 2 showed that EU citizenship attitudes cluster in six distinct groupings: a single Identity factor; two Representation factors (Institutional Trust and Political Efficacy); and three Scope of Governance factors (EU policy competence now and in the future, and preference for extending the EU's geographical scope). In trying to explain why individuals differ in their attitudes along these six dimensions and in their patterns of support for the EU, we advanced four main sets of theoretical claims. The specific hypotheses that we derived from these various theories, together with the indicators used to operationalize each of them, are summarized in Table 9.1.

The first theoretical approach was what can be characterized as *'hard' instrumental rationality*. Derived from classical rational choice theory, this approach suggests that if people believe that they and/or their country have *on balance clearly benefited* from EU membership, then they are more likely to feel a sense of European *identity*, to believe that the EU effectively *represents* their political concerns, and to approve an extension of the EU's policy and geographical *scope*. A positive cost/benefit assessment will also make them more likely to

Table 9.1. Theories, hypotheses and signature variables in this chapter

---

'Hard' Instrumental Rationality Theory
- EU Identity, Representation, Scope, and Support vary positively with perceptions of benefits accruing from the EU
- *Signature variables:* EU Personal Benefits; EU National Benefits; Positive Economic Perceptions

'Soft' Heuristic or Cueing Rationality Theory
- EU Identity, Representation, Scope, and Support vary positively with *transfer* cueing
- *Signature variables:* National Institutional Confidence; National Parliament Trust; Government Trust; Left–Right Ideology; Identification with Pro-EU Political Party
- Identity, Representation, Scope, and Support vary negatively with *substitution* cueing
- *Signature variables:* National Institutional Confidence; National Parliament Trust; Government Trust

Affective/Identitarian Theory
- *Complementary multiple identities:* EU Identity, Representation, Scope, and Support vary positively with national and subnational identities
- *Competing identities:* EU Identity, Representation, Scope, and Support vary negatively with national and subnational identities
- *Signature variables:* National Identity; Regional Attachment; Local Attachment; Trust in Other Europeans

Cognitive Mobilization Theory
- EU Identity, Representation, Scope, and Support vary positively with Cognitive Mobilization
- *Signature variables:* Political Influence; Media Exposure; Political Sophistication; Social Trust; EU Visits; Non-Electoral Participation

---

express their general support for the EU 'project' as a whole. In all cases, the transmission mechanism that generates these expectations is simple. If I believe that both my country and I have benefited from EU membership, then I am more likely to want to preserve, or even enhance, those EU institutional arrangements that I believe have operated in my/my country's *interests*. This belief, in turn, will make me more positively disposed toward the EU in terms of identity, representation, and scope. It will, in short, endow me with a stronger overall sense of European citizenship and a greater willingness to express my general support for the EU itself.

A second theoretical position that we have employed relates to *'soft' cueing or heuristic rationality*. The key idea here is that many people have neither the time nor the interest to expend a great deal of effort acquiring the necessary knowledge about political objects that they either need or wish to evaluate. In these circumstances, these people use what has been described as 'low-information rationality' in order to make decisions. This involves people using heuristics or cognitive shortcuts in order to arrive at judgements that otherwise would be difficult to make. When confronted with a situation where they have limited information, 'soft rationality' utility-maximizers will typically take a 'cue' from an individual or institution with which they are familiar in order to arrive at a judgement. In deciding between political parties, for example, such people will frequently base their voting choices on their assessments of the party leaders, rather than on a detailed and considered analysis of rival party platforms. Similarly, when confronted with a potentially difficult or complex issue, such people typically take positions based on 'cues' provided by prominent individuals or, especially, political parties in which they have confidence.

We argued, across various chapters, that there are potentially a large number of 'cueing' mechanisms, or heuristics, that European citizens might employ in order to make sense of how they think and feel about the EU and its institutions. An obvious one is *party identification*. People who identify with a clearly pro-EU party, *absent other information*, are likely to take a cue from that party and in consequence to adopt pro-EU positions across a range of different attitude domains.[1] Equally, those who identify with 'Eurosceptic' parties, again absent other information, are likely to be 'cued' into a more anti-EU stance.

A second, related, heuristic is *left–right ideology*. Here, two rival hypotheses present themselves. From the 1950s through to the late 1970s, the EU was seen primarily as a project of the political centre. Antagonism towards the EEC/EC was strongest among those on the far right and the far left; the former because of fears that the EEC/EC was seriously weakening national identity and sovereignty; the latter because it was suspected that the EEC/EC was merely a 'capitalists' club'. Given that calculations of this sort can outlast the circumstances that bred them, it would be expected that ideological positions at either *extreme* of the left–right spectrum would cue individuals to adopt anti-EU attitudes and dispositions. A rival hypothesis reflects the changes that have overtaken Europe's far left and radical parties since the collapse of the Soviet Union. Since the early 1990s, far left organizations have tended to embrace the European project, seeing it increasingly as a vehicle for protecting workers' wages and conditions and for advancing the cause of human rights on the international stage. In these circumstances, ideology would be expected to cue low-information utility-maximizers in a simple linear fashion: the more right wing an individual, the more her/his ideological position should cue her/him to embrace broadly anti-EU attitudinal stances.

A further heuristic that we focused on was people's attitudes towards their own *national institutions*. Like ideology, this heuristic can in principle operate in different ways, implying two rival hypotheses. On the one hand, people who evaluate their own national institutions positively (negatively) may uncritically extend these positive evaluations to the supranational sphere and, as a result, also make positive (negative) evaluations of EU institutions. This *transfer effect* clearly implies a positive relationship between attitudes

---

[1] The 'absent other information' stipulation is important here since a strong Eurosceptic (Europhile) could clearly make her/his *choice* of party on the basis of a party's Eurosceptic or Europhile stance. In this case, it would clearly be the individual's EU stance that was determining her/his party allegiance, rather than the allegiance that was 'cueing' the individual's stance on a complex, low-information issue.

towards national and EU institutions. On the other hand, it is equally possible that people are likely to have more (less) confidence in EU institutions and processes precisely when they evaluate their own national institutions negatively (positively)—which implies a negative *substitution* relationship between attitudes towards national and EU institutions. The competing claims of these two hypotheses cannot be settled by theoretical argument, which is precisely why we subject them to empirical test here.

The third major theoretical approach that we have employed is the *affective/identitarian* model. Political, ethnic, and religious identities vary in importance across individuals, but they variously give meaning to social and political relationships—and sometimes strongly affect the way people think about their lives more generally. We analysed the meanings that people across Europe associate with European and national identities in Chapter 3. Our purpose in subsequent chapters was to explore the ways in which national, regional, and even local identities affected both the development of European identity and people's attitudes towards EU institutions and political processes—though in general, we found little role for either regional or local identities. As with some of the heuristics described above, the consideration of national identities in particular engenders rival hypotheses. Insofar as national and European identities are considered to be in competition with one another, it seems plausible to suppose that people with strong national identities will tend to be less likely to feel that their interests are represented by European institutions and less supportive of extensions of EU policy scope. This hypothesis clearly implies a *negative* correlation between national identity on the one hand and EU Representation and EU Scope of Governance on the other. Yet, if national and European identities are seen as complementary, as different aspects of *multiple* political identities, then a rather different conclusion emerges. In these circumstances, it is entirely possible that a strong sense of national identity can coexist with, and even reinforce, a strong sense of European identity, of feeling European. This hypothesis, in contrast, implies a positive correlation between national and European identities. We test both hypotheses explicitly below.

The final broad theoretical model that we use is *cognitive mobilization*. This approach has been used extensively in political science to explain a wide range of attitudes and behaviours, including turnout in elections, participation in protest activities, voluntary community activity, and even value change. The core idea is that people who are more interested in politics, more engaged with the news media, and better informed about political issues generally, will be more likely to participate in a wide range of political actions and be more open to new ideas and values. In the context of European citizenship and support, people who display relatively high levels of cognitive mobilization would be expected to be less *parochial* in their world views than those with low cognitive mobilization. The highly mobilized should be better placed to understand a complex project like the development of multilevel governance in the EU, and they should accordingly, other things being equal, be more likely to develop a sense of European citizenship and to support the idea of the EU.

These, then, were the four theoretical perspectives that guided much of the empirical analysis that we conducted in previous chapters. In the next section, where we combine the majority of our findings in a single encompassing model, we attempt to assess their relative explanatory power. The results suggest that, although all four theories play an important role, the single most powerful set of explanations derive from the 'soft rationality' cueing model.

The modelling logic employed

A key methodological difficulty that afflicts all empirical social science is the issue of 'endogeneity'. In essence, this problem derives from the possibility that, for almost any model, the predictor variables may not truly be 'independent' or 'exogenous'; they may, in fact, be themselves affected by the variable that is assumed to be dependent or 'endogenous'. Social scientists often circumvent this problem by a combination of theoretical reasoning and assumption. Analysts typically argue (a) that there are strong theoretical reasons for supposing that one variable depends on, or can be explained by, another and that therefore (b), for the purposes of engaging in any analysis at all, one variable can be *assumed* to be *de*pendent, and another (or others) assumed *in*dependent. This was very much the approach taken in earlier chapters of this volume. In the chapter on the sources of EU Identity, we *assumed* that perceptions of EU Representation and attitudes towards EU Scope could be treated as exogenous. Similarly, in the chapter on Representation, we *assumed* that both Identity and Scope measures could be treated as exogenous; and so on. In the EU Support and Turnout chapters, we *assumed* that all three citizenship dimensions—Identity, Representation, and Scope—could be regarded as exogenous. Had we not made these assumptions, it would have been difficult even to start to unpick the complex relationships among the various concepts involved.

But consider, now, what we know from earlier chapters about the various effects of Identity on Scope, of Scope on Identity, of Identity on Representation, and so on. It is clear from the results reported in these earlier chapters that all three dimensions of EU citizenship are reciprocally related; that there is a two-way causal linkage, net of all other estimated effects, between each pair of Identity, Representation, and Scope. We also know from Chapter 7 that measures of all three of these dimensions have important effects on Support for the EU itself. But is it not also possible that EU Support could have an effect on the development of EU Citizenship? After all, the sense of citizenship is something that is likely to develop or change over time. It does not seem unreasonable to argue, for example, that if I support the EU now, this feeling of support may of itself lead me to feel a greater sense of European identity in the future. In other words, there may be a feedback loop going back from EU Support to EU Identity—or, indeed, to either of the other two dimensions of citizenship that we have analysed.

With cross-sectional data—even with very rich cross-sectional data of the sort examined here—it is, of course, very difficult to assess these kinds of dynamic or reciprocal effects. However, it is not impossible. Instrumental variable techniques have been developed precisely for this purpose. Their underlying logic is that, instead of using the 'original', suspected endogenous predictor variable, Y, on the right-hand side of any given equation, this variable is instead 'instrumented', using a linear combination of other, genuinely exogenous, variables. This approach ensures that the error term from the equation where Y is instrumented is uncorrelated with the error term from the equation where Y is the dependent variable—a necessary, assumed feature of simultaneous equation models.

The most common form of instrumental variable estimation is two-stage-least-squares (2SLS). However, in situations where more than two variables are presumed to be endogenous—as with the relationships we analyse here—three-stage-least-squares (3SLS) is known to yield more robust parameter estimates than 2SLS. This is because 3SLS takes account of the observed error structure of the system of equations after the second-stage estimates have been produced. We accordingly estimate the system of equations outlined below with 3SLS.[2]

Note, however, that the specification and estimation of any system of simultaneous equations has to confront the issue of *identification*. This involves ensuring that there are sufficient independent pieces of information in the model for there to be a unique solution for estimating the coefficients. A system of equations can be 'identified' if it meets the 'rank' and 'order' conditions. It can be considered to meet these conditions if there is at least one (and preferably more) exogenous predictor variable(s) in each equation that (a) clearly has an effect on the dependent variable in question and (b) does not appear in any other equation. Variables with the qualities (a) and (b) are *identifying instruments*. Note, in addition, that practical constraints arise in

---

[2] STATA provides no standard facility for estimating robust standard errors (to reflect the clustering of data by country). In collaboration with Vera Troeger at the University of Essex, we sought to estimate a 3SLS solution to our equations with robust standard error estimates. The results (not reported) were not substantially different from those with standard 3SLS, particularly in relation to the effects of macro-level variables.

terms of the number of potentially reciprocal relationships that can be examined in any given system of equations. If there are two endogenous variables in a system, then there are only two potential reciprocal effects that need to be estimated. Unfortunately, the number of potential linkages grows geometrically every time a further endogenous variable is included in the system of equations. If there are three endogenous variables, there are six potential linkages; if there are four endogenous variables, twelve potential linkages; and so on. A further problem in this context is that the more linkages are estimated, the more unstable the coefficient estimates become—unless an increasing number of identifying instruments can be incorporated into the model. The practical difficulty here is that identifying instruments are not easy to find.

Because of this practical difficulty, we follow a *two-step procedure* for analysing possibly reciprocal relationships in our data. We begin by looking at the potentially reciprocal relationships among our three *theoretical* dimensions of EU citizenship—EU Identity, Representation, and Scope. Recall that the factor solution we estimated in Chapter 2 produced six statistical dimensions—one corresponding to Identity, two to Representation, and three to Scope. Even to estimate the interrelationships among Identity, Representation, and Scope, therefore, we are obliged to simplify this six-dimensional schema data by constructing new, uni-dimensional measures of Representation and Scope. We achieve this, first, by additively aggregating our two earlier measures of Representation—Institutional Trust and Efficacy—into a single 0–10 Representation Index. Second, we use the same additive approach to combine two of our earlier Scope measures—preferences for EU policy competence now and in the future—into a single 0–10 Scope Index.[3] This excludes the geographical scope dimension altogether, but we consider this omission to be justifiable on the grounds that this third aspect of scope is qualitatively different from the other policy competence aspects. These simplifications of the data (moving from six dimensions of citizenship to three) obviously imply some 'loss' of information. However, we believe that this is more than compensated for by the fact that we can now estimate a three-equation 3SLS model, rather than the six-equation 3SLS model that would have been required had we retained all six original citizenship dimensions.

The second step of the procedure involves a further simplification. If we were to try to model the potentially reciprocal connections among EU Support and each of the three simplified dimensions of citizenship, we would need to estimate a four-equation 3SLS model that incorporated no less than twelve

---

[3] All intercorrelations among the three dimensions are between 0.31 and 0.35, that is to say not particularly high, which reinforces our claim that they represent three distinct dimensions of European Citizenship.

reciprocal coefficients. Given the scarcity of suitable identifying instruments for such a model, we instead create a combined Citizenship Index, which involves additively aggregating all six empirical citizenship dimensions (Identity, Institutional Trust, Efficacy, Policy Scope Now, Policy Scope Future, and Geographical Scope) into a single scale. This allows us to specify a two-equation model (one for EU Support and one for EU Citizenship), in which each equation contains only one right-hand-side endogenous variable, and which is less demanding in terms of its requirements for identifying instruments.

Specifying a simultaneous three-equation model of identity, representation, and scope

Bearing in mind all of the preceding reasoning, the task of specifying a simultaneous equation model of the three theoretical dimensions of EU citizenship is relatively straightforward. We begin by specifying equations for Identity, Representation, and Scope that include the main predictor variables that were hypothesized to have significant effects in the models tested, respectively, in Chapters 4, 5, and 6. Thus, for example, the key independent variables examined in the models for EU Identity in Chapter 4 were the following:

- *'Hard' Instrumental Rationality theory*: EU Personal Benefits
- *'Soft' Cueing or Heuristic Rationality theory*: National Institutional Confidence, Identifies with Pro-EU Party, Left–Right ideology, Left–Right Extreme Position
- *Affective/Identitarian theory*: Attachment to Locality, Attachment to Region, National Identity, Trust in Other Europeans
- *Cognitive Mobilization theory*: Political Influence, Media Exposure, Political Sophistication, Social Trust, Visits to other EU countries, Non-electoral Participation

Each of these measures was included in the Identity equation of the three-equation model. Note that we *exclude* both micro/micro interactions (such as between Institutional Trust and Political Sophistication in Chapter 5) and cross-level predictors (interactions between micro and macro terms) because in a later section of this chapter we add a large number of additional cross-level predictors and micro/micro interactions so that we can *systematically* analyse the effects of political sophistication. Also *included* are the same sets of demographic control variables (male, age, age squared and education, plus Catholic/not religion) and macro-contextual variables (Communist Past, Quality of Governance, and Trade Openness) that had been included in the original single-equation models in Chapters 4–6. The same principles of including key predictor variables from Chapters 5 and 6, plus demographic and macro controls, were applied, respectively, to the Representation and Scope models.

Crucially, however, two other sets of variables were also included in the first-stage estimation of each equation in the combined model. First, in order to maximize the power of the first-stage estimates, a number of additional demographic variables (such as religion, religiosity, union membership, and employment status) were also included as predictor variables in all three equations. Second, we included all the *identifying instruments* from all three equations. This is standard practice since these instruments are by definition exogenous. We selected identifying instruments for each equation on the basis of theoretical relevance and empirical suitability as follows.

For the Identity equation, we used two measures that relate to respondents' understandings of the 'ascribed' and 'achieved' *meanings* of European identity that were described in Chapter 3. Our expectation was that both these measures would be significantly and positively related to EU Identity in the sense that individuals who respond more intensely to questions about either ascriptive or achieved criteria for 'being European' are more likely than 'weak' responders to think of themselves as European. As we show in section 3 below, these expectations were clearly supported by the data.

For the Representation equation, we used (a) the respondent's sense that it was her/his civic duty to vote in European elections and (b) whether or not s/he identified with the incumbent party (parties) in her/his own country. The reasoning underpinning (a) was that people who feel a stronger sense of European civic duty are also more likely to feel that they are represented by EU institutions. The reasoning underpinning (b) was that, as is well known, people who identify with the governing party(ies) are more likely to feel that they are represented domestically than those who do not, and it is clearly possible that this greater sense of representation could extend to the EU sphere.[4] If this reasoning is correct, then both civic duty and incumbent identification should be positively and significantly related to EU Representation. Again, the empirics that we report in section 3 below bear out both of these suppositions.

Finally, for the Scope equation, we used (a) the respondent's perception as to whether the process of globalization represents a serious threat and (b) her/his preference for 'Social Europe' which emphasizes social welfare provision, as opposed to an 'Economically Competitive Europe', which emphasizes market efficiency. The assumption in relation to (a) was that people who feared globalization would be more likely to see the EU as a protective device against globalization's more negative consequences and would therefore be more

---

[4] We code individuals who identify with the incumbent party (or parties) as + 1 and identifiers with other parties as –1. Non-identifiers are coded as 0.

likely to favour an extension of EU Policy Scope. In relation to (b) we assumed that those who favour Social Europe would see this as more likely if the EU's Policy Scope were to be extended. Again, therefore, we expected to observe significant, positive coefficients for both 'Globalization Threat' and 'Social Europe'—suppositions that were again borne out by the data, as we report below.

Table 9.2 summarizes the full model specification and list of predictors that we employed in our combined 'first-step' three-equation model.

Specifying a simultaneous two-equation model of EU citizenship and support

Recall that the model outlined in Table 9.2 only considers the reciprocal relationships among our three theoretical dimensions of EU Citizenship—Identity,

Table 9.2. Model specification for Three-Equation 3SLS Model

Identity Equation	Representation Equation	Scope Equation
Endogenous Citizenship Variables		
EU Representation	EU Identity	EU Identity
EU Scope	EU Scope	EU Representation
Exogenous Predictor Variables		
EU Personal Benefits	EU Personal Benefits	EU Personal Benefits
National Institutional Trust	EU National Benefits	EU National Benefits
Pro-EU Party Identifier	National Parliament Trust	National Institutional Trust
Left–Right Ideology	Government Trust	Pro-EU Party Identifier
National Identity	Pro-EU Party Identifier	Left–Right Ideology
Political Sophistication	Left–Right Ideology	National Identity
Media Exposure	Media Exposure	Media Exposure
Political Influence	Political Sophistication	Political Sophistication
Social Trust	Social Trust	
Visited EU Countries		
Non-Electoral Participation		
Demographic Control Variables		
Male	Male	Male
Age	Age	Age
Age Squared	Age Squared	Age Squared
Education	Education	Education
Catholic	Catholic	Catholic
Macro-Contextual Controls		
Communist Past	Communist Past	Communist Past
Quality of Governance	Quality of Governance	Quality of Governance
Trade Openness	Trade Openness	Trade Openness
Identifying Instrumental Variables		
EU Identity—Achieved	Civic Duty to Vote in European Elections	Globalization is a Threat
EU Identity—Ascriptive	Identification with Incumbent Governing Party	Social *versus* Competitive Europe

First-stage exogenous variables for all three equations are: Exogenous Predictor Variables, Demographic Control Variables, Macro-Contextual Variables, Identifying Instruments; plus Religiosity, Union membership, Other family member in Union, Household size, Born in country, Number of children, Urbanization, Urbanization squared, Orthodox, Protestant, Self-Employed, Married, Unemployed, Manual Worker

Representation, and Scope. Yet we showed in Chapter 7 that all three of these dimensions have effects on overall *support* for the EU. As noted above, given the limitations of existing data, it would have been a statistical step too far to try to estimate feedback effects from EU support to all of these individual dimensions of Citizenship. However, again as noted, by combining our measures of Identity, Representation, and Scope into a single Citizenship Index, the problem becomes more tractable. Using the same sort of logic that we employed in specifying the model in Table 9.2, we can also devise a testable model for estimating the reciprocal linkages between Citizenship and Support.

The Citizenship-Support model is summarized in Table 9.3. The Citizenship Index is a 0–10 scale constructed by adding together our six individual Identity, Representation, and Scope measures and dividing by six. The EU Support measure is a 0–10 scale in which low scores reflect the belief that the process of European integration has 'gone too far' and high scores the belief that the EU 'should be strengthened'.

As in the previous section, we develop our model specification on the basis of findings reported in previous chapters. First, for our *candidate predictors* in the EU Support equation, we include the key predictors that featured in the models of EU Support that were tested in Chapter 7. For the candidate predictors in the EU Citizenship equation, we include all the independent variables that had significant effects in any of the equations for Identity, Representation, and Scope from the Table 9.2 model that is reported below. The second set of exogenous variables consists of the same demographic controls (such as employment status) and macro-contextual variables (such as Quality of Governance) that were also included in the Table 9.2 model. The only addition is a cross-level interaction between Citizenship and Quality of Governance because in analyses not reported here we consistently found that the effects of the different citizenship dimensions are stronger in countries where the Quality of Governance is high. Third, each of the two equations contains a unique set of *identifying instruments*. For the Citizenship equation, we use the two European Identity meanings variables that we employed before, again with the expectation that they will be *positively* signed. However, since the Citizenship Index is broader than the original Identity measure, we also include the equivalent ascriptive and ascribed National Identity meanings variables. Our supposition here is that people who emphasize ascriptive or achieved criteria for 'being Italian' (or German or whatever) are *less* likely to think of themselves as European citizens, with the implication that these measures will be *negatively* signed. Finally, for the EU Support equation, we use two identifying instruments: the respondent's sense of duty to vote in European elections (with the expectation that this measure will be positively signed); and whether the respondent believes that her/his country's EU membership is a good thing, a bad thing, or neither. This latter variable is converted

Table 9.3. Model specification for Two-Equation 2SLS Model

EU Citizenship Equation	EU Support Equation
Endogenous Variable	
EU Support	EU Citizenship
Exogenous Predictor Variables	
Positive Economic Perceptions	Positive Economic Perceptions
EU Personal Benefits	EU Personal Benefits
EU National Benefits	EU National Benefits
National Institutional Trust	Pro-EU Party Identifier
Government Trust	Left–Right Ideology
Pro-EU Party Identifier	Left–Right Ideological Extremes
Left–Right Ideology	Social *versus* Competitive Europe
National Identity	Globalization is a Threat
Local Attachment	National Identity
Trust Other Europeans	Local Attachment
Political Influence	Political Sophistication
Media Exposure	Social Trust
Political Sophistication	
Social Trust	
Visited EU Countries	
Non-Electoral Participation	
Demographic Control Variables	
Male	Male
Age	Age
Age Squared	Age Squared
Education	Education
Catholic	Catholic
Macro-Contextual Controls	
Communist Past	Communist Past
Quality of Governance	Quality of Governance
Trade Openness	Trade Openness
Macro-Micro Interaction	
	EU Citizenship* Quality of Governance
Identifying Instrumental Variables	
EU Identity—Achieved	Voting in European Elections is Civic Duty
EU Identity—Ascriptive	EU Good Thing
National Identity—Achieved	EU Bad Thing
National Identity –Ascriptive	

First-stage exogenous variables for both equations as in Table 9.2.

into two dummies, EUGood and EUBad ('neither' is the reference category), with the expectation that EUGood will be *positively* signed and EUBad *negatively* signed. Again, as we report below, all these expectations for the signs on the identifying instruments were confirmed by the data.

Estimating a simultaneous model of EU identity, representation, and scope

Table 9.4 reports the results of our 3SLS model of EU Identity, Representation, and Scope. We do not report r-squared values as these are highly misleading

Table 9.4. Estimated model of the interactions between and sources of EU Identity, Representation, and Scope

	EU Identity		EU Representation		EU Scope	
	Coefficient	Std Error	Coefficient	Std Error	Coefficient	Std Error
Endogenous Predictor Variables						
EU Identity			0.27***	0.03	0.40***	0.03
EU Representation	0.45***	0.05			0.83***	0.05
EU Scope	0.53***	0.04	0.49***	0.03		
Instrumental Rationality Variables						
EU Personal Benefits	0.50***	0.04	0.17***	0.04	−0.48***	0.05
EU National Benefits			0.29***	0.04	−0.27***	0.04
Heuristic/Cueing Rationality Theory						
National Institutional Trust	−0.07***	0.02			−0.19***	0.02
National Parliament Trust			0.05***	0.00		
Government Trust			0.07***	0.00		
Pro-EU Party Identifier	−0.01	0.01	0.05***	0.01	−0.04**	0.01
Left–Right Ideology	0.01	0.01	0.02***	0.01	−0.04***	0.01
Affective/Identitarian Theory						
National Identity	0.10***	0.01			−0.06***	0.01
Cognitive Mobilization Theory						
Political Influence	0.01**	0.00				
Media Exposure	0.03***	0.01	−0.01	0.01	−0.01	0.01
Political Sophistication	0.10***	0.01	−0.04***	0.01	−0.03***	0.01
Social Trust	−0.04***	0.01	0.04***	0.01		
Visited EU Countries	0.04***	0.01				
Non-Electoral Participation	0.02***	0.00				
Demographic Control Variables						
Male	−0.13***	0.03	−0.17***	0.03	0.34***	0.03
Age	0.00	0.00	−0.03***	0.01	0.03***	0.01
Age Squared	−0.00	0.00	0.00***	0.00	−0.00***	0.00
Education	0.08***	0.02	−0.02	0.02	−0.03	0.02
Catholic	0.13***	0.03	−0.31***	0.03	0.28***	0.03
Macro-Contextual Control Variables						
Communist Past	0.02	0.06	0.12***	0.06	−0.16**	0.06
Quality of Governance	0.35***	0.03	0.19***	0.03	0.51***	0.03
Trade Openness	−0.00***	0.00	−0.00	0.00	0.00**	0.00
Identifying Instrumental Variables						
EU Identity—Achieved	0.06***	0.01				
EU Identity—Ascribed	0.02***	0.00				
Civic Duty to Vote in Euro Elections			0.01***	0.00		
Identification with Incumbent Party			0.05*	0.02		
Globalization is a Threat					0.04***	0.01
Social versus Competitive Europe					0.06***	0.01
Constant	0.68***	0.15	1.11***	0.12	−1.48***	0.17
Root mean squared error	1.83		1.80		2.21	

N = 16,133. Estimation by 3SLS, robust standard errors reported.
*** p = 0.001; ** p = 0.01; * p = 0.05

with 3SLS estimation, preferring instead to use the regression mean square error (rmse) as a measure of goodness of fit. The model enables us to explore two key themes: (a) the pattern of reciprocal interrelationships among the three key theoretical dimensions of Citizenship; and (b) the extent to which our four explanatory theories explain individual variations in Identity, Representation, and Support. We take each of these themes in turn.

The pattern of reciprocal relationships

The first three rows of coefficients in Table 9.4 report the effects of each pair of endogenous variables on the third. The three endogenous variables are all measured using the same 0–10 scale metric, so the magnitudes of the coefficients are directly comparable with one another. For example, in the Identity equation, Representation (b = 0.45) and Scope (b = 0.53) have significant positive effects of a similar size on people's sense of European Identity. It is clear, looking across all three columns of the table, that all the endogenous relationships are statistically significant and positively signed. It would have been odd if this had not been the case, given that all three endogenous measures are positively correlated with each other, but this simple observation nonetheless gives reassurance about the plausibility of the rest of the model. In substantive terms, it suggests a virtuous circle of causality in which feelings of Identity, Representation, and Scope reinforce one another in the minds of European mass publics. In methodological terms, it suggests that the iterative assumptions we made in earlier chapters about the endogeneity and exogeneity of our core dependent variables were justified (i.e. that the Representation and Scope variables were exogenous in the Identity equation; that the Identity and Scope terms were exogenous in the Representation equations; and that the Representation and Identity terms were exogenous in the Scope equations).

Figure 9.1 provides a summary of the pattern of endogenous effects shown in Table 9.4. The figure gives a clear indication of the dominant direction of each causal relationship. The effect of Representation on Identity (b = 0.45) is almost twice as strong as the effect of Identity on Representation (b = 0.27). Similarly, the effect of Representation on Scope (b = 0.83) is significantly larger than the effect of Scope on Representation (b = 0.49). Finally the effect of Scope on Identity (b = 0.53) is noticeably greater than the effect of Identity on Scope (b = 0.40). Taken as whole, this pattern suggests that people's sense of Representation is perhaps the most fundamental aspect of their sense of EU citizenship. Representation has much bigger effects on both Identity and Scope than either of them has on it. This is not to suggest that the other linkages are unimportant, merely that the most decisive role appears to be played by Representation. Factors that increase (or reduce) people's sense of

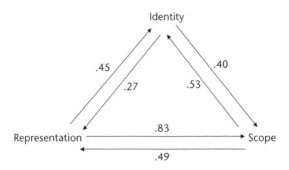

Figure 9.1. Reciprocal effects among EU Identity, Representation, and Scope (based on Table 9.4)

EU Identity or their preferences for EU Scope will clearly have indirect effects on Representation. But the 'virtuous circle' of European citizenship attitudes referred to above is most effectively activated by influencing people's sense of EU Representation—their belief that the EU *represents* them politically.

The merits of the four explanatory theories

The pattern of significant and, in general, correctly signed coefficients reported in Table 9.4 lends modest support to all four theoretical approaches referred to earlier. Note that these coefficient estimates now take full account of the reciprocal causal structure among Identity, Representation, and Scope, so that all observed exogenous predictor effects operate over and above the effects of the endogenous variables. Note also that the coefficients on the identifying instruments in all three equations are significant and correctly signed. In the Identity equation, both 'identity meaning' variables are significant and positive; in the Representation equation, election duty and incumbent identification have positive and significant effects; and in the Scope equation, the coefficients for 'globalization threat' and Social Europe are both positive and significant. This, again, is a reassuring confirmation that the model is well specified.

As Table 9.4 shows, each of the four theories has at least one 'signature variable' that has a significant effect in each of the three equations. So far, so good. However, the effects are rarely identical across equations, and on occasion they are even contradictory. This lends credence to our earlier claim that Identity, Representation, and Scope, though they collectively comprise 'Citizenship', are indeed distinct phenomena in their own right. They are *related*—as our discussion of the reciprocal linkages among them demonstrates—but they are *different*. Moreover, *they are moved by different things* and, on occasion, *moved by the same things in different ways*.

Consider, first, the impact of the 'hard rationality' terms that appear in each of the three equations. In the Identity equation, the EU Personal Benefits coefficient is large, significant, and positive (b = 0.50). In the Representation equation, the benefits terms are also significant and positive (b = 0.17 for EU Personal Benefits and b = 0.29 for EU National Benefits). However, in the Scope equation, although the benefits terms are significant, the *signs* on both of them are *negative*. It clearly makes sense for me to increase my identification with Europe and to feel that the EU's institutions represent my interests if I believe that I, or my country, have benefited from EU membership. It is less easy to see why the belief that the EU has produced benefits should lead me to prefer a *reduction* in the EU's Policy Scope. One possible explanation lies in the recognition that Scope really is different from the two other Citizenship dimensions. It contains an important forward-looking component, since in the policy areas that our survey asked about, the level of EU policy competence is relatively low. It is possible, therefore, that those people who believe that the EU has brought benefits to themselves and/or to their country also believe that it has done so precisely because its policy scope has been relatively modest—and they are consequently the very people who do *not* wish to see the EU's policy scope extended. In short, the status quo has produced benefits; long live the status quo. This may not be a straightforward kind of rationality, but it is still rationality of a sort. In any event, the significance of the 'hard rationality' terms in all three equations suggests that this form of reasoning plays an important role in the development of a sense of European citizenship.

A second set of terms in Table 9.4 concerns the 'signature variables' relating to 'soft', cueing rationality. Recall that, for some of these signature variables, there were 'rival hypotheses' suggested by different theoretical claims about the effects of the various 'cues'. With regard to respondents' *confidence in national institutions*, it was argued that there could be either a 'transfer' effect, in which people extended their national evaluations to EU processes and institutions, or a 'substitution' effect, in which they thought more positively of the EU if they lacked confidence in their own institutions. In the Identity and Scope equations, the national institutional confidence term produces a significant *negative* coefficient (respectively, b = −0.07 and b = −0.19), consistent with the substitution hypothesis. However, in the Representation equation the national institution signature variables—confidence in national parliament and trust in government—both produce significant *positive* coefficients (respectively, b = 0.05 and b = 0.07), consistent with the transfer hypothesis.

A similar ambiguity is also evident in relation to the role played by left–right ideology. In the Scope equation, the effect of left–right is significant and negative (b = –0.04), suggesting that *right*-wingers are, as predicted, less likely to favour an increase in the EU's policy scope. However, in the Identity equation, the left–right term is non-significant and in the Representation equation, it is significant and positively signed (b = 0.02), indicating that it is *left*-wingers who feel less represented by institutions. We cannot provide a definitive explanation for these differences. However, they again reflect the fact that the different dimensions of Citizenship are affected by different things. Indeed, it is perhaps unreasonable to expect Scope and Representation to be affected in the same way by ideology. They are, as we have repeatedly suggested, distinct phenomena. It simply appears to be the case empirically that left-leaning individuals tend to be more critical about Representation in the EU and right-leaning individuals more critical about the EU's Scope. It is possible that this reflects the different priorities accorded by the left and right to these two aspects of Citizenship, with the left paying more attention to issues of representation, and the right focusing more on issues of policy scope.

The final 'cueing' or 'heuristic' variable that yields significant effects is Identification with a Pro-EU Party. Again, however, the effects are not consistent. In the Representation equation, the party cue term is significant and positive (b = 0.05), but in the Scope equation it is significant and negative (b = −0.04). In the Identity equation, the party cue term does not achieve statistical significance. Again, there is no obvious, compelling reason why these differential effects should be observed. They do indicate, however, that the cueing effects of party identification on EU citizenship attitudes are by no means consistent across the different citizenship dimensions.

The third segment of Table 9.4 involves 'affective/identitarian' factors. Here, there is at least consistency in the way the endogenous EU Identity term yields positive and significant coefficients in the Representation and Scope equations (b = 0.32 and b = 0.38 respectively). However, the pattern of coefficients for the National Identity variable is again more wayward. In the Identity equation, the National Identity term is significant and positive (b = 0.10), lending support to the 'multiple identity' thesis that strong (and weak) national and European identities can happily coexist within the same individuals. In the Scope equation, however, the National Identity has a significant negative effect (b = −0.06), suggesting support for the rival hypothesis that European and national identities are in competition—and that more of one implies less of the other. This pattern again points up the distinctive character of the different dimensions of EU citizenship. In this case, while National Identity can readily coexist with, and even enhance, EU Identity, it appears to invoke a less favourable disposition towards EU Policy Scope.

The fourth set of theoretical claims is tested in the Cognitive Mobilization segment of Table 9.4. Here, again, the pattern is variegated. In the Identity equation, four of the Cognitive Mobilization terms (for political influence, media exposure, EU visits, and non-electoral participation) are significant and positive, as predicted. The fifth term, for social trust, is negative and significant. However, the overall balance confirms the claim that the more cognitively mobilized, because they are less parochial in their world views, are more likely to feel a sense of European Identity. Yet, when we turn to the Representation and Scope equations, this relative clarity dissolves. In the Representation equation, although the social trust term yields a significant positive sign (b = 0.04), the political sophistication coefficient is significant and negative (b = −0.04). And in the Scope equation, the only Cognitive Mobilization term—sophistication—is also negative (b = −0.03). Taken together, these results suggest that, while Cognitive Mobilization theory appears to work successfully for the sources of EU Identity, it works perversely or not at all in relation to Representation and Scope.

Finally, Table 9.4 reports coefficients for the demographic control variables and macro-level contextual variables. As with the substantive effects observed above, these effects vary from equation to equation. In all three equations, most of the demographic variables produce significant coefficients with plausible signs, though the effects of age are non-significant in the Identity equation and those of education non-significant in the Scope equation. The effects of the macro-level controls, however, are more varied. Communist Past is non-significant in the Identity equation but has a positive effect on Representation and a negative effect on Scope. Quality of Governance has a positive effect on both Identity and Representation but a negative effect on Scope. Trade Openness has positive effects on Identity and Scope, and no effect on Representation. Even at the macro level, therefore, we find more evidence that the different dimensions of citizenship are affected in different ways by the same exogenous variables.

Where does this leave us? Is it possible to discern a general pattern in this diverse set of empirical findings? The answer to this latter question is both 'no' and 'yes'. It is 'no' in the sense that we cannot offer an overarching theoretical account that explains why certain mechanisms appear to operate in some contexts and not in others, or why some variables appear to affect one citizenship dimension positively and another negatively. Yet the answer is also 'yes', in two senses: first, in that there are areas of *consistency* that tell important theoretical stories; and second, in that there is still an important general lesson that can be derived from the inconsistency and diversity that we have described. We deal briefly here with each of these in turn.

One important area of consistency is the account of European Identity that is furnished by the evidence reported in Table 9.4. The results reported show that European Identity grows as people have more confidence in the representativeness of EU institutions and as they develop a preference for EU Policy Competence. It grows as people rationally recognize the benefits of the EU (which evinces 'hard' rationality) and when people have limited confidence in their own national institutions ('soft *substitution* rationality'). A strong sense of European Identity can easily coexist with strong feelings of National Identity (the 'identitarian' approach), and it is even stronger among the 'cognitively mobilized'. In short, all four theoretical accounts contribute to the story of EU Identity formation in plausible ways.

Now consider the account of EU Representation provided by Table 9.4. Again, the sense of being represented grows with both EU Identity (evincing identitarian theory) and the belief that the EU's policy competence should expand. It grows with the rational recognition that the EU brings benefits (instrumental rationality) and with the cues provided by national institutions (soft *transfer* rationality) and by political parties (heuristic rationality). It is higher among people with higher levels of social trust (consistent with cognitive mobilization theory) though it is lower among the political sophisticated (which contradicts cognitive mobilization theory). Again, all four theoretical approaches make a contribution, though perhaps less decisively than in relation to Identity.

And what of Scope? Even here, the story provided is not implausible. Preferences for EU Policy Scope are clearly reinforced by both EU Identity and Representation. Scope preferences are lower among those who perceive benefits from the EU, but even this can be interpreted as a (hard, instrumental rational) response to the desire to preserve the policy competence status quo that has generated those perceived benefits. Scope preferences are also lower among those who value their own national institutions (soft *substitution* rationality) and among right-wingers (soft cueing rationality). A strong sense of national identity (affective/identitarian perspective) dampens preferences for EU Policy Scope since in some circumstances national attachments can clearly be in competition with European ones. Media exposure and political sophistication both reduce preferences for EU Scope, rather than increasing it, as cognitive mobilization theory would suggest. With the exception of cognitive mobilization theory, therefore, the theoretical models we outlined earlier all play a role in explaining preferences for EU Policy Scope.

The general lesson that can be derived from the irregularities and contradictions in all of these relationships is that, in the midst of overarching patterns, there is almost always inconsistency and even confusion. In trying to make sense of public attitudes towards the EU, there is always a temptation to see all EU orientations and attitudes as being driven by the same set of factors; to assume that if one exogenous variable affects one EU attitude in a particular way, then it will also affect others in the same way. We have shown here that this is not the case. Just as the EU itself is complex and multifaceted, so too are citizens' attitudes towards it. People's views about Europe are often uncertain, changing, inconsistent, variegated, and complicated—just like they are themselves. As we have repeatedly asserted, Identity, Representation, and Scope are all dimensions of the underlying notion of Citizenship. But they are all different. We should not be surprised if people's views in each domain are driven by different factors or even if the same factors have different consequences in different domains. People are rarely consistent in either their attitudes or behaviours. In their orientations towards European Citizenship, there is clear evidence that people do weigh different factors differently across domains. It is the task of future research to discover what drives these differences of emphasis.

EU citizenship, EU support, and European election voting

Table 9.5 estimates the reciprocal model of the relationship between EU Citizenship and Support that was specified in Table 9.3. Estimation is by 2SLS, with robust standard errors to take account of the clustering of cases by country. Both models are reasonably well determined and the identifying instruments in both equations are all significant and correctly signed. As anticipated, the coefficients on the endogenous variables indicate that EU Citizenship and EU Support are reciprocally related. The dominant effect is of Citizenship on Support (b = 0.94), though there is also a positive feedback effect of Support on Citizenship (b = 0.51).

Controlling for these reciprocal effects, what does Table 9.5 reveal about the explanatory relevance of the four theoretical accounts that we advanced earlier? Consider first the Citizenship equation. As with the separate models of Identity, Representation, and Scope that were estimated in the previous section, the results are by no means clear-cut—though they do tend to support the hard and soft rationality approaches. Citizenship is affected positively by perceptions of personal EU benefits (b = 0.24), indicating a clear role for 'hard' instrumental rationality. Citizenship is also cued positively by national institutional trust (b = 0.15) and (as predicted) negatively by left–right ideology (b = −0.03), all of which suggests support for heuristic 'soft' rationality. At the same time, however, trust in national government has a negative effect (b = −0.04), suggesting that national-level cues have mixed effects on EU Citizenship. The position with regard to identitarian factors is even weaker, with none of the three signature variables (National Identity, Local Attachment, and Trust Other Europeans) achieving statistical significance. Cognitive mobilization theory similarly derives no support from the Citizenship equation. Of the six candidate signature variables in the equation, five are non-significant, and the sixth (media exposure) is incorrectly signed. In short, the sense of EU Citizenship, insofar as it is not explained by Support for the EU itself, is largely the result of rational calculation on the part of European mass publics. They consider themselves EU citizens primarily because they see benefits accruing

Table 9.5. Estimated model of the interaction between and sources of EU Citizenship and EU Support

	EU Citizenship		EU Support	
	Coefficient	St. err.	Coefficient	St. err.
Endogenous Predictor Variables				
EU Support	0.51***	0.04		
EU Citizenship			0.94***	0.14
Instrumental Rationality Variables				
Positive Economic Perceptions	0.03	0.02	−0.02	0.02
EU Personal Benefits	0.26***	0.02	0.32*	0.13
EU National Benefits	0.06	0.06	−0.03	0.08
Heuristic/Cueing Rationality Theory				
National Institutional Trust	0.15***	0.02		
National Parliament Trust				
Government Trust	−0.04***	0.01		
Pro-EU Party Identifier	−0.03	0.02	0.06**	0.02
Left–Right Ideology	−0.03***	0.01	0.03*	0.01
Left–Right Ideological Extremes			0.01***	0.00
Social versus Competitive Europe			0.12	0.07
Globalization is a Threat			−0.12**	0.03
Affective/Identitarian Theory				
National Identity	0.02	0.02	−0.03	0.03
Local Attachment	−0.06	0.04	0.05	0.06
Trust Other Europeans	0.02	0.01		
Cognitive Mobilization Theory				
Political Influence	0.02	0.01		
Media Exposure	−0.01*	0.00		
Political Sophistication	0.02	0.01	−0.03*	0.01
Social Trust	−0.00	0.01	0.01	0.02
Visited EU Countries	−0.00	0.01		
Non-Electoral Participation	0.00	0.01		
Demographic Control Variables				
Male	0.06	0.03	0.00	0.06
Age	−0.00	0.01	−0.00	0.01
Age Squared	0.00	0.00	0.00	0.00
Education	0.02	0.02	0.01	0.03
Catholic	0.24	0.13	−0.19	0.10
Macro-Contextual Control Variables				
Communist Past	−0.51*	0.25	0.47*	0.22
Quality of Governance	−0.37*	0.15	−0.82	0.42
Trade Openness	0.00	0.00	−0.00	0.00
Identifying Instrumental Variables				
EU Identity—Achieved	0.04**	0.01		
EU Identity—Ascribed	0.03*	0.01		
National Identity—Achieved	−0.04**	0.01		
National Identity—Ascribed	−0.03**	0.01		
Civic Duty to Vote in Euro Elections			0.03*	0.01
EU a Good Thing (EUGood)			0.30**	0.10
EU a Bad Thing (EUBad)			−0.42**	0.12
Macro-Micro Interactions				
Citizenship*Quality of Governance			0.25**	0.08
Constant	4.18***	0.27	−3.86***	0.64
Rmse	1.41		2.45	

N = 16,133. Estimation by 2SLS, robust standard errors reported.
*** p = 0.001; ** p = 0.01; * p = 0.05

to themselves from the EU and because national institutional and ideological cues encourage them to think of themselves in terms of EU Citizenship.

Turning to the EU Support equation in Table 9.5, it is clear that by far the strongest effect is produced by the respondent's sense of EU Citizenship (b = 0.94). Note, however, that the *multiplicative interaction* between Citizenship and Quality of Governance is also positive and significant (b = 0.23), which indicates that the effect is even stronger in countries with high Quality of Governance. In relation to the four theories outlined above, the results are mixed. There is support for 'hard' rationality in the form of the significant positive coefficient for EU National Benefits (b = 0.32). 'Soft' rationality heuristics also feature significantly in the model. As expected, people who identify with pro-EU parties (b = 0.06) are more likely to support the EU. However, the signs on the Ideological Extremes (b = 0.01) and Globalization is a Threat (b = –0.12) terms are both in the opposite direction to that anticipated. These results suggest, respectively, that individuals on both the extreme right and extreme left are more likely than those in the centre to support the EU, and that those people who most fear globalization are the least likely to see the EU as a solution. These findings are clearly not consistent with particular soft rationality 'cueing' claims that were made earlier. However, given that these relatively modest 'reverse cueing' effects operate over and above the strong effects of Citizenship, their importance should not be exaggerated. When we consider the coefficients on the Identitarian and Cognitive Mobilization variables in the EU Support equation, the position is even weaker. Both of the Identity terms (National Identity and Local Attachment) and both of the Cognitive Mobilization terms (Social Trust and Political Sophistication) are non-significant. The Sophistication term is close to significance at conventional levels, but it is wrongly signed.

All of this goes to suggest that both EU Citizenship and EU Support, and the reciprocal relationship between them, is best explained by instrumental rational calculation and by heuristic cueing responses on the part of mass publics. In terms of rational calculation, Citizenship is most strongly influenced by perceptions of the *personal benefits* that accrue from the EU while Support is driven more by perceptions of *national benefits*. This difference perhaps reflects the fact that the notion of 'being a European citizen' involves *feelings* that are by definition *personal* whereas statements of support (or otherwise) for the EU itself are much more concerned with public policy discourses and their national and international consequences. In any event, the difference exists empirically and it certainly raises an interesting issue for future research. In terms of cueing heuristics, the results in Table 9.5 indicate that Citizenship attitudes are cued primarily by *ideological position* and by perceptions of *national institutional performance*, while EU Support is mainly influenced by the cues provided by respondents' *identifications* with pro- (or anti-) EU parties.

Explaining this difference is also a matter for further research. What perhaps requires less attention in future are the two theoretical perspectives—Identitarian and Cognitive Mobilization—that feature so feebly in the results reported in Table 9.5. On the basis of these findings, it must be concluded that neither of these perspectives, although they undoubtedly play a role in explaining EU Identity, Representation, and Scope, has much to offer in terms of explaining the *overarching* relationship between EU Citizenship and Support.

An aside: EU citizenship, support, and voting

The analyses we have attempted to synthesize so far in this chapter have focused exclusively on the relationships among different attitudes, preferences, and dispositions about the EU. As we noted in Chapter 1, however, we have also been concerned to establish if EU Identity, Representation, or Scope, or indeed support for the EU, affect European citizens' political *behaviour* in terms of whether or not people vote in European elections. Our analysis in Chapter 8 showed that in fact people's orientations towards Europe play no role whatsoever in their turnout decisions in such elections. On the contrary, our analysis confirmed the findings of earlier studies—that most people decide whether or not to vote in European elections almost exclusively on the basis of purely domestic political considerations.

But if Identity, Representation, Scope, and Support do not affect European election turnout, is it perhaps the case that the act of voting itself could reinforce any or all these orientations towards the EU? In other words, could participation in the EU democratic process strengthen people's feelings towards the EU itself?

We can explore this question very straightforwardly by making use of the model specifications that we developed and tested in the previous section. Since we know from Chapter 8 that voting in European elections is not affected by any of our Citizenship measures or by EU Support, we do not need to worry about possible 'endogeneity' effects if we simply add a series of EU voting terms to the model specifications described in Tables 9.2 and 9.3. As in Chapter 8, we use two measures of 'voting in European elections': one that simply distinguishes between people who voted in Europe and those who did not; and one that distinguishes between (a) people who voted in both national and European elections and (b) those who voted in national elections only—the latter group being 'voters' who abstain from voting in Europe.

The consequences of re-estimating the models reported in Tables 9.4 (for Identity, Representation, and Scope) and 9.5 (for Citizenship and Support) are summarized in Table 9.6. The table reports only the coefficients on the two measures of European election voting. The results are very easily interpreted. None of the coefficients is even close to statistical significance; in fact, for all

Table 9.6. The consequences of adding Voting in European Elections terms to the models in Table 9.4 and Table 9.5

	Voted in European Elections		Voted in National and European Election versus Voted only in National Election	
	b	St. err.	b	St. err.
Dependent Variable				
EU Identity (3SLS model)	0.04	0.04	0.01	0.06
EU Representation (3SLS model)	0.04	0.04	−0.01	0.05
EU Scope of Governance (3SLS model)	−0.08	0.05	0.01	0.07
EU Citizenship (2SLS model)	0.02	0.05	0.07	0.08
EU Support (2SLS model)	0.02	0.08	−0.04	0.11
N	15,128		12,539	

Table entries are regression coefficients with robust standard errors.
*** $p = 0.001$
** $p = 0.01$
* $p = 0.05$

but one of the ten effects the significance level is greater than 0.30. Quite simply, participating in European elections has *no effect whatever* on EU Citizenship, on any of its subdimensions, or on EU Support. In short, at least as far as voting is concerned, participating in the European democratic process has no effect on people's feelings about or evaluations of the European project.

The modifying/confounding role of political sophistication

One of the theoretical and empirical themes that emerged frequently in Chapters 4–7 was the tendency for political sophistication to interact significantly with other predictor variables, thereby producing differential-effect magnitudes for different levels of political sophistication. In the model specifications that we developed in sections 3 and 4 of this chapter, we deliberately avoided the inclusion of such interaction terms because here we engage in a *systematic* examination of political sophistication's potential confounding effects. Note that political sophistication is often presented as a component of the Cognitive Mobilization model that we concluded earlier did not display much explanatory power in relation to either EU Citizenship or Support. In this section we treat sophistication as a free-standing concept, divorced from its Cognitive Mobilization theory connotations. In testing systematically for political sophistication interaction effects, we are simply seeking to establish if, in terms of EU Citizenship attitudes and Support, thoughtful well-informed people calculate differently from less thoughtful and ill-informed people.

Our approach first involves distinguishing between politically 'sophisticated' and 'unsophisticated' respondents. Given that sophistication is measured on a 0–10 scale, we define 'sophisticated' as being above the midpoint (5) of the scale. This definition is less arbitrary than it might appear. The results we report below are virtually identical if cut-offs of 4, 5, 6, or 7 are employed to differentiate between sophisticated and unsophisticated individuals. With sophistication thus defined as a dummy variable, we then generate a series of multiplicative interaction terms between sophistication and each of the micro-level predictor variables used in the models shown in Tables 9.4 and 9.5. We then add each interaction term to the relevant model. If an interaction term is significant, this indicates that, for sophisticated respondents, the effect of the predictor variable in question is either greater (in the case of a positively signed interaction term) or lesser (in the case of a negative sign) than the effect for non-sophisticated respondents.

An illustrative example of the approach is described in Table 9.7. The core model of EU Identity is the same as that reported in the Identity column in Table 9.4. The coefficients of interest, however, are those on the sophistication interaction terms. The coefficient on the Personal Benefits* Sophistication interaction, for example, is significant and negative (b = –0.23). This does not mean, however, that the effect of Personal Benefits on Identity is *negative* for political sophisticates. Rather, this coefficient measures the *deviation* from the 'parent' Personal Benefits coefficient (which now measures the effect for the *un*sophisticated) of b = 0.62. This means that the net effect of Personal Benefits on Identity for sophisticates is b = 0.62 – 0.23 = 0.39. This is still a positive effect, but it implies that sophisticated individuals give less weight to instrumental rationality considerations in their feelings of European Identity than do their less sophisticated counterparts.

Rather than overburden the reader with all the details of these models, Table 9.8 summarizes the significant sophistication interaction effects that are produced by adding a full set of sophistication interactions to the models estimated in Tables 9.4 and 9.5. Table 9.8 also summarizes the magnitudes of the 'parent' effects for unsophisticated respondents and the consequent 'net effect' for sophisticates. The table suggests several conclusions. First, sophistication has only modest effects. It affects only two coefficients in the Identity model (*i.e.* two significant interactions), three in the Scope model, and two in Representation. The EU Support and Citizenship equations yield no significant interactions at all. In the case of the Citizenship equation, the loss of detail resulting from aggregating the separate Identity, Representation, and Scope measures clearly washes out the moderating effects of sophistication altogether. Second, for some variables, the parent term loses significance (see, for example, the parent coefficient for media exposure in the Representation equation). In these circumstances, it is reasonable to conclude that the observed effect operates only for the sophisticated, whereas for the unsophisticated the effect is zero. Third, in the Identity and Scope equations, the sophistication terms

Table 9.7. Estimated impact of Political Sophistication on coefficients in the 3SLS Model of EU Identity

	Parent Coefficient		Coefficient on Interaction between Independent Variable and Political Sophistication	
	Coefficient	St. err.	Coefficient	St. err.
Endogenous Predictor Variables				
EU Support	0.44***	0.05		
EU Scope	0.54***	0.04		
Instrumental Rationality Variables				
EU Personal Benefits	0.62***	0.05	−0.23***	0.06
Heuristic/Cueing Rationality Theory				
National Institutional Trust	−0.04*	0.02	−0.03	0.02
Pro-EU Party Identifier	−0.03	0.02	0.03	0.02
Left–Right Ideology	0.02*	0.01	−0.01	0.01
Affective/Identitarian Theory				
National Identity	0.08***	0.01	−0.02	0.01
Cognitive Mobilization Theory				
Political Influence	0.02**	0.01	−0.01	0.01
Media Exposure	0.02**	0.01	0.01	0.01
Political Sophistication	0.11***	0.01		
Social Trust	−0.04***	0.01	−0.01	0.01
Visited EU Countries	−0.05***	0.01	−0.02*	0.01
Non-Electoral Participation	0.02***	0.01	−0.01	0.01
Demographic Control Variables				
Male	−0.14***	0.03		
Age	0.00	0.00		
Age Squared	−0.00	0.00		
Education	0.08***	0.02		
Catholic	0.12***	0.03		
Macro-Contextual Control Variables				
Communist Past	0.03	0.06		
Quality of Governance	0.29***	0.04		
Trade Openness	−0.00***	0.00		
Identifying Instrumental Variables				
EU Identity—Achieved	0.06***	0.01		
EU Identity—Ascribed	0.02***	0.00		
Politically Sophisticated	−0.11	0.19		
Constant	0.68***	0.15		
Rmse	1.83			

N = 16,133. Estimation by 3SLS, robust standard errors reported.
*** p = 0.001
** p = 0.01
* p = 0.05

generally *attenuate* the effects of the parent variable. This can be seen by the fact that signs of the respective parent and interaction terms are almost always in the opposite direction in both these equations. For example, the parent National Institutional Trust term in the Scope equation is negative (b = −0.23) but the interaction for sophisticates is positive (b = 0.05), leading to an attenuated net effect for sophisticates of b = −0.18. There is one notable instance where this sort of sign reversal does not appear. In the Scope equation both the parent EU National Benefits coefficient and the interaction term are significant and negative, indicating that sophistication *exaggerates* the effects of the parent variable.

The overall message of Table 9.8, however, is that political sophistication has very modest mediating effects on the Identity, Representation, and Scope. Most of the net changes in coefficient magnitudes associated with the sophistication interaction terms are very small, and there appears to be no unifying logic that explains why the politically sophisticated and unsophisticated should differ in these various respects. The only major differences in coefficient magnitudes between the sophisticated and unsophisticated are for the EU Personal Benefits term in the Identity equation and the EU National Benefits term in the Scope equation. These two interaction effects, however, represent only two coefficients in three models that estimate a total of twenty-eight interaction parameters. Purely on the basis of chance, we might expect to find one large interaction effect in a model of this size. In these circumstances, probably the safest inference to draw from Table 9.8 is that the case for serious mediating effects on the part of political sophistication in the determination of EU attitudes remains 'not proven'. Sophistication occasionally modifies the way that people think about European citizenship and EU support but it does not do so in a robust or consistent way. Whether they are politically sophisticated or not, people tend to weigh the different factors that affect citizenship and support in more or less the same way.

Table 9.8. *Summary of significant Political Sophistication interaction terms in 3SLS Model of EU Identity, Representation, and Scope

	Coefficient for Politically Unsophisticated	Coefficient Change for Politically Sophisticated	Net Effect for Politically Sophisticated
Identity Equation			
EU Personal Benefits	0.62	−0.23	0.39
Visited EU Countries	0.05	−0.02	0.03
Representation Equation			
EU National Benefits	0.20	0.19	0.39
Media Exposure	0.01 (non-significant)	−0.03	−0.02
Scope Equation			
EU National Benefits	−0.15	−0.24	−0.39
National Institutional Trust	−0.23	0.05	−0.18
Media Exposure	−0.03	0.03	0.00
EU Support Equation	No interactions significant		
Citizenship Equation	No interactions significant		

Summary and conclusions

This chapter has covered a lot of ground. It could be concluded that, in trying to provide unifying and simplifying models of EU Citizenship and Support, we have merely added complexity to what was already a highly diverse and variegated canvass. We trust that this has not been the outcome of this chapter's modelling efforts. The analysis in this chapter is not intended in any sense to override either the detailed substantive findings—including the country-specific and East/West/South Europe regional analyses that we have presented—or the theoretical conclusions reached in previous chapters. Rather, it has constituted an attempt to provide both an overview of the general mechanisms that appear to operate in the different domains of European Citizenship and a general evaluation of the explanatory power of the rival theories that have been advanced to explain various aspects of people's orientations towards the EU.

The conclusions suggested by our analysis can be stated quite straightforwardly. First, as suggested in earlier chapters, there are causal links among the different dimensions of European Citizenship. European Identity, the sense that the EU represents the individual's interests, and people's preferences with regard to the Scope of EU Governance all interact with one another. In all of these reciprocal relationships, Representation has bigger effects on Identity and Scope than either of them has on Representation. This finding carries the implication that policymakers who wish to see the development of a broad sense of European citizenship would do well to focus on ways of convincing European mass publics that EU institutions can genuinely represent their interests.

A second and related conclusion is that, when the 'endogenous' links among Identity, Representation, and Scope are explicitly incorporated into the relevant statistical models, the four general theoretical perspectives that we have used throughout this volume to explore EU citizenship and support— instrumental rationality, heuristic rationality, affective/identitarian theory, and cognitive mobilization—all display some explanatory power. It is often the case with 'rival theories' in political science models that the 'rivals' offer a better explanation in combination than they do separately. This was certainly the case both with our separate models of Identity, Representation, and Scope, and when we combined these three separate dimensions in a single Citizenship scale. In all of our Citizenship models in Tables 9.4 and 9.5, 'signature' variables associated with each of the four theories exerted significant effects on the dependent variable in question. This said, the *largest* effects on citizenship, however we measured it, were consistently associated with the *instrumental rationality* and *heuristic rationality* signature variables. This tendency was particularly evident when we 'simplified' the citizenship measure by combining the Identity, Representation, and Scope measures into a single index. This is not to say that European mass publics are unaffected by identitarian or cognitive mobilization factors, but rather that they respond more, and more consistently, to instrumental calculation about personal and national interests and to heuristic 'cues' provided by national institutions, ideologies, and political parties.

The third conclusion concerns the relationship between EU Citizenship and Support. Here, again, we established that they are reciprocally connected—though the influence of Citizenship on Support is greater than the reverse effect. Crucially, as we showed in Table 9.5, when appropriate account is taken of the joint endogeneity of Citizenship and Support, support for the EU is driven primarily by considerations of National Benefits and by Party Cueing. In short, EU Support—like EU Citizenship—is driven primarily by instrumental and heuristic rationality.

Our fourth conclusion can be stated with similar brevity. In view of our findings in Chapter 8, which showed that voting in European elections is unaffected by our measures of either Citizenship or Support, we considered the possibility that the act of participation might itself influence either or both of these EU 'orientations'. We established clearly that it does not. When EU voting terms are added to any of our Citizenship or Support models, they invariably fail to exert any significant statistical effect.

Finally, we explored the potentially confounding role played by political sophistication in the genesis of public attitudes towards the EU. We found, as in earlier chapters, that although there are some discernible effects in particular contexts—for example, that the less sophisticated are more moved by perceptions of personal benefits in developing a sense of European Identity than are their sophisticated counterparts—these effects are far from widespread. Indeed, the relative paucity of confounding sophistication effects lends weight to the notion that sophisticated and unsophisticated people respond in very similar ways to the factors that drive European Citizenship and EU Support. This in turn supports the idea that a *single* model—albeit a relatively complex one of the sort presented in our 3SLS and 2SLS equations—is all that is needed in order to describe and explain the complexity that underpins the development of EU Citizenship and Support.

10

Conclusions

David Sanders, Paolo Bellucci, Gábor Tóka, and Mariano Torcal

It is widely acknowledged that the process of European integration was, from the outset, an elite-driven project. The Schuman Plan, which initiated the integration process in the early 1950s, was a conscious attempt by a small political elite to generate a set of economic and political conditions in which armed conflict in (at that time, Western) Europe would become impossible. At the heart of the project was the idea that, if elites could generate mechanisms of economic and political cooperation and construct appropriate supranational institutions to support this process, the world views of European mass publics would gradually shift from being exclusively focused on their own nation towards a greater awareness of the benefits of a unified economic space and stronger political cooperation. In the process, this would result in the development of a stronger sense of common interests, shared destiny, and joint identity centred on Europe. This was not to suggest that national identities would disappear, but rather, that they would increasingly be complemented by a sense of a wider, 'European' citizenship. In short, European mass publics would gradually come to think of themselves also as citizens of an emerging European *polis* and members of a single European *demos*. To this end, the introduction of direct elections to the European parliament in 1979 was intended to give European citizens a symbolic channel of participation in European affairs and allow them to seek accountability from the elites that were leading the process. It was also supposed to increase their sense of representation at the supranational level and increase their attachment to European institutions.

In an effort to further move citizens of member countries to see themselves as members of common European *demos*, all citizens of EU member state countries were formally accorded *legal* EU citizenship in 1993. Apart from its symbolic effect, this step awarded EU citizens a range of rights, including the freedom to settle and work across the EU and the right to vote for, and be represented by, local governments and MEPs in other member states. This step took place at a time when the 'permissive consensus' (Lindberg and Scheingold 1970; Wilgden and Feld 1976) between elites and masses, which had characterized the integration process since its inception in the 1950s began to weaken, and when European integration was becoming an increasingly politicized issue for mass publics in many member states (Katz 2001; Hooghe and Marks 2008). The increase in the scope and quantity of EU legislation, combined with the increased politicization of the EU integration process required the creation of more durable links between the European polity-in-the-making and the mass publics of its constituent states. Thus, as European integration has become less and less the preserve of national political elites, issues of attachment to the EU and the representativeness and accountability of its institutions have become increasingly important. In such a setting, the critical questions that remain are how far these 'legal' citizens feel that they are actually part of a functioning European political system and how much they *think* of themselves as EU citizens. In this volume, we have sought to answer three key questions. How widespread is this sense of European citizenship? What are its core drivers? And what consequences does it have, if any, for EU support and for active political participation in EU politics?

We begin this chapter by reviewing the way in which EU citizenship is conceptualized and measured throughout this volume. The following section outlines the main theoretical ideas that have informed our analysis. Section 3 summarizes the key specific empirical findings we have presented relating to the causal factors that underpin the development of EU citizenship, together with its main consequences. The final section discusses the general implications of these findings for understanding the development of EU citizenship. It also reflects on the stability of EU citizenship in the face of the economic crisis that afflicted the European and world economies during the course of 2008.

Conceptualizing and measuring European citizenship

Our central theoretical claim is that citizenship should not be conceived in uni-dimensional terms. If we wish to know the extent to which Europeans feel that they are citizens of an EU *polis*, it is not enough just to ask them if they view themselves as citizens of the European Union. To understand what citizens consider under this arguably vague notion, we need to understand what underpins the subjective feeling of being an EU citizen. Thus we need to take the abstract notion of EU citizenship and break it down into component parts, each of them more clearly defined conceptually and empirically measured. In this we follow Benhabib (2002) in distinguishing three distinct but related dimensions of citizenship. The first two—*identity* and *representation*—correspond to what would typically be expected of a sense of citizenship at the national level. The third—attitudes towards the *scope* of different levels of governance—is more explicitly related to questions of citizenship in the EU as complex polity.

The first dimension—identity—is probably the least contentious. Whether an individual is thinking of her/his national political system or of a developing supranational system like the EU, s/he needs to have a sense of common identity with other members of that system if s/he is to feel a sense of common citizenship. It is this shared identity, often linked to the idea of 'shared fate' at the national level, that is central to the development and maintenance of welfare state and progressive taxation policies typical of most advanced democracies, in which transfer payments are used to redistribute income (and sometimes wealth) across different socio-economic groups. Thus our simple supposition in this context is that, at the supranational level, a sense of European identity, as a feeling of belonging to a single community with a shared destiny and of having a sense of solidarity with its other members, is an essential precondition for the development of a full sense of European citizenship.

The second dimension of EU citizenship relates to people's sense that they are represented by a political system. The more they feel that the system effectively represents their values, interests, and concerns, the stronger their sense of citizenship. Again, it is easy to see how this might apply at both the national and the supranational level. Modern representative democracies provide citizens with opportunities at the national level to vote for (or to reject) political parties that aim and claim to represent their interests. To the extent that people believe that their individual and/or collective interests are represented by the governments that are duly elected, they are likely to feel a sense of citizenship towards their respective national political systems. At the EU level, where a long-standing 'democratic deficit' made it difficult for voters to hold EU policymakers directly to account, the same principles nonetheless apply. To the extent that mass publics consider that the political institutions of the EU effectively represent their interests, the more likely they are to consider themselves European citizens.

The third dimension in our conceptualization of European citizenship—policy scope—is perhaps less relevant in the context of *national* citizenship, since in most democracies (even in federal systems) it is usual practice for the national government to be ultimately responsible for the most important (if not all) areas of public policy. Indeed, in many national contexts, the question of the policy competence of the nation state is a non-issue. However, in the context of the European Union, there is a clear tension between the pre-existing policy competencies of national governments and the issue of extending the policy competencies of the EU itself. The question of EU policy scope accordingly acquires a distinctive importance for people's sense of European citizenship. People who wish to see a diminution of EU policy scope are likely to feel a weak or non-existent sense of EU citizenship; those who wish to see an extension of EU scope are more likely to think of themselves as citizens of that wider community. This does not mean that they do not continue to see themselves as national citizens; merely that such national citizenship is increasingly supplemented by a sense of belonging to a more extensive supranational *polis* as well.

With these distinctions in mind, we conducted a series of surveys across the EU that sought to capture the extent to which mass publics in different European countries thought of themselves in terms of European identity, representation, and policy scope. As we showed in Chapter 2, a factor analysis of some twenty-two different survey items covering these three areas indicates the existence of six distinct factors: one relating to European identity; two relating to representation (trust in EU institutions and personal political efficacy); and three relating to scope (preferences for EU policy scope now, for EU policy scope in the future, and for a geographical extension of the EU itself). Note, moreover, that these six empirical factors emerge no matter how the data are divided up—either by East/West Europe, by EU accession wave, or by demographic category. Crucially, the six empirical factors map very clearly onto our three conceptual dimensions of citizenship. The fact that the dimensions are empirically distinct from one another reinforces the idea that they need to be differentiated from one another theoretically. It supports the idea that European citizenship should be conceptualized in multidimensional terms, such that different individuals can display different patterns of citizenship depending on their positions in a three-dimensional space, the axes of which are defined by their sense of EU identity, EU representation, and EU scope. In principle, it is possible for individuals to be located at any point in this space—even though there might be strong clusters of individuals in particular sectors. The importance of this observation is that, in line with our theoretical distinctions, European mass publics appear to differentiate among identity, representation, and scope. An important consequence of this differentiation, as we show below, is that Europeans' views on identity, representation and policy scope are driven by different (though partially overlapping) sets of predictors.

What does our analysis reveal about the strength of European Citizenship across the EU? Table 10.1 provides a summary answer. It reports the average scores for EU Identity, Representation, and Scope—and for the summary measure of EU Citizenship—on our 0–10 'constant range' scales.

The average scores for the whole sample suggest that levels of European Identity (4.84) and preferences for EU Policy Scope (4.83) are slightly higher

Table 10.1. Mean scores on 0–10 scales, EU and National Citizenship measures

Accession Wave	EU Identity	EU Representation	EU Policy Scope	EU Citizenship	National Identity	National Representation
Founder	5.12	4.58	4.82	4.84	7.64	4.64
Join 1970s	4.63	4.44	3.96	4.34	7.31	5.26
Join 1980s	5.13	4.74	5.44	5.10	7.79	4.48
Join 1994 +	4.60	4.23	4.85	4.56	8.23	4.14
All	4.83	4.44	4.84	4.70	7.89	4.46

Total N = 16,133; for Founders, N = 4023; for Join 1970s, N = 2000; for Join 1980s ('Southern Wave'), N = 3002; for Join 1994 +, N = 7108

than the average sense of EU Representation (4.44). However, the differences are not particularly marked, and they collectively produce an EU Citizenship average score of 4.70. The question that arises, of course, is whether the glass is half full or half empty—whether figures at this sort of level imply a relatively strong or a relatively moderate or even a relatively weak sense of EU citizenship. To throw light on this issue, the table also reports the average levels of National Identity and sense of National Representation, both measured on the same 0–10 constant range scales. The average National Identity score is 7.89—substantially higher than the equivalent European measure. The average National Representation score, however, is only 4.46—virtually identical to the EU Representation average score of 4.44. These comparisons collectively suggest that, although the sense of European Identity is still not particularly well developed, average confidence in European political institutions is just as high as confidence in their national counterparts. Each citizen can easily assess relatively whether s/he feels attachment to Europe or not, whereas it is not so easy to establish if one's interests are adequately represented by a particular level of governance in a multilevel political system.[1] All of this implies that the glass of EU citizenship is perhaps best regarded as half full rather than half empty.

Note, finally, that Table 10.1 also reports the variations in the various average citizenship measures by EU Accession Wave. These figures are reported simply to reiterate a point that has been made in successive chapters. There is no systematic connection between the length of time that countries have belonged to the EU and the average levels of EU citizenship recorded by their populations. The average highest levels of EU Identity, Representation, and Scope are registered in the Southern Wave accession states (Greece, Spain,

---

[1] As discussed in Chapter 5 of the present volume, the similarity of national supranational representation scores could be the result of a transfer of evaluations from national institutions, or the consequence of a tendency to evaluate national and European institutions as a single institutional set. This might further indicate that citizens are willing to accept European institutions and treat them as an equal part of the governance package.

and Portugal), which joined in the 1980s; the lowest are found in the countries that joined in the 1970s (in our sample, Britain and Denmark). Although the average scores are also relatively high in the founding member states, it is clear that length of membership alone cannot explain the cross-national variations in our EU citizenship measures.[2] The task of the contributing chapters in this volume was to establish the factors that do account for variations in the positions of EU mass publics on various citizenship dimensions, using the theoretical framework reviewed below.

Towards explanation: theoretical perspectives

In a companion volume to the present study, we report evidence which shows that levels of European identity, sense of EU representation and preferences for EU policy scope among European mass publics did not trend strongly in any particular direction during the period between 1975 and 2007 (Sanders et al. forthcoming-a). There are nonetheless interesting variations in these measures of EU citizenship both across individuals and across countries that were described in detail in earlier chapters—and these variations clearly require explanation. The substantive chapters of this book have used a range of theoretical perspectives to generate testable hypotheses about the sources of the different phenomena that they have respectively sought to explain. Four main perspectives have been employed: 'hard' instrumental rationality; 'soft' cueing rationality; identitarian attachment; and cognitive mobilization. Here, we briefly review the core theoretical claims of each of these perspectives and illustrate the ways in which our substantive chapters employed them in their analyses.

'Hard' instrumental rationality

The idea that people's views and preferences reflect rational, 'economic' calculations about their own or their countries' interests is widespread in the analysis of public attitude formation and change. Instrumental (economic or institutional) rationality assumes that, when faced with a choice, people will weigh the perceived costs and benefits of each option in order to judge between them (Gabel 1998c; Anderson and Reichert 1996; Tucker, Pacek, and Berinsky 2002; Hix 2007). Since it is difficult directly to observe people engaging in this kind of 'weighing' activity, individual- and aggregate-level research typically has to make assumptions in order to test for the effects of

---

[2] For a similar argument see (Sanders et al. forthcoming-a).

instrumental rationality. In Chapters 4 (European Identity), 5 (EU Representation), 6 (EU Policy Scope), 7 (EU Support) and 9 (Combined Model) individual-level tests are conducted which assume that instrumental rationality can be operationalized by examining people's beliefs about the relative costs and benefits (economic or political) that have accrued either to them personally or to their respective countries as a result of EU membership. The simple empirical proposition tested is that those who believe that either they or their country have benefited will be more likely to take a pro-European stance than those who believe otherwise.

'Soft' cueing rationality

In recent years, rational choice analysts have increasingly recognized the possibility that individuals with access to very limited information might still behave rationally, by using heuristics or 'cognitive shortcuts' in order to make decisions (Lau and Redlawsk 2001). They might, in short, use 'cues' with which they are relatively familiar in order to make judgements about issues and objects with which they are relatively unfamiliar. In electoral research, one classic heuristic or cue for individuals who have neither the time nor inclination to familiarize themselves with the detailed policy stances of rival parties is to focus on the likely managerial capabilities of rival party leaders (Clarke et al. 2004, 2009). There are two main sorts of cueing effect that relate to mass attitudes towards the EU: *substitution* and *transfer* cueing. Substitution cueing occurs when an individual evaluates domestic institutional performance negatively (positively) and therefore assumes that it would be desirable (undesirable) for more (fewer) decision-making powers to be ceded to supranational institutions (Kritzinger 2003; Christin 2005). Reasoning of this sort is assumed to operate in Chapter 6, where it is hypothesized that trust in national institutions has a negative effect on EU policy scope. The core idea is that if things are badly run at home, people are more likely to look to Europe; if they are well run at home, Europe is not so important. The second type of cueing is 'transfer cueing'. This sort of cueing is based on the idea that people who evaluate their own national institutions positively (negatively) may uncritically extend these positive (negative) evaluations to the supranational sphere and, as a result, also make positive (negative) evaluations of EU institutions (Anderson 1998). In contrast to substitution cueing, this *transfer effect* clearly implies a *positive* relationship between attitudes towards national and EU institutions. This sort of transfer effect is hypothesized to operate in Chapters 5 and 7, where trust in domestic political institutions is hypothesised to have a positive cueing effect, respectively, on people's sense of EU representation and on general support for the EU. Transfer cueing is also hypothesized to operate in Chapter 5, where people's identification with a pro-EU political party is considered to contribute positively to their evaluations of EU political institutions: people are more likely to feel that the EU represents their interests if they identify with a party that adopts a broadly pro-EU stance (Ray 2003a; Steenbergen, Edwards, and de Vries 2007).

In addition to all of these individual-level cueing effects, our analysis considered the possible cueing effects of a key macro-level country characteristic (Brinegar and Jolly 2005; Christin 2005)—the Quality of Governance, a measure that combines a number of features of domestic political systems, including (the absence of) corruption and the transparency of decision-making. Two rival sets of hypotheses were identified in relation to this variable in Chapters 4 to 7. On the one hand, following the logic of substitution cueing, Quality of Governance could be negatively associated with the various EU citizenship measures, on the grounds that people living in countries with poor governance are more likely to assume that 'things are better' at the European level. On the other hand, following the logic of transfer cueing, Quality of Governance could have a positive effect on EU citizenship, on the grounds that people living in countries with sound governance are more likely to assume that their domestic experience will be reproduced at the European level (see for instance Chapter 5). Given that both hypotheses have some *a priori* plausibility, both were tested, either explicitly or implicitly, in the empirical analysis conducted in the various substantive chapters.

Affective/identitarian factors

The suggestion that people might have affective feelings towards political objects that can influence their attitudes and preferences just as strongly as rational calculations is neither novel nor contentious. It is clear from a large number of psychological and attitudinal studies that people's feelings and sense of political and social identity can have profound effects on their political attitudes and choices, especially when lack of information obliges citizens to fall back on these basic attitudes when they make up their minds (Zaller 1992). The notion of identity has been widely used in analyses of EU attitudes (McLaren 2002; Carey 2002; Luedtke 2005) and it is used in two contrasting ways in the chapters in this volume. In Chapter 4, national and European identities are seen as complementary. A strong sense of national identity constitutes a positive resource that can coexist with, and even strengthen the development of, a *European identity*. National identity is accordingly predicted to have a positive effect on European identity. In contrast, in Chapter 6, a strong sense of national identity is regarded as a constraint on people's preferences with regard to EU policy competence; in this latter context, national identity is predicted to have a negative effect on *EU policy scope*.

Cognitive mobilization

The basic claim of cognitive mobilization theory is that, as people become more informed about politics through greater education and exposure to political information (the latter often through the mass media), they are more likely to take a more progressive, cosmopolitan view of politics, policy, and political institutions (Inglehart 1970). Inglehart used cognitive mobilization theory in order to explain the developing sense of European identity that was emerging during the 1960s, arguing that rising levels of cognitive mobilization—of education and knowledge—were stimulating an increase in support for the then EEC. This core idea is used in two of the chapters here—in the discussion of the sources of European Identity in Chapter 4 and in the discussion of EU Support in Chapter 5. Both chapters explore the extent to which educated and informed individuals exhibit stronger EU orientations than their less educated and uninformed counterparts. This theme is taken up more explicitly in Chapter 9, in the discussion of the potentially confounding role of 'political sophistication'. A related argument is presented in Chapter 5, which tests the proposition that instrumental calculation plays a more important role in the determination of trust in the European Parliament among people with relatively high levels of political awareness.

It is clear from the foregoing discussion that a range of theoretical perspectives has been used in a diverse set of ways in different chapters. We regard this eclectic approach as entirely appropriate. The phenomena that the different chapters seek to analyse, though often empirically related, are conceptually distinct. It would be decidedly odd if a single theoretical perspective—or even a single set of perspectives—could satisfactorily account for all of the individual and cross-national variation that we have described in our substantive chapters. In the next section, we offer a summary account of the major factors that our analysis suggests are responsible for individual- and country-level variations both in EU Citizenship attitudes and in EU Support. As we will see, although the various theories outlined above all play a role, they by no means provide—even in combination—a full explanation of the complex and diverse pattern of variation that we have outlined.

Empirics: the sources of EU citizenship

Because we provided, in Chapter 9, a summarizing, 'combined' model of the different empirical effects observed in earlier chapters, we can be relatively brief here in outlining the main empirical findings about the causes and consequences of EU Citizenship that emerge from our study. The first set of findings that merits attention concerns the interlinkages among the three dimensions of citizenship itself. As discussed in Chapter 9, although EU Identity, Representation, and Scope are all reciprocally related, some of the linkages among them are stronger than others. Figure 10.1 reprises Figure 9.1. The coefficient magnitudes reported in the figure are all directly comparable with each other since the variables are all measured on the same 0–10 scale. The implications of the figure are clear. The effects that Representation has on both Identity and Scope are almost twice as large as the effects that they exert on Representation. As we suggested in Chapter 9, this implies that it is the representation dimension that is key to the development of a generalized sense of citizenship at the EU level. This in turn places a significant premium on the need to address popular doubts about the EU's 'democratic deficit'. Without a greater sense that the EU effectively represents their interests, European mass publics will be reluctant either to strengthen their identification with Europe or to approve an extension of EU policy competence. In short, they will be unprepared to think of themselves as genuine citizens of a functioning European-wide *polis*.

The second set of core findings that requires brief review relates to the main factors that drive each of our three component dimensions of EU citizenship, over and above the reciprocal effects that they exert on each other. Our analysis of *European Identity* shows that it is affected by factors associated with all four of the theoretical approaches outlined earlier. The positive effects of perceptions of *personal benefits* accruing from EU membership show that Identity is in part a reflection of 'hard' rational calculation. The negative effects of *national institutional trust* indicate that there is also a role for 'soft' rationality 'substitution cueing'.[3]

The positive effects of *national identity* on European Identity support the idea advanced earlier that national and European identities are complementary rather than in competition. Finally, we find that European Identity is also positively affected by cognitive mobilization. As Inglehart argued some forty years ago, more informed, interested, and educated Europeans are more likely to identify themselves as 'European'. But if the sources of Identity lend credence to all four of our theoretical perspectives, the same cannot be said of EU Representation. Here, only rational calculation, in both its 'hard' and 'soft'

---

[3] We should point out here that this negative relationship between Trust in National Institutions and EU Identity only appears in models that also include Trust in EU institutions as a controlling variable. Trust in *national* institutions has a clear positive effect on EU identity through trust in *EU* institutions (see Chapter 6). However, when trust in EU institutions is included in the model, national institutional trust has also a small negative direct effect on EU Identity (see Chapter 4 and this concluding chapter). This implies that Trust in National Institutions, when not transferred into Trust in EU institutions, does indeed have a small negative effect on EU identity. To put it another way, *supranational attitudinal transferring* is the dominant cueing mechanism that we observe, but there is also a modest amount of *attitudinal substitution* as well.

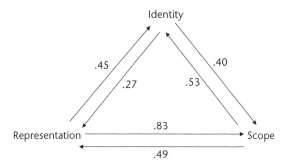

Figure 10.1. Reciprocal effects among EU Identity, Representation, and Scope (based on Table 9.4)

forms, seems to play a role. Our analysis of EU Representation suggests, first, that it is positively affected by instrumental calculations about the *benefits to the individual's country* that derive from EU membership (though this relationship is conditioned by levels of political awareness). Second, Representation is also affected positively by two 'transfer-cueing' mechanisms: higher levels of *national institutional trust* and *identification with a pro-EU political party* also translate into a stronger sense of EU Representation. Finally, our analysis of EU Scope demonstrates a role for both instrumental-rational and identitarian factors. In terms of 'hard' rationality, perceptions of both *national* and *personal benefits* from EU membership have *negative* effects on Scope. We interpret this finding as indicating the distinctiveness of mass publics' views about EU Policy Scope, as opposed to Identity and Representation. This in turn reflects the likelihood that individuals who perceive that the EU has benefited them and/or their countries also want to preserve the status quo position on EU policy competence that generated the benefits from EU membership in the first place. In terms of 'soft' rationality, Scope is also affected, negatively, by *national institutional trust*—a classic example of substitution cueing, in which people who believe that their own national institutions are ineffective place a greater trust in those of the EU. Lastly, Scope is influenced negatively by *national identity*: those individuals who strongly identify with their national political systems are less likely to favour either current levels of EU policy competence or to support an extension of EU competence to new policy areas.

One issue that arises from these different patterns of effect is why 'substitution' cues appear to operate in some contexts while 'transfer' cues operate in others. One possible response is to observe simply that people are inconsistent and that there does not have to be a particular reason or set of reasons why they take one sort of cue in one context and a different sort in another. However, we can take the argument a little further. We suspect that the predominance of substitution cueing in relation to Scope and the predominance of transfer cueing in relation to Identity and Representation reflect a fundamental difference in the way that people think about these different aspects of EU Citizenship. Identities—whether they are national, European, subnational, religious, or whatever—are not really in competition with each other. They can coexist precisely because people can carry multiple social and political identities, just as they can perform multiple social and economic roles—as daughter, mother, consumer, employer, worshipper, patient, and so on. Identities, in short, are not in a zero sum relation with one another. On the contrary, they are in a variable sum relationship. I can be Umbrian, Italian, and European without any contradiction. The same general position holds for Representation. It is perfectly possible (though obviously not necessarily the case) that my interests can be 'represented' effectively by several different levels of governance simultaneously—local, regional, national, and even supranational. Again, these different levels of representation are not in a zero sum competition with one another in terms of representing my interests. Now, consider the contrasting question of Policy Scope. Here, the position is much more akin to a zero sum competition. If one level of governance is competent in a given policy area, then the other level(s) *cannot* be. Individuals know, therefore, that if they prioritize one governance level, then they must downgrade another or others. It follows from all this that substitution cueing is much more likely in situations of zero sum competition, where discreet choices have to be made. In contrast, where choices can be avoided—in variable sum situations—transfer cueing is more likely to be the norm. Identity and Representation develop in variable sum contexts in which national-level and EU-level considerations are not mutually exclusive; Identity and Representation are accordingly affected primarily by transfer cueing. Scope perceptions, in contrast, develop in zero sum contexts and hence substitution cueing predominates.

Our final set of empirical findings relate to the *consequences* of EU Citizenship. The results of our models here are very clear. General Support for the EU itself is strongly influenced by the extent of people's sense of European Citizenship, where Citizenship is conceived as an aggregation of the individual's scores on EU Identity, Representation, and Scope. In addition, there is a feedback effect from Support to Citizenship—if I support the EU, I am more likely to feel a strong sense of EU citizenship—but it is nothing like as strong as the effect of Citizenship on Support. In terms of *exogenous* effects on Support, we find evidence of both 'hard' and 'soft' rationality. Instrumental calculation features strongly in our Support models, with perceptions of *personal benefits* from EU membership exerting a powerful positive effect. Transfer cueing also strongly affects support, with *national institutional trust* displaying a similar positive effect. As with Identity and Representation, EU Support is in a non-zero sum relation with, for example, national government support, so transfer (rather than substitution) cueing makes very good sense in this context.

But if EU Support is influenced by EU Citizenship, the same cannot be said for its behavioural counterpart, turnout in European elections. Our empirical results here, reported in detail in Chapter 8, demonstrate comprehensively that people's orientations towards the EU have no impact whatsoever on their inclination to vote in elections to the European Parliament (EP). The decision whether or not to cast an EP vote is driven much more by domestic political considerations—including the factors that move people to vote in national elections—than by anything related to the EU. It is sometimes thought the simple act of participating in the political process can change the way people think and feel about the political systems to which they belong. The evidence that we reported in Chapter 9 suggests that this is certainly not the case in relation to voting in EP elections. Our models show that such voting has no effect on EU Support, on our aggregate measure of EU Citizenship, or any of the three constituent dimensions (Identity, Representation, and Scope) of that Citizenship. MEPs may well feel that the more people vote in European elections, the greater the legitimacy of the decisions that the Parliament takes. However, they should not delude themselves into thinking that this participation in itself signifies anything very much—or that it will contribute significantly to the development of a sense of EU Citizenship among EU citizens.

Conclusions

Throughout this volume, we have sought to describe and analyse the individual- and country-level variations in the citizenship perceptions of EU mass publics. There are, of course, significant variations at both levels. The populations of some countries—like the UK and Denmark—are consistently more Eurosceptic than average; in others, as in Italy and Spain, most people are much more Europhile. There are also differences in the sense of EU Citizenship between Western Europe and the newer member states of the East. Mass publics in the East are generally more enthusiastic about extensions to EU Policy Scope—primarily because of institutional failings at home—but they have obviously had less time as members to develop as great a sense of EU Identity and Representation as is evident among their counterparts in the West. In spite of these differences in 'national' levels of EU sympathy, our statistical analyses suggest similar cognitive processes across EU mass publics in the determination of EU Citizenship perceptions and EU Support. In the various substantive chapters, we have explored the possibility that the calculus of Citizenship and Support might vary from country to country, from EU Accession Wave to Wave, or from East Europe to West. We found no such variations exist. The same broad mechanisms and factors appear to operate across all of the countries that we have examined. A similar conclusion is in order in relation to the *calculations* of different types of people within countries, even though there are some minor differences in Citizenship and support *levels* across different socio-demographic groups. In terms of the determinants of their EU Citizenship and Support attitudes, men do not appear to think differently from women. Old people do not think differently from young people. Cognitively sophisticated people do not differ in their calculations from their less politically informed 'unsophisticated' counterparts. We could go on, but we trust that the general point is made. People develop (or fail to develop) a sense of EU Citizenship in more or less the same way across the EU. They do so primarily on the basis of rational calculations about the costs and benefits that accrue to them and their countries as a result of EU membership. They use heuristics—substitution cues and transfer cues—to guide them in their judgements when they lack the necessary detailed information to make a more informed assessment. Much less important—though still significant—they also use their sense of national identity as a (negative) guide to their EU thinking, particularly in relation to EU Policy Scope. Finally, if people are more involved in politics and cognitively mobilized they are more likely to feel a sense of European Identity, though this effect does not extend to Representation, Scope, or Support.

Where does this leave us? We have shown that the sense of EU Citizenship among European mass publics is quite extensive. We have also argued that, against comparable standards of 'national citizenship', the European Citizenship glass is probably best viewed as half full rather than half empty. But how stable is the set of EU attitudes and orientations that we have reported? The detailed analysis that we have conducted here relates to a set of surveys that was carried out in the spring of 2007. As a follow-up, we also asked a similar set of core questions to a similar cross-national sample in the late summer of 2008. In the period between the two surveys, the world economy was hit by a banking crisis that was initially labelled 'the credit crunch', but which developed into a full-blown world recession. By the time of our second survey, the world economy—and the European economy with it—was already in recession. By comparing EU Citizenship and Support patterns across the two waves, we can very clearly assess the impact of the crisis on mass public attitudes. In short, we can make use of a 'natural experiment' to determine whether on not the 'external shock' of the worst economic crisis since the Second World War affected the stability of our measures of Citizenship and Support.

Table 10.2 reports the simple comparison across all of our sixteen sampled countries, before and after the 'shock'. The magnitude of the economic shock itself on popular perceptions can be seen in the first segment of the table, which reports the percentage of people who thought that the economic situation had got worse/the same/better over the previous twelve months.

Table 10.2. Comparison of economic perceptions and EU orientations, sixteen-country averages, 2007–9

	2007	2009	Change
Economic Perceptions			
Economic Conditions in the last 12 months:			
Got worse	43.8	85.2	+41.4
Stayed the same	30.8	11.1	−19.7
Got better	25.4	3.7	−21.7
EU Support			
EU Membership is:			
A good thing	70.5	70.1	−0.4
Neither good nor bad	14.7	14.2	−0.5
A bad thing	14.8	15.7	+0.9
EU Identity			
See self as:			
National only	38.9	39.5	+0.6
National and European	47.9	47.3	−0.6
European and National	7.2	7.1	−0.1
European only	3.9	4.0	+0.1
EU Representation			
Satisfaction with the way democracy works in the EU:			
Satisfied	66.1	63.4	−2.7
Dissatisfied	33.8	36.6	+2.6
Trust the European Commission (score over 5 on 0–10 scale)	40.0	36.7	−3.3
Trust the European Parliament (score over 5 on 0–10 scale)	39.8	37.2	−2.6
Strengthen the EU (score over 5 on 0–10 scale)	49.1	49.3	+0.2
EU Policy Scope			
Prefer EU decision-making in:			
Fighting unemployment	22.4	27.1	+4.7
Immigration	43.4	46.4	+3.0
Environment	46.2	47.6	+1.4
Fighting crime	39.1	41.5	+2.4
Health	21.5	20.9	−0.6

Note: Table entries are column percentages (within each segment) shown. N for 2007 = 16,133; N for 2009 = 16,614.

The change is extraordinary (and unprecedented on an annual basis with data of this sort). The percentage of respondents who thought the economic situation had worsened increased from 43.8 per cent to no less than 85.2 per cent—an increase in pessimism of no less than 42.4 percentage points. Clearly, people knew that a serious economic crisis had occurred. Indeed, if EU attitudes were unstable, then we would certainly expect to find that an economic shock of this magnitude would disturb them noticeably. Yet when we look at the figures for EU Support, we see that the percentage of respondents who consider that the EU is 'a good thing' is in effect constant—it falls from 70.5 per cent in 2007 to 70.1 per cent in 2008. This is well within any conceivable margin for sampling error (which we estimate at +/− 3 per cent). Similar patterns are evident when comparisons are made in terms of EU Identity (the percentages in the various identity categories are virtually identical across both columns of the table); and in terms of EU Representation (satisfaction with democracy at the EU level falls only 2.6 points to 63.4 per cent; the institutional trust levels on average fall less than 3 points; and the percentage expressing a preference for 'Strengthening the EU' actually increases marginally to 49.3 per cent). In terms of Scope, the percentages preferring EU competence again *increase* across four of the five policy categories—most noticeably in relation to unemployment and immigration.

What all of this suggests is that the sense of EU Citizenship among European mass publics is remarkably stable. Not only is the EU Citizenship glass half full, but not much—if any—of it was spilt even in the face of the 2008 recession. For good measure, Table 10.3 breaks down the results shown in Table 10.2 by East and West and Europe. The results shown in the table illustrate perfectly the central theme of this book. The pattern of radical change in economic perceptions but stability in EU attitudes is clearly evident

Table 10.3. Comparison of economic perceptions and EU orientiations, East and West European averages, 2007–9

	East		West	
	2007	2009	2007	2009
Economic Perceptions				
Economic Conditions in the last 12 months:				
Got worse	39.4	81.9	47.2	87.7
Stayed the same	34.7	13.9	27.8	9.0
Got better	25.9	4.2	25.0	3.4
EU Support				
EU membership is:				
A good thing	65.3	63.2	73.9	74.4
Neither good nor bad	10.7	24.5	8.6	7.8
A bad thing	24.0	12.4	17.4	17.8
EU Identity				
See self as:				
National only	45.5	47.1	33.8	33.8
National and European	44.0	43.4	50.9	50.3
European and National	5.8	5.1	8.2	8.6
European only	2.2	2.3	5.2	5.2
EU Representation				
Satisfaction with the way democracy works in the EU:				
Satisfied	67.6	64.3	65.1	62.7
Dissatisfied	32.4	35.7	35.0	37.3
Trust the European Commission (score over 5 on 0–10 scale)	37.4	33.1	41.9	39.3
Trust the European Parliament (score over 5 on 0–10 scale)	34.7	33.9	43.3	39.4
Strengthen the EU (score over 5 on 0–10 scale)	45.1	46.8	51.8	51.0
EU Policy Scope				
Prefer EU decision-making in:				
Fighting unemployment	21.0	25.1	23.2	28.3
Immigration	41.8	46.3	44.4	46.4
Environment	40.7	42.6	49.8	50.6
Fighting crime	40.6	42.8	38.1	40.6
Health	18.4	20.0	20.4	21.5

Note: Table entries are column percentages (within each segment). N for 2007 = 16,133; N for 2008 = 16,614.

in both East and West. The *levels* of EU sympathy are different in some areas (though they are not that different), but the *responses* to the economic crisis in terms of the pattern of attitude *change* are virtually identical. Mass publics across Europe tend to make their judgements about the EU in very similar ways. Their sense of EU Citizenship and the extent of their Support for the EU are driven by the same common set of factors, regardless of their regional or national backgrounds. It may be the case, of course, that our 2009 survey was fielded too early for the global economic crisis to impact fully on the structure of EU beliefs. However, from what we have observed so far we would argue that, if the EU delivers, and is perceived to deliver, clear benefits for its citizens, and if its political institutions effectively represent its mass publics, then the currently stable half-full glass of EU Citizenship will continue progressively to fill.

Sampling and Data, Variable Description, Data Weighting, and Missing Value Imputation

1. Sampling and Fieldwork Information

The analysis in this volume is based on survey data collected within the framework of the IntUne project. The dataset analysed in this book derives from representative mass surveys collected, using face-to-face or phone interviews, in spring 2007 in sixteen EU member states (we have not considered Serbia and Turkey which are also included in the project). The average number of respondents per country is around 1000 and the total number of respondents in the dataset is 16,133. The details about the fieldwork, sampling methods, interview, and the response rate are listed in Table A1 below.

2. Variable description

The following variable description includes most of the variables used in the chapters of this volume. The description and distribution of dependent and key independent variables are already provided in Chapters 2 and 3. Unless specified in the various chapters, variables follow the definitions here provided. This appendix brings description and coding of individual-level variables as they appear in the original IntUne survey. All variables listed below included two categories for missing values indicating respondent's refusal to answer (refused) or inability to answer (don't know).

Micro Variables

DEPENDENT VARIABLES

Our dependent variables in Chapters 4 to 9 are derived from dimensions of EU citizenship described in Chapter 2. In different chapters some of these variables are also used as predictors.

EUROPEAN IDENTITY is a variable composed from four items forming a scale ranging from 0–10. The items included in a scale are:

Table A1. Sample and fieldwork information for INTUNE Mass Survey I, 2007

Country	Fieldwork start–end	Method	Sampling	Number of contacts	Achieved sample size	Response rate	Number of call-backs/visits
AUT	09–19 May	CATI	regionally stratified proportional-to-size/random dialling of phone numbers	1902	1002	53%	min. 5 call-backs
BEL	23–9 March	CATI	geographically stratified random generator of phone numbers	4883	1004	20.5%	max. 8 call-backs
BUL	24 March–30 April	PAPI	multi-staged stratified random sampling of sampling units/random route selection of respondents	1562	1005	64%	3 call-backs/4 visits
DEN	20 March–17 April	CATI	random generation of telephone numbers from the open series	11,404	1000	8.8%	max. 8 call-backs
EST	21 March–13 April	CATI	regionally stratified proportional-to-size selection of phone numbers	1511	1000	66%	N/A
FRA	26 March–06 April	CATI	random selection of phone numbers/regional and urban/rural stratification	5084	1007	19.8%	8 call-backs
GER	21 March–04 April	CATI	randomized last digits selection/stratified by district and community size	4179	1000	23.9%	max. 10 call-backs
GRE	26 March–05 April	CATI	systematic random sample stratified by geographical area and settlement size	5669	1000	17.6%	max. 8 call-backs
HUN	04 –23 April	CAPI	sampling points selected proportional to region and settlement size/random route	1249	1002	80.1%	3 call-backs/4 visits
ITA	03–13 April	CATI	random sample stratified by geographical area and settlement size	7125	1012	14.2%	8 call-backs
POL	23 March–02 April	CAPI	random route selection of households/Kish method for selecting respondents	N/A	1000	N/A	3 call-backs/4 visits
POR	22 March–12 April	CATI	random digit dialling method	6074	1000	16.5%	6 for the first connection + 2
SLK	24 March–15 April	PAPI	regionally and population size stratified selection of sample points/random route	1772	1082	61%	4 visits (1st visit + 3 call-backs)
SLO	21–8 March	CATI	regionally stratified random sampling of phone numbers	13,345	1018	7.6%	max. 8 call-backs
SPA	22 March–02 April	CATI	regionally and population size stratified/random phone sample	5180	1002	19.3%	max. 10 call-backs
UK	23 March–01 April	CATI	random digit dialling method	9381	1000	10.7%	max. 8 call-backs
TOTAL					16,133		

1. People feel different degrees of attachment to their town or village, to their region, to their country and to Europe. What about you? Are you (1) not at all attached, (2) not very attached, (3) somewhat attached, or (4) very attached to EUROPE.
2. Do you see yourself as . . . ? (1) (NATIONALITY) only, (2) (NATIONALITY) and European, (3) European and (NATIONALITY), (4) European only.
3. How much does being a European have to do with how you feel about yourself in your day-to day-life? (1) Not at all, (2) Not very much, (3) Somewhat, (4) A great deal.
4. How far do you feel that what happens to Europe in general has important consequences for people like you? (1) Not at all, (2) Not very much, (3) Somewhat, (4) A great deal.

EUROPEAN REPRESENTATION is measured with two scales: *EU REPRESENTATION—INSTITUTIONAL TRUST*, and *EU REPRESENTATION—EFFICACY*.

EU REPRESENTATION—INSTITUTIONAL TRUST is a scale—scored from 0 to 10—composed of four items tapping satisfaction with the way democracy works in the EU, trust in EU institutions and decision-makers. The question wording is:

1. On the whole, how satisfied are you with the way democracy works in the European Union? Are you: (1) very dissatisfied, (2) somewhat dissatisfied, (3) somewhat satisfied, (4) very satisfied.
2–3. Please tell me on a scale of 0 to 10, how much you personally trust each of the following institutions to usually take the right decisions. '0' means that 'you do not trust an institution at all' and '10' means 'you have complete trust': (a) the European Parliament, (b) the European Commission.
4. Those who make decisions in the European Union are competent people who know what they are doing: (1) strongly disagree, (2) somewhat disagree, (3) neither agree nor disagree, (4) somewhat agree, (5) strongly agree.

EU REPRESENTATION—EFFICACY is a scale—scored from 0 to 10—composed of two items measuring the responsiveness of the European Union, with following question wording: I am going to read a few statements on politics in (OUR COUNTRY) and in Europe: (1) Those who make decisions in the European Union do not care much what people like me think, (2) Those who make decisions in the European Union do not take enough account of the interests of (OUR COUNTRY). Could you please tell me whether you (1) strongly agree, (2) somewhat agree, (3) neither agree nor disagree, (4) somewhat disagree, (5) strongly disagree with each of them?

TRUST IN EUROPEAN PARLIAMENT is measured with an item asking respondent: Please tell me on a scale of 0 to 10, how much you personally trust each of the following institutions (the European Parliament) to usually take the right decisions. '0' means that 'you do not trust an institution at all' and '10' means 'you have complete trust'.

TRUST IN EUROPEAN COMMISSION is measured with an item asking respondent: Please tell me on a scale of 0 to 10, how much you personally trust each of the following institutions (the European Commission) to usually take the right decisions. '0' means that 'you do not trust an institution at all' and '10' means 'you have complete trust'.

SCOPE OF THE EU is measured with two scales indicating preference for the current policy scope of the EU and future policy scope of the EU.

Measure of the *PRESENT EU SCOPE* is made from the following six items asking respondent: In most European countries today, political decisions are made at three different levels of government: at the regional level, at the national level, and at the level of the European Union. In your opinion who should be responsible for each of the following policy areas? (1) Regional level, (2) National level, (3) EU level, (4) Not an area to be dealt with by any level of Government, (5) More than one.

1. Fighting unemployment.
2. Immigration policy.
3. Environment policy.
4. Fight against crime.
5. Health care policy.
6. Agriculture policy.

The measure of the *FUTURE EU SCOPE* is made from the following four items asking respondent: Thinking about the European Union over the next ten years or so, can you tell me whether you are in favour or against—(1) Strongly in favour, (2) Somewhat in favour, (3) Somewhat against, (4) Strongly against, (5) Neither in favour nor against—the following:

1. A unified tax system for the EU.
2. A common system of social security in the EU.
3. A single EU foreign policy toward outside countries.
4. More help for EU regions in economic or social difficulties.

SUPPORT FOR EUROPEAN INTEGRATION is measured with the following variable asking respondent: Some say European unification has already gone too far. Others say it should be strengthened. What is your opinion? Please indicate your views using a 10-point scale. On this scale, '0' means unification 'has already gone too far' and '10' means it 'should be strengthened'. What number on this scale best describes your position?

TURNOUT is measured with two variables: the first variable measures reported turnout in national elections and the second measures reported turnout in European elections.

TURNOUT IN NATIONAL ELECTIONS is measured by the following item: Which party did you vote for in the last (OUR COUNTRY) general election in (YEAR)? (1)–(28) (PARTY NAME), (29) Other party, (30) Vote in blank/null and void, (31) Did not vote, (32) Don't know/can't remember, (33) Refusal.

TURNOUT IN EUROPEAN ELECTIONS is measured with the following item: Which party did you vote for in the last election for the European Parliament in 2004? (1)–(28) (PARTY NAME), (29) Other party, (30) Vote in blank/null and void, (31) Did not vote, (32) Don't know/can't remember, (33) Refusal.

INDEPENDENT VARIABLES

AGE and *AGE SQUARED* are measured with the variable asking what is the respondent's year of birth, in some chapters recoded into six age categories (18–24, 25–34, 35–44, 45–54, 55–64, and 65+).

SEX is measured with a variable coded as 1 for Male and 2 for Female.

EDUCATION is measured with a question asking respondent: Which of the following best describes your level of education? (1) Did not go to school, (2) Completed primary (elementary) education, (3) Completed basic secondary education (middle school), (4) Completed secondary education with vocational qualifications, (5) Completed secondary education with A-level qualifications, (6) College, university, or other degree, (7) Still a student, (8) Other qualification, (9) Refusal.

OCCUPATIONAL STATUS is measured with an item measuring respondent current employment and occupational status: As far as your current occupation is concerned, would you say you are self-employed, an employee, a manual worker, or would you say that you do not have a paid job? (1) Self-employed, (2) Employee, (3) Manual worker, (4) Without a paid job, (5) Don't know, (5) Refusal.

If a respondent indicated s/he is self-employed the following categories were offered: (1) Farmer, forester, fisherman, (2) Owner of a shop, craftsman, (3) Professional (lawyer, medical practitioner, accountant, architect, etc.), (4) Manager of a company, (5) Other.

If respondent indicated s/he is an employee the following categories were offered: (1) Professional (employed doctor, lawyer, accountant, architect, etc.), (2) General management, director, or top management, (3) Middle management, (4) Civil servant, (5) Office clerk, (6) Other employee (salesman, nurse, etc.), (7) Other.

If respondent indicated s/he is a manual worker the following categories were offered: (1) Supervisor/foreman (team manager, etc.), (2) Skilled manual worker, (3) Unskilled manual worker, (4) Other.

If respondent indicated s/he is without a paid job the following categories were offered: (1) Looking after the home, (2) Student (full time), (3) Retired, (4) Seeking a job, (5) Other.

MANUAL WORK is a variable constructed from the above variable by coding the respondents who are manual workers as 1 and all others as 0.

UNEMPLOYED is a variable constructed from the above variable by coding unemployed respondents as 1 and all others as 0.

RELIGION is measured with an item asking respondent: What is your religion, or don't you have one? (1) Catholic, (2) Orthodox, (3) Protestant, (4) Other Christian, (5) Jewish, (6) Muslim, (7) Sikh, (8) Buddhist, (9) Hindu, (10) Atheist/Non-believer/ Agnostic, (11) Other, (12) Don't know, (13) Refusal.

CATHOLIC is a variable constructed from the above variable by coding all respondents who declared themselves as Catholic as 1 and all others as 0.

RELIGIOSITY is measured with an item asking respondent: Apart from weddings or funerals, about how often do you attend religious services? (1) More than once a week, (2) Once a week, (3) About once a month, (4) Once every 2 or 3 months,

(5) Only on special holy days, (6) About once a year, (7) Less often, (8) Never, (9) Don't know, (10) Refusal.

URBANIZATION is a subjective measure of urbanization of the area where respondent lives and is measured with an item asking respondent: Could you give me the size of the area you live in? (1) Less than 2,000 inhabitants, (2) From 2,000 to 4,999 inhabitants, (3) From 5,000 to 19,999 inhabitants, (4) From 20,000 to 99,999 inhabitants, (5) 100,000 inhabitants and more.

LEFT–RIGHT IDEOLOGY is measured with an item asking respondent: In politics people sometimes talk of 'left' and 'right'. Where would you place yourself on a scale from 0 to 10 where '0' means 'the left' and '10' means 'the right', and '5' means 'neither left nor right'?

LEFT–RIGHT (IDEOLOGICAL) EXTREME is calculated from the above variable by taking the squared deviation of the left–right self-placement from the midpoint of the scale.

IDENTIFICATION WITH A PRO-EU PARTY is created by assigning to each respondent the value of the position on European integration taken from Chapel Hill expert survey from 2006 (ranging from 1 to 7) of the party s/he identifies with.

IDENTIFICATION WITH AN INCUMBENT PARTY is a variable created by coding respondents who identified with an incumbent party at the last national elections the value of 1 and respondents who voted for other parties at the last national elections the value of 0.

STRENGTH OF PARTISAN IDENTIFICATION is measured with an item asking respondent: Do you feel very close to this party, somewhat close, or not very close? . . . (1) Very close, (2) Somewhat close, (3) Not very close.

PARTISAN DIVIDE OVER EUROPE is measured as the standard deviation in estimates of experts from Chapel Hill expert survey about party position over European integration of the party the respondent identifies with.

POLITICAL INFLUENCE is a variable asking respondent: On a scale from 0 to 10, where '10' means 'a great deal of influence' and '0' means 'no influence', how much influence do YOU have on politics? 0 no influence to 10 a great deal of influence.

MEDIA EXPOSURE is measured by two items asking respondent how frequently s/he follows news on television and reads newspapers, forming an additive scale ranging from 0 to 10. The wording of the items is as follows: (1) Normally, how many days a week (0–7) do you watch the news on television? (2) Normally, how many days a week (0–7) do you read about politics in the newspaper?

POLITICAL SOPHISTICATION is measured with four items where respondent was asked to provide answers to factual questions and an item measuring self-reported interest in politics. First three items measuring factual knowledge are asking respondent to answer (yes, no, don't know, refusal) whether three countries (The Netherlands, Malta, and Croatia) are members of the EU. The fourth item measuring factual knowledge is asking respondent to answer how many countries are members of the EU nowadays (on a scale ranging from 1 to 31 states). The item measuring self-reported political interest is measured with an item asking: How much interest do you generally have in politics? Would you say: (1) A lot, (2) Some, (3) Not very much, (4) None at all.

SOCIAL TRUST is measured with an item asking respondent: Generally speaking, would you say that most people can be trusted or that you need to be very careful in dealing with people? Please use a number between 0 and 10, where '0' means that 'you need to be very careful in dealing with people', and '10' means that 'most people can be trusted'.

NATIONAL INSTITUTIONAL CONFIDENCE is a 0–10 index composed from variables measuring *SATISFACTION WITH DEMOCRACY*, *NATIONAL INSTITUTIONAL TRUST*, and *POLITICAL EFFICACY*.

SATISFACTION WITH DEMOCRACY is measured with an item asking: On the whole, how satisfied are you with the way democracy works in (OUR COUNTRY)? Are you . . . ? (1) Very satisfied, (2) Somewhat satisfied, (3) Somewhat dissatisfied, (4) Very dissatisfied.

NATIONAL INSTITUTIONAL TRUST is measured with items asking if respondent trusts national parliament, national government, and local government. The text of the question is as follows: Please tell me on a scale of 0 to 10, how much you personally trust each of the following institutions to usually take the right decisions. '0' means that 'you do not trust an institution at all' and '10' means 'you have complete trust' in:

a. The (NATIONALITY) Parliament.
b. The (NATIONALITY) Government.
c. The regional or local Government.

POLITICAL EFFICACY is measured with two items asking: I am going to read a few statements on politics in (OUR COUNTRY) and in Europe. Could you please tell me whether you strongly agree (1), somewhat agree (2), somewhat disagree (3), or strongly disagree (4) with each of them?

1. Those who make decisions in (OUR COUNTRY) do not care much what people like me think.
2. Those who make decisions in (OUR COUNTRY) are competent people who know what they are doing.

INTEREST IN POLITICS is measured with an item asking respondent: How much interest do you generally have in politics? Would you say: (1) A lot, (2) Some, (3) Not very much, (4) None at all.

EU INSTITUTIONAL TRUST is measured with items asking respondent: Please tell me on a scale of 0 to 10, how much you personally trust each of the following institutions to usually take the right decisions. '0' means that 'you do not trust an institution at all' and '10' means 'you have complete trust in . . .' (a) The European Parliament, (b) The European Commission.

NON-ELECTORAL PARTICIPATION is measured with four items asking respondent: In the last 12 months . . .

A. Have you worked for a party or a political candidate, Yes/No?
B. Have you worked actively with an organization or group of people to address a public issue or problem, Yes/No?

C. Have you been active in a voluntary organization, such as a community association, a charity group, a sports club, etc., Yes/No?

D. Have you boycotted certain products or services for political or ethical reasons, Yes/No?

ECONOMIC PERCEPTIONS is measured with an item asking respondent: How do you think the general economic situation in (OUR COUNTRY) has changed over the last 12 months? (1) Got a lot worse, (2) Got a little worse, (3) Stayed the same, (4) Got a little better, (5) Got a lot better.

NATIONAL IDENTITY is measured as an index composed from variables measuring attachment to national, regional and local community. The wording of the item is as follows: People feel different degrees of attachment to their town or village, to their region, to their country and to Europe. What about you? Are you very attached (1), somewhat attached (2), not very attached (3), or not at all attached (4) to the following?

a. Your town/village.
b. Your region.
c. (OUR COUNTRY.)

EXCLUSIVE NATIONAL IDENTITY is measured with an item asking respondent: Do you see yourself as...? (1) (NATIONALITY) only, (2) (NATIONALITY) and European, (3) European and (NATIONALITY), (4) European only, and (5) None of the above—where first category (NATIONALITY only) is coded as 1 and remaining 4 categories are coded as 0.

REGIONAL ATTACHMENT, LOCAL ATTACHMENT, EUROPEAN ATTACHMENT are measured with above-mentioned items asking respondent: People feel different degrees of attachment to their town or village, to their region, to their country, and to Europe. What about you? Are you very attached (1), somewhat attached (2), not very attached (3), or not at all attached (4) to the following?

a. Your town/village.
b. Your region.
c. (EUROPE.)

TRUSTS OTHER EUROPEANS is measured with an item asking respondent: Please tell me on a scale of 0 to 10, how much you personally trust each of the following groups of people (PEOPLE IN OTHER EUROPEAN COUNTRIES). '0' means that 'you do not trust the group at all' and '10' means 'you have complete trust'.

GENERAL TRUST is measured with four items, asking respondent first: Generally speaking, would you say that most people can be trusted or that you need to be very careful in dealing with people? Please use a number between 0 and 10, where '0' means that 'you need to be very careful in dealing with people' and '10' means that 'most people can be trusted'. This item is combined with three other 0–10 scale items that ask the respondent: Please tell me on a scale of 0 to 10, how much you personally trust each of the following groups of people. '0' means that 'you do not trust the group at all' and '10' means 'you have complete trust': (a) [Nationality], (b) People in other European countries.

EU VISITS is measured with an item asking respondent: How many times have you visited another EU country in the last 12 months? (Answer is a scale from 1 to 5 and more.)

EU NATIONAL BENEFITS (or *'EU BENEFITS NATION'*) is measured with an item asking respondent: Taking everything into consideration, would you say that (OUR COUNTRY) has on balance benefited (1) or has not benefited (2) from being a member of the European Union?

EU PERSONAL BENEFITS (or *'EU BENEFITS ME'*) is measured with an item asking respondent: And what about people like you? Have people like you on balance benefited (1) or not benefited (2) from (OUR COUNTRY)'s EU membership?

EU DEMOCRACY SATISFACTION is measured with an item asking respondent: On the whole, how satisfied are you with the way democracy works in the European Union? Are you...? (1) Very satisfied, (2) Somewhat satisfied, (3) Somewhat dissatisfied, (4) Very dissatisfied.

SOCIAL OR COMPETITIVE EUROPE is measured with an item asking respondent: I'm going to read you two statements. Please tell me which of them comes closest to your view: (1) The main aim of the EU should be to make the European economy more competitive in world markets, (2) The main aim of the EU should be to provide better social security for all its citizens.

ACHIEVED NATIONAL IDENTITY is measured with three items asking respondent: People differ in what they think it means to be (NATIONALITY). In your view, how important is each of the following to be (NATIONALITY)? (1) Very important, (2) Somewhat important, (3) Not very important, (4) Not at all important...

A. To respect (NATIONALITY) laws and institutions.
B. To master (COUNTRY LANGUAGE); IF MULTILANGUAGE COUNTRY: to master one of the official languages of (OUR COUNTRY).
C. To exercise citizens' rights, like being active in the politics of (OUR COUNTRY).

ASCRIBED NATIONAL IDENTITY is measured with three items forming an additive scale ranging from 0–100: People differ in what they think it means to be (NATIONALITY). In your view, how important is each of the following to be (NATIONALITY)? (1) Very important, (2) Somewhat important, (3) Not very important, (4) Not at all important...

A. To be a Christian.
B. To be born in (OUR COUNTRY).
C. To have (NATIONALITY) parents.

THREAT OF GLOBALIZATION is measured with an item asking respondent: Nowadays, people, money, and ideas travel across national boundaries very quickly. Because of this, a number of (NATIONALITY) believe the country now faces serious threats to our cultural values and way of life. What do you think? Is this...? (1) A very serious threat, (2) A somewhat serious threat, (3) Not a very serious threat, (4) Not a threat at all.

CIVIC DUTY TO VOTE IN EUROPEAN ELECTIONS is measured with an item asking respondent: Please tell me whether you strongly agree, somewhat agree, somewhat disagree or strongly disagree with the following statement: I would be seriously neglecting my duty as a citizen if I didn't vote in elections for the European Parliament ... (1) Strongly agree, (2) Somewhat agree, (3) Somewhat disagree, (4) Strongly disagree, (5) Neither agree nor disagree.

CIVIC DUTY TO VOTE IN NATIONAL ELECTIONS is measured with an item asking respondent: Please tell me whether you strongly agree, somewhat agree, somewhat disagree, or strongly disagree with the following statement: I would be seriously neglecting my duty as a citizen if I didn't vote in (OUR COUNTRY)'s general elections: (1) Strongly agree, (2) Somewhat agree, (3) Somewhat disagree, (4) Strongly disagree, (5) Neither agree nor disagree.

Macro Variables

LENGTH OF EU MEMBERSHIP measured as duration of EU membership in years.

DEMOCRATIC HISTORY measured in number of years country was under a democratic regime since 1900 for all years in which country has POLITY score of 6 or higher.
Source: Polity IV dataset.

COMMUNIST PAST indicating former Communist countries coded as 1 when indicating former Communist countries and 0 for others.

COMPULSORY VOTING indicating if country has compulsory vote requirement, coded as 1 for countries which have compulsory voting and 0 for others.
Source: Administration and cost of elections project (ACE) *Electoral Knowledge Network comparative data.*

SUNDAY VOTING indicating if elections in a country are held on Sunday, coded as 1 for countries which have Sunday voting and 0 for others.
Source: Administration and cost of elections project (ACE) *Electoral Knowledge Network comparative data.*

POSTAL VOTING indicating if postal voting is available to all eligible voters in national elections, coded as 1 for countries which have postal voting and 0 for others.
Source: Administration and cost of elections project (ACE) *Electoral Knowledge Network comparative data.*

TURNOUT IN LAST NATIONAL ELECTIONS measured as turnout in last national elections measured as % of number of registered voters.
Source: IDEA turnout database.

POPULATION SIZE measured as size of the population in millions in 2006.
Source: World Bank.

INTRA-EU TRADE measured as trade with EU countries as a % of total trade.
Source: Eurostat.

SOCIAL EXPENDITURE—public social expenditure as % of GDP in 2005.
Source: Eurostat.

NET EU TRANSFERS—net transfers from EU budget as % of GNI in the given calendar year.
Source: European Commission EU Budget Financial Report 2008.

QUALITY OF GOVERNANCE index based on an estimate of first principal component of the World Bank Governance Indicators: (1) Voice and accountability, (2) Political stability, (3) Regulatory quality, (4) Control of corruption, (5) Government effectiveness, (6) Rule of law.

GROSS NATIONAL INCOME measured in USD per capita in 2006 current prices.
Source: World Bank.

3. Data Weighting and Missing Value Imputation

IntUne dataset uses three sets of weights:

1. W1 is a national weighting factor which is used to make national samples representative of the population they are drawn from.
2. W2 is a total weighting factor used to make a full sample of 16 countries representative of the population of 16 countries included in IntUne survey.
3. W3 is extrapolated weighting factor based on the real population of 16 countries in IntUne survey.

The micro data file used in the analysis in this volume had missing values imputed with multiple imputation of missing values, using Amelia 2 package for R. The imputations were done country by country and resulted in five separate datasets for each country. All five are identical as far as non-missing values are concerned, but have different values imputed to each missing value on each variable. All country files from separate imputations are pooled subsequently in a single file. Whereas the original IntUne 16-country file has N = 16133 the imputed dataset has 5 times the number of cases and it equals N = 80665. Since each case in the imputed dataset turns into five separate cases that have different values on those variables where the case in question had a missing value in the original file, this multiplication of cases artificially reduces the standard errors of any estimates to a considerable extent. Nearly all of this distortion is eliminated, however, if statistical procedures are using weight variables adjusted for the fact that we have a fivefold increase in the number of cases in the analysis. The new variable Weight is a constant of 1/5, and the original weight variables, w1, w2, and w3, supplied with the IntUne data, are also adjusted by this constant (i.e. their value is always one-fifth of what it was for the respective individual in the original IntUne file). Thus any weight variable has an unweighted mean of 1 in the original file and an unweighted mean of 0.2 in the multiply imputed dataset.

4. The INTUNE questionnaire

INTUNE 2007 MASS WAVE 1 SURVEY (TNS 5189)
English Master Questionnaire

B   Country Code
        (PLEASE USE CODES MENTIONED IN THE INSTRUCTIONS)

        [|]

C   Our survey number
        (PLEASE WRITE 5189)

        | 5 | 1 | 8 | 9 |

D   Interview number
        (HAS TO BE UNIQUE — ONE NUMBER PER INTERVIEW)

        [| | | | |]

E   SPLIT BALLOT

        A   1
        B   2
        C   3

D2a   Could you please tell me the year in which you were born?
        (PLEASE USE 4-DIGITS YEAR—IF 'DK' CODE '9999'—IF 'REFUSAL' CODE
        '9998' AND ASK D2b)

        [| | |]

        ASK D2b IF 'REFUSAL' IN D2a

D2b   Could you please tell me to which age category you belong to?

        18-24   1
        25-34   2
        35-44   3
        45-54   4
        55-64   5
        65 +   6
        Refusal (SPONTANEOUS)   7

D14a Could you tell me how many people live in your household, yourself included?
(WRITE DOWN EXACT NUMBER—MINIMUM 1 AS WE ARE TALKING
ABOUT 'YOU INCLUDED')

D14b Could you tell me how many are below age 18?
(WRITE DOWN EXACT NUMBER)

Q1 How do you think the general economic situation in (OUR COUNTRY) has
changed over the last 12 months?
(READ OUT—ONE ANSWER ONLY)

Got a lot worse	1
Got a little worse	2
Stayed the same	3
Got a little better	4
Got a lot better	5
DK (SPONTANEOUS)	6
Refusal (SPONTANEOUS)	7

Q2 How much interest do you generally have in politics? Would you say ...?
(READ OUT—ONE ANSWER ONLY)

A lot	1
Some	2
Not very much	3
None at all	4
DK (SPONTANEOUS)	5
Refusal (SPONTANEOUS)	6

Q3 On the whole, how satisfied are you with the way democracy works in (OUR
COUNTRY)? Are you ...?
(READ OUT—ONE ANSWER ONLY)

Very satisfied	1
Somewhat satisfied	2
Somewhat dissatisfied	3
Very dissatisfied	4
DK (SPONTANEOUS)	5
Refusal (SPONTANEOUS)	6

Q4 Generally speaking, would you say that most people can be trusted or that you need to be very careful in dealing with people? Please use a number between 0 and 10, where '0' means that 'you need to be very careful in dealing with people', and '10' means that 'most people can be trusted'. You can use any number from zero to ten.
(PLEASE USE A SCALE FROM 0 TO 10 ON FIELD AND CODE 1 TO 11 IN YOUR DATA FILE)

Need to be very careful				Most people can be trusted						
1	2	3	4	5	6	7	8	9	10	11

DK (SPONTANEOUS)   12
Refusal (SPONTANEOUS)   13

Q5 Please tell me on a scale of 0 to 10, how much you personally trust each of the following institutions to usually take the right decisions. '0' means that 'you do not trust an institution at all' and '10' means 'you have complete trust'.
(ONE ANSWER PER LINE) (PLEASE USE A SCALE FROM 0 TO 10 ON FIELD AND CODE 1 TO 11 IN YOUR DATA FILE)

(READ OUT—ROTATE PAIRWISE)	No trust at all	1	2	3	4	5	6	7	8	9	Com- plete trust	DK (SPONTA- NEOUS)	Refusal (SPON- TANE- OUS)
1 The (NATIONALITY) Parliament	1	2	3	4	5	6	7	8	9	10	11	12	13
2 The European Parliament	1	2	3	4	5	6	7	8	9	10	11	12	13
3 The (NATIONALITY) Government	1	2	3	4	5	6	7	8	9	10	11	12	13
4 The European Commission	1	2	3	4	5	6	7	8	9	10	11	12	13
5 The regional or local Government (USE THE APPROPRIATE NAME IN YOUR COUNTRY)	1	2	3	4	5	6	7	8	9	10	11	12	13

Q6 On a scale from 0 to 10, where '10' means 'a great deal of influence' and '0' means 'no influence', how much influence do YOU have on politics? (PLEASE USE A SCALE FROM 0 TO 10 ON FIELD AND CODE 1 TO 11 IN YOUR DATA FILE)

No influence						A great deal of influence				
1	2	3	4	5	6	7	8	9	10	11

DK (SPONTANEOUS)   12
Refusal (SPONTANEOUS)   13
DO NOT ASK Q7a, Q8a and Q9a in SERBIA—SERBIA GO TO Q7b

Q7a Generally speaking, do you think that (OUR COUNTRY)'s membership of the European Union is...?
(READ OUT—ONE ANSWER ONLY)

A good thing   1
A bad thing   2
Neither good nor bad (SPONTANEOUS)   3
DK (SPONTANEOUS)   4
Refusal (SPONTANEOUS)   5

Q8a Taking everything into consideration, would you say that (OUR COUNTRY) has on balance benefited or not from being a member of the European Union?

Has benefited   1
Has not benefited   2
DK (SPONTANEOUS)   3
Refusal (SPONTANEOUS)   4

Q9a And what about people like you? Have people like you on balance benefited or not from (OUR COUNTRY)'s EU membership?

Have benefited   1
Have not benefited   2
DK (SPONTANEOUS)   3
Refusal (SPONTANEOUS)   4
ASK Q7b, Q8b and Q9b ONLY in SERBIA - OTHERS GO TO Q10

Q7b Generally speaking, do you think that the accession of Serbia in the European Union would be...?
(READ OUT—ONE ANSWER ONLY)

A good thing	1
A bad thing	2
Neither good nor bad (SPONTANEOUS)	3
DK (SPONTANEOUS)	4
Refusal (SPONTANEOUS)	5

Q8b Taking everything into consideration, would you say that Serbia would on balance benefit or not from being a member of the European Union?

Would benefit	1
Would not benefit	2
DK (SPONTANEOUS)	3
Refusal (SPONTANEOUS)	4

Q9b And what about people like you? Would people like you on balance benefit or not from Serbia's EU membership?

Would benefit	1
Would not benefit	2
DK (SPONTANEOUS)	3
Refusal (SPONTANEOUS)	4
ASK ALL	

Q10 How much does being a European have to do with how you feel about your-self in your day-to-day life?

(READ OUT—ONE ANSWER ONLY)	
A great deal	1
Somewhat	2
Not very much	3
Not at all	4
DK (SPONTANEOUS)	5
Refusal (SPONTANEOUS)	6

Q11   People feel different degrees of attachment to their town or village, to their
       region, to their country and to Europe. What about you? Are you very
       attached, somewhat attached, not very attached or not at all attached to
       the following?
       (ONE ANSWER PER LINE)

	(READ OUT)	Very attached	Some-what attached	Not very attached	Not at all attached	DK (SPONT ANEOUS)	Refusal (SPONT ANEOUS)
1	Your town\ village (INT.: IF RESPON-DENT ASKS 'where you live')	1	2	3	4	5	6
2	Your region (INT.: IF RESPON-DENT ASKS 'what-ever you understand by your region')	1	2	3	4	5	6
3	(OUR COUNTRY)	1	2	3	4	5	6
4	Europe	1	2	3	4	5	6

Q12   Do you see yourself as...?
       (READ OUT—ONE ANSWER ONLY)

(NATIONALITY) only	1
(NATIONALITY) and European	2
European and (NATIONALITY)	3
European only	4
None of the above (SPONTANEOUS)	5
DK (SPONTANEOUS)	6
Refusal (SPONTANEOUS)	7

Q13 People differ in what they think it means to be (NATIONALITY). In your view, how important is each of the following to be (NATIONALITY)?
(ONE ANSWER PER LINE)

	(READ OUT— ROTATE)	Very important	Somewhat important	Not very impor- tant	Not at all impor- tant	DK (SPONT ANEOUS)	Refusal (SPONTA NEOUS)
1	To be a Christian	1	2	3	4	5	6
2	To share (NATIONALITY) cultural traditions	1	2	3	4	5	6
3	To be born in (OUR COUNTRY)	1	2	3	4	5	6
4	To have (NATIONALITY) parents	1	2	3	4	5	6
5	To respect (NATIONALITY) laws and institutions	1	2	3	4	5	6
6	To feel (NATION-ALITY)	1	2	3	4	5	6
7	To master (COUNTRY LANGUAGE) (IF MULTI-LANGUAGE COUNTRY "to master one of the official languages of (OUR COUNTRY))	1	2	3	4	5	6
8	To exercise citizens' rights, like being active in the politics of (OUR COUNTRY)	1	2	3	4	5	6

Q14   And for being European, how important do you think each of the
      following is...?
      (ONE ANSWER PER LINE)

	(READ OUT— ROTATE)	Very important	Somewhat important	Not very impor- tant	Not at all impor- tant	DK (SPONTA NEOUS)	Refusal (SPONTA NEOUS)
1	To be a Christian	1	2	3	4	5	6
2	To share European cultural traditions	1	2	3	4	5	6
3	To be born in Europe	1	2	3	4	5	6
4	To have European parents	1	2	3	4	5	6
5	To respect European Union's laws and institu- tions	1	2	3	4	5	6
6	To feel Euro- pean	1	2	3	4	5	6
7	To mas- ter any European language	1	2	3	4	5	6
8	To exercise citizens' rights, like being active in politics of the Euro- pean Union	1	2	3	4	5	6

Q15   Please tell me whether you are in favour of or against the enlargement of the European Union to include new countries.
(READ OUT—ONE ANSWER ONLY)

Very much in favour	1
Somewhat in favour	2
Somewhat against	3
Very much against	4
DK (SPONTANEOUS)	5
Refusal (SPONTANEOUS)	6

DO NOT ASK Q16a in SERBIA—SERBIA GO TO Q16b

Q16a   Please tell me whether you strongly agree, somewhat agree, somewhat disagree or strongly disagree with the following statement: I would be seriously neglecting my duty as a citizen if I didn't vote in elections for the European Parliament.
(READ OUT—ONE ANSWER ONLY)

Strongly agree	1
Somewhat agree	2
Somewhat disagree	3
Strongly disagree	4
Neither agree nor disagree (SPONTANEOUS)	5
DK (SPONTANEOUS)	6
Refusal (SPONTANEOUS)	7

ASK Q16b ONLY in SERBIA—OTHERS GO TO Q17

Q16b   Please tell me whether you strongly agree, somewhat agree, somewhat disagree or strongly disagree with the following statement: If Serbia were a member of the European Union, I would be seriously neglecting my duty as a citizen if I didn't vote in elections for the European Parliament.
(READ OUT—ONE ANSWER ONLY)

Strongly agree	1
Somewhat agree	2
Somewhat disagree	3
Strongly disagree	4
Neither agree nor disagree (SPONTANEOUS)	5
DK (SPONTANEOUS)	6
Refusal (SPONTANEOUS)	7

ASK ALL

Q17 How far do you feel that what happens to Europe in general has important consequences for people like you?
(READ OUT—ONE ANSWER ONLY)

A great deal	1
Somewhat	2
Not very much	3
Not at all	4
DK (SPONTANEOUS)	5
Refusal (SPONTANEOUS)	6

Q18 Normally, how many days a week do you watch the news on television?
(WRITE DOWN 0 TO 7 DAYS. IF 'DK', CODE '9'. IF 'REFUSAL', CODE '8')

☐ DAYS

Q19 Normally, how many days a week do you read about politics in the newspaper?
(WRITE DOWN 0 TO 7 DAYS. IF 'DK', CODE '9'. IF 'REFUSAL', CODE '8')

☐ DAYS

Q20 In politics people sometimes talk of 'left' and 'right'. Where would you place yourself on a scale from 0 to 10 where '0' means 'the left' and '10' means 'the right', and '5' means 'neither left nor right'?
(PLEASE USE A SCALE FORM 0 TO 10 ON FIELD AND CODE 1 TO 11 IN YOUR DATA FILE)

Left							Right			
1	2	3	4	5	6	7	8	9	10	11

DK (SPONTANEOUS)	12
Refusal (SPONTANEOUS)	13

Q21 Some say European unification has already gone too far. Others say it should be strengthened. What is your opinion? Please indicate your views using a 10-point scale. On this scale, '0' means unification 'has already gone too far' and '10' means it 'should be strengthened'. What number on this scale best describes your position?
(PLEASE USE A SCALE FORM 0 TO 10 ON FIELD AND CODE 1 TO 11 IN YOUR DATA FILE)

Gone too far					Strengthen					
1	2	3	4	5	6	7	8	9	10	11

DK (SPONTANEOUS)	12
Refusal (SPONTANEOUS)	13

Q22   Some say that we should have a single European Union Army. Others say every country should keep its own national army. What is your opinion?
(READ OUT—ONE ANSWER ONLY)

Have a national (NATIONALITY) army	1
Have a European Union army	2
Have both national (NATIONALITY) and a European Union army	3
Neither (SPONTANEOUS)	4
DK (SPONTANEOUS)	5
Refusal (SPONTANEOUS)	6

Q23   Please tell me on a scale of 0 to 10, how much you personally trust each of the following groups of people. '0' means that 'you do not trust the group at all' and '10' means 'you have complete trust'.
(ONE ANSWER PER LINE)

(READ OUT)	No trust at all										Complete trust	DK (SPONTA NEOUS)	Refusal (SPONTA NEOUS)
1 (NATIONALITY)	1	2	3	4	5	6	7	8	9	10	11	12	13
2 People in other European countries	1	2	3	4	5	6	7	8	9	10	11	12	13
3 People outside Europe	1	2	3	4	5	6	7	8	9	10	11	12	13

Q24   I am going to read a few statements on politics in (OUR COUNTRY) and in Europe. Could you please tell me whether you strongly agree, somewhat agree, somewhat disagree or strongly disagree with each of them?
(ONE ANSWER PER LINE)

(READ OUT— ROTATE ITEMS 1 and 2 and 3 and 4 - ITEM 5 MUST NOT BE ROTATED)	Strongly Agree	Some- what agree	Somewhat disagree	Strongly disagree	Neither agree nor disagree (SPONTA NEOUS)	DK (SPONTA NEOUS)	Refusal (SPONTA NEOUS)

1	Those who make decisions in the European Union do not care much what people like me think	1	2	3	4	5	6	7
2	Those who make decisions in (OUR COUNTRY) do not care much what people like me think	1	2	3	4	5	6	7
3	Those who make decisions in the European Union are competent people who know what they are doing	1	2	3	4	5	6	7
4	Those who make decisions in (OUR COUNTRY) are competent people who know what they are doing	1	2	3	4	5	6	7

5	Those who make deci-sions in the European Union do not take enough account of the interests of (OUR COUNTRY)	1	2	3	4	5	6	7

Q25 On the whole, how satisfied are you with the way democracy works in the European Union? Are you...?
(READ OUT—ONE ANSWER ONLY)

Very satisfied	1
Somewhat satisfied	2
Somewhat dissatisfied	3
Very dissatisfied	4
DK (SPONTANEOUS)	5
Refusal (SPONTANEOUS)	6

DO NOT ASK Q26a in SERBIA—SERBIA GO TO Q26b

Q26a In most European countries today, political decisions are made at three dif-ferent levels of government: at the regional level, at the national level, and at the level of the European Union. In your opinion who should be respon-sible for each of the following policy areas?
(ONE ANSWER PER LINE)

	(READ OUT— ROTATE)	Regional level	National level	EU level	Not an area to be dealt with by any level of Government (SPONTA NEOUS)	More than one (SPON-TANE-OUS)	DK (SPON-TANE-OUS)	Refusal (SPON-TANE-OUS)
1	Fighting unem-ployment	1	2	3	4	5	6	7

2	Immi-gration policy	1	2	3	4	5	6	7
3	Environ-ment policy	1	2	3	4	5	6	7
4	Fight against crime	1	2	3	4	5	6	7
5	Health care policy	1	2	3	4	5	6	7
6	Agri-culture policy	1	2	3	4	5	6	7

ASK Q26b ONLY in SERBIA—OTHERS GO TO Q27

Q26b   In most European countries today, political decisions are made at three different levels of government: at the regional level, at the national level, and at the level of the European Union. In your opinion, if Serbia were a member of the European Union, who should be responsible for each of the following policy areas?
(ONE ANSWER PER LINE)

	(READ OUT—ROTATE)	Regional level	National level	EU level	Not an area to be dealt with by any level of Government (SPON-TANE-OUS)	More than one (SPONTA-NEOUS)	DK (SPON-TANE-OUS)	Refusal (SPON-TANE-OUS)
1	Fighting unem-ployment	1	2	3	4	5	6	7
2	Immi-gration policy	1	2	3	4	5	6	7

3	Environ-ment policy	1	2	3	4	5	6	7
4	Fight against crime	1	2	3	4	5	6	7
5	Health care policy	1	2	3	4	5	6	7
6	Agricul-ture policy	1	2	3	4	5	6	7

ASK ALL

Q27 Thinking about the European Union over the next ten years or so, can you tell me whether you are in favour of or against the following.
(ONE ANSWER PER LINE)

	(READ OUT— ROTATE)	Strongly in favour	Some-what in favour	Some-what against	Strongly against	Neither in favour nor against (SPONTA-NEOUS)	DK (SPONTA-NEOUS)	Refusal (SPON-TANE-OUS)
1	A unified tax system for the EU	1	2	3	4	5	6	7
2	A com-mon system of social security in the EU	1	2	3	4	5	6	7
3	A single EU foreign policy toward outside countries	1	2	3	4	5	6	7

4	More help for EU regions in economic or social difficulties	1	2	3	4	5	6	7

Q28   I'm going to read you two statements. Please tell me which of them comes closest to your view.
(READ OUT—ONE ANSWER ONLY)

The main aim of the EU should be to make the European economy more competitive in world markets   1
The main aim of the EU should be to provide better social security for all its citizens   2
DK (SPONTANEOUS)   3
Refusal (SPONTANEOUS)   4

ASK Q29a ONLY TO SPLIT BALLOT A—SPLIT BALLOT B GO TO Q29b—SPLIT BALLOT C GO TO Q29c

Q29a   Nowadays, people, money, and ideas travel across national boundaries very quickly. Because of this, a number of (NATIONALITY) believe the country now faces serious threats to our national security. What do you think? Is this...?
(READ OUT—ONE ANSWER ONLY)

A very serious threat   1
A somewhat serious threat   2
Not a very serious threat   3
Not a threat at all   4
DK (SPONTANEOUS)   5
Refusal (SPONTANEOUS)   6

ASK Q29b ONLY TO SPLIT BALLOT B—SPLIT A GO TO Q30—SPLIT C GO TO Q29c

Q29b   Nowadays, people, money, and ideas travel across national boundaries very quickly. Because of this, a number of (NATIONALITY) believe the country now faces serious threats to our economic well-being and jobs. What do you think? Is this...?
(READ OUT—ONE ANSWER ONLY)

A very serious threat	1
A somewhat serious threat	2
Not a very serious threat	3
Not a threat at all	4
DK (SPONTANEOUS)	5
Refusal (SPONTANEOUS)	6

ASK Q29c ONLY TO SPLIT BALLOT C—SPLIT BALLOT A and B GO TO Q30

Q29c   Nowadays, people, money, and ideas travel across national boundaries very quickly. Because of this, a number of (NATIONALITY) believe the country now faces serious threats to our cultural values and way of life. What do you think? Is this...?
(READ OUT—ONE ANSWER ONLY)

A very serious threat	1
A somewhat serious threat	2
Not a very serious threat	3
Not a threat at all	4
DK (SPONTANEOUS)	5
Refusal (SPONTANEOUS)	6

DO NOT ASK Q30a in SERBIA - SERBIA GO TO Q30b

(IF CODE 3 or 4 in Q29, PLEASE DO NOT READ 'In order to deal with this threat' in the following question)

Q30a   In order to deal with this threat, should the powers of the European Union be increased, even if this means reducing the power of the (NATIONALITY) Government?
(READ OUT—ONE ANSWER ONLY)

Yes, increase EU powers	1
No, do not increase EU powers	2
It depends (SPONTANEOUS)	3
DK (SPONTANEOUS)	4
Refusal (SPONTANEOUS)	5

ASK Q30b ONLY in SERBIA—OTHERS GO TO Q31

Q30b   If Serbia were a member of the European Union, in order to deal with this
        threat, should the powers of the European Union be increased, even if this
        means reducing the power of the (NATIONALITY) Government?
        (READ OUT—ONE ANSWER ONLY)

Yes, increase EU powers	1
No, do not increase EU powers	2
It depends (SPONTANEOUS)	3
DK (SPONTANEOUS)	4
Refusal (SPONTANEOUS)	5

        ASK ALL

Q31   How much does being a European have to do with how you feel about your-
        self in your day-to-day life?
        (READ OUT—ONE ANSWER ONLY)

A great deal	1
Somewhat	2
Not very much	3
Not at all	4
DK (SPONTANEOUS)	5
Refusal (SPONTANEOUS)	6

Q32   Generally speaking, do you think that Turkey's membership of the European
        Union would be a good thing or a bad thing?
        (READ OUT—ONE ANSWER ONLY)

A good thing	1
A Bad thing	2
Neither good nor bad (SPONTANEOUS)	3
DK (SPONTANEOUS)	4
Refusal (SPONTANEOUS)	5

Q33   Now a few questions about how active you are in politics and community
        affairs. In the last 12 months...?
        (ONE ANSWER PER LINE)

	(READ OUT)	Yes	No	DK (SPONTA-NEOUS)	Refusal (SPONTA-NEOUS)
1	Have you worked for a party or a political candidate?	1	2	3	4
2	Have you worked actively with an organisation or group of people to address a public issue or problem?	1	2	3	4
3	Have you been active in a voluntary organisation, such as a community association, a charity group, a sports club, etc.?	1	2	3	4
4	Have you boycotted certain products or services for political or ethical reasons?	1	2	3	4

Q34 Please tell me whether you strongly agree, somewhat agree, somewhat disagree or strongly disagree with the following statement: I would be seriously neglecting my duty as a citizen if I didn't vote in (OUR COUNTRY)'s general elections.
(READ OUT—ONE ANSWER ONLY)

Strongly agree	1
Somewhat agree	2
Somewhat disagree	3
Strongly disagree	4
Neither agree nor disagree (SPONTANEOUS)	5
DK (SPONTANEOUS)	6
Refusal (SPONTANEOUS)	7

Q35 Do you usually think of yourself as being close to any particular political party?
(READ OUT—ONE ANSWER ONLY)

Yes	1
No	2
DK (SPONTANEOUS)	3
Refusal (SPONTANEOUS)	4

ASK Q36 IF 'NO, DK OR REFUSAL', CODE 2 to 4 IN Q35—OTHERS GO TO Q37

Q36 Do you feel yourself to be a little closer to one of the political parties than the others?
(READ OUT—ONE ANSWER ONLY)

Yes	1
No	2
DK (SPONTANEOUS)	3
Refusal (SPONTANEOUS)	4

ASK Q37 AND Q38 IF 'YES', CODE 1 IN Q35 OR IN Q36—OTHERS
GO TO Q39

Q37 Which political party do you feel closest to?
(DO NOT READ OUT—CODE IN THE PRECODED LIST   ONE ANSWER
ONLY—PUT NEXT TO PARTY NAME THE NAME OF THE LEADER)

Local party 1	1
Local party 2	2
Local party 3	3
Local party 4	4
Local party 5	5
Local party 6	6
Local party 7	7
Local party 8	8
Local party 9	9
Local party 10	10
Local party 11	11
Local party 12	12
Local party 13	13
Local party 14	14
Local party 15	15
Local party 16	16
Local party 17	17
Local party 18	18
Local party 19	19
Local party 20	20
Local party 21	21
Local party 22	22
Local party 23	23
Local party 24	24
Local party 25	25
Local party 26	26

Local party 27	27
Local party 28	28
Local party 29	29
Local party 30	30
Local party 31	31
DK (SPONTANEOUS)	32
Refusal (SPONTANEOUS)	33

Q38 Do you feel very close to this party, somewhat close, or not very close?
(READ OUT—ONE ANSWER ONLY)

Very close	1
Somewhat close	2
Not very close	3
DK (SPONTANEOUS)	4
Refusal (SPONTANEOUS)	5
ASK ALL	

Q39 Which party did you vote for in the last (OUR COUNTRY) general election in (YEAR)?
(DO NOT READ OUT—CODE IN THE PRECODED LIST—ONE ANSWER ONLY—PUT NEXT TO PARTY NAME THE NAME OF THE LEADER)

Local party 1	1
Local party 2	2
Local party 3	3
Local party 4	4
Local party 5	5
Local party 6	6
Local party 7	7
Local party 8	8
Local party 9	9
Local party 10	10
Local party 11	11
Local party 12	12
Local party 13	13
Local party 14	14
Local party 15	15
Local party 16	16
Local party 17	17

Local party 18	18
Local party 19	19
Local party 20	20
Local party 21	21
Local party 22	22
Local party 23	23
Local party 24	24
Local party 25	25
Local party 26	26
Local party 27	27
Local party 28	28
Other party	29
Vote in blank/null and void	30
Did not vote (SPONTANEOUS)	31
DK/can't remember (SPONTANEOUS)	32
Refusal (SPONTANEOUS)	33

DO NOT ASK Q40 in BG and SERBIA

Q40   Which party did you vote for in the last election for the European
       Parliament in 2004?
       (DO NOT READ OUT—CODE IN THE PRECODED LIST—ONE ANSWER
       ONLY—PUT NEXT TO PARTY NAME THE NAME OF THE LEADER)

Local party 1	1
Local party 2	2
Local party 3	3
Local party 4	4
Local party 5	5
Local party 6	6
Local party 7	7
Local party 8	8
Local party 9	9
Local party 10	10
Local party 11	11
Local party 12	12
Local party 13	13
Local party 14	14
Local party 15	15
Local party 16	16

Local party 17	17
Local party 18	18
Local party 19	19
Local party 20	20
Local party 21	21
Local party 22	22
Local party 23	23
Local party 24	24
Local party 25	25
Local party 26	26
Local party 27	27
Local party 28	28
Other party	29
Vote in blank/null and void	30
Did not vote (SPONTANEOUS)	31
DK/can't remember (SPONTANEOUS)	32
Refusal (SPONTANEOUS)	33

DEMOGRAPHICS

ASK ALL

D1   Gender

Male	1
Female	2

D3   Which of the following best describes your level of education

Did not go to school	1
Completed primary (elementary) education	2
Completed basic secondary education (middle school)	3
Completed secondary education with vocational qualifications	4
Completed secondary education with A-level qualifications	5
College, university, or other degree	6
Still a student	7
Other qualification (SPONTANEOUS)	8
Refusal (SPONTANEOUS)	9

D4a   As far as your current occupation is concerned, would you say you are self-employed, an employee, a manual worker or would you say that you do not have a paid job?
(READ OUT—ONE ANSWER ONLY)

Self-employed	1
Employee	2
Manual worker	3
Without a paid job	4
DK (SPONTANEOUS)	5
Refusal (SPONTANEOUS)	6

IF 'SELF-EMPLOYED', CODE 1 IN D4a

D4b   Self-employed—that is to say...
(READ OUT—ONE ANSWER ONLY)

Farmer, forester, fisherman	1
Owner of a shop, craftsman	2
Professional (lawyer, medical practitioner, accountant, architect, etc.)	3
Manager of a company	4
Other (SPECIFY)	5

IF 'EMPLOYEE', CODE 2 IN D4a

D4c   Employee—that is to say...
(READ OUT—ONE ANSWER ONLY)

Professional (employed doctor, lawyer, accountant, architect, etc.)	1
General management, director or top management	2
Middle management	3
Civil servant	4
Office clerk	5
Other employee (salesman, nurse, etc.)	6
Other (SPECIFY)	7

IF 'MANUAL WORKER', CODE 3 IN D4a

D4d   Manual worker—that is to say...
(READ OUT—ONE ANSWER ONLY)

Supervisor/foreman (team manager, etc.)	1
Manual worker	2
Unskilled manual worker	3
Other (SPECIFY)	4

IF 'WITHOUT A PROFESSIONAL ACTIVITY', CODE 4 IN D4a

D4e   Without a paid job—that is to say...
(READ OUT—ONE ANSWER ONLY)

Looking after the home	1
Student (full time)	2
Retired	3
Seeking a job	4
Other (SPECIFY)	5

ASK ALL

D5   To which of the following categories do you feel you belong?
(READ OUT—ONE ANSWER ONLY)

The upper class	1
Upper middle class	2
Lower middle class	3
The working class	4
None of this (SPONTANEOUS)	5
DK (SPONTANEOUS)	6
Refusal (SPONTANEOUS)	7

D6   Which of the following best corresponds to your marital status?
(READ OUT—ONE ANSWER ONLY)

Single	1
Married	2
Separated—divorced	3
Living with a partner	4
Widowed	5
Refusal (SPONTANEOUS)	6

D7   What is your religion, or don't you have one?
(DO NOT READ OUT—DO NOT SHOW CARD—CODE IN THE PRECODED
LIST—ONE ANSWER ONLY)

Catholic	1
Orthodox	2
Protestant	3
Other Christian	4
Jewish	5
Muslim	6
Sikh	7
Buddhist	8
Hindu	9
Atheist / Non believer / Agnostic	10
Other (SPONTANEOUS)	11
DK (SPONTANEOUS)	12
Refusal (SPONTANEOUS)	13

D8   Apart from weddings or funerals, about how often do you attend religious
services?
(READ OUT—ONE ANSWER ONLY)

More than once a week	1
Once a week	2
About once a month	3
Once every 2 or 3 months	4
Only on special holy days	5
About once a year	6
Less often	7
Never	8
DK (SPONTANEOUS)	9
Refusal (SPONTANEOUS)	10

D9   Are you or is someone else in your household a member of a trade union or
staff association?

No	1
Respondent is member	2
Other person in household is member	3
Both respondent and other person are members	4
DK (SPONTANEOUS)	5
Refusal (SPONTANEOUS)	6

D10 You personally, were you born...?
(READ OUT—ONE ANSWER ONLY)

In (OUR COUNTRY)	1
In another Member Country of the European Union	2
In Europe, but not in a Member Country of the European Union	3
In Asia, in Africa, or in Latin America	4
In Northern America, in Japan, or in Oceania	5
Refusal (SPONTANEOUS)	6

D11 How many times have you visited another EU country in the last
12 months?
(WRITE DOWN—IF 'NONE', CODE '000'. IF 'DK' CODE '999'.
IF 'REFUSAL', CODE '997')

			times

D12 Can you tell me which of the following countries are members of the European Union (European Community)?

	(READ OUT)	Yes	No	DK (SPONTA-NEOUS)	Refusal (SPONTA-NEOUS)
1	The Netherlands	1	2	3	4
2	Malta	1	2	3	4
3	Croatia	1	2	3	4

D13 How many member states are there in the European Union nowadays?
(WRITE DOWN. IF 'DK', CODE '99'. IF 'REFUSAL', CODE '97')

		states

INTERVIEW PROTOCOLE

P1 DATE OF INTERVIEW

		DAY

		MONTH

P2 TIME OF THE BEGINNING OF THE INTERVIEW
(INT.: USE 24-HOUR CLOCK)

		HOUR

		MINUTES

P3 NUMBER OF MINUTES THE INTERVIEW LASTED

			MINUTES

P6 Size of locality
(LOCAL CODES)

P7 Region
(LOCAL CODES)

P8 Postal code

P9 Sample point number

P10 Interviewer number

P11 Weighting factor

P14 Could you give me the size of the area you live in?
(PLEASE ADAPT THE NOTION OF 'AREA' TO YOUR COUNTRY)

Less than 2,000 inhabitants	1
From 2,000 to 4.999 inhabitants	2
From 5,000 to 19.999 inhabitants	3
From 20,000 to 99.999 inhabitants	4
100,000 inhabitants and more	5
DK	6

References

Ahrens, J., Meurers, M., and Renner, C. (2007), 'Beyond the Big-Bang Enlargement: Citizens' Preferences and the Problem of EU Decision Making', *Journal of European Integration*, 29, 447–79.

Alesina, A., Angeloni, I., and Schuknecht, L. (2005), 'What Does the European Union Do?', *Public Choice*, 23, 275–319.

—— and Wacziarg, R. (1999), 'Is Europe Going Too Far?', *Carnegie-Rochester Conference Series on Public Policy*, 51, 1–42.

—— (2008), 'Europe Was Going Too Far', <http://www.voxeu.org/index.php?q=node/1258>, accessed 23 June 2008.

Almond, G. and Verba, S. (1963), *Civic Culture: Political Attitudes and Democracy in Five Nations* (Princeton: Princeton University Press).

Anderson, C. J. (1998), 'When in Doubt, Use Proxies: Attitudes Toward Domestic Politics and Support for European Integration', *Comparative Political Studies*, 31, 569–601.

—— and Kaltenthaler, K. (1996), 'The Dynamics of Public Opinion Toward European Integration, 1973–1993', *European Journal of International Relations*, 2, 175–99.

—— and Reichert, S. (1996), 'Economic Benefits and Support for Membership in the EU: A Cross-National Analysis', *Journal of Public Policy*, 15, 231–49.

Aspinwall, M. (2002), 'Preferring Europe: Ideology and National Preferences on European Integration', *European Union Politics*, 3, 81–111.

Banducci, S., Karp, J., and Loedel, P. (2003), 'The Euro, Economic Interests and Multi-level Governance: Examining Support for the Common Currency', *European Journal of Political Research*, 42, 685–703.

Battistelli, F. and Bellucci, P. (2002), 'L'identità degli italiani tra euroscetticismo e euro-pportunismo', *Il Mulino*, 1, 77–85.

Bednar, J., Ferejohn, J., and Garrett, G. (1996), 'The Politics of European Federalism', *International Review of Law and Economics*, 16, 279–94.

Bellucci, P., Memoli, V., and Sanders, D. (forthcoming), 'The Determinants of Democracy Satisfaction in Europe', in D. Sanders, P. Magalhães, and G. Toka (eds.), *Citizens and the European Polity: Mass Attitudes Towards the European and National Polities* (Oxford: Oxford University Press).

Benhabib, S. (2002), 'Political Theory and Political Membership in a Changing World', in I. Katzelson and H. V. Milner (eds.), *Political Science: The State of the Discipline* (New York and London: W. W. Norton), 404–32.

References

Blais, A. (2000), *Vote or Not to Vote? The Merits and Limits of Rational Choice Theory* (Pittsburgh: University of Pittsburgh Press).

Blondel, J., Sinnott, R., and Svensson, P. (1998), *People and Parliament in the European Union: Participation, Democracy and Legitimacy* (Oxford and New York: Oxford University Press).

Börzel, T. (2005), 'Mind the Gap! European Integration Between Level and Scope', *Journal of European Public Policy*, 12, 217–36.

Brambor, T., Clark, W. R., and Golder, M. (2006), 'Understanding Interaction Models: Improving Empirical Analysis', *Political Analysis*, 14, 63–82.

Brinegar, A. P. and Jolly, S. K. (2004), 'Integration: Using the Eurobarometer to Measure Support', in J. G. Geer (ed.), *Public Opinion and Polling Around the World* (Santa Barbara, CA: ABC-CLIO), 497–503.

———— (2005), 'Location, Location, Location: National Contextual Factors and National Support for European Integration', *European Union Politics*, 6, 155–80.

———— and Kitschelt, H. (2004), 'Varieties of Capitalism and Political Divides Over European Integration', in G. Marks and M. Steenbergen (eds.), *European Integration and Political Conflict* (Cambridge: Cambridge University Press), 62–98.

Bruter, M. (2005), *Citizens of Europe?: The Emergence of a Mass European Identity* (Basingstoke: Palgrave Macmillan).

—— (2009), 'Time Bomb? The Dynamic Effects of News and Symbols on the Political Identity of European Citizens', *Comparative Political Studies*, 42, 1498–536.

Bunce, V. (2005), 'The National Idea: Imperial Legacies and Post-Communist Pathways in Eastern Europe', *East European Politics and Societies*, 19, 406–42.

Campbell, A., et al. (1960), *The American Voter* (New York: John Wiley & Sons).

—— Gurin, G., and Miller, W. (1954), *The Voter Decides* (Evanston, IL: Row, Peterson and Co.).

Campbell, D. T. (1958), 'Common Fate, Similarity, and Other Indices of the Status of Aggregates of Persons as Social Entities', *Behavioural Science*, 3, 14–25.

Caplanova, A., Orviska, M., and Hudson, J. (2004), 'Eastern European Attitudes to Integration with Western Europe', *Journal of Common Market Studies*, 42, 271–98.

Carey, S. (2002), 'Undivided Loyalties: Is National Identity an Obstacle to European Integration?', *European Union Politics*, 3, 387–413.

Carling, J. B., Galati, J. C., and Royston, P. (2008), 'A New Framework for Managing and Analyzing Multiply Imputed Data in Stata', *Stata Journal*, 8, 49–67.

Carruba, C. J. (2001), 'The Electoral Connection in European Union Politics', *Journal of Politics*, 63, 141–58.

Castano, E. (2004), 'European Identity: A Social Psychological Perspective', in R. K. Hermann, T. Risse, and M. B. Brewer (eds.), *Transnational Identities: Becoming European in EU* (Lanham, MD: Rowman & Littlefield), 40–58.

—— Yzerbyt, V. Y., and Bourguignon, D. (2003), 'We are One and I Like It: The Impact of Ingroup Entitativity on Ingroup Identification', *European Journal of Social Psychology*, 33, 735–54.

Castiglione, D. (2009), 'Political Identity in a Community of Strangers', in J. T. Checkel and P. J. Katzenstein (eds.), *European Identity* (Cambridge: Cambridge University Press), 29–51.

Catellani, P. and Milesi, P. (1998), 'Identità regionale, nazionale, europea', in A. Quadrio Aristarchi (ed.), *Nuove questioni di psicologia politica* (Milano: Giuffré), 219–72.

Checkel, J. T. and Katzenstein, P. J. (2009), 'The Politicization of European Identities', in J. T. Checkel and P. J. Katzenstein (eds.), *European Identity* (Cambridge: Cambridge University Press), 1–25.

Chierici, C. (2005), 'Is There a European Public Opinion? Public Support for the European Union, Theoretical Concepts and Empirical Measurements', *Working Paper, POLIS* (Paris).

Christin, T. (2005), 'Economic and Political Bias of Attitudes Towards the EU in Central and East European Countries in the 1990s', *European Union Politics*, 6, 29–57.

Chryssochoou, X. (1996), 'How Group Membership is Formed: Self-Categorisation or Group Beliefs? The Construction of a European Identity in France and Greece', in G. M. Breakwell and E. Lyons (eds.), *Changing European Identities: Social Psychological Analyses of Social Change* (Oxford: Butterworth-Heinemann), 297–314.

Cichowski, R. (2000), 'Western Dreams, Eastern Realities: Support for the European Union in Central and Eastern Europe', *Comparative Political Studies*, 33, 1243–78.

Çiftçí, S. (2005), 'Treaties, Collective Responses and the Determinants of Aggregate Support for European Integration', *European Union Politics*, 6, 469–92.

Citrin, J. and Sides, J. (2004), 'More than Nationals: How Identity Choice Matters in the New Europe', in R. K. Herrmann, M. B. Brewer, and T. Risse (eds.), *Transnational Identities: Becoming European in the EU* (Lanham, MD: Rowman & Littlefield), 161–85.

Clarke, H. D., et al. (2009), *Performance, Politics, and the British Voter* (Oxford: Oxford University Press).

—— (2004), *Political Choice in Britain* (Oxford: Oxford University Press).

Coleman, J. S. (1990), *Foundations of Social Theory* (Cambridge: Belknap Press).

Converse, P. E. (1972), 'Changes in the American Electorate', in A. Campbell and P. E. Converse (eds.), *The Human Meaning of Social Change* (New York: Russell Sage), 263–331.

Cotta, M. and Isernia, P. (2009), 'Citizenship in the European Polity: Questions and Explorations', in C. Moury and L. De Sousa (eds.), *Institutional Challenges in Post-Constitutional Europe* (London and New York: Routledge), 71–94.

Crespo, N. and Fontoura, M. P. (2007), 'Integration of CEECs into EU Markets: Structural Change and Convergence', *Journal of Common Market Studies*, 45, 611–32.

Dahl, R. (1971), *Polyarchy, Participation and Opposition* (New Haven: Yale University Press).

Dalton, R. J. and Eichenberg, R. C. (1998), 'Citizen Support for Policy Integration', in W. Sandholz and A. Stone Sweet (eds.), *European Integration and Supranational Governance* (Oxford: Oxford University Press), 250–82.

De Vreese, C. H. (2007), 'A Spiral of Euroscepticism: The Media's Fault?', *Acta Politica*, 42, 271–86.

—— and Boomgaarden, H. G. (2006), 'Media Effects on Public Opinion About the Enlargement of the European Union', *Journal of Common Market Studies*, 44, 419–36.

—— et al. (2006), 'The News Coverage of the 2004 European Parliamentary Elections Campaign in 25 Countries', *European Union Politics*, 7, 477–504.

De Vries, C. and Edwards, E. (2009), 'Taking Europe to Its Extremes: Extremist Parties and Public Euroscepticism', *Party Politics*, 15, 5–28.

—— and van Kersbergen, K. (2007), 'Interests, Identity and Political Allegiance in the European Union', *Acta Politica*, 42, 307–28.

De Winter, L. and Swyngedouw, M. (1999), 'The Scope of EU Government', in H. Schmitt and J. Thomassen (eds.), *Political Representation and Legitimacy in the European Union* (Oxford: Oxford University Press), 47–73.

Deutsch, K. V. (1957), *Political Community and the North Atlantic Area* (Princeton: Princeton University Press).

Díez Medrano, J. (2003), *Framing Europe: Attitudes to European Integration in Germany, Spain, and the United Kingdom* (Princeton: Princeton University Press).

—— and Gutiérrez, P. (2001), 'Nested Identities: National and European Identity in Spain', *Ethnic and Racial Studies*, 24, 753–78.

Duch, R. and Taylor, M. (1997), 'Economics and the Vulnerability of the Pan-European Institutions', *Political Behavior*, 19, 65–79.

Duchesne, S. and Frognier, A. P. (1995), 'Is there a European Identity?', in O. Niedermayer and R. Sinnot (eds.), *Public Opinion and Internationalized Governance* (Oxford: Oxford University Press), 193–226.

Easton, D. (1953), *Political System* (New York: Knopf).

—— (1975), 'A Re-Assessment of the Concept of Political Support', *British Journal of Political Science*, 5, 435–57.

—— (1965), *A Systems Analysis of Political Life* (New York: Wiley).

Ehin, P. (2001), 'Determinants of Public Support for EU Membership: Data from the Baltic Countries', *European Journal of Political Research*, 40, 31–56.

Eichenberg, R. C. and Dalton, R. J. (1993), 'Europeans and the European Community: The Dynamics of Public Support for European Integration', *International Organization*, 47, 507–34.

—— (2007), 'Post-Maastricht Blues: The Transformation of Citizen Support for European Integration, 1973–2004', *Acta Politica*, 42, 128–52.

Eijk, C. van der and Franklin, M. N. (2004), 'Potential for Contestation on European Matters at National Elections in Europe', in G. Marks and M. Steenbergen (eds.), *European Integration and Political Conflict* (Cambridge: Cambridge University Press), 32–50.

—— —— (2006), 'The Sleeping Giant: Potential for Political Mobilization of Disaffection with European Integration', in W. van der Brug and C. van der Eijk (eds.), *European Elections and Domestic Politics: Lessons from the Past and Scenarios for the Future* (South Bend, IN: University of Notre Dame Press), 212–35.

—— —— (2009), *Elections and Voters* (London: Palgrave Macmillan).

—— —— and Marsh, M. (1996), 'What Voters Teach Us About Europe-Wide Elections: What Europe-Wide Elections Teach Us About Voters', *Electoral Studies*, 15, 149–66.

Epstein, R. A. and Sedelmeier, U. (2008), 'Beyond Conditionality: International Institutions in Post-Communist Europe After Enlargement', *Journal of European Public Policy*, 15, 795–805.

Ethier, D. (2003), 'Is Democracy Promotion Effective? Comparing Conditionality and Incentives', *Democratization*, 10, 99–120.

Fauvelle-Aymar, C. and Stegmaier, M. (2008), 'Economic and Political Effects on European Parliamentary Electoral Turnout in Post-Communist Europe', *Electoral Studies*, 27, 661–72.

Flickinger, R. S. and Studlar, D. T. (2007), 'One Europe, Many Electorates? Models of Turnout in European Parliament Elections After 2004', *Comparative Political Studies*, 40, 383–404.

Fligstein, N. (2009), 'Who are the Europeans and How Does this Matter for Politics?', in J. T. Checkel and P. J. Katzenstein (eds.), *European Identity* (Cambridge: Cambridge University Press), 132–66.

Franklin, M. N. (2001), 'How Structural Factors Cause Turnout Variations at European Parliament Elections', *European Union Politics*, 2, 309–28.

——Eijk, C. van der, and Marsh, M. (1995), 'Referendum Outcomes and Trust in Government: Public Support for Europe in the Wake of Maastricht', *Journal of Common Market Studies*, 32, 455–72.

——— and Oppenhuis, E. (1996), 'The Institutional Context: Turnout', in C. van der Eijk and M. N. Franklin (eds.), *Choosing Europe* (Ann Arbor: University of Michigan Press), 306–31.

——Marsh, M., and McLaren, L. (1994), 'Uncorking the Bottle: Popular Opposition to European Unification in the Wake of Maastricht', *Journal of Common Market Studies*, 32, 455–72.

Frognier, A. (2002), 'Identity and Electoral Participation: For a European Approach to European Elections', in P. Perrineau, G. Grunberg, and C. Ysmal (eds.), *Europe at the Polls: The European Elections of 1999* (New York, Houndmills: Palgrave), 43–58.

Fukuyama, F. (1995), *Trust: The Social Virtues and the Creation of Prosperity* (New York: Free Press).

Gabel, M. J. (1998a), 'Economic Integration and Mass Politics: Market Liberalization and Public Attitudes in the European Union', *American Journal of Political Science*, 42, 936–53.

——(1998b), 'Public Support for European Integration: An Empirical Test of Five Theories', *Journal of Politics*, 60, 333–54.

——(1998c), *Interests and Integration: Market Liberalization, Public Opinion, and European Union* (Ann Arbor: University of Michigan Press).

——and Anderson, C. J. (2004), 'The Structure of Citizen Attitudes and the European Political Space', in G. Marks and M. Steenbergen (eds.), *European Integration and Political Conflict* (Cambridge: Cambridge University Press), 13–31.

——and Hix, S. (2004), 'Defining the EU Political Space: An Empirical Study of the European Election Manifestos, 1979–1999', in G. Marks and R. Steenbergen (eds.), *European Integration and Political Conflict* (Cambridge: Cambridge University Press), 93–119.

——and Palmer, H. D. (1995), 'Understanding Variation in Public Support for European Integration', *European Journal of Political Research*, 27, 3–19.

——and Scheve, K. F. (2007), 'Mixed Messages: Party Dissent and Mass Opinion on European Integration', *European Union Politics*, 8, 37–59.

——and Whitten, G. D. (1997), 'Economic Conditions, Economic Perceptions, and Public Support for European Integration', *Political Behavior*, 19, 81–96.

Garry, J. and Tilley, J. (2009), 'The Macroeconomic Factors Conditioning the Impact of Identity on Attitudes towards the EU', *European Union Politics*, 10, 361–79.

Genna, G. M. (2005), 'Public Perceptions of the European Power Hierarchy and Support for a Common Foreign and Security Policy', *EUSA Ninth Biennial International Conference* (Austin, Texas).

Geys, B. (2006), 'Explaining Voter Turnout: A Review of Aggregate-level Research', *Electoral Studies*, 25, 637–63.

Green, D. P., Palmquist, B., and Schickler, E. (2002), *Partisan Hearts and Minds: Political Parties and the Social Identities* (New Haven & London: Yale University Press).

Haller, M. and Ressler, R. (2006), 'National and European Identity: A Study of Their Meanings and Interrelations', *Revue française de sociologie*, 47, 817–50.

Haughton, T. (2007), 'When Does the EU Make a Difference? Conditionality and the Accession Process in Central and Eastern Europe', *Political Studies Review*, 5, 233–46.

Hermann, R. K. and Brewer, M. B. (2004), 'Identities and Institutions: Becoming European in the EU', in R. K. Hermann, T. Risse, and M. B. Brewer (eds.), *Transnational Identities: Becoming European in the EU* (Lanham, MD: Rowman & Littlefield), 1–23.

Hix, S. (2005), *The Political System of the European Union* (2nd edn; London: Palgrave Macmillan).

—— (2007), 'Euroscepticism as Anti-Centralization: A Rational Choice Institutionalist Perspective', *European Union Politics*, 8, 131–50.

Holmes, D. R. (2009), 'Experimental Identities (After Maastricht)', in J. T. Checkel and P. J. Katzenstein (eds.), *European Identity* (Cambridge: Cambridge University Press), 52–80.

Hooghe, L. (2003), 'Europe Divided?: Elites vs. Public Opinion on European Integration', *European Union Politics*, 4, 281–304.

—— (2004), 'Does Identity or Economic Rationality Drive Public Opinion on European Integration', *PS: Political Science and Politics*, 37, 415–20.

—— (2006), 'Europe's Blues: Theoretical Soul-Searching After the Rejection of the European Constitution', *PS: Political Science and Politics*, 39, 247–50.

—— Bakker, R., Brigevich, A., De Vries, C., Edwards, E., Marks, G., Rovny, J., Steenbergen, M., and Vachudova, M. (2010), 'Reliability and Validity of Measuring Party Positions: The Chapel Hill Expert Survey of 2002 and 2006', *European Journal of Political Research*, 49, 687–703.

—— and Marks, G. (1999), 'The Making of a Polity: The Struggle over European Integration', in H. Kitschelt et al. (eds.), *Continuity and Change in Contemporary Capitalism* (Cambridge: Cambridge University Press), 70–97.

———— (2001), *Multi-level Governance and European Integration* (Lanham, MD: Rowman & Littlefield).

———— (2005), 'Calculation, Community and Cues: Public Opinion on European Integration', *European Union Politics*, 6, 419–43.

———— (2008), 'A Postfunctionalist Theory of European Integration: From Permissive Consensus to Constraining Dissensus', *British Journal of Political Science*, 39, 1–23.

———— and Wilson, C. J. (2002), 'Does Left/Right Structure Party Positions on European Integration?', *Comparative Political Studies*, 35, 965–89.

———— (2004), 'Does Left/Right Structure Party Positions on European Integration?', in G. Marks and M. Steenbergen (eds.), *European Integration and Political Conflict* (Cambridge: Cambridge University Press), 120–40.

Huber, J. D. and Inglehart, R. (1995), 'Expert Interpretations of Party Space and Party Locations in 42 Societies', *Party Politics*, 1, 73–111.

Huddy, L. (2001), 'From Social to Political Identity: A Critical Examination of Social Identity Theory', *Political Psychology*, 22, 127–56.

—— (2003), 'Group Identity and Political Cohesion', in D. O. Sears, L. Huddy, and R. Jervis (eds.), *Oxford Handbook of Political Psychology* (Oxford and New York: Oxford University Press), 511–58.

Hug, S. and Sciarini, P. (2000), 'Referendum and European Integration: Do Institutions Matter in the Voter's Decision?', *Comparative Political Studies*, 33, 3–36.

Huici, C., et al. (1997), 'Comparative Identity and Evaluation of Socio-political Change: Perceptions of the European Community as a Function of the Salience of Regional Identities', *European Journal of Social Psychology*, 27, 97–113.

Hurwitz, J. and Peffley, M. (1987), 'How are Foreign Policy Attitudes Structured? A Hierarchical Model', *American Political Science Review*, 81, 443–68.

Inglehart, R. (1970), 'Cognitive Mobilization and European Identity', *Comparative Politics*, 3, 45–70.

—— (1977a), *The Silent Revolution: Changing Values and Political Styles Among Western Publics* (Princeton: Princeton University Press).

—— (1977b), 'Long-Term Trends in Mass Support for European Unification', *Government and Opposition*, 12, 150–77.

—— (1979), 'The Impact of Values, Cognitive Level and Social Background', in S. H. Barnes and M. Kaase (eds.), *Political Action* (Beverly Hills: Sage), 343–80.

—— and Rabier, J.-R. (1978), 'Economic Uncertainty and European Solidarity: Public Opinion Trends', *Annals of the American Academy of Social and Political Science*, 440, 66–97.

———— and Reif, K. (1987), 'The Evolution of Public Attitudes Toward European Integration 1970–1986', *Journal of European Integration*, 10, 135–55.

Isernia, P., et al. (forthcoming), 'But Still It (Does Not) Move: Functional and Identity-Based Determinants of European Identity', in D. Sanders, P. Magalhães, and G. Toka (eds.), *Citizens and the European Polity: Mass Attitudes Towards the European and National Polities* (Oxford: Oxford University Press).

Janssen, J. (1991), 'Postmaterialism, Cognitive Mobilization and Public Support for European Integration', *British Journal of Political Science*, 21, 443–68.

Kaase, M. (1990), 'Mass Participation', in M. Jennings and J. van Deth (eds.), *Continuities in Political Action* (Berlin, New York: de Gruyter), 23–64.

Kaltenthaler, K. and Anderson, C. J. (2001), 'Europeans and Their Money: Explaining Public Support for the Common European Currency', *European Journal of Political Research*, 40, 139–70.

Karp, J., Banducci, S., and Bowler, S. (2003), 'To Know is to Love It? Satisfaction With Democracy in the European Union', *European Journal of Political Research*, 36, 271–92.

Katz, R. (2001), 'Models of Democracy: Elite Attitudes and the Democratic Deficit in the European Union', *European Union Politics*, 2, 53–79.

Kaufmann, D., Kraay, A., and Mastruzzi, M. (2009), 'Governance Matters VIII: Aggregate and Individual Governance Indicators, 1996–2008', Policy Research Working Paper, SSRN eLibrary (Washington, DC: World Bank).

Kelman, H. C. (1969), 'Patterns of Personal Involvement in the National System: A Social Psychological Analysis of Political Legitimacy', in J. N. Rosenau (ed.), *International Politics and Foreign Policy: A Reader in Research and Theory* (New York: The Free Press), 276–88.

Kersbergen, K. van (2000), 'Political Allegiance and European Integration', *European Journal of Political Research*, 37, 1–17.

Killian, M., Schoen, R., and Dusso, A. (2008), 'Keeping Up With the Joneses: The Interplay of Personal and Collective Evaluations in Voter Turnout', *Political Behavior*, 30, 323–40.

Klingemann, H.-D. (1999), 'Mapping Political Support in the 1990s', in P. Norris (ed.), *Critical Citizens: Global Support for Democratic Governance* (Oxford: Oxford University Press), 31–56.

Knutsen, O. (1995), 'Value Orientations, Political Conflicts, and Left-Right Identification: A Comparative Study', *European Journal of Political Research*, 28, 63–93.

Kriesi, H. (2008), 'Rejoinder to Liesbet Hooghe and Gary Marks, "A Postfunctional Theory of European Integration: From Permissive Consensus to Constraining Dissensus"', *British Journal of Political Science*, 39, 221–4.

—— Grande, E., Lachat, R., Dolezal, M., Bornschier, S., and Frey, T. (2008), *West European Politics in the Age of Globalization* (Cambridge: Cambridge University Press).

Kritzinger, S. (2003), 'The Influence of the Nation-State on Individual Support for the European Union', *European Union Politics*, 4, 219–41.

Kumlin, S. and Rothstein, B. (2005), 'Making and Breaking Social Capital: The Impact of Welfare State Institutions', *Comparative Political Studies*, 38, 339–65.

Kymlicka, W. (2002), *Contemporary Political Philosophy: An Introduction* (Oxford: Oxford University Press).

Laffan, B. (2004), 'Transnational Identities: Becoming European in the EU', in R. K. Hermann, T. Risse, and M. B. Brewer (eds.), *The European Union and its Institutions as 'Identity Builders'* (Lanham, MD: Rowman & Littlefield), 75–96.

Lau, R. R. and Redlawsk, D. P. (2001), 'Advantages and Disadvantages of Cognitive Heuristics in Political Decision Making', *American Journal of Political Science*, 45, 951–71.

Lazarsfeld, P. F., Berelson, B., and Gaudet, H. (1968), *The People's Choice: How the Voter Makes Up His Mind in a Presidential Campaign* (3rd edn; New York and London: Columbia University Press).

Lilli, W. and Diehl, M. (1999), 'Measuring National Identity', Working Paper, Mannheimer Zentrum für Europäische Sozialforschung, Mannheim.

Lindberg, L. N. and Scheingold, S. A. (eds) (1970), *Europe's Would-be Polity: Patterns of Change in the European Community* (Englewood Cliffs, NJ: Prentice-Hall).

Lipset, S. M. and Rokkan, S. (1967), *Party Systems and Voter Alignments: Cross-National Perspectives* (2nd edn; New York and London: The Free Press/Collier-Macmillan).

Loveless, M. and Rohrschneider, R. (2008), 'Public Perceptions of the EU as a System of Governance', *Living Reviews in European Governance*, 3. <http://www.livingreviews.org/lreg-2008-1>.

Lowenthal, D. (2000), 'European Identity: An Emerging Concept', *Australian Journal of Politics and History*, 46, 314–21.

Lubbers, M. and Scheepers, P. (2005), 'Political Versus Instrumental Euro-scepticism: Mapping Scepticism in European Countries and Regions', *European Union Politics*, 6, 223–42.

Luedtke, A. (2005), 'European Integration, Public Opinion and Immigration Policy: Testing the Impact of National Identity', *European Union Politics*, 6, 83–112.

Luhtanen, R. and Crocker, J. (1992), 'A Collective Self-Esteem Scale: Self-Evaluation of one's Social Identity', *Personality and Social Psychology Bulletin*, 18, 302–18.

Lupia, A. (1992), 'Busy Voters, Agenda Control and the Power of Information', *American Political Science Review*, 86, 390–404.

—— (1994), 'Shortcuts Versus Encyclopedias: Information and Voting Behavior in California Insurance Reform Elections', *American Political Science Review*, 88, 63–76.

—— and McCubbins, M. (1998), *Democratic Dilemma: Can Citizens Learn What They Need to Know?* (Cambridge: Cambridge University Press).

Magalhães, P. (forthcoming), 'Europe à la Carte: Public Support for Policy Integration in an Enlarged European Union', in D. Sanders et al. (eds.), *Citizens and the European Polity: Mass Attitudes Towards the European and National Polities* (Oxford: Oxford University Press).

Manin, B. (1997), *The Principles of Representative Government* (Cambridge: Cambridge University Press).

Marcus, G. (2002), *The Sentimental Citizen: Emotion in Democratic Politics* (University Park, PA: Pennsylvania State University Press).

Markowski, R. and Tucker, J. A. (2005), 'Pocketbooks, Politics and Parties: The 2003 Polish Referendum on EU Membership', *Electoral Studies*, 24, 409–33.

Marks, G. (1999), 'Territorial Identities in the European Union', in J. Anderson (ed.), *Regional Integration and Democracy. Expanding on the European Experience* (Lanham, MD: Rowman & Littlefield), 69–94.

Marks, G. and Steenbergen, M. R. (eds.) (2004), *European Integration and Political Conflict* (Cambridge: Cambridge University Press).

Marks, G., et al. (2006), 'Party Competition and European Integration in the East and West: Different Structure, Same Causality', *Comparative Political Studies*, 35, 155–75.

Marshall, T. H. (1950), *Citizenship and Social Class* (Cambridge: Cambridge University Press).

Mattila, M. (2003), 'Why Bother? Determinants of Turnout in the European Elections', *Electoral Studies*, 22, 449–68.

—— and Raunio, T. (2006), 'Cautious Voters – Supportive Parties: Opinion Congruence Between Voters and Parties on the EU Dimension', *European Union Politics*, 7, 427–49.

McLaren, L. (2002), 'Public Support for the European Union: Cost/Benefit Analysis or Perceived Cultural Threat', *Journal of Politics*, 64, 551–66.

—— (2006), *Identity, Interests and Attitudes to European Integration* (London: Palgrave Macmillan).

McLaren, L. (2007a), 'Explaining Mass-Level Euroscepticism: Identity, Interests, and Institutional Distrust', *Acta Politica*, 42, 233–51.

——(2007b), 'Explaining Opposition to Turkish Membership of the EU', *European Union Politics*, 8, 251–78.

McManus-Czubinska, C., et al. (2003), 'Understanding Dual Identities in Poland', *Political Studies*, 51, 121–43.

Milbrath, L. W. (1965), *Political Participation* (Chicago: Rand McNally).

Mlicki, M. and Ellemers, N. (1996), 'Being Different or Being Better? National Stereotypes and Identification of Polish and Dutch Students', *European Journal of Social Psychology*, 26, 97–114.

Moreno, L. (2006), 'Scotland, Catalonia, Europeanization and the Moreno Question', *Scottish Affairs*, 54, 1–24.

Niedermayer, O. (1995), 'Trends and Contrasts', in O. Niedermayer and R. Sinnott (eds.), *Public Opinion and Internationalized Governance* (Oxford: Oxford University Press), 53–72.

Norris, P. (1999), 'The Political Regime', in H. Schmitt and J. Thomassen (eds.), *Political Representation and Legitimacy in the European Union* (Oxford: Oxford University Press), 74–89.

——(2010), *Critical Citizens Revisited* (New York: Cambridge University Press).

Oppenhuis, E. (1995), *Voting Behavior in Europe: A Comparative Analysis of Electoral Participation and Party Choice* (Amsterdam: Het Spinhuis).

Pattie, C., Seyd, P., and Whiteley, P. (2004), *Citizenship in Britain: Values, Participation and Democracy* (Cambridge: Cambridge University Press).

Peter, J. (2004), 'Our Long "Return to the Concept of Powerful Mass Media" —A Cross-National Comparative Investigation of the Effects of Consonant Media Coverage', *International Journal of Public Opinion Research*, 16, 144–68.

Pharr, S. and Putnam, R. (2000), *Disaffected Democracies: What is Troubling the Trilateral Countries* (Princeton: Princeton University Press).

Pitkin, H. (1967), *The Concept of Representation* (Berkeley: University of California Press).

Pop-Eleches, G. (2007), 'Between Historical Legacies and the Promise of Western Integration: Democratic Conditionality After Communism', *East European Politics and Societies*, 21, 142–61.

Popkin, S. (1991), *The Reasoning Voter* (Chicago: University of Chicago Press).

Przeworski, A. (2010), *The Limits of Self-Government* (Cambridge: Cambridge University Press).

Putnam, R. (1993), *Making Democracy Work: Civic Traditions in Modern Italy* (Princeton: Princeton University Press).

——(1995a), 'Bowling Alone: America's Declining Social Capital', *Journal of Democracy*, 6, 65–78.

——(1995b), 'Tuning In, Tuning Out: The Strange Disappearance of Social Capital in America', *Political Science and Politics*, 28, 664–83.

——(2000), *Bowling Alone: The Collapse and Revival of American Community* (New York: Simon & Schuster).

Rattinger, H. (2009), *Einführung in die Politische Soziologie* (München: Oldenbourg).

Ray, L. (1999), 'Conversion, Acquiescence or Delusion: The Contingent Nature of the Party Electorate Link', *Political Behavior*, 21, 325–47.

—— (2003a), 'When Parties Matter: The Conditional Influence of Party Positions on Voter Opinion About European Integration', *Journal of Politics*, 65, 978–94.

—— (2003b), 'Reconsidering the Link Between Incumbent Support and Pro-EU Opinion', *European Union Politics*, 4, 259–79.

—— (2004), 'Don't Rock the Boat: Expectations, Fears and Opposition to EU-Level Policy Making', in G. Marks and M. Steenbergen (eds.), *European Integration and Political Conflict* (Cambridge: Cambridge University Press), 51–61.

Reif, K. (1984), *European Elections 1979/81 and 1984: Conclusions and Perspectives from Empirical Research* (Berlin: Quorum).

—— (1997), 'European Elections as Member State Second-Order Elections Revisited', *European Journal of Political Research*, 31, 115–24.

—— and Schmitt, H. (1980), 'Nine Second-Order National Elections: A Conceptual Framework for the Analysis of European Election Results', *European Journal of Political Research*, 8, 3–44.

Risse, T. (2004), 'European Institutions and Identity Change: What Have We Learned?', in R. K. Hermann, T. Risse, and M. B. Brewer (eds.), *Transnational Identities: Becoming European in the EU* (Lanham, MD: Rowman & Littlefield), 247–72.

Rohrschneider, R. (2002), 'The Democracy Deficit and Mass Support for an EU-Wide Government', *American Journal of Political Science*, 46, 463–75.

—— (2005), 'Institutional Quality and Perceptions of Representation in Advanced Democracies', *Comparative Political Studies*, 38, 850–74.

—— and Whitefield, S. (2004), 'Support for Foreign Ownership and Integration in Eastern Europe: Economic Interests, Ideological Commitments and Democratic Context', *Comparative Political Studies*, 37, 313–39.

—— —— (2006a), 'Political Parties, Public Opinion and European Integration in Post-Communist Countries: The State of the Art', *European Union Politics*, 7, 141–60.

—— (eds.) (2006b), *Public Opinion, Party Competition and the European Union in Eastern Europe* (London: Palgrave-Macmillan).

Rosema, M. (2007), 'Low Turnout: Threat to Democracy or Blessing in Disguise? Consequences of Citizens' Varying Tendencies to Vote', *Electoral Studies*, 26, 612–23.

Roth, D. (2004), 'Europa und die Deutschen: Die untypische Wahl am 13. Juni 2004', *Politik und Zeitgeschichte*, 54, 46–54.

Ruiz-Jiménez, A., et al. (2004), 'European and National Identities in EU's Old and New Member States: Ethnic, Civic, Instrumental and Symbolic Components', *European Integration online Papers (EIoP)*.

Sadurski, W. (2004), 'Accession's Democracy Dividend: The Impact of the EU Enlargement upon Democracy in New Member States of Central and Eastern Europe', *European Law Journal*, 10, 371–401.

Sánchez-Cuenca, I. (2000), 'The Political Basis of Support for European Integration', *European Union Politics*, 1, 147–71.

Sanders, D., Magalhães, P., and Toka, G. (forthcoming-a), 'Europe in Equilibrium: Unresponsive Inertia or Vibrant Resilience?', in P. Magalhães, D. Sanders, and

G. Toka (eds.), *Citizens and the European Polity: Mass Attitudes Towards the European and National Polities* (Oxford: Oxford University Press).

Sanders, D., Magalhães, P., and Toka, G. (eds.) (forthcoming-b), *Citizens and the European Polity: Mass Attitudes Towards the European and National Polities* (Oxford: Oxford University Press).

Sanders, D. and Price, S. (1995), 'Party Support and Economic Perceptions in the UK 1979–87: A Two-Level Approach', in D. Broughton et al. (eds.), *British Elections and Parties Yearbook, 1994* (London: Frank Cass), 45–72.

Scharpf, F. (1999), *Governing in Europe* (Oxford: Oxford University Press).

Scheuer, A. (1999), 'A Political Community?', in H. Schmitt and J. Thomassen (eds.), *Political Representation and Legitimacy in the European Union* (Oxford: Oxford University Press), 25–46.

——(2005), *How Europeans See Europe: Structure and Dynamics of European Legitimacy Beliefs* (Amsterdam: Amsterdam University Press).

——and van der Brug, W. (2007), 'Locating Support for European Integration', in W. van der Brug and C. van der Eijk (eds.), *European Elections and Domestic Politics: Lessons from the Past and Scenarios for the Future* (Notre Dame: University of Notre Dame Press).

Schimmelfenning, F. (2008), 'EU Political Accession Conditionality After the 2004 Enlargement: Consistency and Effectiveness', *Journal of European Public Policy*, 15, 918–37.

——Engert, S., and Knobel, H. (2003), 'Costs, Commitment and Compliance: The Impact of EU Democratic Conditionality on Latvia, Slovakia and Turkey', *Journal of Common Market Studies*, 41, 495–518.

Schmitt, H. (2005), 'The European Parliament Elections of June 2004: Still Second-Order?', *West European Politics*, 28, 650–79.

——and Eijk, C. van der (2003), 'Die politische Bedeutung niedriger Beteiligungsraten bei Europawahlen. Eine empirische Studie über die Motive der Nichtwahl', in F. Brettschneider, J. van Deth, and E. Roller (eds.), *Europäische Integration in der öffentlichen Meinung* (Opladen: Leske + Budrich), 279–302.

——and Mannheimer, R. (1991), 'About Voting and Non-Voting in the European Parliament Elections of June 1989', *European Journal of Political Research*, 19, 31–54.

Schmitt, L. (2003), 'Vertrauenskrise in der EU? Ausmaß, Struktur und Determinanten des Vertrauens in die zentralen Institutionen der EU unter besonderer Berücksichtigung des Europäischen Parlaments', in J. van Deth and E. Roller (eds.), *Europäische Integration in der öffentlichen Meinung* (Opladen: Leske + Budrich), 57–82.

Schopflin, G. (1993), *Politics in Eastern Europe* (Oxford: Blackwell).

Schuman, H. and Presser, S. (1996), *Questions and Answers in Attitude Surveys: Experiments on Question Form, Wording and Context* (Thousand Oaks, London, and New Delhi: Sage Publications).

Schumpeter, J. (1942), *Capitalism, Socialism and Democracy* (New York: Harper).

Sedelmeier, U. (2008), 'After Conditionality: Post-Accession Compliance with EU Law in East Central Europe', *Journal of European Public Policy*, 15, 806–25.

Shulman, S. (2002), 'Challenging the Civic/Ethnic and West/East Dichotomies in the Study of Nationalism', *Comparative Political Studies*, 35, 554–85.

Sides, J. and Citrin, J. (2007), 'European Opinion About Immigration: The Role of Identities, Interests and Information', *British Journal of Political Science*, 37, 477–504.

Sinnott, R. (1995), 'Policy, Subsidiarity, and Legitimacy', in O. Niedermayer and R. Sinnott (eds.), *Public Opinion and Internationalized Governance* (Oxford: Oxford University Press), 246–76.

—— (2005), 'An Evaluation of the Measurement of National, Subnational and Supranational Surveys', *International Journal of Public Opinion Research*, 18, 211–23.

Smith, A. D. (1998), *The Ethnic Origin of Nations* (Oxford: Blackwell Publishers).

Sniderman, P. M., Brody, R. A., and Tetlock, P. E. (1991), *Reasoning and Choice: Explorations in Political Psychology* (Cambridge: Cambridge University Press).

Steenbergen, M., Edwards, E., and De Vries, C. (2007), 'Who's Cueing Who? Mass-Elite Linkages and the Future of European Integration', *European Union Politics*, 8, 13–35.

—— and Jones, B. S. (2002), 'Modelling Multilevel Data Structures', *American Journal of Political Science*, 46, 218–37.

—— and Marks, G. (2004), 'Introduction: Models of Political Conflict in the European Union', in G. Marks and M. Steenbergen (eds.), *European Integration and Political Conflict* (Cambridge: Cambridge University Press), 1–10.

—— and Scott, D. J. (2004), 'Contesting Europe? The Salience of European Integration as a Party Issue', in G. Marks and M. Steenbergen (eds.), *European Integration and Political Conflict* (Cambridge: Cambridge University Press), 165–92.

Steinbrecher, M. (2009), *Politische Partizipation in Deutschland* (Baden-Baden: Nomos).

—— Huber, S., and Rattinger, H. (2007), *Turnout in Germany: Citizen Participation in State, Federal, and European Elections Since 1979* (Baden Baden: Nomos).

Stråth, B. A. (2002), 'European Identity: To the Historical Limits of a Concept', *European Journal of Social Theory*, 5, 387–401.

Szczerbiak, A. and Taggart, P. (2004), *Choosing Union: The 2003 EU Accession Referendums* (London: Frank Cass Publishers).

—— (2008), *Opposing Europe?* (Oxford: Oxford University Press).

Tajfel, H. (1981), *Human Groups and Social Categories: Studies in Social Psychology* (Cambridge: Cambridge University Press).

—— and Turner, J. C. (1986), 'The Social Identity Theory of Intergroup Behaviour', in W. Worchel and W. G. Austin (eds.), *Psychology of Intergroup Relations* (Chicago: Nelson Hall), 7–24.

Tanasoiu, C. and Colonescu, C. (2008), 'Determinants of Support for European Integration', *European Union Politics*, 9, 363–77.

Thomassen, J. and Schmitt, H. (1999), 'Introduction: Political Representation and Legitimacy in the European Union', in H. Schmitt and J. Thomassen (eds.), *Political Representation and Legitimacy in the European Union* (Oxford: Oxford University Press), 3–20.

Todorova, M. (1992), 'Ethnicity, Nationalism and the Communist Legacy in Eastern Europe', *East European Politics and Societies*, 7, 135–54.

Torcal, M. and Montero, J. R. (2006), 'Political Dissatisfaction in Comparative Perspective', in M. Torcal and J. R. Montero (eds.), *Political Dissatisfaction in*

Contemporary Democracies: Social Capital, Institutions and Politics (London: Routledge), 3–20.

——Munoz, J., and Bonet, E. (forthcoming), 'Trust in European Parliament: From Affective Heuristics to Rational Cueing', in D. Sanders, P. Magalhães, and G. Toka (eds.), *Citizens and the European Polity: Mass Attitudes Towards the European and National Polities* (Oxford: Oxford University Press).

Tsebelis, G. and Garrett, G. (2000), 'Legislative Politics in the European Union', *European Union Politics*, 1, 9–36.

Tucker, J. A., Pacek, A. C., and Berinsky, A. J. (2002), 'Transitional Winners and Losers: Attitudes Toward EU Membership in Post-Communist Countries', *American Journal of Political Science*, 46, 557–71.

Turner, J. C. (1985), 'Social Categorization and the Self-Concept: A Social Cognitive Theory of Group Behaviour', in E. J. Lawler (ed.), *Advances in Group Process* (2nd edition; Greenwich, CT: Jai Press), 77–122.

Tverdova, Y. and Anderson, C. J. (2004), 'Choosing the West? Referendum Choices on EU Membership in East-Central Europe', *Electoral Studies*, 23, 185–208.

Vachudova, M. A. (2009), 'Corruption and Compliance in the EU's Post-Communist Members and Candidates', *Journal of Common Market Studies*, 47, 43–62.

Verba, S. and Nie, N. H. (1972), *Participation in America: Political Democracy and Social Equality* (New York: Harper & Row).

——Schlozman, K., and Brady, H. (1995), *Voice and Equality: Civic Voluntarism in American Politics* (Cambridge, MA and London: Harvard University Press).

Vetik, R., Nimmerfelft, G., and Taru, M. (2006), 'Reactive Identity Versus EU Integration', *Journal of Common Market Studies*, 44, 1079–102.

Vliegenthart, R., et al. (2008), 'News Coverage and Support for European Integration, 1990–2006', *Journal of Public Opinion Research*, 20, 415–39.

Vössing, K. (2005), 'Nationality and the Preferences of the European Public Toward EU Policy-Making', *European Union Politics*, 6, 445–67.

Weale, A. (2007), *Democracy* (2nd edn; London: Palgrave Macmillan).

Weiler, J. H. (1999), *The Constitution of Europe: Do the New Clothes Have an Emperor? and Other Essays on European Integration* (Cambridge: Cambridge University Press).

Wessels, B. (1995), 'Development of Support: Diffusion or Demographic Replacement', in O. Niedermayer and R. Sinnott (eds.), *Public Opinion and Internationalized Governance* (2nd edition; Oxford: Oxford University Press), 105–37.

——(2004), 'Staatsaufgaben: gewünschte Entscheidungsebene für acht Politikbereiche', in J. van Deth (ed.), *Deutschland in Europa* (Wiesbaden: VS Verlag für Sozialwissenschaften), 257–73.

Westle, B. (2003), 'Europäische Identifikation im Spannungsfeld regionaler und nationaler Identitäten: Theoretische Überlegungen und empirische Befunde', *Politische Vierteljahresschrift*, 44, 453–82.

——(2007a), 'Political Beliefs and Attitudes: Legitimacy in Public Opinion Research', in A. Hurrelmann, S. Schneider, and J. Steffek (eds.), *Legitimacy in an Age of Global Politics* (London: Palgrave Macmillan), 93–125.

—— (2007b), 'European Identity and European Democracy: Analyses Concerning the "Democratic Dilemma" of the European Union', *INTUNE Working Paper* (Marburg: University of Marburg).

Wilgden, J. K and Feld, W. J. (1976), 'Evaluative and Cognitive Factors in the Prediction of European Unification', *Comparative Political Studies*, 9, 309–34.

Zaller, J. (1992), *The Nature and Origins of Mass Opinion* (New York: Cambridge University Press).

Index